THE
FOUR GLORIOUS YEARS
1918-1921

By

FRANK GALLAGHER

(First edition used his *nom de plume*, David Hogan)

BLACKWATER PRESS

ISBN 1-84131-784-5

© Ann Gallagher 2005

Editorial Committee for the republication of this book:

Ann Gallagher, Liam Cullen and Séan Sherwin

First Published 1953 and Reprinted 1954

Printed and Bound in Ireland by Cahill and Co. Ltd. Dublin for Irish Press Ltd.

Second Edition Published 2005

Blackwater Press, c/o Folens Publishers, Hibernian Industrial Estate, Greenhills Road, Tallaght, Dublin 24. www.folens.ie

An Taoiseach, Eamon de Valera T.D. and Frank Gallagher, director of the Government Information Bureau, working together.

FOREWORD

The years 1918–21 represent the white heat of the furnace that cast the foundations of modern Ireland; these were indeed four glorious years. At the beginning of 1918, Ireland had a Proclamation of Independence and a considerable desire for liberty. At the end of 1921 Ireland had forced the then world superpower, Great Britain, to the negotiating table; the potential for self-determination had improved greatly. When pondering the distance between these two positions, it never ceases to amaze me how such progress was made in a relatively short period of time. Frank Gallagher's excellent book provides a fascinating personal insight into the day-to-day work that brought about this miraculous transformation of national fortunes. Many may initially question the relevance of such a book to Ireland in 2005. I would have little time for those who would so glibly dismiss a work that contains fascinating details of the evolution of the Irish nation. It is my firm belief that if we are to chart a prudent path into the future, it is first vital that we understand our past. Frank Gallagher's book is a key factor in our understanding of this most turbulent period in our long history.

Gallagher's narrative is both deeply personal and simultaneously national in terms of subject and content. His ability to switch from an account of schooldays and boyhood cares to a reasoned criticism of the operation of military censorship in Ireland is quite remarkable. The juxtaposition of the personal and the national is one of the most endearing aspects of *The Four Glorious Years*. The sense of excitement that engulfed Dublin between 1918 and 1921 can still be felt in the city today.

Throughout the book the reader witnesses the coming of age of a young, idealistic and committed republican, Frank Gallagher. The movement to bring about Irish independence developed in unison with the author. Gradually, Gallagher drifted away from the city of his birth, Cork, and the Home Rule politics of his early mentor, William O'Brien. When he moved to Dublin in early 1917, Gallagher, like the country as a whole, had become more impatient with the well-worn path of Westminster-based politics. It was time to forge a new way: if Ireland was to gain the ultimate prize of independence, it would have to be done through a parliament in Ireland.

The establishment of Dáil Éireann provided the country as a whole with a fulcrum, around which the independence movement revolved. Gallagher was at the heart of this activity, working as deputy director in the Dáil Department of Publicity. In this capacity, he was responsible for producing the remarkable publication *The Irish Bulletin*. This daily news-sheet exposed the full extent of enemy atrocities during the War of Independence. It is fascinating to read Gallagher's descriptions of how an entire Dáil department was forced to relocate with less than a half an hour's notice as the security forces closed in on their secret location. With success, came the inevitable counter-offensive from those opposed to Irish self-determination. Arrests, imprisonments and deportations became the order of the day. Gallagher was not immune from the campaign of repression. He provides a heart-rending account of the personal burden borne by so many who struggled for Irish freedom. In particular, his account of his arrest and detention in April 1920 is a clear illustration of the cost one had to endure in the pursuit of the ultimate ideal. Towards the latter half of 1921, Gallagher revealed the increasing sense of uncertainty in Ireland as the pace of events accelerated considerably.

The nature of the sacrifice made by Gallagher is possibly best summarised in the words of Eamon de Valera, who, on the occasion of the death of Gallagher in 1962, wrote the following:

> Frank Gallagher's love for his country and for the liberty of its people stood the constant testing of close on fifty years. He played fully his part as a Volunteer and as a member of the Republican Army. His devotion to what he thought right made compromise for him almost impossible: for him the good was but a poor substitute for the best.

The Four Glorious Years is an insider's view of the forces that shaped the country we live in today. Frank Gallagher has been relatively neglected by historians of twentieth-century Ireland. He was, by nature, a discreet man who liked to stay out of the spotlight. So much so that when *The Four Glorious Years* was first published in 1953 Gallagher used the *nom de plume* of David Hogan to avoid widespread public recognition. However, it would be a mistake to confuse Gallagher's self-effacing nature for a marginal position. He was at the centre of the republican administration. Among his close personal friends were people such as Eamon de Valera and Erskine Childers.

It is my fervent hope that by republishing *The Four Glorious Years* the book will be read widely by those who have an interest in Ireland and all things Irish. I have read and reread portions of this book over the years. As Taoiseach, this book serves as a constant reminder of the considerable debt modern Ireland owes to the founding generation of the country we live in today. In one sense, what appeared common during those 48 months – curfews, arrests, travel restrictions and death – seem completely alien in 2005. I would argue that it is vital to remember that the liberties we now tend to take for granted were earned only by the considerable sacrifices of a group of selfless patriots. *The Four Glorious Years* is the story of one of those patriots. Gallagher's story of the years 1918–21 is honest, witty, chilling and, at times, heart-breaking. I have no doubt that this book will enhance the understanding of this pivotal period in the gestation of our country. It is for this reason I make a point of recommending *The Four Glorious Years* to anyone who asks me about the origins and development of the Irish state.

An Taoiseach, Bertie Ahern T.D., October 2005

Publisher's Note

The chapters of this book have been reproduced exactly as they were in the First Edition of *The Four Glorious Years* in 1953.

Many of the photographs that were, in the first edition, dispersed throughout the text have been substituted by others from the same era and placed in a photograph section in the middle of the book. These, together with a foreword, a note on the author and two new photos in the preliminary section are the only additions to the original work.

At the time that this book was first published, Frank Gallagher, as a civil servant, felt it inappropriate to publish comments on political events under his real name, choosing instead to use the *nom de plume*, David Hogan. As those considerations no longer apply, his work is published here under his real name for the first time.

Frank Gallagher and his wife Cecilia in 1952, attending the wedding of Erskine Hamilton Childers, who went on to become Uachtarán na hÉireann.

ABOUT THE AUTHOR

James J. Gallagher worked as an accountant in Cork city; he was employed by the Dwyer family, who were involved in textile, tanning and shoe manufacturing concerns throughout the city. James and his wife Kathleen decided to locate their family in Bloomfield Terrace on the Western Road. In the last decade of the nineteenth century, the Western Road had developed into an impressively groomed, middle-class suburb. Large, bright, well-appointed houses were the norm, with plenty of room in the immediate vicinity for children's adventures and only a short walk from the city centre. On 22 February 1893, Bloomfield Terrace welcomed a new resident: Frank B. Gallagher. The sixth child of ten children born to Kathleen and James J. Gallagher, Frank made his presence felt. While he was still young, prior to attending school, the family moved from the Western Road to St Patrick's View on the elevated, north-eastern side of the city. The move to such a salubrious area was a definite expression of the social advancement of the Gallagher family. The semi-rural setting allowed the children to roam with greater freedom, building forts, fighting battles and having a general whale of a time.[1] It was during this time that Frank developed a lasting bond with his brother Jim, who was only a year older than him. The two boys were inseparable; they treated the hills around Tivoli as their wild west, scorching up and down the slopes as if their very existence depended upon the success of the particular campaign. This horseplay provided vital training for the thrilling Dublin adventures to be undertaken by the two brothers during the course of 1917 and 1918.

This interlude of boyhood pleasure was brought to a close when the need to attend school arose; in this regard, the desires of an ambitious father came to the fore. Richard, the eldest in the family, had been sent to the Presentation Brothers College – 'Pres'. When the time came for Jim and Frank to begin their schooling, their father ignored institutions closer to the family home. He insisted that the boys traverse the length of the city. The curriculum pursued by the faculty at 'Pres' at this time was, in relative terms, adventurous: boys were prepared for entrance to the nearby university and for responsible employment in fields abroad. It must be pointed out that the educational landscape in Ireland in the early decades of the twentieth century was very different to the present

---

[1] Interview with Ann Gallagher, daughter of Frank Gallagher, conducted 8 July 2003.

day. In terms of their educational opportunity, the Gallaghers were very much the elite. It has been estimated that by 1911, the year Frank left 'Pres', only 6 per cent of the school-going population of Ireland was enrolled at secondary schools. While at 'Pres', Frank met Michael Saunders, a classmate of his elder brother Jim; little did Frank know that 20 years later, Michael Saunders would become his brother-in-law (Frank Gallagher married his long-time sweetheart Cecilia Saunders on 22 May 1922).

In the later stages of his scholastic career, Frank developed into a talented author of compositions. He wrote clearly and with a sense of humour which was employed liberally in his writing. In 1911, Frank joined the proofreading department of the *Cork Free Press*. The first issue of the *Cork Free Press* was published on 11 June 1910. The staff of the publication was relatively small, which was advantageous to an ambitious young man attempting to make a mark for himself in the world of journalism. The new employee was, within six months of his appointment, transferred from the proofreading department to take up the post of junior reporter. Frank's initial promotion may have had as much to do with the relatively low rate of pay he received and the resultant cost-effectiveness as to do with his journalistic ability.

William O'Brien, the owner of the *Cork Free Press*, regarded Frank's early writing as promising and fiery. Frank quickly assumed the role of O'Brien's protégé and the elder man warmed greatly to his teenage employee. A central feature of the *Cork Free Press* was the 'London Letter'. It consisted of a dispatch giving an insight into the behaviour of the protagonists of the Westminster parliamentary community. The tone was that of a gossip column, set against the background of parliamentary political wrangling. O'Brien wished to inject some vitality into the 'London Letter'; Frank was chosen to go to London. Thus, within a year of joining the staff of the *Cork Free Press*, Gallagher had risen to become the paper's London correspondent. He was immersed into a world of parliamentarians, lobby correspondents and their entourages; he was still only 19 years of age.

The time spent in London, and more importantly Westminster, was central to the development of Frank's political beliefs because he saw at first hand how the British parliamentary system operated. Concurrently, Frank's bond with William O'Brien began to strengthen considerably.

In *The Four Glorious Years*, Frank said of the relationship:

> A relationship had developed between us almost of father
> and son. When we met he would lead me to one of the
> further wings of the library, where his favourite place of
> conversation was a long, red-carpeted passage between
> twelve-foot-high shelves laden with law books. Up and
> down that passage we walked many a night, putting the
> world through our hands. He talked of people and books, of
> movements and memories; he told me of his party troubles,
> he sketched his plans and invited my views. He was then
> sixty-one years of age, and I had just turned twenty.[2]

The eventual passage of the Third Home Rule bill in 1912, the
suspension of the legislation in 1914, and the assurances of an aging and
increasingly marginalised O'Brien caused Frank to become progressively
more frustrated and impatient with the particular brand of Home Rule
advocated by O'Brien. Frank had listened to and learned from O'Brien
for the best part of three years. For his part, O'Brien in 1914 still viewed
Frank as a suitable candidate for the post of editor of the *Cork Free Press*.

As early as 1913, Frank's political views had begun to harden. However,
his involvement in physical force republicanism remained minor until
early 1918. By 1916, the brutality of the First World War, combined
with the failure to resolve the Irish question, meant that support was
growing in certain quarters for dramatic political action. O'Brien's
failure to appreciate the tidal change in the direction of the zeitgeist
was such that post-Rising his political stance was to become increasingly
marginalised. In the immediate aftermath of the Rising, Frank, in his
capacity as editor of the *Cork Free Press*, realised one of the most pressing
issues was to influence O'Brien's response to the events of Easter week.
More so than O'Brien, Frank appreciated that the Rising would, in time,
change the public mood. In order to convince O'Brien of this, Frank
travelled to London to meet with his employer and increasingly distant
mentor. In *The Four Glorious Years* Frank described how:

> William had received only the anti-Irish story of the Rising.
> He believed from it that this was a Socialist revolt and that
> only those behind it were the *sans-culottes* and the down-
> and-outs.[3]

---

[2] David Hogan [*nom de plume* used by Frank Gallagher], *The Four Glorious Years*
(Dublin, 1953), pp. 222-23.

[3] Hogan, *The Four Glorious Years*, p.225.

Frank feared that O'Brien would utilise the *Cork Free Press* to attack the leaders of the Rising. In order to prevent this, he had in his possession a letter of mass resignation signed by the entire editorial department of the *Cork Free Press*. There was a blazing row between the two men, but ultimately Frank succeeded. In the editorial which was published on 29 April 1916, O'Brien curtailed his anger. The overwhelming tone of the piece is one of remorse at the nature of events. O'Brien wrote:

> The government [in Westminster] must bear a heavy part of that burden. For the past two years it has made it its object to wage a war of prosecution against this wing of the volunteers. For the gunmen of Mr. Carson there was nothing but smiles and compliments. For the gunmen of Mr. Redmond there was nothing but smiles and compliments. But for the Irish Volunteers suppression, raids, secret arrests and deportations were good enough.[4]

In the latter half of 1916 the political distance between Frank and William O'Brien grew greater almost by the day. On the 13 December 1916, Frank found out that the *Cork Free Press* was to cease publication due to financial difficulties. Frank was somewhat shocked by this news. His private papers suggest that Frank had considered the possibility of resigning from the paper, however financial considerations had prevented him from doing so.

With the closing of the paper, Cork city contained little opportunity for such an ambitious and idealistic young man of considerable experience. In mid-January 1917, armed with his considerable severance payment, Frank left Cork for Dublin. With the assistance of his brother Jim, Frank began to find his feet in what was, at the time, a highly charged city. By July he had joined the staff of the P.J. Little-owned weekly paper *New Ireland*. The paper, despite being relatively moderate in its views, received a great deal of attention from the British censors. Frank was quickly assigned to deal directly with the censors in an attempt to counter the constant interference in relation to content. Frank's letters during these months reveal his continuous frustration. However, he learned a number of lessons. In the following years, he used these encounters with the censor and his experience on the *Cork Free Press* when he was operating as a propagandist for the republican movement. Through his dealings with the censor, Frank became aware of topics which the British administration in Ireland found sensitive.

---

4 *Cork Free Press*, 29 April, 1916.

His journalistic ability and propagandist potential came to the notice of the republican leadership. In October 1917 he was offered the editorship of a Galway newspaper purchased by Sinn Féin, *The Galway Express*. The remuneration for the post was generous at £2 10 per week, however Frank turned down the proposition as he felt he would be moving away from the epicentre of activity. The three days from 25–27 October 1917 were dramatic and pivotal in terms of the emergence of a united republican front in Ireland. Over the course of these three days, Eamon de Valera managed to secure the leadership of Sinn Féin and the Irish Volunteers. Clearly, a series of events with wide-reaching consequences had begun. In *The Four Glorious Years* Frank portrayed the election of de Valera as president of Sinn Féin as follows:

> ...that serious convention promptly gave way to rejoicing, it was not in partisan triumph that one man rather than another had been chosen, but that in this new Ireland men knew how to smother their ambitions that the nation proudly knit might face the world.[5]

In the latter half of 1917, Frank began what was to be a lifelong friendship with Eamon de Valera; the two men had begun to work in closer proximity. Frank also became an active election worker for the resurgent Sinn Féin; during the south Armagh by-election, he travelled to the constituency and worked as a propagandist. Whilst on the campaign trail, he met several individuals who were destined to have pivotal influences on the direction of Irish politics for a generation to come. In south Armagh, Frank met and worked alongside Robert Barton, Desmond Fitzgerald and Ernest Blythe.

In May 1918, the British administration in Ireland made a concerted effort to blunt the progress of the resurgent republican leadership through the tried and trusted method of arrests and deportations to England. These actions were justified on the basis that members of the leadership were in contact with German agents operating in Ireland. The campaign became known as the 'German Plot' and appeared extremely successful at first. The list of those arrested read like a who's who of the republican leadership, among them Eamon de Valera, Arthur Griffith, Countess Markievicz, Madame Maude Gonne MacBride, Seán MacEntee, Tom Hunter, Frank Fahy, Joe McGrath and Páidín O'Keeffe.[6] In the days immediately following the arrests, it became apparent that the

---

5 Hogan, *The Four Glorious Years*, p.22.
6 Hogan, *The Four Glorious Years*, p.29.

policy was counter-productive from a British perspective. Rather than weakening the commitment of the republicans, the 'German plot' arrests strengthened the resolve of those who remained at large to continue the struggle. The first manifestation of this desire was during the east Cavan by-election; polling day was set for 21 June 1918. The Sinn Féin candidate was Arthur Griffith. At the time of the election he was in Reading Jail. Frank had evaded arrest during the 'German plot' campaign. The loss of so many key personnel meant that those who remained at liberty were thrust into responsible positions. During the east Cavan by-election Frank again remained in Dublin, writing propaganda and meeting foreign press delegates.

Griffith won the east Cavan seat and a clear signal was sent by Frank and others to the outside world: that message was that Sinn Féin had arrived and would make its presence felt. In *The Four Glorious Years* Frank recalled the national significance of the events of May and June 1918: he wrote,

> A new wave of arrests began. But it was too late now. Sinn
> Féin had met the challenge, and, in facing it, had re-found
> its highest courage.[7]

The scene was set for the inevitable general election – a contest that would be a fundamental indicator of the position of Irish political opinion.

In late 1918 Frank began to do less work for *New Ireland* and spend more of his time travelling around the country speaking at anti-conscription rallies and pro-Sinn Féin meetings. His position within Sinn Féin was formalised on 7 September – he was appointed as an assistant in the Press Bureau. In addition to Frank's journalistic and propagandistic skills, the organisational and logistical expertise he had acquired during the by-election campaigns were also exploited when, in late September, he was appointed as Director of Publicity for the Dublin area. On 20 November 1918, the British administration in Ireland sought to blunt the impact being made by Sinn Féin with a fresh round of arrests targeting the organisational staff of the party. Again, Frank managed to evade capture and, again, liberty resulted in increased responsibility.

In the final run into the 1918 general election and less than two years after he had first moved to Dublin, Frank had assumed control of the propaganda activities of Sinn Féin. He performed his tasks to an extremely

---

[7] Hogan, *The Four Glorious Years*, p.33.

high standard. In relation to his work and character, Bob Brennan wrote: 'I was lucky to enrol Frank Gallagher for publicity. He was and is a prodigious worker, painstaking and sincere'.[8] Frank described the 1918 general election result as a 'sweeping victory'. Little did he know that for himself and Sinn Féin the problems were just beginning.

The resounding success of the December 1918 general election afforded Sinn Féin the opportunity to mount a formidable challenge to continued British direct rule in Ireland. During the first three months of 1919, Dáil Eireann began to sit and establish a parallel administration to rival the British administration. In *The Four Glorious Years* Frank described the gravity of the meeting of Dáil Eireann held on 21 January 1919: 'In that two hours Ireland was given a sovereignty, a parliament, and a programme to raise up the people and make for them at home and in the world an honoured place'.[9] Dáil Eireann began to put in place a republican civil service and in April 1919 it was decided to create a Dáil Department of Publicity; the first director of this department was Laurence Ginnell. On 5 April, Frank was appointed as the deputy director, a post which gave him a salary of £4 per week.

The importance of international support for the Dáil was paramount. In early July the Department of Publicity began to issue a weekly list entitled, *The acts of aggression committed in Ireland by the military and police of the usurping English government, as reported in the Daily press, during the week ending, July 12th 1919*. This publication was drafted by Frank and it occupied the bulk of his time throughout the Anglo-Irish War of Independence. The publication was not intended for distribution in Ireland. It was sent to foreign press correspondents, members of the opposition in other countries (particularly in England), union leaders and high-ranking religious figures. Throughout its three-year run, the *Irish Bulletin* was particularly fond of quoting British service men and ex-service men who expressed disquiet in relation to British policy in Ireland. For example, on the evening of 30 July 1919, a meeting was held in the British army barracks in Thurles, County Tipperary. According to the *Irish Bulletin*, the soldiers present thought that contemporary Ireland was under more strict militarism 'than they had seen in Belgium during the German occupation'.[10] Statements such as this were of considerable propaganda value because they represented a criticism of a system from within that system, in this case the British army.

---

[8] Bob Brennan, *Allegiance* (Dublin, 1950), p.167.
[9] Hogan, *The Four Glorious Years*, p.62.
[10] *Irish Bulletin*, 2 August 1919.

In early 1920, the *Irish Bulletin* was heavily revamped, it was published on a daily basis, six days a week. Writing to Cecilia, Frank referred to this increased work load:

> As well as having to write the Bulletin every day I am in control of an office with eight people in it. The ordinary organisation and overseeing of that takes me all day and in the evening I have to turn around and produce 2,000 or 3,000 words of original stuff.[11]

The nature of the work was hazardous, the success of the *Irish Bulletin* is apparent from the desire of the British administration to seize those responsible for the production of the daily news-sheet. Frank described how, on three consecutive days, the staff of the publicity department were forced to abandon the office in case they were raided by the police or military. The pressure and grave danger faced by the staff of the publicity department is described by Frank in graphic detail in chapter fifteen of *The Four Glorious Years*.

On 26 March 1920, Alan Bell was taken from a tram on his way home and shot by members of the IRA. Bell, at the time of his killing, had been conducting a successful investigation into the financial support structure of Dáil Eireann – work that represented a considerable threat to the republican movement. The British authorities responded to the killing of Bell with a prolonged campaign of arrests. Early on the morning of 27 March 1920, Frank was arrested and taken to the Bridewell barracks and subsequently transferred to Mountjoy jail.[12] While in Mountjoy, Frank led a hunger strike, which ultimately resulted in a nationwide two-day labour strike and the release of over 100 republican prisoners. In 1928, Frank published his hunger strike diary *Days of Fear*, describing the events between his arrest and eventual release on 20 April 1920.[13] This book is a remarkable piece of writing as it illuminates the fragility, insanity and venerability that a hunger striker must endure. When Frank was writing *The Four Glorious Years* 20 years after *Days of Fear*, he removed much of the horror and fear which formed such a large portion of the earlier work. For Frank, *Days of Fear* was a much rawer book; *The Four Glorious Years* was a more considered reflection on events.

Following his release from prison, Frank rested for a number of weeks

---

11 TCDMS, *FG and CS Papers*, Ms 10050/125(a).
12 For Frank's graphic depiction of the events surrounding his arrest and imprisonment see: Hogan, *The Four Glorious Years*, pp.149-59.
13 Frank Gallagher *Days of Fear*, (London, 1928).

and then returned to producing the *Irish Bulletin* and generally making a propaganda nuisance of himself. Often it is difficult to gauge the impact of propaganda on the target audience. However, in the case of the *Irish Bulletin*, there are a number of instances that illustrate the success of the publication and the skill of Frank in this regard. In terms of penetration, the *Irish Bulletin* was a huge success. C.S. Andrews wrote of the value of the publication to the morale of those involved in the struggle for the establishment of a republic.

> The *Bulletin* was one of the most important weapons of the Republican Movement. It was worth several flying columns…Had it not been for the exposures of the *Bulletin*, the British campaign of terror could have been conducted relatively quietly and the measure of resistance of the IRA would never have been known to the outside world.[14]

Perhaps the most glowing endorsement of Frank's work on the *Irish Bulletin* came from an unlikely source, Sir Hamar Greenwood, the Chief Secretary for Ireland. On 24 November 1920, Greenwood responded to a statement made by former British Prime Minister Herbert Asquith. Asquith had criticised tainted official sources. Greenwood utilised the opportunity to launch a blistering attack on members of parliament who relied on the '*Irish Republican Bulletin*' as a source of information in regard to the situation in Ireland. Greenwood alleged that republican representatives had circulated copies of the *Irish Bulletin* in the lobby of the House of Commons; in response to this he thundered:

> I consider it a loathsome alliance that men whose hands are red with blood of gallant soldiers and policemen should come into the lobby of this House and be allowed to circulate their hideous documents of falsehood…I repeat that an organ prohibited by the law and used as a basis of newspaper reports condemning his Majesty's Government out of the mouths of those responsible for the murder campaign in Ireland is not a publication that ought to be accepted. I say it is a tainted source.[15]

Two elements of this debate illustrate the extent to which the *Bulletin* succeeded in its aims. Firstly, that such an esteemed figure as Asquith would utilise it to attack government policy in Ireland was testament to

---

[14] C.S. Andrews, *Dublin Made Me*, (Dublin, 2001), p.188.
[15] *The Parliamentary Debates: Official Volume*, Fifth Series, Volume 135 (London, 1920) Col.487.

the accuracy and reliability of the material contained within its pages. The *Irish Bulletin* was clearly being read and utilised by its target market, the opinion-makers in other countries. Secondly, the amount of bile directed towards the *Irish Bulletin* by Greenwood illustrated the impact that Frank's propaganda work had on the British administration.

In the white heat of the initial hours after the signing of the Anglo-Irish Treaty, Frank's private correspondence reveals that he was confused as to what position he should take. After a week of frenetic activity Frank again wrote to Cecilia; this time, he was in little doubt as to the course of action he intended to take. It was in the days immediately following the signing of the Treaty that the lifelong bond between Frank and Eamon de Valera was cemented. On the evening of Thursday 8 December, following a long cabinet meeting, Frank went to de Valera and informed the president that he intended to support him in whatever course the president saw fit to adopt.

Frank wrote *The Four Glorious Years* over 30 years after the Anglo-Irish Treaty was signed and that must be remembered when reading the book. As a researcher, it is very interesting to compare Gallagher's initial reaction to the agreement with the one he published in *The Four Glorious Years*. The final two chapters of *The Four Glorious Years* are devoted to the national reaction to the Anglo-Irish Treaty of 1921. Here, Frank was very cautious in the language and interpretation of events he included, not wanting to add to the hurt and division caused by the Treaty. His opening lines reflect his desire to avoid confrontation, 'The days that followed the signing of the Treaty were days swaying between hope and despair'.[16] Frank went on to describe the Dáil debates on the Treaty, again stressing the tragedy of events, 'None of those who attended them will forget those crowded, painful days'.[17] His retrospective magnanimity is apparent when he wrote, 'As the discussions of the Treaty continued the scene was marked more by sadness than by the anger which so often glowed on the surface'.[18] Frank's poignant conclusion to his final chapter is still difficult to read. Today, each reading resonates with the waste of the Civil War: those who died, those who lived a myopic existence in the aftermath, those who emigrated, and the stunted nature of the early decades of a country which found it difficult to make peace with itself.

---

[16] Hogan, *The Four Glorious Years*, p.364.
[17] Hogan, *The Four Glorious Years*, p.368.
[18] Hogan, *The Four Glorious Years*, p.370.

I think these were some of the thoughts going through Frank's head when, in 1952, he wrote:

> The men in that room, nearly all young soldiers, knew
> the vastness of the tragedy that had overwhelmed them.
> A British statesman had divided the men of Ireland who
> had held together so magnificently, had divided them
> irrevocably, uncontrollably. Those who for four years had
> fronted every danger, never yielding, never quailing, never
> parting, were now at one another's throats despite every
> effort to turn this English victory aside. The passing
> of the Treaty which saw Irish unity melt away and the
> nation lie helpless at last before the will of her enemy, was
> greeted only by tears.

> It was the chief protagonist of the Treaty that described
> the scene. The *Irish Independent* reported:
> "The painful silence was soon broken in every part of the
> Chamber, and not only women, but stalwart men, sobbed
> and wept like children."
> Then the house rose. The Four Glorious Years were over.[19]

Many of the protagonists of *The Four Glorious Years* went on to exert considerable influence on the manner in which Irish society developed. The repercussions of events that took place during the years 1918–21 are still being felt in Ireland today. *The Four Glorious Years* also informs the reader about the Ireland of the 1950s. It is an account written by one particular participant of the Anglo-Irish War of Independence, looking back on the events of these years with the benefit of hindsight. In particular, the concluding chapters are fascinating. The arrogance and zeal of the young man are replaced with a poignant sense of wasted opportunity and perhaps an element of 'what if'. That is not to say that in later life Frank regretted the choices he made as a young man; he most certainly did not. However, when one reads these chapters one cannot help feeling the depth of the tragedy of the Irish Civil War.

Declan Jackson, University of Limerick
(Declan Jackson is currently completing a Ph.D. on Frank Gallagher.)

---

[19] Hogan, *The Four Glorious Years*, p.376.

CONTENTS

LIST OF ILLUSTRATIONS

ACKNOWLEDGMENTS

My thanks are due to many that this book has been published. Most of all, I owe gratitude to Lieutenant-Colonel Matt Feehan, who, as Editor of the *Sunday Press*, first suggested the setting down of reminiscences which, in time, grew to this full record. I had intended but a few articles of recollection. He would be satisfied with nothing but the whole story insofar as one humble participant could recall it. A young man himself, he wished his own generation to understand the men and the movement of those heroic years. Often when I would have ceased, he begged me to go on, and I am deeply grateful to him. To the officials of the National Library, I offer thanks too, for I had to confirm my memory by many consultations, of books and papers, and I found them courteous and tireless in my aid. To hundreds of correspondents, who wrote to me as the series was passing through the *Sunday Press*, I am greatly obliged. Some strongly disagreed with what I had written, some gave me details of a forgotten fact, many wrote just to say that the story I had to tell made them prouder than ever of being Irish. To my good friend and former colleague, Mr. Angus O'Daly, I owe a special debt. He volunteered to read the proofs and his wide knowledge saved me from many a slip. To all, I say that their encouragement, their help and their letters enabled me to pay a more worthy tribute to the dead and the living who made Ireland's name shine to the world in those years of great endeavour.

To *my Daughters*

ANN and MARY

CHAPTER I

THE REAWAKENING

IN many a city parlour or farmhouse kitchen when the night grows old and men have time to talk, minds go questing to those years when Ireland was in revolt. If there be a few veterans in the company they are soon in the thick of it all and their talk is full of treasure. That Ireland of theirs lives again, and around the fire the younger ones share, wide-eyed, in the tumult, the daring and the humour of the days from 1917 to 1921, when the nation made its bravest effort for freedom. In these recollections my mind will, in the same way as that fire-side talk, go in and out among the events of those four glorious years.

The first of my unbidden memories is of the courage of the common people, of which in the year that followed the Insurrection of 1916 there were two unique manifestations. One was a meeting and the other a funeral.

The Rising had been crushed. The leaders were dead or toiling shaven-headed in their broad arrows beside the lags of English convict prisons, those abodes of rigour and silence. Thousands of others were in internment. To the British Government the Irish were greater enemies and had fewer rights than the Germans with whom they were officially at war.

The nation at home was leaderless under stark military government. General Maxwell, slayer of the signatories of the Easter Week Proclamation, was king. All journals and newspapers that would not conform were censored or suppressed. The singing of a rebel song, the shouting of a slogan for liberty, even in one case, " a humbugging sort of a smile" at a policeman meant jail.

The people had no means of expressing what was in their minds.

At last a chance came. After the Rising many little parties sprang into existence to fill the vacuum of Redmondism, which was dead, and Republicanism which was in prison. All were conscious now that 1916 had spoken the deeper thoughts of the race and men set out to organise that rebirth to freedom.

Among the organisations that mushroomed into life was the Nation League. One Sunday in September, 1916, the Nation League called a meeting for the Phœnix Park. In order to exist at all, the League had to step warily. It gave itself the immediate objective of opposition to Partition, which was Lloyd George's latest " solution " to that eternal Irish Question.

To emphasise the national resistance to dismemberment the League brought speakers, clergy and laity, from the four corners of Ireland.

As it turned out, what the speakers said—and they were eloquent and sincere—did not matter a farthing, but what the audience did was a revelation. Perhaps the speakers, when they saw the citizens of Dublin pouring into the Park that Sunday afternoon, felt that their movement had already been a triumph. The meeting itself must have looked astonishing from the platforms, for the crowd stood packed out over the open spaces.

I was in the crowd, and during the speeches I moved about. There were several platforms, else half that gathering would have heard nothing in those days before loudspeakers. The cheers and the shouts of the audience may have meant one thing to the speakers. They meant another to me, for that crowd cheered from their hearts only when the dead of Easter Week were named, and shouted their devotion only at references to the prisoners.

And the songs they sang as they marched from the Park were the songs of the Volunteers. It was all orderly and " legal," but it had been turned by the common will into a manifestation, electric in its quality, of the people's real feeling.

I tramped out of the Park with the multitude that evening in September, and I noticed that as the horse-drawn brakes of speakers, riding like boats on the sea of humanity, made their slow way to the gates, the singing crowds neither lifted their eyes nor their voices.

They parted to let the vehicles through, but they were looking straight ahead and many were marching in step.

Later came the second heralding of what the years were to bring. It came now with less surprise, for Ireland had got back her leaders. The funeral of Thomas Ashe, on the last day of September, 1917, was the symbol of a union between the people and the prisons that was to remain unbroken for almost a decade.

The British had set up in Dublin an " Irish Convention," so selected that its personnel was overwhelmingly opposed to independence, and the world was then told to observe that the Irish were free to choose their own form of Government. The men sentenced after the Rising had been amnestied in June to create the impression of a change of heart, and the first name on the official list of those set free was Thomas Ashe.

If the British thought the releases would soften the Irish people's attitude to the Convention, the people soon disabused them and military repression was resumed.

As the jails became fuller the tension inside them grew sharper. Every prisoner knew the fight must be carried on inside the jails as well as out. They demanded the status of political prisoners. It was refused and they smashed their cells. They were put in irons and began a hunger strike. That was to be the rhythm throughout those years.

Ashe had taken part in the Rising and had been sentenced to death, a sentence afterwards commuted to penal servitude for life. Like all who were amnestied, Ashe had thrown himself back into the struggle and was arrested and sentenced by a courtmartial to a year's hard labour for a speech. He was sent to Mountjoy, where Austin Stack, his fellow-countyman, was Commandant of the prisoners.

These two undaunted men organised their comrades and resumed the fight. An effort to treat them as criminals set off the explosion. The hunger-strike was launched. Ashe was ordered to eat; he refused until the prisoners' demands for political status were granted. They seized him, strapped him to a chair, and, shoving rubber tubes down his throat, forcibly fed him.

It was horrible, but these men knew they had to endure all things for freedom, and day after day the ghastly struggle went on. At last, Thomas Ashe collapsed and was rushed to hospital. The food had been pumped into his lungs and he was soon dead of pneumonia.

Although British troops, in full war kit, were everywhere ready to suppress any demonstration, there was a spontaneous decision of Volunteer Executive, Trades Unions and all the National organisations to do homage to Ashe, no matter what the consequences.

It was the first full-scale challenge to the British power since the Rising. A year before, the people, as individuals, had used the Nation League meeting to show where they stood. Now there was to be an organised assertion that Ireland belonged to the Irish.

The body of Thomas Ashe lay in state in Dublin's City Hall for two days and tens of thousands passed before it, many weeping, many angry, all sharing a new pride. Men were dying again for Ireland.

In secret drill-halls, in G.A.A. clubs, in trade union branches, in homes and offices the other side of the mourning was being prepared.

The day came, and through Dublin passed a cortége the like of which had not been seen since the death of Parnell. Leading the marching host were volunteers in full uniform, carrying rifles. There was a hush over the city at the daring of it. Everyone wondered would the challenge be accepted; would the troops suddenly bar the way of the Volunteers?

The coffin was carried from the City Hall on the shoulders of Ashe's comrades. Nearly two hundred priests in their white surplices, mayors and councillors in their red robes, fell in behind the mourners, and as they moved slowly away, the great contingents took their places in the procession from the neighbouring streets ; teachers, labourers, athletes, football and hurling leagues, Sinn Féin clubs, Cumann na mBan, Foresters in their colourful uniforms, and many others. The slow beat of drums, the caoining of war pipes, the cry of funeral music filled the air.

Soon one sound overcame them all : the beat of marching feet. The footpaths from the City Hall to Glasnevin were packed tight ; the windows were crowded ; every statue and vantage point on the way had its watchers, but it was the swing of the Volunteers, in brigades, battalions, companies, and of the 10,000 members of the trade unions, led by the Citizen Army, that dominated everything.

The Volunteers had come from all over the country : Sligo, Donegal, Cork, everywhere. Kerry, Ashe's county, sent 700 to mourn him. The trade unions represented every craft in Ireland, and at their head, in their uniforms, marched 1,000 men of the Postmen's Federation.

The memory of it stands sharply outlined in the mind, even after 35 years—that and the scene near Findlater's Church on Parnell Square, when all might have been lost.

There was that day all through Dublin the tension that gives rumour its chance. People could not believe that the British, whose troops held the city, would permit the proscribed uniform, the "treasonable" arms.

Near the Rotunda there came down from the hill a strange murmuring among the packed watchers on the pavements. It strengthened, and soon the high-pitched note of it drowned even the marching feet. It was rumour being called from mouth to mouth. The British had mobilised ; they were on the move ; they had blocked the road to Glasnevin ; they were advancing against the Volunteers ; they would fire at any moment !

Like lightning, the cries went through the watchers, and at that moment the procession stopped. It seemed to confirm the rumours, and the crowd panicked and broke and a mass of rushing humanity swept down the hill on to the funeral procession.

It was a moment of destiny ! A fleeing mob has an incomparable strength of its own, and, with its power of communicating terror to all around it, can sweep away anything in its path. Under its trampling feet the whole demonstration of national discipline could have vanished. But suddenly the Volunteers resumed their marching : moving up the hill rhythmically again, while on either side of them the milling crowd swept in the other direction, filling the air with that extraordinary sound of mass fear.

Then, like a flash, it changed. The runners, seeing the undisturbed marchers swinging ever up the hill to where the imagined danger lay, stopped, turned, and then strode with them. It was over ! Thomas Ashe had led to triumph the new Ireland which had sprung up beneath the feet of the Army of Occupation.

The rest was as a peroration to a great speech. To the beat of muffled drums, the host of mourners slow-marched through the cemetery gates, and there stood in endless ranks, while around the grave the priests were chanting. Then the sound of spades, and the hollow noise of falling clay chilled the heart.

Clear into the air the trumpets flung the salute of the Last Post, and as the final note wavered into silence, there came sharp commands, and the three volleys were fired, to be echoed challengingly from near-by houses as every Volunteer stiffened at the sound of Irish arms being used again in Ireland's name.

A tall, handsome, pale-faced man stepped forward. He was in the uniform of a Volunteer officer. Few at that time knew him, and had to learn his name from the next day's papers : " Vice-Commandant M. Collins." He spoke a funeral oration characteristic of the new Ireland that had been born :

" The volley we have just heard is the only speech it is proper to make above the grave of a dead Fenian."

CHAPTER 2

THE BYE ELECTIONS

W HO will ever recapture the magic of those days when Sinn Féin won its first bye elections? To all old Republicans, the names North Roscommon, South Longford, East Clare and Kilkenny City still have a halo in the very sound of them. They were the first real fruits of the Rising.

Everything was against a Republican victory—yet the Republicans won. The new movement (it had not even become a movement) faced a party experienced in fifty years of electioneering, rich in funds, influential with all those sections of the community who can create a powerful local machine and provide transport, organisers, propagandists and orators. The Irish Parliamentary Party had given Ireland its leaders for half a century. They knew all the pitfalls.

Ninety per cent. of the workers for the new movement had never been in public life before. They were unknown to the people and untrained in approaching them. They had no funds, no organisation, no local influence. Yet, one after another, those four seats were taken from the Party, and thereafter everybody knew that the first General Election would end that long-dominant political power. For youth and idealism were on the side of the new and made it invincible.

North Roscommon fell vacant in January, 1917, and some time later an elderly man, resident in Dublin, received a letter. He was George Noble Count Plunkett, and the letter began:

> "We, the undersigned Irishmen, living within the Parliamentary Constituency of North Roscommon, declare our adhesion to the doctrine of Ireland a nation which has come down to us from our forefathers. We believe that the Irish nation has as much right to freedom and the same kind of freedom as any other nation . . . ."

Common enough words later, brave words then, when the graves and the jails were full of men who had asserted just that. The letter went on to say that the signatories had studied who amongst Irishmen might speak and act for that freedom, and they regarded Count Plunkett as the most fitted, by his learning, his national spirit and his gift of tongues. They invited him to stand in their name, and Count Plunkett accepted.

It was the depth of a bitter winter when that contest warmed the heart of the nation. Snow covered the constituency for most of the campaign. The old man, for he was already well over sixty, had, with his wife, Countess Plunkett, been deported to Britain after the Rising. He was dismissed from his post as Director of the Science and Art Museum, Dublin, because one brave son had been executed and two made convicts for their part in the Rising.

To mark its disapproval of any father who allowed his sons to sacrifice everything for Ireland, the Royal Dublin Society erased his name from its roll of members, he who was among the most cultured men in Ireland. The *Irish Times* began a leading article on the election with the words :

" Count Plunkett is a person of no importance."

They, and many others, were to learn a lot in the next few months.

How was the election to be conducted, where were the speakers to come from, the organisers, the committee men ? But, as a magnet draws flecks of steel, so the word of a contest, with a man of the Rising as candidate, drew to Roscommon from the ends of Ireland men and women burning to prove their devotion to the newly dead.

They set up Committee Rooms, learning as they worked ; they went over those frozen roads canvassing, canvassing, canvassing. They cycled in bitter winds, spreading the new gospel from village to village. Those who could speak went from platform to platform all the day long until night came, and their voices had become hoarse whispers.

As has happened so often to Ireland in a crisis, men and women, until then unheard of, proved to have the very gifts required for victory. At the moment most needed came an orator, whose name and voice were soon to be known in every parish in the country—a young priest from Crosna in that very County of Roscommon, Father Michael O'Flanagan.

His presence, like his courage, was magnificent, his gift of words was magical. His voice deep and musical, his mind strong and subtle, he could speak with humour or with passion, with moving tenderness or bitter anger, but, above all, he understood the hearts of the young.

He and Arthur Griffith and Larry Ginnell criss-crossed North Roscommon with argument and appeal and the assertion of Ireland's right to be free.

What their hearers thought we do not now know, except by their votes. They were listening to a new oratory, for there were few like Fr. O'Flanagan. The speechmaking of Sinn Féin was in a new vogue, calm, blunt, factual, statistical even, without any attempt to embellish arguments with graceful words. Nothing was more marked than the difference between this and the ornate, flamboyant and, at its best, noble oratory of the Redmondite movement.

Yet. the new style had an effectiveness at least as great as the old. On the eve of the poll, Count Plunkett said at the last rally :

> " It was the usual thing for a candidate to promise astonishing things. He was not going to appoint anybody postmaster, to promote any policeman, to go lobbying and wire-pulling in the House of Commons ; but when they wanted a strong voice saying no uncertain things for Ireland, they could count on him."

Although so many had come forward to work for him; nobody really believed that, with the restricted franchise of those days, Count Plunkett could win the seat. But they could show Britain there were plenty of people uncowed in Ireland still.

There might have been some chance of putting the unpopularity of the Parliamentary Party to use if a third candidate had not been nominated, the famous Jasper Tully, owner of newspapers and ferocious opponent of the Party and of T. J. Devine, the Party nominee. To make matters worse, the young people were not on the register at all, and as for their elders, the snow was heavy on the roads and winds of ice swept the countryside. The ballot boxes were opened without any belief anywhere that this might be the beginning of an epoch.

Soon it was clear that the unanticipated had happened. Word of it went into the streets of Boyle, and around the courthouse where the count was on the crowd swelled. News spread outside the town, and country people began to flow in. The victory of Count Plunkett had become a possibility, and messages were sent throughout Ireland. At first they were not credited. All through the campaign, the British censor had ensured that only the briefest reports of the speeches had appeared. It was true that by now the Irish people were adept at reading between the lines, but there were so few lines that the figures came as a complete surprise :—

Count Plunkett	...	...	...	...	... 3,022
T. J. Devine	...	...	...	...	... 1,708
Jasper Tully	...	...	...	...	... 687

An all-over majority ! The Dublin Corporation was in session when a Sinn Féin member carried in the figures. Cheering broke out in the gallery and the chamber, though an effort to adjourn the house was defeated. Kilkenny Corporation promptly decided to confer the Freedom of the City on the victor " as an answer to the British Government and the Royal Dublin Society." Sligo Corporation congratulated the electors of Roscommon, and through the nation went a golden chain of bonfires, Volunteers paraded, the bells of Father O'Flanagan's church at Crosna were rung by his devoted people.

Back at Boyle, Count Plunkett was thanking the electors at a great meeting. He foreshadowed the new era :

> " My place henceforth will be beside you in my own country for it is in Ireland with the people of Ireland that the battle for Irish liberty is to be fought."

Arthur Griffith said of the victory that it was the greatest since Clare elected O'Connell.

The heavy hand came down again after the Roscommon election, and deportations recommenced. On Washington's birthday, 22nd February, British forces arrested men prominent in the national and language movements, and shipped them off to English villages, where they must reside or go to prison. Among them from Dublin were " Sceilg " (J. J. O'Kelly) Sean T. O'Kelly, Liam Pedlar, Micheál Ó Foghludha, Barney Mellows. From Cork two were taken whose names were to be linked for ever with Ireland's story—Tomás Mac Curtáin and Terence MacSwiney. There were many more.

Less than two months later matters were put to the test once more. South Longford became vacant. It was an area strong in its support of the Parliamentary Party. If that nut could be cracked, the whole tree might come down. This time the Republicans nominated Joseph McGuinness, then doing penal servitude in Lewes Jail.

It had been said that the issue was not really clear in Roscommon ; that the people had voted for Count Plunkett because he had been an old Fenian and an old Parnellite. Very well then, there would be no doubt this time. It would be a shaven convict against the most powerful party in Ireland. Griffith stated the issue in his first speech :

> " The fight is between the Irish nation and the English power."

From everywhere the contesting groups brought in their reserves. The Parliamentary Party chose Patrick McKenna, a man of substance in Longford Town. They provided him with an elaborate machine. Dillon and Devlin, as well as a score of other M.P.s, came to help him.

On his side, too, was an element that now entered Irish politics for the first time and was to create a problem for the young movement—the " Separation Women," as they were called ; the wives of men serving in the British army who received large separation allowances. They became the victims of the forces hostile to Irish nationalism, and being organised by them, were thrown into the first few elections in a way that disturbed many.

They and the rowdy element delivered savage attacks on supporters of McGuinness and on cars flying the tricolour. Many were injured, Countess Plunkett among them.

Sinn Féin, as in Roscommon, had few cars, little money. From Dublin, a hundred miles away, cycled 200 workers. Others hurried in, packing the trains from North, South, East, and West. The bereaved of the Rising came, Mrs. Pearse, Mrs. Clarke, Miss O'Hanrahan, Countess Plunkett and her daughters.

From Kerry came members of the County Council and the Urban Councils. The Liverpool Irish and the Manchester Irish sent money. Sinn Féin had the better gift for publicity. For McGuinness they used many slogans, but the pride of them was " Put him in to get him out."

As polling day drew near the hotels were crowded to the doors, election workers slept in billiard rooms and boxrooms and even in baths. Many slept by the kerb in their cars. It was late spring. The deportees slipped back from England and took a hand. The widows and mothers of the 1916 men went from door to door endlessly canvassing. Old John Sweetman wrote a letter to the papers :

" After nearly eight centuries of English rule . . . Ireland has at last a good chance . . . to gain her freedom." There was no difference, he went on, when both candidates undertook to go to the British Parliament, but now the elector " can show England and the world that it is for the freedom of the Irish Nation that he is voting."

On the eve of the poll Sinn Féin workers wore tricolour armlets—with a crêpe band, for these days were the first anniversaries of the executions !

Then came a second letter. It was from another veteran like John Sweetman. It was signed William J. Walsh, Archbishop of Dublin. It told the people that the plot to partition Ireland was all but complete. They would have to act now—" The country is practically sold." In a matter of hours that short letter, in great posters, was on every spare hoarding in South Longford and on the bonnet and back of every Sinn Féin car. It turned the scales.

On 10th May the count took place. There has been no count like it in the history of elections. In the first hour of checking the votes, during which they were grouped in bundles of 100, Sinn Féin were jubilant and signals from the windows brought hundreds of tricolours into the air above the packed masses waiting for the result. Then slowly McKenna drew level. There were areas in which Sinn Féin polled hardly a vote. When the last bundle was taken up McKenna was twenty ahead. The count ended. He had won.

Through the window the crowd were told by signs and now was the moment of Redmondite triumph, and songs and banners and processions filled Longford town. The Sinn Féin scrutineers demanded a recount. The sub-sheriff counted the votes himself. The result was

McKenna	1,457
McGuinness	1,445

Sinn Féin representatives refused to allow the announcement to be made. They must have another recount. They felt somehow that votes were missing. But, no, there was a difference but the result was the same :

McKenna	1,459
McGuinness	1,448

An older movement would have given up. Every voting paper, Sinn Féin insisted, would have to be examined again, separately. The bundles were checked for the third time, and then it was found that in a bundle of McGuinness's votes supposed to number only 100, there were actually 150. It changed the totals, and for Sinn Féin it changed the world. To the window came the sheriff. He gave the figures :

McGuinness	1,498
McKenna	1,459

Never did a result have such reverberations. It cast the Party into Stygian gloom ; but resurgent Ireland was delirious. In one of the strongest centres of Redmondism, as Griffith said at the declaration of the poll, the movement with no means but an ideal had routed the movement which had behind it influence, money, " a corrupt Nationalism and a strong Unionism."

Across the Channel, the *Manchester Guardian* lamented that the result was equivalent to a " serious defeat of the British army in the field."

CHAPTER 3

THE EAST CLARE VICTORY

AT the declaration of the poll in Longford the defeated Redmondite candidate had said that the fires of Roscommon had dwindled in South Longford and soon the spark would be out. One month later that prophecy was put to the test.

In a speech in the British House of Commons in the spring of 1917, Major Willie Redmond, Member for East Clare, pleaded with Britain to be just to Ireland. He said he spoke as one of those " about to die." On 7th June, 1917, Major Redmond was killed in action at Messines.

A few days later as he stepped from Pentonville Prison back into the world, Eamon de Valera was handed a telegram. He had been selected to contest East Clare.

De Valera was chosen not for any political gifts, for those at home knew as yet of none; nor for being an orator, for he had never addressed a public meeting; nor for any capacity for organising a great political movement, for that lay hidden in the future. His choice was dictated by one thing only : the brother of the leader of the old movement was dead. There was needed to contest such a seat somebody of standing. De Valera had a status nobody else had—he was the last surviving commandant of the Rising.

After the election was over, a Unionist wrote to the *Irish Times.* He held a Commission from His Majesty King George V, as the editor sharply reminded him in a footnote to the letter. But he had watched events in Clare and somehow he sensed a portent.

The picture then given the world of Sinn Féin was of " wild men and women," blazing-eyed fanatics who would stop at nothing. It was a truer picture which Colonel O'Callaghan-Westropp drew for the *Irish Times.*

He first stated his authority to write : " May I say that in 1892 I was Unionist candidate selected to contest East Clare."

It was he whom Willie Redmond had defeated 25 years earlier, and so the years were spanned. He added he was a Unionist still and would not vote for de Valera.

But, he went on, the gospel of Sinn Féin as he heard it in East Clare, " was wholly free from incitements to class and religious hatred, from abuse of opponents and from personalities of the bitter

and objectionable kind which formerly characterised similar contests."
He gave an example:

"I was myself a witness of proceedings which gave many a
vote to Sinn Féin. Both sides held meetings in the same village.
The constitutional party formed a column before any speeches
were delivered and with bands playing marched right through
the de Valera meeting which Professor MacNeill was then
addressing. Yet, though this was done a second time ten minutes
later, not a blow was struck nor an offensive expression made
use of. When decent people saw the restraint and good temper
of those they had been warned against as rowdies, a quite natural
revulsion of feeling set in."

Something new had come into Irish politics, and it was to be
seen again and again in the coming months—in Kilkenny, in East
Cavan, in South Armagh, in East Tyrone, wherever the tricolour
was raised.

When de Valera reached Dublin from Pentonville, he discussed
his proposed candidature for Clare. He would stand on two conditions: that a Republic was stated to be the aim and that Eoin
MacNeill would appear on his platform.

These were daring conditions in the atmosphere of thirty-five
years ago. To declare for a Republic might be resented by the many
good people whose ideas of that form of Government came from
revolutionary France rather than from America. To have MacNeill
on his platforms would be resented by many Volunteers who still
condemned his calling-off of the Easter Sunday mobilisation which
restricted the Rising to Dublin, Wexford and Galway.

Would it not be better, the cautious ones asked, merely to say we
wanted freedom and still better to leave MacNeill at home? But
the prospective candidate pressed his point. The people wished for
full national independence and the Rising had crystallised that into
the Republic. They of the Rising stood for that: why not be open
with the people and tell them so? The word freedom had been
abused into meaning the most meagre form of Home Rule. Better
make clear at once that it was the old ideal that the new movement
had made its own.

As to MacNeill—they must have unity. Here was a rift already in
their ranks. Why not close the wound before it went so deep that
it crippled the nation? He had his way. He went to Clare: MacNeill
went with him and in his first speech de Valera cited the Proclamation
of Easter Week.

Into Clare, after de Valera, came every Volunteer in Ireland who
could get free, and it was there that the new fashion in electioneering
really took form.

In Clare nobody knew him. But his name was so strange and his legend from the prisons so full of colour and courage that they came in curiosity to see and hear him. He was no orator : words came too slowly to fit all his ideas. He spoke at length and patiently, carefully, without passion. Yet those country people had little difficulty in understanding him. They felt his sincerity. He did not mystify them. When he wished to tell them that he stood for an Ireland freely governing itself, he said, " I told the prison authorities in England that the only law I recognised was the law of the Irish people."

Out from Ennis went word of this new leader, who spoke so quietly and did not abuse anyone. Curiosity to see a young man who had been sentenced to death for Ireland coupled with the fact that his mother was a Limerick girl, made them come to his meetings, and when they had been at one, they wanted to be at others.

Soon the whole county was on the move, and at Sixmilebridge began the concourses that were to mark out this election from any in the decades gone by. To Sixmilebridge they came in every vehicle that would carry them—butt and cart, trap and wagonette, float and dray, on bicycle and horse, in motor-cars and trains. People set out in the early forenoon, to get a good place near his platform. There were others who came marching and singing : the young men of the new Volunteers, and the young women of Cumann na mBan.

Soon, everywhere the Sinn Féin speakers went there was a body-guard of young men for them, carrying hurley-sticks as rifles. But if Irishmen marched, the English marched, too ; and into Clare were drafted troops, with machine-guns, which were set up at street corners. The Royal Irish Constabulary came in quadrupled strength, with hands itching for the batons. At any excuse, the batons were out and, at first, the young men broke. Then they began to stand their ground.

The leaders saw how easily all this could drift into a useless conflict, especially when the " Separation Women " in the towns and the corner-boys began to stone the cars and tear down the Tricolour as in South Longford. One day the car in which de Valera, Stephen O'Mara, and others were travelling, found the road blocked and, as they drew up, the car was fired on. At his next meeting de Valera made a proposal to the people of Clare—that they take a little self-government on themselves :

"If the police would withdraw, both sides could carry on their meetings in perfect order. They did not need the military who had been brought down to Ennis. They would maintain the public peace themselves."

Clare rose to this plan. Soon those eager Volunteers, who in a previous generation would have been thrown at one another's throats in faction fights had learned the magic of order.

"Do not indulge in violence," the tall leader told them, " or you will be described to the world as a rabble, and Ireland's name will be hurt."

The words were heeded. It was the most orderly election old people could remember. But it was more than orderly: it was clean. De Valera insisted on civil tongues: hard hitting on policies, respect for persons. Somebody had brought out a poster with a cartoon showing a member of the Irish Party as a hangman. De Valera considered it offensive and had it destroyed.

By nomination day, the whole campaign had been affected by these methods: the constabulary stood by while the meetings policed themselves. And, as the two candidates went with their nomination papers (one of de Valera's nominators was T. V. Honan, Chairman of the Ennis Urban Council), their groups met, and it was jests, not stones, that were thrown, a remarkable thing at that time. Nor was de Valera's candidature hurt when the day before polling he saw a runaway horse and trap. The former athlete " jumped from his motor-car and giving chase captured the animal," as the prosaic Press report said.

Stunned by South Longford, few of the Redmondite M.P.s. came to help the Party candidate, a Claremar Patrick Lynch, K.C. Those who did failed to understand the way the people's thoughts were moving. They made the wrong kind of speeches: " de Valera was unknown and unheard of until the disastrous fiasco of Easter Week." They referred to the Volunteers as " de Valera and his handful of children." They warned the old people that if they voted for this man out of jail they would lose their old age pensions.

On polling day, 10th July, a veritable passion to vote swept the constituency. Many refused lifts and, gathering at the cross-roads, marched to the voting places, some with bands or pipers at their head. When night came down and the polling stations closed, Sinn Féin knew they had won. They did not dream that the majority would be so decisive. The unknown and unheard-of man polled 5,010 votes and the Clare K.C. 2,035. At the count de Valera wore the banned uniform of a Commandant. He spoke to an audience greater than Ennis had seen since the days of O'Connell:

"What shall I say to you?" he began with emotion. "I shall simply say that you are men of Clare and that you are worthy descendants of the Claremen who fought under Brian Boru, with the same spirit in your hearts to-day as your forefathers had a thousand years ago. This victory is one which will be celebrated all over the world—a victory for Ireland. This victory will show the world that Irishmen if they had a ghost of a chance would fight for the independence of Ireland and for an Irish Republic."

As the new M.P. came back to Dublin he saw from the windows of the train a nation celebrating. Everywhere there were parades, bonfires, flags. In Dublin a vast meeting flowed from O'Connell Street to College Green. One of the speakers was Thomas Ashe, who so soon was to fill these very streets with mourners. What Ashe said described it all:

"We had heard whispers in prison that a new Ireland had arisen, but we never dreamt anything like the reality we have seen."

Hardly had the rejoicing over East Clare ended than the Whip of the Irish Party, Pat O'Brien, M.P. for Kilkenny City, died. Sinn Féin knew now that rural Ireland was with them, but what of the cities? Kilkenny was the first urban contest.

The choice fell again on a man of Easter Week. At the Convention in Kilkenny at which he was selected the man who proposed him soon paid for his hardihood—E. T. Keane, Editor of the *Kilkenny People*. Within a week his paper was suppressed.

Keane said:

"The candidate is Councillor W. T. Cosgrave of Dublin, lately released from Lewes Jail, where he was condemned to penal servitude for life, the courtmartial having first determined his execution. Roscommon returned the father of three rebels, South Longford returned a rebel prisoner, East Clare returned one of the finest soldiers that ever fought for the cause of Ireland, and now Kilkenny will return a rebel as its representative. We have adopted a man to-night who is worth fighting for, and we shall fight for him as he fought for us."

And thus began the best organised election Sinn Féin had yet contested. They knew now where they were going. They had become veterans of the hustings. Before the Party had even chosen their nominee, Sinn Féin had its headquarters open and its posters up. They brought Dan MacCarthy into the constituency as Director of Elections, Dan, whose name as an "organiser of victory" was already made. The night he arrived he made a typical speech:

"I merely want to say the committee rooms will be open to-morrow morning in High Street, and I want the very best workers in Kilkenny to turn in there and work."

It would be a tough job bringing this city into the new fold, for there was only a tiny register of about 1,200 electors, a great majority of them old. They would be hard to change, but Sinn Féin burned with its own faith, and the moving of mountains was nothing.

It was fortunate in its candidate. He was a city man too, a man well versed in public life, for he had been long a Sinn Féin member of the Dublin Corporation. He understood finance and economics, and he was a vigorous and eloquent speaker.

So they set to work. Soon they had the city blazing with their signs, and it was there that were first introduced the little tri-colour celluloid badges with the candidate's photograph on them. After a few days it seemed half the city had them in their button holes with the slogan "Vote for Cosgrave."

The Redmondites chose a member of the City's Corporation, Councillor Magennis, a Kilkenny man. To meet this challenge, they would make an appeal to local patriotism. But fewer than ever of the Irish Party members came to help, as if they knew their day was over.

Wherever their canvassers called, Sinn Féin had been before them, not talking against anyone, but for a cause. "Come out and vote anyway," the Republican canvassers said, "even if you vote against us." It was new advice and the electors liked it.

On 10th August, the eve of the poll, Dan MacCarthy announced that Sinn Féin would win, perhaps by two to one. Every voter had been asked, and the carefully checked totals gave 786 for Sinn Féin. Those who could not be shaken from the Party allegiance were about 400.

As happened on many occasions afterwards, the prediction made possible by Dan MacCarthy's methods was almost exactly fulfilled. Cosgrave got 776 votes and Magennis 380.

At the declaration of the poll there was a scene in Kilkenny City that opened the eyes of the many English correspondents who had come to see the new movement take its stiffest hurdle. Almost every house was burnished with tricolour and green flags. As the victor came out on the balcony of the courthouse the crowd below cheered him passionately, affectionately. After a little while, de Valera joined him, and as they shook hands there was, as the reporters recorded, "frantic enthusiasm."

Cosgrave made a simple and moving speech, ending with the words :

" In the name of the men who fought and died for Ireland, I thank you for having recorded your approval of the sacrifices they have made."

De Valera said :

" One of the grand things this movement is doing, and will continue to do, is to lift up politics in this country from the degradation to which they have been brought."

The victors found Dublin tense with excitement when they arrived. The Castle had ordered the suppression of the victory meeting planned for Westmoreland Street, and had packed the street with police. The Sinn Féin offices were raided, and as outside the cordons the crowds refused to move on, a clash seemed inevitable. But suddenly a stirring began, and quietly the throngs melted away, as young men passed among them telling them to go to James's Street. There a multitude gave a deep voiced welcome to Cosgrave, and rebel songs from fifty thousand voices were darkly heard in Dublin Castle.

CHAPTER 4

THE FIRST ÁRD-FHEIS

WITHIN a month of the lowering of Ashe's coffin into the dark earth, within two months of the Kilkenny victory, the new Sinn Féin organisation was founded. Not since the days of Young Ireland had such an assembly been seen in Dublin. Into the great circular room of the Mansion House, built to honour King George IV, there gathered that day in October, 1917, two thousand delegates bent on making Ireland a Republic. The British army marched through the streets outside, while inside the greatest popular movement since the time of O'Connell was given the objective of independence.

From six a.m. the queues had begun in Dawson Street. By eight they stretched far down towards Nassau Street. By nine, the street was packed, and Volunteers in mufti had taken over the regulation of the crowds, and the police quietly withdrew. At ten, the First Árd-Fheis of the new Sinn Féin was called to order.

It was the fruit of long preparation, and it was in the jails and in the internment camps that the first steps were taken. There the men of the Rising, and thousands of others from the provinces who had had no chance to be " out," laid the plans that now brought into being this national Convention.

The men in prison had known that a new Ireland was coming into being, and that it could be strong only if disciplined and united. So in Frongoch, in Lewes Jail, in Dartmoor, in Knutsford, Irish leaders thought over and wrestled with problems as O'Donovan Rossa, Tom Clarke and Michael Davitt had done in their prison-cells a generation before. As this man and that of the rank and file were released, they hurried back to their towns and parishes, and began building the civil arm of resurgent Ireland.

They had, as yet, no name for the organisation. The British had in contempt called the insurrection the " Sinn Féin Rising." The Parliamentarians had dismissed the whole movement as " the hopping of fleas." And to tell the truth, Sinn Féin itself, before the Rising, was numerically of little moment. Its strength lay rather in those who made it up, young men and women of fine minds who passionately believed in Arthur Griffith's doctrine of Self-Reliance and spread it by public debate and lecture, and through the journals Griffith edited.

For twelve years he had preached his new evangel. He would take the Irish M.P.s out of the British Commons, where they were permanently outnumbered, and set them up in Ireland as its National Council. If Griffith seemed to achieve little that was dramatic, and if the Árd-Fheis of his movement was a yearly gathering of a few score, there was at work among the people a new ferment.

In many a hamlet and farmstead, in many a little room behind a city shop, young men crowded round a winter's fire to hear Griffith's paper read as they had crowded in Davis's day to hear the brave doctrine of *The Nation*. The Irish Parliamentary Party remained undisturbed in their mastery, with triumphant meetings and colourful processions, filling the squares and the streets with music and rich speech. Yet it was Griffith's words, read in the flickering light, that had unction.

The founding of the Irish Volunteers in November, 1913, was part of the same slow reawakening. Those with the deeper insight had made the Rising, and suddenly the spell of Redmondite oratory fell to pieces, and to the sound of the volleys of execution, Ireland got up off its knees.

Then the little gatherings around the fire became the spokesmen of their villages and their streets, and all these small groups together became the nucleus of the new national movement. As yet it was leaderless, without cohesion, unorganised. It has not even a clear-cut policy.

It was Lloyd George who solved these difficulties. With his " Irish Convention " he hit upon a new way of deceiving those naive Americans, who thought that if the war was a war for freedom, Britain ought to take her grip off Ireland.

At 3,000 miles distance he hoped that the Convention would bear the same appearance as the First Congress. He gave it the task of drafting an Irish constitution, having taken care that its hand-picked membership would allow no such thing. And then he released the long-term men.

The busiest political days in Ireland were those immediately after that amnesty. The Redmondites, the Unionists, the Dominion Home Rulers were arguing in the Convention about preserving imperial supremacy. The leaders of all the groups that shared the spirit of the Rising were planning the supremacy of Ireland. What was to be the name of the new movement? There were many to urge that it be not Sinn Féin. Sinn Féin had not even been Republican, but had stood for a semi-independent Ireland linked to Britain through the person of a joint monarch. It seemed impossible to fit the growing young Republican giant into that garment. But there was wisdom in keeping a name and using a movement already founded. Besides, was not the name Sinn Féin, if even in error, given to the Rising?

There were some, too, who thought that to Griffith, for his long and lonely work, was owed the tribute of keeping the name. There must, of course, be a new policy. What was that to be? Griffith said the people alone had the right to decide. The Volunteers replied that a Republic had already been declared. After much discussion, the new Constitution of Sinn Féin stated the objective thus:

> "Sinn Féin aims at securing the international recognition of Ireland as an independent Irish Republic.
> "Having achieved that status the Irish people may by Referendum freely choose their own form of Government."

During the conferences, which thus harmonised the past and the present, Griffith had been observing the M.P. for East Clare. He had not met de Valera in such circumstances before, but now as he listened and watched, he took a decision which he did not disclose publicly until half-way through the Árd-Fheis over which he presided.

Griffith's short stocky figure filled the chair as, veteran of many conventions, he looked down at the 2,000 delegates. Behind him sat the tall young man to whom politics were a new science. On the platform also was Count Plunkett, the oldest man present, stately, courteous, straight out of an Italian painting, and Fr. O'Flanagan, the orator of the new movement, typically Irish, tall, a more handsome Daniel O'Connell.

The other better-known leaders were there: William Cosgrave, Constance Markievicz, Eoin MacNeill, Cathal Brugha. Joseph McGuinness, victor of Longford, had marched to the Árd-Fheis at the head of his county's delegation.

As President of Sinn Féin, Griffith, in his speech, surveyed the years of pioneering. His labours in a twelve-year wilderness had at least something to do with this tremendous gathering. One fundamental principle of the old Sinn Féin policy had certainly been realised:

> "Ireland had renounced the British Parliament and with that renunciation had destroyed the moral sanction of English authority in this country."

He urged the delegates to realise that they were making history. The Press tables were crowded as Griffith spoke, and these journalists from many lands must have thought it one of the strangest political conventions they had seen. The vast majority of the delegates were young men and young women in their early twenties. There were hardly more than a dozen grey heads.

There were not even fireworks, for that age was dead too. Punctuality, brevity, order were the notes of this assembly. There was enthusiasm and eagerness, but subordinate to the commonsense of men and women who had work to do.

The first break with the past came early on the opening day. Some of the candidates for office on the National Executive were seen canvassing among the country delegates. A young man protested to the platform. He drew from de Valera the revealing reply: "Beginning a new Ireland, it will not be necessary to resort to such methods any more."

Somebody proposed that the Press, which had been almost unanimously hostile to Ireland's independence, should be excluded. The platform answered: "We are not a secret organisation and are afraid of no man."

When the aims of Sinn Féin were being debated, two of the older delegates proposed that the phrase undertaking to establish Irish freedom by "every means available" be qualified by adding "which in the judgment of the National Council are deemed legitimate and effective." Otherwise, the delegates said, it would be insinuated that the movement was revolutionary and anarchic. De Valera urged the Árd-Fheis to hold to the unqualified words "for Ireland must no longer truckle to insinuators." Here, assuredly, was a new breath blowing through the politics of Ireland.

A president for the organisation had to be chosen. This is what the newspapers waited for. Now there would be the coat-trailing and shillelaghs. The new movement, everybody outside it was assured, was already split: Griffith had the Sinn Féin clubs to force him in; Count Plunkett had the Liberty Clubs; de Valera had the Volunteers—they would stage the biggest faction fight in Irish history.

The chairman called the item on the agenda: "Election of President." The hall grew very still. Griffith rose. He announced the decision he had already taken that he would withdraw his name in favour of the M.P. for East Clare.

"De Valera," he said, "is a man of cool judgment. In him, as President, we will have a statesman as well as a soldier."

Count Plunkett rose immediately. He, too, begged leave to withdraw. And if that serious convention promptly gave way to rejoicing, it was not in partisan triumph that one man rather than another had been chosen, but that in this new Ireland men knew how to smother their ambitions that the nation proudly knit might face the world.

Before the session ended, another event occurred that was to set an example to every Árd-Fheis that followed. Since the Rising, as the preliminaries to East Clare had shown, a controversy had raged about the personality of Eoin MacNeill. Many had urged that this cleavage be not brought on to the floor of the Assembly.

But Countess Markievicz decided that she could not be silent when Eoin MacNeill's name appeared on the ballot paper. She asked that it be struck off. This was the man of whom James Connolly said " he cut the ground from under our feet." Griffith stood as passionately by Eoin MacNeill, and said he himself would stand or fall by him. De Valera quoted Pearse's tribute to MacNeill, and said that MacNeill had acted as a good Irishman : " Had I the slightest doubt of that he would not have been on my platform in Ennis."

The delegates listened, realising that in this new movement there was free speech and the courage to face even the most delicate problems if they affected Ireland. When each side had had its say, the delegates took a hand. Although that first Árd-Fheis was overwhelmingly in favour of those who participated in the Rising, MacNeill headed the poll.

Seldom in a national organisation was a breach of opinion among the leaders dealt with so patiently and then so decisively.

Then the officers of Sinn Féin were elected. Arthur Griffith and Father O'Flanagan were the Vice-Presidents ; William Cosgrave and Larry Ginnell, Hon. Treasurers ; Austin Stack and Darrell Figgis, Hon. Secretaries, and the members of the new Executive included several other names that were to be famous : Cathal Brugha, Michael Collins, Seán T. O Kelly, Seán MacEntee, Harry Boland, J. J. Walsh, Mrs. Tom Clarke.

Arthur Griffith vacated the chair, and the delegates rose in tribute as the new President came forward, a little shyly. It was the first time many of those present had heard him speak, and what they heard was so different from the colourful oratory of the old movement that it left them glancing at one another. It was direct, calm, quietly spoken—Griffith's was the same—with here and there a momentary burst of passion which, the contrast was so great, swept the delegates into demonstrations of support. The last words of the President's address brought them again to their feet.

He had talked of the need for a symbol of their unity. They had it, he told them, in the flag.

> " . . . the flag of the Republic. . . . I ask you to salute that flag, nailed to the mast, which we shall never lower—to salute the flag and in Grattan's words to say : ' Esto perpetua.' "

The Pressmen listened to the deep note in the cheering, and next day they wrote that Sinn Féin had in it something of which the British Government had better beware.

CHAPTER 5

THE MANSION HOUSE CONFERENCE

LIFE in any part of Ireland in the early months of 1918 was tense. The Convention was sitting more fruitlessly than ever in Trinity College. Lloyd George, when he heard there was likely to be agreement on a form of Dominion Home Rule, promptly changed the terms ! The letter in which he did so was dated 25th February, 1918. It provides a clue to when the British Premier came to the decision to take Irishmen by force into the British army.

The war was going desperately for England. Her armies were being forced back in a German offensive into which the Kaiser was putting his last remaining strength. The losses were so heavy that Lloyd George thought that soon there would be no reserves.

In this moment of fear, the enemies of Ireland had his ear. Sir Henry Wilson, Chief of the Imperial General Staff, himself frantically opposed to Irish freedom, pressed Conscription on him.

There were 150,000 Irishmen to be had for the taking, he told Lloyd George —advice which could only be called criminally insane. Every organisation in Ireland that could approach the Cabinet, pleaded that this madness be discarded, even a Convention sub-committee of which the Duke of Abercorn was a member. But Lloyd George was determined. He would get those Irish as soldiers somehow.

The wisdom of Easter Week was now proven beyond all doubt, even the material wisdom of it. The strength that the Irish people were able to pit against Lloyd George in this contest was the strength of a nation re-awakened to its rights. They had been given back by the Rising the one thing the people then needed, their own sense of the moral right to resist injustice in arms.

The Volunteers had, ever since the first releases, been rebuilding their organisation. It was no easy service. Volunteers, as will be told more fully later, worked at their ordinary employment by day and learned to be soldiers by night. All over the cities there were drill halls, mostly dance halls, and these were hired in the name of some innocent body—the Shop Assistants' Social Club, the Rathgar Literary Society, the Bricklayers' Union.

There was no lack of personnel to train this new army. Ireland never was at a loss for Sergeants from the British Army. If Dublin

Castle could have got near enough to those halls or to the clefts in the hills, where field training went on, they would have heard many a familiar voice disciplining Young Ireland.

One night I was in such a drill hall, this time in a basement, when Jack MacDonagh, whom I had often met in the Hardwicke Street Theatre, came down the stairs. We were standing to attention as he came in and I heard him ask for me. Called from the ranks, I was told to go to speak at a meeting which had been banned in a proclamation by the Military Governor of Dublin.

A Volunteer in those days just did what he was told, and a few minutes later I was in a packed hall in 41 York Street offering defiance to Major-General Friend and all his aides and accomplices.

It was a wonderful meeting. Young men with eager faces, girls ready for any danger, older men and women thoughtfully applauding, everywhere an air of resolution which could almost be felt. When it was over, and we had broken another enemy law and brought his proclamations into deeper disrepute, I went back to the drill hall and learnt the mechanism of the rifle.

As Lloyd George went ahead with his plan to take young Irishmen, the drill halls turned into munition factories. I recall many an evening spent in a loft in Corrigan's undertaking premises in Lower Camden Street. There—suitably near the coffins—my company, K of the Third, made bombs.

To most of us it was new, this cutting of sticks of gelignite with wooden knives, knowing there was always a chance of soaring heavenwards, accompanied by the now unnecessary coffins, if a piece of grit met with the wrong kind of cutter.

We were warned that gelignite must on no account be allowed to become affected by the cold. So in the evenings, when frost hung in the air, we put the sticks inside our shirts so that the gentle heat of the body could thaw them fully before we began to cut. It took time, and we turned to something else as the human oven did its work.

One evening, swathed in gelignite, I went to tea at a D.B.C. restaurant in Westmoreland Street, myself and my brother, who so soon afterwards was to be killed at rifle practice during Sunday manoeuvres.

Who should come to sit at our table—for the restaurant was crowded—but the Most Reverend Dr. Crozier, Lord Archbishop of Armagh, Protestant Primate of All Ireland. He greeted us and we fell to discussing the Convention, of which he was a member.

There were never in Ireland quieter disputants than the two of us. While not agreeing with everything he said, we expressed our dissent with such deference that he went away marvelling at the tolerance and courtesy in the Republican movement.

What if he knew that he was sitting beside half a hundredweight of gelignite and that our affability was due to the fact that we dare not disagree out loud with anybody on anything!

What we were doing among the coffins, Volunteers were doing in all kinds of odd places around Ireland. The British Government were determined to fetch us to die in France for them: we thought it was far more convenient to do the dying at home for Ireland. So did the mass of the people, who showed it in one of those demonstrations of national determination that can overawe an Empire, even an Empire at war.

The Irish Party resisted every line of Lloyd George's Conscription Bill, but were solidly voted down. Typically, Lloyd George taunted them with having supported the declaration of war in 1914 which, he said, was tantamount to assuming a responsibility for supplying troops!

The Bill passed, and the Irish M.P.s left the House in a body and came to Ireland on 16th April to participate in the people's resistance.

Just at this time two bye elections went against Sinn Féin, with results that might have been disastrous. John Redmond died on 6th March.

The bye election in Waterford on 22nd March was won by Redmond's son, after a contest which tried Sinn Féin's policy of restraint to the full. A fortnight later, on 4th April, Seán Milroy was defeated in East Tyrone.

Lloyd George, as always, jumped to conclusions. Ireland was turning against Sinn Féin! He brushed aside a warning he had just got from President Wilson that conscripting Irishmen would cause profound resentment in the United States; he put the Report of the Convention (8th April) into his pocket without reading it—he had kept the Irish talking!—and ordered full speed ahead with Conscription.

The Irish were ready. The Lord Mayor of Dublin called a Conference, and the Mansion House suddenly became the seat of what was in all but name, a Government: John Dillon and Joe Devlin for the Irish Party; Arthur Griffith and Éamon de Valera for Sinn Féin; William O'Brien, of Mallow, for the All-For-Ireland League; Tim Healy for the Independents; William O'Brien, of Dublin; Michael Egan and Tom Johnson, for Labour. The people talked of it as a National Cabinet, and so for the period of crisis it was.

If the Sinn Féin leaders found themselves in strange company, there was still a bond between almost all who sat around Lord Mayor O'Neill's table. For Dillon had been in prison in the Land Wars, and so had William O'Brien, and the Labour leaders had been comrades of James Connolly.

With patience and care it was possible to get resolute leadership for the crisis. It was de Valera who got it. It was he who steered those conflicting minds to the simple declaration that knit every man and woman in Ireland :

> " Denying the right of the British Government to enforce compulsory service in this country, we pledge ourselves solemnly to one another to resist conscription by the most effective means at our disposal."

It was blessing No. 1 on those bombs we had been making.

The Catholic Hierarchy were then sitting at Maynooth, and the whole National Conference went off to plead with them not to declare against armed resistance. The speeches made to their lordships were in private, but it became known that it was Dillon's speech that won the day. The Bishops, in their Joint Declaration, said :

> " We consider that conscription forced in this way upon Ireland is an oppressive and inhuman law, which the Irish people have a right to resist by every means that are consonant with the law of God."

It was blessing No. 2 on those bombs. Every Volunteer knew now that, in fact, he had been recognised as a soldier of Ireland, fighting justly against tyranny.

There followed a Solemn League and Covenant. On Sunday, 21st April, three days before the Second Anniversary of the Rising, at church gate, town hall, at people's doors, in every place where men and women gathered, two million people signed the declaration pledging themselves to one another to resist conscription if necessary with their lives.

A song ran through Ireland :

> " We'll set Ireland free from the sod to the sky on you :
> There's a surprise for you, David Lloyd George ! "

And the Trade Unions added their hammer blow. On 23rd April a General Strike was called. The whole of Ireland, outside parts of four counties, responded with a demonstration that had never before been seen. Trams stopped, factory wheels stood still, no meals were served in hotels, no office doors opened. Wealthy visitors over for Punchestown offered fabulous prices to taximen to drive them to the racecourse. They were refused. Theatres, cinemas and publichouses closed, even the myriad little huckster shops.

The British Cabinet received reports of Ireland's grim resolve gloomily. Dublin Castle had told them that they would need three army corps to get one out of Ireland. Now they knew they would probably need five. But they would go on.

To show they meant business, they appointed Lord French as Viceroy; Lord French, who had been the Commander of all the British War armies in France. He soon made it known that imposing Conscription was a mere bagatelle to him.

A change in the leading personnel of the military and police forces was made. New men, tough enough to face the holocaust Conscription must mean, took office. In the British Cabinet the Chief Secretary, Duke, was removed and replaced by Edward Shortt, who was thought to have the " grit " to see this thing through.

Ireland, too, got ready. For the first time since the Rising there were raids on British posts for arms. Drilling was carried on openly. An Anti-Conscription Fund was opened, and when it had reached £100,000 it was still climbing. A Woman's Day was held in every part of Ireland, on which the women went through the streets in procession and then attended special religious services to implore God's help in this hour of trial.

At Christ Church Cathedral many Protestant women of Dublin had a chilly reception, but they gathered in the gardens of the Cathedral and there prayed for Ireland's safety. Great meetings were held, and at one of these, at Ballaghaderreen, John Dillon and de Valera spoke from the same platform the united mind of the people.

The middle of May came, and then Britain seemed suddenly to realise the magnitude of what she was attempting, and in desperation she struck.

CHAPTER 6

THE " GERMAN PLOT "

DUBLIN was seething with rumours on the afternoon of 17th May 1918. There was nothing tangible, but something like a commonly-shared intuition. The British Government was about to take action in some way. Warnings went out to Volunteer leaders. As the evening drew on, the activity of the G-men (as Dublin Castle's political police were called) confirmed the darkly-expectant mood.

That night the Executive of Sinn Féin met as usual in the Head-quarters of 6 Harcourt Street. The talk soon reflected the belief that wholesale arrests were to be made. It was decided that Sinn Féin would carry on as if there were to be no change.

The alternative was for the movement to go underground, but what Ireland needed now was a national organisation working in the open for freedom. As they left Harcourt Street for their homes, the leaders wondered where they would be on the morrow.

In fact, they were on a cruiser speeding to a long imprisonment in Britain. It had been a night of sensations. As de Valera's train to Greystones stopped at Bray, armed police got into the compartment just behind his and, when he got out at his destination, he was sur-rounded and taken prisoner.

Arthur Griffith was in bed in the early morning when police raided his home in Fairview and told him they had orders for his arrest and deportation. Countess Markievicz, with an English visitor, was on her way back from an evening with AE when she was taken into custody on the Rathmines Road. Madame Maud Gonne MacBride was arrested in her home. Seán MacEntee and Denis McCullough were seized in Belfast. Tom Hunter, with many others, in Cork. Count Plunkett was taken at Amiens Street Station as he arrived back from visiting his re-imprisoned son in Derry. With every half-hour the list grew—Frank Fahy, Joe McGrath, Páidín O'Keeffe, the shrewd and pugnacious secretary of Sinn Féin.

As the papers next morning carried the news to the people, a pilgrimage began to Dun Laoghaire, and there by the quay lay the cruiser. Already there were fifty leaders aboard and others were coming hourly.

The people had also come, and had filled the whole west pier, and as each new batch of prisoners arrived they were hurried aboard to the sounds of songs of defiance and cheers of encouragement. Now and again a light-hearted captive would wave to the great crowd, and then everyone started happily off again filling the port with rebel airs.

Sinn Féin issued a statement:

> " Anticipating such action, the Standing Committee of Sinn Féin nominated substitutes to carry on the movement during the enforced and, what may be, the temporary exile of our leaders. The country may rest assured that no matter how many leaders may be arrested, there will be men and women to take their places. All that we need is to continue to follow the latest advice of de Valera, namely, to remain calm and confident."

It was signed " Michael O'Flanagan, C.C."

The same newspapers that carried the story of the arrests published a pompous proclamation from Lord French, the new Viceroy. It announced the discovery of a " German Plot," but those who could read between the lines knew it was something else that had been discovered—that the people's will to resist conscription was unbreakable. This was the revenge. The Proclamation began:

> " WHEREAS it has come to our knowledge that certain subjects of His Majesty the King domiciled in Ireland have conspired to enter and have entered into treasonable communication with the Germany enemy . . .
>
> AND WHEREAS drastic measures must be taken to put down this German Plot. . . .
>
> NOW THEREFORE we, the Lord Lieutenant General and General Governor of Ireland have thought fit to issue this our Proclamation declaring and it is hereby declared as follows . . ."

What followed, called on " all loyal subjects " to crush the conspiracy and secure the effective prosecution of the war. And then came the tell-tale conclusion:

> " That as a means to this end we shall cause still further steps to be taken to facilitate and encourage voluntary enlistment in Ireland in His Majesty's Forces."

It should have been disastrous to Ireland's cause among the Allied nations that the British Government had " unearthed " a conspiracy between the great new national movement and Germany. The British people themselves were fighting for their lives. The French were all but bled to death by terrible losses, and in this new German advance they saw their homeland once more ravaged and their now scarce sons falling ever faster. American mothers, so long inured to peace, were sorrowing over loved ones sailing to slaughter.

The proclamation of the German plot should consequently have made Ireland's name hateful. There were very many in Europe and America who believed the story, but there were millions who did not. Ireland's resistance to conscription had touched the hearts of freedom-loving peoples everywhere, and these brought a deeper sympathy to Ireland.

Soon the plot story started of its own weight to fall to pieces. Edward Shortt, the new Chief Secretary, was asked why, if Ireland were so deeply implicated, was the Viceroy calling for still more recruits from those " treasonable " Irish. He had to placate a puzzled Commons with the admission that the " number of Irishmen and women who are in active co-operation with the German enemy is very small, but many of them might unwittingly become involved."

From all over the world came a call to Lloyd George to produce the proofs. The *New York Times* urged that he substantiate his statements, as " Sinn Féiners here are saying that it is a concoction," and there were a few million Sinn Féiners in America. The English Press, a little hoarse from its anti-Irish denunciations, felt embarrassed too, and began to demand a public trial for the deported men—" to convince doubters." But the thing the British Premier wished above all to avoid was a trial, and, using his gift for hypocrisy to the full, he told the Commons that he had read through the evidence, and it was " a sad unpleasant story to any friend of Ireland—but it could not be published."

The demand for proof went on, and at last the British published a statement. But it was all words and it failed to connect Sinn Féin with anything later than the Rising, and it was now that the Sinn Féin leaders who were supposed to be conspiring with Germany.

The whole fabrication collapsed a few weeks later when Lord Wimborne, the Viceroy who had been removed to make room for Lord French, told the House of Lords that he did not believe a word about any German plot, and that it had all the appearance of being thought up by the " new broom " to show how clever he was.

As for the Irish people, they went on with their anti-conscription preparations. The fund reached £200,000 while Lloyd George was fumbling with his " evidence." And then came the real purpose behind the plot.

Now that Ireland was leaderless and, it was hoped, the sympathy for her abroad had been killed, Britain felt sure her young men dare not resist enlisting. Lord French issued another Proclamation. He asked for 50,000 recruits before 1st October and for 2,000 to 3,000 a month after that. There was to be a nice bribe for everyone who would come forward !

"Those who fight for their motherland," the Proclamation said, " are entitled to share in all that their motherland can offer. Steps are therefore being taken to ensure as far as possible that land shall be available for men who have fought for their country."

At that the house fell around Lord French's ears. The English, Scottish and Welsh asked : " What will we get ? " The men with land in Ireland, and the sons of farmers, asked " Whose land ? " The situation was not improved by the *Morning Post's* suggestion that land should be taken from Sinn Féiners as a penalty for treason.

In the House of Commons, M.P.'s jumped up like flies to ask by what right the Viceroy made a promise which would need legislation and about which the House had not been consulted let alone agreed. Lloyd George wriggled, but the bribe had to be withdrawn. And now British statecraft tried to strike a bargain. If Irishmen volunteered, Conscription would be dropped.

To aid recruitment, the British and their friends in Ireland prepared a great drive, beginning with an appeal over the names of A. M. Sullivan, Stephen Gwynn and M. Dockrell, in which they used the old Nationalist ideal of fighting for liberty to get young Irishmen to volunteer. But if they did not—! A Recruiting Council of Ireland was formed, and Gwynn, addressing the Galway Urban Council, said that if Irishmen did not do their share voluntarily, " all the machinery was ready for Conscription."

Serjeant Sullivan, K.C., another member of the Recruiting Council, told the Limerick Chamber of Commerce : " Within 24 hours the military could clear every available man out of Clare and put him in a barbed-wire cage in France."

Every organisation favourable to Britain was roped in. The recruiting meetings were to be the most impressive gatherings ever held in Ireland. There would be bands and marches and real oratory. The Volunteer Executive decided that there would also be a few uninvited guests.

Just at the right moment a fillip came, in the form of another bye-election. East Cavan fell vacant, and the British watched it eagerly in the hope that Sinn Féin might be defeated.

There was hardly a Sinn Féiner who could put two words together, or one who could handle a register, or a canvasser who could argue, but poured into East Cavan. Though the cream had been whipped off by the deportations, they made a goodly crowd. Day and night they struggled with the people's minds, for they knew what was at stake.

It amazed many of us young men, from counties where Sinn Féin was opposed only by the old, to see the processions of young Hibernians marching against the new Ireland. It made the task harder and the fight more violent, but Sinn Féin grew in that struggle, and under Father O'Flanagan's leadership the energy put into the contest was terrific.

Arthur Griffith was the candidate ; he was now in Gloucester Jail, one of the plot prisoners. To get him elected for this Ulster county would be the sharpest answer to Lord French and the British Cabinet. Men and women abandoned their offices, and some their employment, to achieve that.

Fr. O'Flanagan spoke five or six times a day : the election workers were out at dawn, and were still at it in village and townland and hillside farm when dark fell. They did it. Arthur Griffith, even in this Hibernian stronghold, got 3,785 votes and the Irish Party's O'Hanlon 2,581.

The victory was the more striking, as the Irish Party, under its leader John Dillon, threw every ounce they had left of their energy and influence into the contest. The declaration of the poll was the signal for a demonstration throughout Ireland which showed Britain how triumphantly Sinn Féin had survived the great blow struck at it.

A new wave of arrests began. But it was too late now. Sinn Féin had met the challenge, and, in facing it, had re-found its highest courage.

CHAPTER 7

SEDITION OPEN, MERRY AND UNABASHED

IN all my memories of the Four Glorious Years, there are none so vivid as the capturing of the recruiting meetings.

Ireland was then more tightly in the grip of military repression than ever. The new Viceroy, having cooked up the German plot and swept away the leaders, now struck at everything that reflected the national ideal. Anybody locally prominent in Sinn Féin or the Volunteers, Cumann na mBan or the Gaelic League was arrested.

So rapidly did the arrests grow that they became the main work of the police, who were by now police only in name : they had become part of the active Army of Occupation.

After the Recruiting Council had been set up with the task of : " 50,000 before October 1st or else ——," the Viceroy felt the opposition of the people stiffen. He decided to break this national stubbornness.

On 15th June, sixteen Irish counties and cities were declared " proclaimed districts " under the Permanent Coercion Act of 1887. Three days later, other parts of Ireland were scheduled as " Special Military Areas," which brought them under British War legislation and suppressed all meetings, even fairs.

Then on 4th July—no doubt to celebrate the American Declaration of Independence—the major national organisations were declared to be " dangerous associations"—every Sinn Féin club, every branch of the Irish Volunteers, of the Gaelic League and Cumann na mBan, membership of any of these four organisations, in which almost the whole of Ireland's nationalist youth was then enrolled, became a crime.

Orders were issued by the Castle that local R.I.C. chiefs were to decide whether any gathering of any kind would be permitted. At Ballymacoda, Co. Cork, the local D.I. told the Gaelic League organiser of the O'Neill Crowley Féis : " I will not allow an address in Irish : I am here to stop any such thing." The organiser promptly gave his address in French. All G.A.A. games were stopped and the spectators dispersed. Even Camogie games were banned.

Then the Irish people decided this thing had gone far enough, and they showed what can be done by a nation that has its share of courage. In the first week of August, G.A.A. teams in every parish in the country went to their sports' grounds and played the forbidden games. Some were broken up, but as there were nearly fifteen hundred of them, there were not enough R.I.C. and troops to go round.

On 15th August, Sinn Féin organised a perfectly-timed defiance of a similar kind. At the one hour throughout the whole land the local Sinn Féin Cumann held a public meeting. There were nearly 2,000 Cumainn. In almost every townland, and in the cities in almost every street, the people gathered and defied the big and little military governors.

Each meeting was timed to last fifteen minutes, and as soon as word of it came to the local British headquarters and troops and police had been assembled to disperse it, the meeting was over. In Dublin, Constabulary hurried from street to street noting who was speaking, who was listening. Soon they realised that it was all Dublin which was defying them, and, in the country, all Ireland. They threw up their hands—what could be done with a people like that?

Meanwhile, the Recruiting Council was beginning to encounter rough weather. The more notable members of it, Capt. Stephen Gwynn, M.P.; Col. Arthur Lynch, M.P.; Capt. James O'Grady, M.P., had been appearing before public bodies, making their recruiting speeches. Then the people asserted themselves there too. First, Sligo Corporation refused to hear Colonel Lynch; then Waterford Corporation rescinded a motion to hear Capt. Gwynn, and soon that prairie was on fire also, and no public body would hear any of them.

One morning, well-designed posters appeared all over Dublin. the real business of getting Irish reinforcements for the British armies had begun. The first great recruiting rally was fixed for Kildare Place on 24th August. It was to be the grand send-off to a passion of fire and oratory—and so it was, but the goods were not as advertised.

Thousands came to that first meeting, and their mood was quiet. Some had come on the heels of the parading bands, some because they believed in the British cause. But many came because they wanted to know if there was really a way of equating the war for freedom for small nations with military repression, the crammed jails, deported leaders, endless midnight raids, outlawed associations.

Colonel Lynch was the principal orator that night. He had been a member of the Irish Brigade that fought for the Boers; he had been a lifelong champion of Home Rule. The crowd were not unfriendly to him though they tossed him an odd interjection. One of those interruptions was his Waterloo. A voice asked: " Why not stop in Ireland and share our dangers?" There was cheering at this because it so reflected the mood of the moment. Lynch waited until the cheers died down. Then he said : " Stop in Ireland and share your cowardice ! " These seven words not only undid him but the whole recruiting campaign.

Michael Collins and Harry Boland, who had escaped the widecast net of the German Plot, were somewhere at the edge of that first meeting. Joe Stanley, who ran the Juverna Press, and myself, were asked to meet Mick and Harry. It was decided that, instead of allowing the meetings to dissolve into unorganised hostility, they should be captured for Sinn Féin.

Henceforth, Joe and I—and others, too, for I remember Mrs. Joseph Plunkett and Seán O'Duffy—were to be standing beside the platform, and when the opportunity came we were to climb up and carry the meeting away from whatever Captain or Colonel was in charge that night.

The picture of the meeting at the fountain in James's Street stays brightly in my mind. Joe Stanley and I decided we would present Colonel Lynch, who was the main speaker, with a letter.

It was a very polite letter. It reminded him that he had said in Kildare Place that it was the dearest hope of his life to induce some Sinn Féiners to join the British army. We asked to be given the courtesy of his platform " to enable the position of Sinn Féin to be explained and to defend the young men of Ireland against the imputation of cowardice."

It was a lovely autumn evening. The military bands in full regalia had marched through the city, and had the pleasure of seeing hundreds, then thousands march with them. Everybody was on his way to James's Street Fountain. The street was packed from side to side, and, as I recall it, melting away into the distance was the sea of faces.

The crowd were good-humoured, and while waiting for the speakers, sang national songs against the harmless tunes of the military bands. There was no hostile demonstration when the military speakers arrived in their khaki and gold braid. The band struck up some Irish air that had no Fenian associations, and then Col. Lynch stepped forward.

At the same time, Joe Stanley mounted one of the wheels and, calling him, handed him the letter. He put it into his pocket without reading it. He faced the crowd and the thunderstorm broke.

Not one word was he allowed to speak. The vast crowd cheered, sang, shouted, danced even. Colonel Lynch stood facing them, and suddenly a lull came. Before he could use it, another speaker's voice arose over the heads of the crowd. Away on the far side of the street there was a float, and who was on it but Pádraic Ó Conaire and he speaking in Irish ! The cheer that shot up rent the heavens, and Colonel Lynch's chance to get even one word in was lost.

He stood facing that sea of noise and protest, still smiling and it seemed still hoping. We called on him to open the letter. Instead, at some signal we did not see, he and the others turned and hurriedly left the platform. Before they had disappeared, Joe and I were up and that vast crowd was now as still as a Wicklow lake, and our voices were echoed back from the houses opposite.

It certainly was good to be alive and in Ireland on that strange night. All meetings had been suppressed. All speakers were instantly seized and clapped into prison. Batons, and if necessary bayonets, were out if a crowd would not break up quickly enough. And here were we, in the heart of Ireland's capital, talking sky-high treason to a multitude that could not be dispersed because this was a meeting to attract recruits to the British army!

So we spoke to our heart's content, and there was never a readier audience to salute every sturdy thing we said. It was not far from midnight when that great crowd broke up and went marching back to the centre of the city.

The next meeting was fixed for Portland Row, and if James's Street was dramatic, there was high tension here. Word had gone round that as soon as the Captains and the Kings departed, Sinn Féin would be there. It became like the eve of a general election. Wherever the recruiters were to be, there the people came in endless procession. Every face was smiling. Remembering the furtive fifteen minutes of 15th August, this was glorious. Sedition open, merry and unabashed.

Capt. Gwynn was the orator for that night. His tall figure and handsome face would have interested any other audience, but this throng had but one thing to do : to sing the rebel songs until those gold-braided soldiers bowed themselves out.

Joe and I were again below, calling for the letter to be read, copies of which had been sent to Recruiting Council's headquarters. But even if it had been produced, it would not have been listened to that night.

Eventually they bowed to the storm, and Joe and I had to be quickly up, as there were the beginnings of anger as the military moved away, and we must see that they be given a safe conduct and be free from jibes. They went, and then again a vast meeting heard Sinn Féin's answer.

This time I noticed that the number of R.I.C. men scattered through the crowd was much greater, and here and there near the platform was a " G " man. What they thought of the reasons we gave from His Britannic Majesty's recruiting platform, why Irishmen should *not* join the Army, none of us knew, but their presence was a sign that these glorious opportunities might not last.

They didn't. I forgot now how many more meetings we turned

D

into Sinn Féin rallies and concerts of lusty rebels. But the last of them still is silhouetted in my memory.

The crowd was stretched out before me. The sky was brilliant with evening light, now deepening into red whose glow tinged all those eager, up-turned faces and gave to that last meeting the picturesqueness of a surrealist painting.

The military orators, who in many nights had not spoken one clearly audible word, had done. As they prepared to go, Col. Lynch went close to the Pressmen, hardly two yards below him, and began to dictate a speech. The crowd at that moment saw what he was doing, and not even the journalists heard anything. Then it was over: their car sped back to the Kildare Street Club or wherever silenced recruiters go.

Joe Stanley had spoken, and I had just begun when I noticed among all those lit-up faces one coming closer to the platform. It had caught my glance because of the jet-black moustache. It came closer. I was fascinated by it. As I warmed to my speech, I had noticed that the R.I.C. were now almost in a cordon around the platform, and that the " G " men were still more numerous. But all that, and what it might have meant, was lost in the jet curves of that moustache.

The left eye above it winked as its bearer stopped just beyond the R.I.C. cordon. And then I recognised him. It was Harry Boland —in disguise ! And at that moment I heard his voice, sharp, with a tone of command. " Jump, over the cordon, quick."

I was of lesser weight then. I rose as birds to the sound of a gun. Many hands came up to receive me, and I was passed bodily over the heads of the crowd out towards the edge of the meeting. Harry Boland was beside me when I was put down on my feet, and he said merely : " Get home as quick as you can."

As I turned the corner I looked back at the platform. It was crowded with R.I.C. men. The cordon had closed just too late.

Not anywhere else in the world could there have been such strange recruiting meetings in the midst of a war as those in the heart of Dublin in the August of 1918. Sinn Féin, so censored everywhere else, said its say without let or hindrance, and Lord French never got a tenth of his 50,000.

CHAPTER 8

BAFFLING THE CENSOR

THE people of to-day have no chance of knowing how hard it was to get the truth into print during those years. Censorship is inseparable from war, and if Ireland had to submit only to what all warring States impose on themselves it might have been tolerable. But soon after the war started, the British added a political to a military censorship, and with every month the censors' realm grew wider. Lists of instructions went to every editor, telling him not only what he must not publish at all, but also what he must not publish until it bore the censor's initials.

What did survive was headed " Passed by Censor," and neat rows of dots showed where cuts had been made. These were warnings to everybody that much was hidden. But soon the dots themselves were censored, and then the legend " Passed by Censor " vanished. Thereafter, nobody knew where the news had been cut, and eventually many forgot there was a censorship at all.

Endlessly the Independence movement tried to find ways to get inside the censor. It became a considerable part of the national struggle, for it was regarded as vital to get any means of reminding the people that there *was* a censorship. Mainly the reminders were given through what was known as the Mosquito Press. Who gave it that name I don't know, but it neatly fitted the journals to which it was applied—small, difficult to kill, and with a bite that was remembered. Though I forget to what periods they belonged, I remember many names : *Old Ireland, New Ireland, Young Ireland, Honesty, The Republic, The Irish Nation, Irish Opinion, The Irish Volunteer, The Spark, The Voice of Freedom, Nationality, Scissors and Paste, The Watchword of Labour, An Saoghal Gaedhealach, The Voice of Labour, The Irishman, The Tribune, Liberator*. There were others, I'm sure.

Arthur Griffith was the great initiator of this underground journalism. No sooner was one paper suppressed, than he had started another. The cleverest of all was his *Scissors and Paste*. This consisted mainly of items already passed by the censor. It broke no law, therefore, but by the method of juxtaposition it conveyed a tremendous lot to the people, and brought many an outburst in the censor's office. What Griffith did was simple ; he placed two news items side by side, making no comment whatever himself. One told of British arrests in Ireland. The one next to it of German arrests in Belgium. That was all, but the people had the parallel. Or a British newspaper's account of the Germans using Czechs in the most dangerous part of the line was followed by the latest total of Irish war casualties. The censors didn't know what to do, and so after a few months, *Scissors and Paste* disappeared overnight, joining the growing ranks of the suppressed, no reason given.

Griffith, and others of the Sinn Féin journalists, were past-masters, too, at the historical allusion. Comparisons which entirely escaped the censors, who knew little Irish history, would be an eloquent comment for the Irish reader. The use of the word Mullaghmast next to some British account of " massacre " by the enemy, or the one word Drogheda in reference to propaganda about burning of churches.

Griffith's greatest triumph was the leading article in which he described the fate of a mythical small nation held down by a great Power. No country was named, but the article was so worded that the censor would think immediately of some of Germany's victims. It was a passionate and indignant article, and when the censor had read it, he, no doubt, thought of those paradoxical Sinn Féiners—they would not join in the war, and yet they felt deeply about the sufferings of the peoples the Germans had invaded. Everybody else had no trouble in recognising the country whose fate Griffith described so movingly. It was Ireland, the Ireland of that very day. The young man who so painstakingly initialled that article was back in England by the next boat, for even Dublin Castle had no trouble in recognising the land of which Griffith wrote.

What were they like, these gentlemen of the blue pencil? I had a great deal to do with them, for it was my job for over a year to bring them all the contents of one of the Republican weeklies every Tuesday evening. P. J. Little, editor and publisher of *Old Ireland*, was one of the Old Guard, and to us, younger men, his name was honourable indeed. He had done many a brave thing for the men of the Rising and their successors, and his writing now had sturdiness and courage in it. My task was to get as much of what Paddy Little wrote, and something of the few pieces I wrote myself, through the big Grafton Street office.

The Censor-in-Chief was the Rt. Hon. Lord John Graham Hope de la Poer Beresford, the Baron Decies—big, bluff, patronising if you let him; typical Anglo-Irishman of the " huntin', fishin' and shootin' " tradition. He was completely British in his way of thinking, and was blessed, thank God, with little subtlety. His predominant passion was racing. He had a string of horses himself, and a few years before had won the Irish Derby with, I think, Ballaghtobin. He probably never discovered how those horses were his undoing as a censor. His staff included a number of university dons, whom we, benighted Republicans, thought should be at the front. They were not quite so simple as his Lordship, and I insisted on dealing with Lord Decies. We became friends, he and I, but mine was not a disinterested friendship. I knew he would want to get away to the Kildare Street Club as the evening drew on, and I would appear just an hour or so earlier with my bundle of proofs. As I laid them on his desk I would ask casually about some horse of his that was either running that week or was in training, or one that he had just bought. " You know, Hogan . . ." he would begin, and, lighting a cigar, would consume it and a good deal of his time as he told me all the merits of that horse, and it is only an owner who knows how many merits a horse really has. Then I would drop a sympathetic word about the hard luck a horse of his had recently, and questioned whether the weight he had to carry was really fair. Milord always rose to this commiseration, and we almost wept together as the clock ticked a little more. It was always I who said : " But, my lord, we should be at the proofs." " Gracious, so we should," he would say, and would apologise for talking so much and would settle down to censorship.

There would not be much to cut in the great bulk of what I brought and that, too, was part of the game, for if we brought a little it would get more attention. Somewhere towards the end of the bundle was the proof which was " dangerous " that week. Club-time would almost be on us, and his Lordship would be getting just a little impatient when he came to it. I would suggest that he should read that particular proof himself. He hated doing this, but his pencil would faithfully travel from line to line, and then as he came near the paragraph we dearly wanted in, I would say something about income tax. Lord Decies was chairman of the Income Tax Payers' Society, and if he felt passionately about horses, he felt wildly about income tax. The pencil would still go on, but his Lordship's thoughts and words would be about something very different, and soon I would be sailing back to Paddy Little with one proof that should have been " killed."

It was a great game, and was played with infinite variety. Another part of the technique was to place the " dangerous " proof just below three or four others which we knew he would never pass ; some of them, indeed, would have been set up specially to be suppressed. He would strike out the first. I would say : " You are very stern to-night, milord." He would suppress the second and third to the cries of my despair, and then feeling a little guilty himself, he would come to the proof we wanted to get through at all cost. If he paused, I'd say : " But if you touch that one, too, there'll be nothing left for the paper." It did not always work, as witness one leading article which, when published, began with the word " Secondly." But the percentage of victories made it worth trying.

Because Lord Decies was fundamentally honest, it was easy to persuade him with a good argument. In one article, in which we were giving the Viceroy a drubbing, we referred to him as " Lord French, hero of the Mons retreat." Milord reacted violently. " You can't say that." I told him his judgments were sometimes hasty, and he did not let himself see the real meaning of the words he wanted to cut. " You can't deny," said I, " that he was the hero of the Mons retreat. It was a very difficult withdrawal, milord." " Difficult," he exploded; " it was the most masterly military manœuvre of the whole war ! " " Well," said I, " that's what we're saying : ' Lord French, hero of the most masterly military manœuvre of the whole war.' " " Yes," the poor man said, puzzled, " but you don't mean that." " But you have just said yourself, Lord Decies, that that's what the words mean." He gave me a long, pained and baffled look, but the phrase was saved.

Another phrase rescued in the same way was a reference to the loop line which had been built across the Liffey just above the Custom House. It destroyed the view from O'Connell Bridge of that beautiful building, and in a description I wrote of the triumphal progress of Madame Markievicz on her return from Holloway Prison I referred to it as " like the blue daub of the censor on a great idea." " That must go," he said firmly. " By no means," I replied; " it has nothing to do with war or politics; it is not seditious or treasonable; it is just a perfect phrase and if you had any poetry in your soul you would pass it, my lord." He hesitated, and I asked him to tell me what he thought of that wretched bridge in front of that lovely building. He was quite eloquent himself, and as he wrote his initials, he looked sideways at me and said : " I shouldn't be doing this, for you mean it as a criticism of the censorship." And so, of course, I did, and as a way of reminding the people that a censorship existed.

Naturally, there were many stories of this breezy Lord and his war-work. One of these was of P. J. Lynch, then editor of the *Sunday Independent*. P.J., who was a stout old Republican, had a halt in his speech which he could use with devastating effect.

It is the fate of all evening papers that they must go to press without the result of the last race. So when the staff of the *Sunday* take over, there are many 'phone calls by punters for the name of the winner. To wheedle an answer, the 'phoners say they are a first cousin of the owner or a brother of the Chairman of the Board or the son of this Director or that. The tempers of the *Sunday* staff after half-a-dozen rings, begin to get short. One Saturday evening, P. J. Lynch was in the newsroom when call after call came in. At last, at about the tenth, he said, " I'll fix that one," and grabbed the 'phone. " W-W-Well, and w-w-who is it this t-t-time ? " he asked, expecting someone to say he was the Lord Mayor of Dublin. Instead the voice said, " This is the Chief Censor." " W-W-Well, that's t-t-the b-b-best lie t-t-to-day," said P.J., adding with infinite scorn, " and I s-s-suppose you want to know t-t-the name of the w-w-winner of the l-l-last r-r-race ? " Lord Decies, for it was he, was delighted : " Thanks very much, that's very kind of you, who won ? " " B-B-Buy to-morrow's *S-S-Sunday*," answered P.J., and slammed down the 'phone. Five minutes later an armoured car was outside the office with a special order milord had wished to communicate by 'phone.

The news items which never survived the blue pencil often decorated the newspaper office walls. The best was the recruiting speech of Michael O'Leary's father in his native Inchigeela. For incredible bravery, his son had won the Victoria Cross, and the War Office took the father on to the recruiting platforms, or rather platform, for he did not last more than one meeting. His speech, as the censor killed it, was something like this :

> " Mr O'Leary, senior, father of the famous V.C., speaking in the Inchigeela district, urged the young men to join the British army. ' If you don't,' he told them, " the Germans will come here and will do to you what the English have been doing for the last seven hundred years."

But it was not all laughter, for many a plucky Irish printer, who, despite the censorship, tried to get the truth to the people or to print what would sustain their hearts in a bitter hour, had his printing house invaded by the Royal Engineers and his machinery dismantled. His way of livelihood was gone and his workers could starve or, if they didn't like that, join the British army.

Yet despite it all the facts were got to the people, by secretly printed leaflet, by the Mosquito Press, by innocent-seeming letters to the daily papers and they led to the most spectacular victory in the history of Irish politics.

CHAPTER 9

THE GENERAL ELECTION

THERE was never a general election in Ireland like that of December, 1918. It was not that it was carried out in a country under military repression ; nor that most of the Sinn Féin candidates were in prison and never saw the electors ; nor that right through it arrests were going on of key-election workers.

From the beginning there was about it a sense of the parting of the ways. Something was being done that would change everything. The present was going out and not only the future but the past was coming in.

A vivid kinship arose between Sinn Féin and all who had fallen for freedom, a national communion of souls. The by-gone generations seemed to be standing beside this generation whose banners flew so bravely. The election workers felt this presence of the past : of the Croppies in their mass graves, the Famine dead under the tumbled roofs, the distraught wearers of the pitch-caps, the gaunt parents who from the woods saw their ripe corn burning under Carew's torches and pressed their famished children to their sides.

This is no exaggeration or lyricism. There was that feeling in the election of 1918—that Tone was driving in from the sea, triumphant now ; that Davis had not died but was young and eager amongst us ; that Mitchel's angry heart was coining words for the speakers ; that the meanness which had tortured Parnell was being cleansed away for ever.

Remember we were but two-and-a-half years from the Rising ; that in every month of that time people were punished for their fidelity to freedom, that now as the election progressed there was open tyranny at every corner : the R.I.C. man with his rifle and his note-book near the platforms of even the small meetings. Wherever the constabularly got the excuse they clubbed the people unmercifully, their long, stone-hard batons rising and falling.

I remember one day—it was somewhere in the Midlands—when the local military satrap proclaimed one of the early Sinn Féin meetings before the election date was fixed. Father O'Flanagan was to be the principal speaker. As usual a procession met him at the station and was marching towards the meeting-place. As we turned a corner we found, across the road, a line of troops with fixed bayonets. There was a moment of hesitation and then Fr. O'Flanagan squared his shoulders and, stepping out a little in front of us all, led us to that line of pointed steel.

He said nothing : we said nothing. In complete silence he walked on. If there were shouts of " Halt," as I suppose there must have been, they meant nothing to us. Our eyes were on that buff cordon and the black square shoulders of the priest. Fr. O'Flanagan seemed to add to his great height as he all but met the bayonets and without turning gave one commanding gesture to us that come what may we must go forward. The barrier of bayonets broke as he walked into them, all of us now almost beside him, and we passed through in the same hard silence.

Then suddenly and spontaneously there arose a shout of victory, the like of which I did not ever hear in my life before or since. It was not only of the triumph of the unarmed over the armed, it was of the fierce determination of the unarmed to drive out the armed. And in a second that note was gone, too, and we were swinging along chorusing somebody in " Kelly, the Boy from Killanne."

There was that spirit everywhere : a refusal to be daunted, and the quiet and the meek showed it as well as the vocal and the strong. There had been a series of setbacks in the bye elections : the defeats of Waterford, South Armagh, East Tyrone.

Yet nobody was downcast : we all felt now that set-backs meant nothing, and East Cavan came to prove it. A general victory might not be easy, for the Irish Party was still a powerful organisation and, as is the way of many Irishmen, its followers clung to it more tightly now that it seemed to be going down. It would fight, and fight hard, and yet that, too, seemed to mean nothing.

Ever since the First Árd-Fheis in October, 1917, it became the practice of Sinn Féin to hold after-Mass meetings. Each week-end Dublin denuded itself of speakers, who went in all directions into the country to speak to the congregations as they left the rural churches, telling them of this new doctrine of self-reliance. As time went on it became easier to hold those worshippers, for the arrests and the batonings made many of the old want to hear what the young men had to say, and thereafter Sinn Féin was stronger.

The dynamism in the new movement was inexhaustible. There was not a Feis or an Aeridheacht, a local commemoration or a monthly fair, but there there was a Sinn Féin speaker. What was done from Dublin was done also from Cork and Belfast, Limerick, Galway, Waterford, Drogheda, Derry, every big town at each week-end or Sunday morning poured its speakers into the country, and Ireland was laced with ceaseless propaganda, and better still the young orators paid their own way everywhere.

The machinery, built up out of the experience of the bye elections was never let rust. Bob Brennan, the night after the German Plot arrests, had been nominated National Director of Elections as well as Director of Publicity. I went to Harcourt Street to work with him sometime in the Fall of 1918. Both of us as journalists knew the value of the printed word, and as the election came nearer we lived in a snowstorm of handbills and pamphlets, leaflets and posters.

Bob had the gift of the sharp, bright phrase and nearly all the good slogans were his. He, like many others at the top, knew the rural as well as the city mind, and it was that community with the countryside which saved Sinn Féin from ever becoming a Dublin movement or a city movement. Redmondism had shown how far apart from the people a " popular " movement can grow.

Sinn Féin, because of its strong local organisation, never really separated itself from the farm and the village. This local as well as national character became one of the pivots of our publicity. Though we had propaganda to suit all parts of Ireland, we sent draft handbills and posters to each county and each big town applying Sinn Féin doctrine to the facts the people there already knew. These were printed locally and brought home points of policy which, nationally stated, would not have been half so impressive.

Many an uproarious night we spent at these leaflets, for Bob had a delicious sense of humour and the slogans that did *not* get into print were even better than those that did.

Thanks to the way Sinn Féin was organised, it was possible to get publicity to the whole country hot on the heels of some event or some unwise admission by our opponents. Since O'Connell's day there was no movement so closely knit yet so flexible. It began in the street or the townland, came up through the parish, the constituency, the county, the province, all joining like the rays to a star at the National Headquarters. An order from Dublin would be in operation within a week in 2,000 Cumainn areas. If there was pressure for time and motor-cars were used, publicity wet off the machines in Dublin on a Wednesday would be in the hands of the people as they came from Mass on Sunday in Dingle or Dungloe, Ballycastle or Youghal. Sinn Féin was not content only with posters and local facts. It gave the electors names and personalities, too. As early as September it had its candidates chosen, a Fitzgerald, a Hayes, a Little, a Galligan, so that each constituency could work for a man as well as for a movement.

As the war drew to a close and the papers were filled with the tumblings of empires, new hope inspired the election workers. It need not be the " enemy " empires only that one day would topple. As freedom came to the Czechs and the Poles, the military power clamped down harder on us, but each small nation free seemed to be a step nearer liberty to ourselves and ever more people flocked to the Sinn Féin Committee rooms begging for some way of helping.

It was the time of the Great 'Flu. Ireland, in common with all Europe, was in the grip of the deadliest epidemic in the memory of man. Throughout the world it swept away in six months more young lives than war had taken in four years. In Ireland before it was over there were few who had not lost a relative. As we travelled the country on our speech-making, we saw from the train windows funerals everywhere. Gravediggers could not work hard enough to keep up with the flow of coffins and they had to wait on the unopened sward. In Dublin in one week over 200 people died of war 'flu, and Dublin was less hit than most parts of the nation.

The fears of parents and wives flew at once to the prisons. They knew that every jail was crowded and that the poor food and constant prison struggles had lowered the men's vitality. One hundred of the prisoners in Belfast Jail were down with 'flu, and Cumann na mBan appealed to Tim Healy, M.P., to demand their release. Tim did, and in protest at their continued imprisonment, resigned his seat.

Doctors in Dublin, unable to cope with the calls on them, pleaded with the British to release the medical men among the prisoners. That was refused, too. Then a formal demand was made on the British Government to set free the men who had been chosen as candidates, that they might at least be able to conduct their campaign. A Scottish Communist was set free for the election in Britain, but the Irish must stay in jail. Not only were they not released, but no word of politics was permitted to appear in their letters.

De Valera wrote from Lincoln acknowledging his selection as candidate. He said :

> " As you are aware my views I may not give. The world has to be made safe for democracy and the British Government could not risk the cause of small nations rightly struggling to be free by tolerating political references in our correspondence."

Having referred vaguely to news percolating into the prison which gave them some idea of what was happening outside he went on in this entirely non-political letter :

> " From what we know, then, we are confident that every true son and every true daughter of Ireland is mindful of what the honour of the motherland demands in the time that is upon us."

The Irish people smiled when they read that letter : the English were surely a naïve race, especially their prison censors.

When the Sinn Féin Election Manifesto came out in the first week of October it was badly mutilated. Happily the censor allowed the gaps to be represented by neat black rows which became more effective than the most seductive promises.

On 11th November the war ended. The Armistice was celebrated in Dublin, too, but with a difference. Before the war had been a year in progress the soldier and ex-soldier were being organised against the national movement. The actual organisers did not show themselves, but whenever there was need they were able to throw these ex-service men against Sinn Féin.

They did so on the night of the Armistice. Mobs flying a hundred Union Jacks filled the streets and converged on the nearest Sinn Féin Committee rooms. Windows were battered in and fittings scattered in the roadway. On some order, the processionists swung towards Harcourt Street and the National Headquarters.

Showers of stones demolished the windows ; blazing inflammables were thrown through the gaping casements and once the building went on fire but the flames were quenched. Volunteers from the Third Battalion came on the double to save what could be saved and, as the police watched, the men of the Third gave back as good as they got.

In among the howling mobs were troops on furlough urging the wreckers on, using their belts on suspected Sinn Féiners, but there were others in khaki, too, standing there looking at what they had been fighting for—young Americans on leave, learning that there were more meanings than the Yankee one to the word " democracy."

Next morning it looked as if a hurricane had struck No. 6 and Dubliners passing by swore they would vote for Sinn Féin. Then just when Parliament was dissolved and the fight was on at last, the British raided these same headquarters and Bob Brennan, National Director of Elections, was carried off untried to Gloucester Jail.

It was a knavish blow but James O'Mara with his terrific energy took over and, in any case, a campaign was under way that nothing could stop.

The Parliamentarians were no weak rivals. They held 73 seats to Sinn Féin's 6. Of seven contested bye elections the Redmondites had won three. They had a core of trusty followers, men of standing. John Dillon himself took over the leadership of the Party fight and announced that he would use every weapon at his disposal.

There were other imponderables : one movement was free, the other tied. One could hold any meetings it liked, do what it liked, say what it liked : the other had its leaders, speakers, organisers arrested, its key men hunted, its voice strangled in censorship. And worse still, the Party had the nine points of the law, they were in possession of an overwhelming majority of the seats.

And there was an entirely new element in this election—women over 30 had been enfranchised. What would be the effect on them of the incessant Party propaganda that a vote for Sinn Féin would be a vote for war.

But nomination day gave a hint of how shaky the Parliamentary structure was. Old William O'Brien of the All-For-Ireland League yielded to the new movement all the seats his party held. Twenty Irish Party members looking out of their constituency windows saw only Sinn Féin Flags and gave up, among them Captain Stephen Gwynn and Colonel Arthur Lynch, who only a few weeks before had been the orators of the hour.

On that first day de Valera was in for Clare with Brian O'Higgins as his colleague ; Arthur Griffith was in for Cavan with Paul Galligan. Cork had elected without a contest men who were to have a notable part in all that followed : Terence MacSwiney, Michael Collins, Páidín O'Keefe, Tom Hunter, Dáithí Kent. Liam Mellows was in for Galway, Cosgrave for Kilkenny, and Austin Stack for Kerry.

The six Sinn Féin M.P.'s had become twenty-six, but these very victories enabled the Party to concentrate on the many seats they were defending and Sinn Féin had not only to meet them but also Unionists, Orangemen and Hibernians, for Sinn Féin contested every seat except six in the Six Counties, where they stood down so that Unionists would not win on a split Nationalist vote. John Dillon was opposed by de Valera in East Mayo and Devlin was opposed by de Valera in West Belfast : Griffith stood for North-West Tyrone as well as for East Cavan—and neither the leaders nor fifty other candidates could play any part at this turning point of Ireland's history. They sat in English prisons, helpless.

CHAPTER 10

THE SWEEPING VICTORY

IT was from the steps of 6 Harcourt Street that I watched the joy of the crowds as the results of the General Election of 1918 came in.

Outside the second-floor window a notice board had been fixed and as each result was phoned or wired from the counting rooms first the victory and then the figures appeared on it. For those whose names the people knew well, Harry Boland would come to the window and in the silence that immediately fell would call out: " Countess Markievicz is in " or " Seán T. O'Kelly has been elected " or " Alderman Tom Kelly beats them both in Stephen's Green." Then the crowd would demonstrate to its heart's desire.

It was Paddy Sheehan who cried out: " Harry Boland wins South Roscommon " and when Harry came next he had to wait for his silence.

From that narrow street the crowd, growing ever vaster, flowed into St. Stephen's Green. Beside me as we gazed down on that throng were Mrs. Campbell, wife of the poet, Mrs. Mabel Fitzgerald, Desmond's wife, whose inexhaustible energy had ensured his triumph, Anna Fitzsimons (now Anna Kelly) whom the movement knew as " Miss Fitz," Seán and Michael Nunan, Paddy Sheehan with his quips, Fr. O'Flanagan, silent now after a hundred great speeches, Vera MacDonnell, Madge Clifford, oh, and many others !

To the crowd the results were almost unbelievable. Never had a nation so much reason to make a cautious demand and never had it made a more daring one. As the figures poured in and Sinn Féin won with huge majorities it seemed as if with their bare hands the ordinary men and women had seized the cordon of bayonets around Ireland and thrust them aside to call their sovereignty to the world.

There had been no concealment of what Sinn Féin stood for. Every gatepost in the country, carried the Election Manifesto and although chunks had been cut from it it held the three main ideas still :

1. That it was for Ireland a Republic the people were being asked to vote.

2. That those elected would not attend the British Commons but would remain in Ireland to set up a National Assembly.

3. That that assembly would assert full sovereign independence.

All through the campaign those were the notes what were sounded in every kind of propaganda—by speech, by slogan, by leaflet. My friend, Thomas P. O'Neill, the historian, lent me, the other day, a collection of the 1918 handbills and leaflets, now so rare. As I went through them after 33 years it seemed to be only yesterday that on the top floor of No. 6 Bob Brennan and I were composing them.

In one of them our aim was to get into the simplest form the absurdity of looking for freedom from Westminster. It was done through an imagined conversation with a Frenchman. It is a good example of the incisiveness of Sinn Féin propaganda:

The Frenchman: Who are those gentlemen boarding the mail-boat?

The Irishman: Those are the members of the Irish Party. That tall, thin, bearded man is Mr. Dillon. The short, thick-set man, with the fur collar to his coat, is Mr. Devlin.

The Frenchman: These I believe are the leaders of the Irish people: where are they going?

The Irishman: They are going to the English House of Commons.

The Frenchman: For what?

The Irishman: They are going to ask for Home Rule.

The Frenchman: For how long have your leaders been going to England to ask for Home Rule?

The Irishman: For one hundred and eighteen years.

The Frenchman: For a century and eighteen years? Well, really, I don't think the Irish people deserve anything at all. First of all, when other small nations all over the world are asking for independence, they—the oldest—ask for Home Rule, which is only another name for English rule. Then although they have been refused for one hundred and eighteen years, they go on begging as cheerfully as ever. Do you think if Germany held us by force we would send our leaders to Berlin to crave as a favour what is ours by right? No, we would elect them, and having elected them we would keep them in France and obey them only. Why don't you have some national self-respect?

This leaflet is entitled "International Conversations—4." There were many others, each setting down what some other nation with a spirit of independence, would do if it had our problems.

One propaganda method that Sinn Féin used widely seems to

have died out. Many of the election leaflets were ballads written to popular airs. I remember Gerard Crofts and his wife—both with fine voices—singing them to crowded and delighted halls.

Even before the applause died down the song in leaflet form was being distributed among the audience, and the singers went on to the next concert, leaving groups behind in every corner, learning the words and chorusing one another.

The weather during that election blessed us. It was the mildest December for many years, spring-like up to polling day. That meant many outdoor meetings, and anyone who could talk had to sleep as he travelled, for there was no other time.

On the same day I spoke in the forenoon of a fair day at Ballycastle, Co. Antrim, in West Belfast in the afternoon, at Balbriggan at nine o'clock, and somewhere near Swords close to midnight. Others were in the same boat, and no sooner was one meeting over, than the speakers scattered on their separate ways to wherever was next on their lists.

Up to the very eve of the poll the arrests went on, every morning we found a new key-worker gone. In a list I made at the time I find the last name is that of Joe Kennedy, of Castlepollard, Westmeath, whipped into jail two days before polling, a grevous loss to his area, for he was Director of both Meetings and Transport and could least be spared then. Since the widespread Plot raids Sinn Féin had lost 560 men and women by imprisonment. As for the Party, it went down as angry as a wild horse. The leader, John Dillon, a fine orator, was not so blessed with discretion and many of his speeches injured his own cause such as his sneer that he did not know whether to call him " Father O'Flanagan or Michael O'Flanagan, Esquire."

Into East Mayo came 150 Clare Volunteers, men of fine ideals, well-disciplined, yet determined there would be no tearing down of flags, no mob violence by the Ex-soldiers and " Separation Women." John Dillon referred to them as "imported rowdies from Clare brought in to beat and bully the people of East Mayo." That hurt not Sinn Féin but the nation and the people resented it.

Everywhere the R.I.C. tore down Sinn Féin posters.

But it was the North that the speakers from the rest of Ireland found most puzzling. I had, as I said, to speak in West Belfast. It must have been a half-day in the mills and the shipyards, for the audience was a young and merry one, girls from the mills, lads from the yards. Just the material, I thought, for the new doctrine.

They never heard it, for *they* had songs about their Wee Joe that they wanted to sing to *me*, and when they were done singing they had a fife and drum band which made a neat circle of marching men around my platform and smothered my eloquence in an hour of perfect bombination. The drums never paused or halted until I had to bow gracefully and run for my train. If only Capt. Stephen Gwynn or Col. Arthur Lynch could have seen me then!

Our reception from some of the Orangemen was even less gracious and whenever we had to pass through an Orange district from meeting to meeting—and we were always identifiable for we would not lower the tricolour—the old Ford had to be swathed in loose and flowing rugs like a Sheik of Araby, leaving just space enough for the driver to see the road. I thought it absurd until I heard the dull thuds of stones against the embroidery and then I, like the rest, offered up many ejaculations.

Yet even in these hostile places there were rewards. In one of the Armagh constituencies the Sinn Féin Committee rooms had a call one night from a Presbyterian farmer, a short, hard-built man, I remember, with fair hair, about forty.

He asked us many questions. Why had they risen in Dublin: what were those men who had been shot dying for: did they really mean an Independent Ireland, one entirely free, with a free Parliament of its own, with fair play for all men, every citizen being equal in his rights, a Republic for the ordinary people? We answered frankly, every question. " I'll vote for ye," he said at the end of it all.

We must have expressed surprise for he added, " and my neighbours will vote for ye too," and into that polling station, as I learned later, there came on the morning of 14th December some twenty small-farmers, men of the old Presbyterian Liberalism from which it was a short step, and a happy one for them, to the sovereign independence of Ireland.

In between nomination day and polling day the 'flu gave the cause a martyr. Dick Coleman died of pneumonia, following influenza, on 9th December, in the prison of Usk in Wales. Dick was a Volunteer who had fought in the Rising at Ashbourne, had been sentenced to death, did penal servitude, was amnestied and threw himself promptly back into the struggle, was twice again imprisoned and went through two hunger strikes.

Swept away in the Plot arrests he came home now on 11th December in a coffin. He was but 27 years of age; he was handsome. It was as if a goodly knight had fallen in a crusade. The people's tears came quickly for him. The inquest disclosed the utter neglect of the sick in Usk Prison where the many Irish prisoners struck down by the epidemic had only one untrained male nurse to attend to them.

The disclosure horrified all who had men in prison and a telegram was sent to the British Government: " Irish trained nurses ready to leave for English prisons to nurse Irish prisoners stricken with influenza. Wire necessary permits."

E

There were no permits and Dick Coleman's death had a deeper influence than ever.

Hearing of these things, men and women in every contested division pored over the registers for the tenth time. Sinn Féin's method of canvass made history. Every voter had been seen, many twice and three times. Opposite his or her name was " F," " A " or " D "—for, against, doubtful. The morning after the Coleman inquest canvassers sought out those still doubtful and put straight questions to them. How could any but the heartless stand aside now. All over Ireland that night the " D's " were being rubbed out.

The final Dublin rally was in O'Connell Street. There were no loud speakers then and the rally consisted of a march into the city from every constituency, which brought its own speakers in its own wagonette. Down the whole length of the great thoroughfare the nine city meetings were held and over each flew a tricolour with a black cross on every one for Dick Coleman. Thousands wore the enamel badges with their candidate's photograph, draped now in crêpe. Mrs. Pearse presided at the main meeting ; Mrs. Ceannt and others of the 1916 women presided at others. The street echoed with many voices simultaneously.

And so came polling day, 14th December. Everywhere it was like hosts going into action. In Dublin the thousand workers on the great new British aerodrome went to the polls in a fleet of lorries all flying the tricolour. The Dublin dockers marched to the booths behind an advance guard of Citizen Army veterans.

That night we gathered in No. 6 as the first of the shoal of telegrams and reports came in which were to go on all the next day. We went home knowing at least that the turn in Ireland's history had come, but we must wait two weeks before the votes were counted. Probably to convenience the gathering of the ballots of British troops in the field the count was postponed to 28th December.

Sinn Féin was taking no risks ; everywhere it was insisted that the ballot boxes be kept in sealed rooms so placed that they could be seen and so supervised from a window. Volunteers kept this vigil for fourteen days and nights. Then the count began. Those who gathered at No. 6 to hear the figures, to watch the joy of the people, to feel the magnitude of the victory, to think of the men and women in the prisons who now became the rulers of Ireland, to share at last the secret of the calm with which, confident of a new Ireland, the 1916 men died—to stand on those Harcourt Street steps and see all this take substance in figures and names of men and constituencies was an experience beyond telling.

The accuracy of the Sinn Féin method was shown in the totals that Headquarters, in the dead fortnight, whispered to itself lest it boast too soon : Sinn Féin 75, all others 30. In fact it was Sinn Féin 73 (for two seats were lost by split votes), Nationalists elected in agreement with Sinn Féin 4, Irish Party 2, Unionists 26.

To the people the details came as new and thrilling. Sinn Féin estimated they would take nine of the eleven Dublin city and county seats, they took the tenth, thanks mainly to Mabel Fitzgerald. Among the ten victors were Seán T. O'Kelly, Countess Markievicz, Joe McGrath, Gavan Duffy. Paddy Little, who fought both a Unionist and an Irish Party man, would probably have won in Rathmines, if the vote was not split. James O'Mara swept Kilkenny; J. J. Walsh and Liam de Roiste swamped Cork City; Eoin MacNeill took Derry City; Liam Mellows, North Meath; Kevin O'Higgins, Offaly; Dr. Jim Ryan, South Wexford; Robert Barton, West Wicklow; Cathal Brugha captured County Waterford with an immense vote; MacEntee and Blythe took the Monaghan seats. Griffith was in for Tyrone as well as Cavan; Frank Fahy took Galway South with a flourish.

The Irish Party held only Waterford City, where Captain Redmond scraped through with 4,915 against Dr. White's 4,441 ; and West Belfast where Devlin polled 8,438 against de Valera's 3,045. But it was on East Mayo that all eyes were turned : there the new leader had challenged the old. The result was one of the last in. Eamon de Valera : 8,875 ; John Dillon, 4,514.

The Irish Party which for forty years had held Ireland's representation against all challengers had disappeared. Leaders and rank-and-file had vanished together, vanquished by beardless boys and the mere names of imprisoned men.

All over Ireland bonfires blazed and the songs of the Rising were echoed back by the hills.

CHAPTER 11

"NOW, THEREFORE, WE . . ."

THE Declaration of Independence, made by Dáil Éireann on 21st January, 1919, is historically the most important document in the archives of modern Ireland.

The days leading up to that Declaration were hectic days. Sinn Féin never believed in waiting on events : it created them. The energies released from the General Election were harnessed right away for a national protest against men and women lying in jail without charge or trial.

The National Executive organised one hundred meetings to be held on Sunday, 5th January, 1919. These meetings became a demonstration of the strength of this tremendous movement. Every M.P. who was free, and there were thirty of them still at liberty, went to his constituency. For the other meetings the Executive chose the speakers. I remember some on that list : Professor Stockley, Stephen O'Mara, Mrs. Sheehy Skeffington, Professor Clery.

Snow was lying heavy on the country roads. But to be at those meetings the people would have climbed Mount Everest ; and in from far-lying townlands and a thousand villages they came to protest against the foreigner holding those who had served Ireland bravely. I spoke at Mullingar that day and it was the same everywhere : there was an exaltation on the people : they would have followed any call.

"Release the prisoners" became a national slogan. It was printed on windscreen slips, on posters, on great streamers which were regularly stretched across the main streets, particularly streets in which the shops were owned by Unionists. Grafton Street in those days was one of the most "loyal" of streets, and often at night, while those respectable merchants were in their beds, Sinn Féin unrolled its linen legend high up between the roofs, not forgetting that in this street Tone had often walked, and that it was from these pavements that, looking up, he saw fifteen-years-old Matilda Witherington at an upper window and the romance began which gave Ireland one of the greatest of her national books.

The slogan was printed on little tricolour flags which everyone wore although the British had declared the motto seditious. It must have been about this time that I first met that sturdy soul Albinia Brodrick, the Honourable Albinia Brodrick. Her brother, the Viscount Midleton, was as Tory as they make them. He had held high Cabinet rank in the days of Chamberlain and Salisbury and he certainly had no use for rebels, though later he was to see a little of the light.

His sister was a stout-hearted, indomitable Sinn Féiner and one night after a party at Margaret Browne's house I saw her to her hotel, at that time a hostelry that never forgot its imperial destiny. It housed the Anglo-Irish, British Generals and the more *élite* of Dublin Castle. Others could go elsewhere. She told me on the way that she had not booked but they always had a room. We went there.

But from desk-clerk to manager (for, being Albinia, she sent for him) it was the same : " No room," " full to the doors," " booked out." The Hon. Albinia was given to black voluminous gowns and wore on that occasion a little unobtrusive black hat. Eventually as we turned away she said with a chuckle, " If I told them I was Lord Midleton's sister they'd have put me in the Royal suite." " No," said I, " but if you had taken down that, they might have found a corner for you." " That," perched on the very summit of her hat, was one of the tricolour flags with the banned slogan on it. I had noticed the manager's horrified gaze fixed on it. Albinia had many a laugh over that wee flag.

The effect of the General Election on the British was completely to disconcert them. They had no idea what to do next. So insincere were the war aims that the furthest thought from their minds was : " The Irish people have shown us their will ; how may we honour our pledges." The reaction of the British was rather : " Those damned Irish have raised their heads again : we'll show them."

A new bout of repression was the right answer. " Firmness " their Press in Britain and in Ireland called it. There was one other hope—perhaps the elections could be invalidated. The London *Times* recalled the case of John Mitchel. He, as a felon, had been unseated immediately after election. That could be done in the case of MacNeill, de Valera, MacEntee, Dr. Hayes and a dozen others who had been sentenced after 1916 and happily were never pardoned. But the Sinn Féin M.P's. were in scores and most of them though imprisoned had never been charged. Therefore it must be "firmness." Besides there were the Irish papers themselves asking for it, and they ought to know, especially the *Irish Times*, the *Belfast Newsletter*, and the *Northern Whig*. All three had the solution pat. The Big Bear said : " If the country is to be saved at all it must be by the firmness of the British Government in Ireland " ; the Middling Bear said : " The Irish Executive must be empowered to act with firmness and decision"; the Baby Bear said : " It was an occasion for action of a firm and con- sistent kind."

Dublin Castle thought this excellent advice. Cathal Brugha, coming back from his electoral triumph in Waterford, was arrested because he, a Member of Parliament, gave his name to an R.I.C. man as "Cathal" instead of "Charles." William Sears, M.P., was sentenced in Dublin to six months' imprisonment for a phrase in an election speech in South Mayo. A small army of 30 G-men raided Sinn Féin headquarters and ransacked it from cellar to ceiling. Sinn Féin afterwards said that the only "seditious literature" carried off were copies of President Wilson's speeches about "government with the consent of the governed."

Soon there were divided counsels at the Castle, and a series of important conferences were held which the Viceroy, the Law Officers, the British Commander-in-Chief, the Chief of Intelligence and others of the military government attended. Obviously they were discussing ways of preventing the establishment of an Irish Parliament, and sat wrangling far into the night, with couriers speeding between Dublin and Downing Street, as the Cabinet in London tried also to make up its mind.

As the Castle fussed and fumed, the arrangements were openly made for the sitting of the first Dáil. On 7th January, in the Oak Room of the Mansion House, all the M.P's. available met under the presidency of Count Plunkett, the "senior member," and having demanded the release of their thirty-seven colleagues, decided that all representatives elected by the Irish people on 14th December were members of the Parliament and should be summoned to the opening session. And it was decided on 17th January that four days later at 3.30 p.m. Dáil Éireann, the elected Parliament of Ireland, would meet in the Round Room of the Mansion House, Dublin.

Up to the last nobody knew whether the meeting might not be dispersed by force and the remaining Deputies be swept to join their colleagues in Usk and Wandsworth and Reading and Lincoln. What evidently postponed the application of "firmness" was that three days before the First Dáil met there assembled in Paris the great Peace Conference which, under the Presidency of Woodrow Wilson, was to give freedom all round, but above all to little States.

And so on Tuesday, 21st January, 1919, at 3.30 in the afternoon, there assembled in the capital of Ireland the first National Parliament to meet on Irish soil for three hundred years. There were no flags, no fireworks, few cheers even.

Into the Round Room had come the long queues of ticket-holders who, for hours, had stood among the throngs in Dawson Street. Soon after 3 p.m. the House was crowded, floor and galleries, except for a space under the dais separated from the rest of the great room by a light barrier. There the seats for the Deputies were vacant.

Looking through that hall that day, I saw young Ireland as I had seen it at the first Árd Fheis of the new Sinn Féin. There were, again, a few grey heads and some white ones. But the gathering itself was of the young men and women who had brought this day to pass.

They were not solemn, not merry, but serious in a happy way. They could not have foreseen what the years were to bring, or how many of those present were to fall in the struggle. But they did know that this was a day of which every coming generation would be proud, a day of decision, in which the recent past would be forever obliterated and the future forever changed.

There was but one tricolour in the whole hall, that hanging over the Speaker's chair in the centre of the dais. For the rest, there was no decoration, a thing that surprised the seventy Pressmen who sat at long tables flanking the platform, men who had come from Britain, America, the Continent, Australia and South Africa. The audience, as they waited for 3.30, cheered occasionally, as for a group of U.S. naval officers in uniform, but they were too filled with emotion to show their feelings lightly.

At the stroke of the hour the great doors at the back of the hall opened, and then there swept over that audience a passion of demonstration. Standing, each thronged side faced the centre aisle, and as to their cheering the Deputies came slowly up the passage, tall Volunteers who acted that day as stewards stood to attention.

Count Plunkett was at the head of that procession of the people's representatives. Behind him came some known to everybody in that hall, and others known to nobody. Here, too, there were a few grey heads, but the rest were young men in their twenties. They filed through the barrier, turning to left and right in the alphabetical order of their constituencies, leaving the first row of seats vacant. The men and women in prison were the nation's front bench still.

Count Plunkett proposed that Cathal Brugha be elected Speaker, and into the Chair on the dais stepped the stocky figure of the man who two and a half years before had fallen with many wounds, and only yesterday was in enemy hands. Now he was on his feet and turning towards the back of the platform, he said he would ask " the most faithful priest that ever lived in Ireland to call a blessing on that day and its fruits."

Father O'Flanagan came forward and the cry of affection that rose from that audience for him was a strange and moving thing to hear. When it was stilled and all had risen to their feet the deep musical voice in lovely Irish asked that the Holy Ghost should replenish their hearts and grant them the spirit to relish what was right and to rejoice in the consolations of God.

The Dáil appointed four clerks: Diarmuid O'Hegarty, Risteárd Ó Foghludha, Seán Nunan and Paddy Sheehan, and the business of that first Session began. Before it ended the dream which through the long night of persecution had consoled the Gael; the vision which inspired the secret songs by the fireside; the hope which for a century had made a victory out of every defeat; the certainty which made firm the countless steps as they mounted the scaffold— all had, in spirit, been realised. Ireland had declared herself free.

The roll of Deputies was called. To many names the clerks gave answer " *Fé ghlas ag Gallaibh* "—in foreign prisons. So often was that answer given that it became a refrain, a menacing refrain, which ever afterwards rang in the mind as that day was recalled. To other names the answer was simply " Absent." One of these names was Sir Edward Carson. For a moment the audience laughed and then it was realised that Dáil Éireann *was* the assembly of Ireland, embracing all whom the people chose, and that Unionists had the same right to be there as Republicans, and the laugh died out and was not repeated.

It was to Cathal Brugha that the honour fell of giving the Declaration to that hushed audience, which as he proceeded rose quickly to its feet. As the tense voice read the Irish text which so many in that hall could follow, eyes everywhere were immovably fixed on him. The people remained standing as in the same pulsing silence the English version was read by Éamonn Duggan:

" *Whereas the Irish people is by right a free people . . .*

And, whereas, for seven hundred years the Irish people has never ceased to repudiate and has repeatedly protested in arms against foreign usurpation . . .

And whereas the Irish Republic was proclaimed in Dublin on Easter Monday, 1916, by the Irish Republican Army acting on behalf of the Irish people . . .

And whereas at the threshold of a new era in history the Irish electorate has, in the General Election of December, 1918, seized the first occasion to declare by an overwhelming majority its firm allegiance to the Irish Republic . . .

Now, therefore, we the elected Representatives of the ancient Irish people in National Parliament assembled do in the name of the Irish nation ratify the establishment of the Irish Republic and pledge ourselves and our people to make this declaration effective by every means at our command. . . ."

And so to the final passage read in that thronged and silent hall, which, as the words ended, burst into a cry of exaltation :

" In the name of the Irish people, we humbly commit our destiny to Almighty God, Who gave our fathers the courage and determination to persevere through long centuries of ruthless tyranny, and strong in the justice of the cause, which they have handed down to us, we ask His Divine blessing on this the last stage of the struggle we have pledged ourselves to carry through to freedom."

When the Declaration had been read in French by George Gavan Duffy, Cathal Brugha said quietly :

"Deputies, you understand from what is stated in this Declaration that we have cut ourselves free from England. Let the world know it and those who are concerned bear it in mind. For come what may now, whether it be death itself, the great deed is done."

Then speaking in unison the members of the Dáil adopted the Declaration of Independence and dedicated themselves to sustain it.

There followed the choice of three delegates, Éamon de Valera, Arthur Griffith and Count Plunkett, to demand from the Peace Conference the recognition of Ireland's sovereignty.

Two other statements were read. Sceilg read the "Message to the Free Nations of the World," in Irish ; Count Plunkett, in French, and Robert Barton, in English, beginning with the words :

"To the Nations of the World—Greeting.

"The Nation of Ireland having proclaimed her national independence calls through her elected Representatives in Parliament assembled in the Irish Capital on 21st January, 1919, upon every free nation to support the Irish Republic by recognising Ireland's national status and her right to its vindication at the Peace Congress. . . ."

Piaras Béaslaí read the Democratic Programme in soft Kerry Irish and Alderman Tom Kelly read it in English in the voice of a Dublin worker. It laid down the foundations on which the new Ireland would be built "in accordance with the principles of Liberty, Equality and Justice for all, which alone can secure permanence of government in the willing adhesion of the people." In return for allegiance every citizen would have the right to an adequate share of the produce of the nation's labour. The children would be the Republic's special care and "no child shall suffer hunger or cold," and to all there would be opened means to "education and training as citizens of a free and Gaelic Ireland." The degrading poor-law system would be abolished and instead of the aged being regarded as a burthen, they would be treated as "entitled to the nation's gratitude and consideration." The people's health would be safe-guarded, the harbours and waterways, the resources of the soil, minerals, peat-bogs would be developed for the benefit of the Irish people, industries would be built up and "the conditions under which the working-classes live and labour" would be changed through social legislation.

The session ended. In that two hours Ireland was given a sovereignty, a parliament, and a programme to raise up the people and make for them at home and in the world an honoured place.

Many of the journalists who had watched the session had come to sneer, but they had seen an assembly conducted with dignity before a great audience whose behaviour matched the nobility of the occasion. True there was no mace, no sword-bearers, no wigs or robes in this Parliament. There was not even a separate House. But it was clear that it was the representatives of a Democracy who had met and their authority had no need to be symbolised in outer things, for, as the grim years were to show, it rested in the hearts of a people.

CHAPTER 12

THE SECOND SESSION

IT was nearly three months before Dáil Éireann met again. Into that three months were crowded incident and crisis in unbroken succession.

For one thing, de Valera escaped from Lincoln Prison. There have been many dramatic prison escapes in Ireland's history : there have been releases that took the nation by surprise : now and again the jail-gates everywhere have been thrown wide open in amnesty : but there was nothing comparable to that prison-break in the dusk of a February evening in the year 1919.

Britain had refused to set her Irish prisoners free for the elections ; she refused their release for the first meeting of the Irish Parliament ; though the great 'flu was raging she held them still in prison hospitals inadequately staffed. And now, no thanks to her, the head of them all was out. It was heaven to us at home and gall and wormwood to her, and that made our rejoicing brighter still.

The story of the escape has been told too often to need a description here. It had a sequel which was even more important. When Harry Boland, Mick Collins and Frank Kelly waited in the shadows outside the jail to greet de Valera, Seán Milroy and Seán McGarry coming as other shadows through the barbed wire, the perfect escape had been carried through. And then all concerned vanished as if the earth itself had been in the plot.

The news was not known in Ireland for three days. When it burst strangers shook hands with one another in the streets and the ballad writers had broadsheets out almost within the hour. The English Press scolded and raged and then set out on de Valera's track.

He was seen on a boat to France, on a liner to America, in a London street, on a Southampton train, in a fishing smack off the Welsh coast. Being the heads of a democracy, the British Government put a special guard on the House of Commons lest he turn up and claim his seat. Under the lash of criticism, they swore to level the score by his re-arrest and there was never such a search as for this elusive man. But he also knew for what stakes Ireland was playing in his person and for weeks nothing was heard of him. And then the shadow of death fell across the nation again.

On 6th March, Pierce McCann, T.D.* for Tipperary, died of influenza in Gloucester Prison. He was a celebrated rider to hounds, a swimmer who had saved several lives, all-round athlete, but he feared the 'flu deeply. " We will," he wrote a few days before he took ill, " be bad subjects, after our long confinement and the danger will be great." The prison doctors knew it; the Government knew it. The prisoners knew it. And on 6th March, Pierce McCann was dead.

As de Valera's escape had shown the ineffectualness of the British repression, Pierce McCann's death showed its meanness. The British Cabinet, ashamed at last, announced the opening of the jail gates that very night—a living and a dead patriot had between them wrenched aside the prison bars for their comrades.

Out through them the nation's leaders came flocking: they poured into a Dublin and an Ireland which tried in cheering masses along the quays, in thronged railway stations, in great processions, in decorated home-towns, to express to them their devotion and their fealty.

One only did not come. Éamon de Valera remained in hiding. He had had warning of how eagerly he would have been retaken. Bob Barton, who on the historic 21st January had read the Message to the Free Nations, had been re-arrested on 26th February, and Piaras Béaslaí, who had read the Democratic Programme, was taken on 4th March.

Then Sinn Féin announced the date all Ireland was now waiting for. On 26th March, de Valera would be officially welcomed back to Ireland. A ceremony hitherto reserved for royalty was to mark that homecoming. The Lord Mayor of Dublin would go to the city boundary and there he would hand to Éamon de Valera the keys of the capital of Ireland and escort him into the city.

There was a quick response from Dublin Castle. Lieut.-General Shaw, British Commander-in-Chief, issued a proclamation prohibiting, not only the reception, but all meetings, assemblies, and processions in Dublin City and County. It was the challenge.

Troops were rushed into Dublin from the Curragh. Volunteers everywhere got ready. Once more the two nations were face to face. And then to many a young man's consternation it was learned that de Valera had called off the reception and, when others argued with him, had insisted. Sinn Féin issued another announcement:

" Mr. de Valera feels that the occasion is not one which would justify proceeding with the public reception as arranged. We, therefore, wish to inform the public that in deference to Mr. de Valera's urgent request the reception will not be held."

We, the young men, talked of " another Clontarf." He, not so much older, was determined that there was no principle involved

---

* T.D. Teachta Dála: Member of the Dáil, Deputy.

in whether he was welcomed at the city boundary or not and that there were much more important things to be done than giving this chance to the Castle to wipe out in blood all that had been gained. There was a Government to be organised and a Parliament to be put firmly on its feet. If Dublin Castle wanted a contest of wills, it must be over something more essential to liberty than even the keys of Dublin.

It was the first of many lessons that the young men got of the new leader's practicality, and also of his readiness to take decisions, even unpopular ones. And if some of the Volunteers shook their heads, others went back to Davis for comfort, and found there that a nation cannot be demonstrated into freedom—not by processions or parades would Ireland's liberty be won, but by solid work.

However, Volunteers and other workers had not much time for gloomy meditations. There were prisoners still in who had to be got out, and I remember a most successful meeting I addressed at Tinahely, Co. Wicklow, demanding the release of Bob Barton.

It was an impassioned gathering, and the British Government was left in no doubt what would happen if there were a refusal. Next day it was learned, without surprise in Tinahely, that Bob Barton was out. Alas, he was out also before the meeting was held. He had escaped from Mountjoy Jail, leaving a polite note for the Governor that, as the accommodation was not all that he expected, he had to leave.

The warder then learned that the figure in the bed on which he had flashed his torch reassuringly each half-an-hour during the night was neatly compacted of old clothes and suitcases.

That escape, which took place on St. Patrick's Eve, set the ballad writers off again, but it was to be eclipsed within ten days by the most exciting jail-break ever made in Dublin. Thirty Sinn Féin prisoners one Saturday evening were sauntering in apparent indifference to life round one of the exercise rings between the tall wings of Mountjoy. At a signal, all weariness fell from them and they had four warders on the ground. At the same moment a rope came flying over the high wall, and after it a rope ladder. Soon up the ladder the prisoners started to race, and after a moment there, silhouetted against the Dublin evening sky, dropped down to freedom. In the excitement, two of the warders got away, and soon troops came round the corner buildings at the double. But twenty men were gone, and all Ireland felt it was delightful to be alive.

It was in these months, too, that the first blows in the War of Independence were struck : at Soloheadbeg, Dan Breen, Seán Treacy, Seumas Robinson, Seán Hogan, and five others, ambushed an R.I.C. patrol and carried off explosives. In Limerick, Robert Byrne, a hunger-striker was under escort in hospital when his comrades rushed in to rescue him. The R.I.C. guard promptly shot the prisoner and was then shot himself. Although rescued, the prisoner died.

At Collinstown, in Dublin, one of the biggest raids for arms ever carried out, proved a model of organisation. Commando-fashion, the sentries at the great R.A.F. aerodrome were surprised and over-powered by men, who were on them without making a sound, not one of them even spoke. Nobody was injured, and 75 rifles were captured with 4,000 rounds of ammunition. Next day, 800 workers were dismissed, but another company of the Volunteers had been fully armed.

With this cut and thrust as curtain-raiser, Dáil Éireann met again in public on 10th April, 1919. It was in the same room, before nearly the same audience, but there was a gayer spirit somehow, a relief, perhaps, that the great decision had been taken and this was the Republic functioning. Now there were few empty seats in the House. Over sixty T.D.'s came up the aisle to their places, led by the new Speaker, Seán T. O'Kelly, and now many in the hall knew them, and there was a welcome more tumultous than ever. A series of private sessions of the Dáil had already been held. At these the Presidency was established, de Valera being elected to this office on 1st April ; on 2nd April he chose his Ministry :

Arthur Griffith became Minister for Home Affairs ; Cathal Brugha, Minister for Defence ; Count Plunkett, Minister for Fine Arts ; Countess Markievicz—the first woman Cabinet Minister in Europe— was appointed Minister for Labour ; Eoin MacNeill, Minister for Industries ; Michael Collins, Minister for Finance ; W. T. Cosgrave, Minister for Local Government ; Laurence Ginnell, Director of Propaganda, and Robert Barton, Director of Agriculture.

In his statement of policy, de Valera said :

"There is in Ireland at this moment only one lawful authority, and that authority is the elected Government of the Irish Republic. . . ."

He quoted Cardinal Mercier on the relationship between an invaded people and the occupying power, and said of the British :

"We shall conduct ourselves towards them in such a way as will make clear that we acknowledge no right of theirs."

He told the house that ambassadors would be sent from the Republic to other nations to "see that the position of Ireland is understood as it really is, and not as English propaganda would represent it."

Before that day's session closed, the flotation of the first Dáil Loan was announced. It was for £500,000, half to be raised in Ireland and half abroad.

Next day, in a grave and firm speech, de Valera proposed that the R.I.C. be socially ostracised: " They are no ordinary civil force as police are in other countries. The R.I.C., unlike any other police force in the world, is a military body, armed with rifle, bayonet and revolver, as well as baton." They were part of the army of occupation, and must be treated as such.

The House unanimously approved, and then stood in silence, in memory of " the first member of our body," Pierce McCann, to lay down his life for freedom. Many who stood for him that day were to emulate his sacrifice.

Foreign policy was discussed. De Valera pleaded against a harsh peace being imposed on Germany, for otherwise " another war of revenge must surely follow," and he proposed that the Dáil formally resolve to support the principles enunciated at Washington's tomb on 4th July, 1918, by President Wilson.

It was even then becoming clear that Wilson would make no effort to have those principles applied to Ireland. The Dublin Corporation had invited him to become a freeman, and because he heard that to accept might displease Britain, he did not answer the letter for two months, and then declined even to visit Ireland. At Paris, he was asked to permit the Irish delegation to appear before the Peace Conference, and he ignored that request also.

Bishop Fogarty of Killaloe wrote: " For the honour of Ireland, let us hope that this much-lauded man may not turn out to be as big a humbug as the rest of them."

He did.

But Republican Ireland had no illusions. They would have to fight this fight themselves, and win it with their own grit. They needed, above all, for the struggle that was coming, recognition of Ireland's independence by some foreign Power. If that could be achieved, the Volunteers would have belligerent status, and could fight for liberty without the hangman's noose always around their necks, or ill-usage awaiting them in prisons. To seek that recognition, and to get funds to carry on the fight, became the first objectives of Government policy.

When the Dáil met again in May, it was known that the Cabinet had asked de Valera to undertake a task of great magnitude. For more than a month the exact nature of that task remained a secret. Then the world heard that de Valera, as will be told later, had slipped across the Atlantic as a stowaway and landed in the United States on 11th June, 1919.

Meanwhile, those at home had had a foretaste of what was to be Britain's attitude to every constructive effort of Dáil Éireann. Michael Collins, as Minister for Finance, issued the prospectus for the loan. It would be used to state Ireland's case to the world, to create an Irish Civil Service, to set up Consuls abroad to aid Irish trade, to develop fisheries, forestry and industries, to prepare for a policy of land division and to establish arbitration courts.

Every newspaper that published that prospectus was promptly suppressed by the British, and though the provincial papers were afterwards permitted to re-appear, all Labour and Republican papers were closed down permanently—or at least as permanently as ever Britain succeeded in suppressing Ireland's voice; for the mosquito press was reborn, secretly printed and sedulously distributed, to sting and bite ceaselessly.

Dáil Éireann had soon to meet in private, for its members had again become the prey of the Crown forces. It could assemble only by the greatest stealth, for on 10th September, 1919, the Parliament of Ireland, elected by a million Irish voters, was proclaimed an " illegal association " by Dublin Castle, whose supporters in five-sixths of the country would hardly fill a schoolhouse.

The Dáil, mere membership of which was now a crime, had no intention of giving up its mandate. By careful preparation it managed still to hold important sessions. At the session of 29th June, 1920, for instance, Arthur Griffith, then Acting President of the Republic, was able to tell the House that, although coming to that meeting exposed every T.D. to deadly peril, 46 of the 51 members available (the others were abroad or in prison) were present.

That June meeting sat from 9 a.m. to 10.30 p.m. Every moment of that time might have brought a murderous raid. Yet, all day long, plans were discussed, decisions taken, moneys voted. It was decreed that a Land Bank be established, that an Import and Export Company be set up, that Courts of Justice and Equity, and later Courts of Criminal Jurisdiction, be created, and a judiciary appointed.

Changes were made in the Ministry, to fill gaps caused mainly by imprisonment. Austin Stack, who had made a spectacular escape from Strangeways Gaol, Manchester, became Minister for Home Affairs; Kevin O'Higgins, substitute Minister for Local Government; Art O'Connor, substitute Director of Agriculture.

It was decided that, as everything else had failed, the Dáil must decree a boycott of Belfast goods in an effort to bring aid to the persecuted minority there.

Of the Belfast area, Arthur Griffith told the House :

" There were five or six thousand men, representing 40,000 people, thrown out of work, and there was no likelihood of their getting back. A printed form had been prepared which it was sought to compel every workingman to sign before he would be considered for re-instatement.   It contained a repudiation of Sinn Féin."

Outside in the streets, while Ireland's deputies thus sat in national assembly, troops, Auxiliaries, Black-and-Tans, constabulary, and a score of G-men pursued the endless search for " rebels," and the suppression of all liberty.

As the Dáil was carried on despite this universal repression, so the Republican Government also.   Many Departments of State were in full operation.   Their offices were scattered all over Dublin, though their location was a secret most jealously guarded and known to the fewest possible number.   They were disguised as type-writing companies, duplication firms, law offices, benevolent societies, advertising agencies, trade associations.

With infinite care and courage, a real Central Administration was brought into being, with Ministers and staffs, guiding the nation in its fight, supervising local government bodies, supplying the insurgent armies, administering the Republic's finance, surveying industrial developments, organising courts, and through the newly-founded Republican police, protecting the innocent and punishing the guilty.

As a Government, which the nation repudiated, applied terror in an effort to wring compliance with its decrees, this hunted Government of the people wielded the real authority.

CHAPTER 13

COURTS OF THE NATION

THE establishment of the Republican Courts, more than any other single act in the Four Glorious Years, won fame for the Republic abroad and honour for it at home.

It was unanswerable proof of the capacity of the Irish people for self-government, and when later Britain perceived this, and used all the force of her repressive machinery to destroy the courts, their maintenace, often at the cost of life, became an epic of man's devotion to justice.

The setting up of these courts, which re-established law, and in a few critical months saved Ireland from a bitter class-struggle, came about almost naturally.

As the fight for freedom developed, the R.I.C. acted more and more as a military body. I remember in 1923, in the sadness of the war which had followed the signing of the "Treaty," tramping round Gormanston internment camp with George Plunkett. We were looking back into the years and arguing if this sequel had not destroyed all that bravery and self-sacrifice had won. George had no doubts.

" We destroyed the real army of occupation, the R.I.C.," he said. " That was to be done if ever Ireland was to be freed, by us or others. It was a task almost beyond the strength of any one generation and we did it."

And I recalled what Erskine Childers had written two years before in his *Constructive Work of Dáil Éireann*. Having described the organisation and the armament of the R.I.C., he said :

> " In pre-Republican times the average strength of the force was about 11,000 men. Outside Dublin (which had its own special force, the Dublin Metropolitan Police), the R.I.C. were distributed over a vast number of small barracks throughout the country.
>
> " No village or hamlet was too insignificant to be accommodated with a barracks and a garrison of a sergeant and a few constables.
>
> " This force was the most potent of all the weapons used by the British Government in subduing the Irish people, because

it was recruited from the people themselves, and in the work of political repression was able to draw upon intimate local knowledge and strong local influence, as well as upon intelligence and courage which are the common attributes of the Irish race. . . .

"Stripped of all disguise, the R.I.C. stood forth as the Irish portion of the military garrison."

When at last the Republic had to be fought for, it was against this force that the Volunteers had first to turn their arms.

The R.I.C. barracks were attacked systematically. The smaller and more isolated posts were the first victims. They were defended, often heroically, but in a countryside from which the force had alienated itself, they stood no chance. The losses grew, and as each captured barracks helped to arm a new Volunteer platoon, the British began to draw in its outposts.

Nearly five hundred of the smaller barracks were abandoned, and soon these were burned down by the Volunteers (350 on one night) to prevent their reoccupation. The evacuation of the villages and hamlets was followed by withdrawals from the lesser towns, as the attacks of the Volunteers grew bolder.

Eventually, the R.I.C. were quartered only in the sizeable towns. Their retreat blinded the military government, whose eyes and ears they had been, and in revenge that government sought to use them for indiscriminate violence. It was at this point that the force began to disintegrate.

As the R.I.C withdrew from the villages and small towns, they left a vacuum. There were no police : no guardians of the civil law. Soon the law-breaker saw his chance, not the criminal only, but the land-hungry, the cattle drivers, the faction fighters, every group with a grievance. At first, the manifestations of lawlessness were few. Then a body of landless marched to the neighbouring big farm and seized portions of it for themselves. Like the pressing of a switch, this action set landless men in motion all over the south and west of Ireland.

The land hunger at that time was terrible. Britain had never been speedy with land division, and had suspended it altogether during the war. Also it was a time of force : the world had just come through the most terrible war in history, and Ireland was at war, too, and land-hungry men do not believe in gentle methods. So farm after farm, ranch after ranch was taken over. Soon it was not only the huge farms or the vast grazing grounds that were occupied. The uneconomic holders helped themselves to the nearest land whose-ever it was. When the farmer objected, he was boycotted, his crops were sometimes burned, his family set upon.

It was a crisis, and one of great magnitude. If it should go on, it would be proof of everything the British had said—the Irish could never rule themselves. Take away the British police, they had said, and chaos would come immediately—and so at one moment it seemed.

Although the violence and suddenness of this upheaval had taken the nation by surprise, Dáil Éireann had in a measure provided against something like this. By the Decree of June, 1919, it had authorised the establishment of National Arbitration Courts. One area only acted promptly on the Decree, and in the crisis which came to its head in the spring of 1920, the whole country turned to that area for inspiration.

It was West Clare. As soon as the Dáil had authorised the Courts, Brian O'Higgins, T.D. for the area, summoned a conference to discuss how the decree might be put into operation. It was decided to have Parish Arbitration Courts, and above them, for the whole constituency, a District Court. A scheme was carefully worked out —rules of court, scales of fees, costs, form of summons, range of fines. The District Court was first established, consisting of the T.D. for West Clare, the President of the Sinn Féin Comhairle Ceanntair, and three other justices :

> " Within a fortnight," writes Erskine Childers, " the first District Arbitration Court in Ireland since O'Connell's day sat to hear three important cases."

Before 1919 was out, every parish in West Clare had its court, and thereafter, for the rest of the War of Independence, no enemy court functioned in that constituency.

But when almost a class-war was sweeping through half of Ireland in the first six months of 1920, the solution could hardly have been found in courts alone. There was needed, and needed quickly, an efficient police as well, and not efficiently only, but determined ; for the times were getting out of joint, and a bone-setter needs strong as well as supple hands.

Happily for Ireland, the Volunteers had drawn to themselves the pick of the young men. They were young men who in any case would have been respected by their neighbours, upstanding and clean-living. Now with the aura of soldiers of freedom around them, their prestige was high. To these young soldiers, mainly the sons of farmers, and to the courts whose instrument they were, fell the duty of re-establishing order.

The Government, meeting under Arthur Griffith, in March, 1920, took in hand the task of ending the chaos. Austin Stack, as Minister for Home Affairs, speeded up the machinery of justice, and within a month, District Republican Courts were in open session in almost every constituency in Ireland, and Parish Courts were functioning in twenty-seven counties.

The effect was nothing less than phenomenal. To Dublin had come hundreds of aggrieved landowners and large farmers, asking for protection. They were followed by lesser folk, and by many, not themselves wronged, but horrified at what the mounting disorder would mean to Ireland's name and Ireland's cause.

Although most of the landowners who had come were pro-British, they did not go to Dublin Castle. They went to the Headquarters of Sinn Féin, to wherever they knew there was somebody connected with the Dáil.

Though times were bitter and passions strong, they were not repulsed, and many a Unionist who had swallowed the endless press stories of murderers, gunmen, bolsheviki, went wondering away. The details of their cases had been carefully noted, and they were promised protection. Dáil Éireann issued a stern proclamation :

" WHEREAS it has come to our knowledge that claims have been and are being made in various parts of the country to farms and holdings which are being used and worked by the occupiers as Dairy, Agricultural and Residential Holdings, and as such claims are being based on the assertion that the claimants or their ancestors were formerly in occupation of the property so claimed,

" AND WHEREAS these claims are for the most part of old date and while many of them may be well-founded, others seem to be of a frivolous nature and are put forward in the hope of intimidating the present occupiers,

" Now it is DECREED BY DAIL EIREANN in SESSION assembled :

" (1) That the present time when the Irish people are locked in a life and death struggle with their traditional enemy, is ill-chosen for the stirring up of strife amongst our fellow country-men ; and that all our energies must be directed towards clearing out—not the occupier of this or that piece of land—but the foreign invader of our country.

" (2) That pending the international recognition of the Repub-lic no claims of the kind referred to shall be heard or determined by the Courts of the Republic unless by written licence of the Minister of Home Affairs . . . .

" AND IT IS FURTHER DECREED :

" That any person or persons who persists or persist in pressing forward a disputed claim of the nature above referred to shall do so in the knowledge that such action is a breach of this Decree.

"AND IT IS ORDERED that the forces of the Republic be used to protect the Citizens against the adoption of high-handed methods by any such person or persons."

It is probable that nothing but this linking up of the local courts with the struggle for independence could have restored order in the Ireland of 1920 so swiftly and so completely. The tone of the Proclamation set the key. The local court had behind it the Nation's Parliament, and if the law breakers would not desist, the community would use all its strength against them.

The Republican Courts and police had first tackled ordinary crime. Into the unpoliced areas came the professional criminals, out from the cities and many from Britain itself. Residences, shops, post offices, banks were burgled with impunity. In April, 1920, the Volunteers won their first notable victory over these experienced criminals.

Near Millstreet, in the previous November, two bank officials had been held up and robbed of £16,700. The bank turned to the British authorities, who showed little interest. The Volunteers took the case in hands, and after a long and patient piece of detective work, swooped down on Millstreet one night and rounded up one of the best organised criminal gangs Ireland had seen. They were tried, convicted and sentenced, and £9,000 of the stolen money was recovered.

But the Irish Republic had no prisons for major criminals. They had to suit their penalties to this lack, and the gang were sentenced to various terms of deportation. The leader got 15 years, others ten and eight. Later, the leader came back, but was caught again within a week. This time he got 20 years' deportation and was brought by an armed guard to Britain and informed that if he returned again he would be shot out of hand.

The news of this exciting case went broadcast over the country as a warning to the lesser gangs that their day was over, and within two months it was. The Republican Police were now an established force, and acted openly as such. They kept order at race meetings, re-enforced the licensing laws which had fallen into complete desuetude. When their orders were not carried out, they closed all public-houses in the area for a time. They made war on poteen makers, and soon had that degrading trade under control, too. The people turned to them in all kinds of difficulty and trouble; they were the first real police Ireland had known for generations.

Meanwhile the fame of the Courts was spreading. In a matter of weeks they had created for themselves such a reputation that newspapers in many countries sent special correspondents to see them at work.

"These courts," wrote the *Manchester Guardian* on 10th May, 1920, "are the natural result of the strong, common will for national responsibility. Their object is simply the promotion of peace and of economic justice through an authority which derives its sovereignty from the general will."

John Steele, famous correspondent of the *Chicago Tribune*, attended some of the courts. He reported to his paper the magnitude of what had happened:

"It used to be said that the King's writ did not run beyond the Shannon. That is true to-day, but it is also true that another writ runs and runs effectively—the writ of the Irish Republic."

The London *Daily News* said:

"Sinn Féin has accomplished an amazing work in producing law and order in those parts of Ireland in which it is in power. Sinn Féin has a sanction behind it such as no other law in Ireland has had for generations."

Pro-Britishers of all kinds paid their tributes: Lord Monteagle spoke of the courts as "dispensing even-handed justice between man and man, Catholic and Protestant, farmer and shopkeeper, grazier and cattle-dealer, landlord and tenant."

Even the *Irish Times* could not forbear to cheer:

"Confidence in the sanctions of British law and order," it wrote on 2nd June, 1920, "vanished long ago, and whole countrysides now bring their rights and wrongs to the courts of Sinn Féin."

The man from the *Daily Mail* found a new Ireland:

"In scores of miles I never saw a policeman, a row, or a drunken man."

The courts sat in public. Barristers at first were slow to appear. That profession, like others in Ireland at that time, had governing bodies whose majorities were hostile to everything Republican. But there were no cases for lawyers anywhere else. The British courts were empty, and in any case, courageous national lawyers had set the example, and soon famous advocates were arguing great causes in farmhouses and local halls.

CHAPTER 14

" WITHDRAWN, MY LORD "

THE success of the Republican Courts took everyone, even the Dáil, by surprise. At the session of Dáil Éireann at which they were decided upon, Austin Stack had said the country was ready for them ; but nobody appreciated how ready.

After West Clare, one of the earliest courts established was that at Westport. On the bench were Conor Maguire and Eamonn Moane, the same Conor Maguire who is now Chief Justice of Ireland. He was among the moving spirits of the whole scheme, and infected Arthur Griffith with his enthusiasm.

He was also one of the Committee who gave shape and symmetry to this development : a Committee whose names should be nationally treasured—James Creed Meredith, Professor Arthur Clery, Conor Maguire himself, Diarmuid Crowley and Cahir Davitt, all of whom were to become Supreme Court or High Court judges of the Republic. On the Committee was Kevin O'Shiel, who was to head the Land Courts, and Hector Hughes, now an M.P. at Westminster for a Scottish constituency.

These Land Courts were a perfect instrument for their task, and in the course of their work, dealt with hundreds of cases and many thousands of acres. Sales of land under them involved £229,000. They were set up in the very heart of the land agitation area. One of the first was in Tuam, and that in Ballinasloe, whither Art O'Connor was sent by Dáil Éireann with Kevin O'Shiel as Commissioner, became famous and was visited by many foreign Press men.

In May and June, 1920, the Republic was functioning everywhere. In the previous January the municipal elections had led to overwhelming victories for Sinn Féin. The corporations of the cities, as well as the Borough and Urban Councils, now had strong Republican majorities. They took their stand at once, formal resolutions were passed recognising only one Government, that of Dáil Éireann, and refusing to obey any orders or instructions from the British Local Government Board.

The June elections for the rural bodies strengthened that position. There, too, Sinn Féin swept into power in nine-tenths of Ireland, and the local government machinery was soon bringing the authority of Dáil Éireann into every village and town. More than two hundred

Councils transferred their allegiance to the National Assembly. The Government of the Republic had become the *de facto* as well as the *de jure* Government of Ireland.

As the authority of Dáil Éireann rose, that of the Occupying Power collapsed. Cases listed in the British Courts were withdrawn wholesale.

Those who are over forty or so will recall what the Assizes meant to a country town and to the cities, too. The R.I.C. went into full uniform, the hotels were packed with lawyers, the streets were filled with litigants and witnesses, and when his lordship drove through the cities in his red and ermine robes, crowds watched him with respect, and acknowledged his power with courteous welcome. The procession to the court, with mounted bodyguard, was full of colour and, it seemed, of an unbreakable stability. Here was The Law, something that went deep into the lives of the people, something set and immovable. As the judge passed in his long white wig and flowing crimson from his carriage up into the courthouse, court officials bowed, and the local officers of police and military acknowledged his precedence over them all.

But in June and July, 1920, it was not like that. The lawyers were still in the hotels ; and in the streets were the litigants and witnesses. The R.I.C. were stronger than ever, and their silver buttons and helmet-crests shone in the sunshine. The Judge wore his ermine, and his crier went before him. But there were no people to stand in respectful welcome, for they and British law were now going in different directions.

And when his lordship had passed through the doors of the court-house, around which sandbags and machine-gun posts had been erected in unintended symbolism of the separation of the " law " from the people, he entered a deserted courtroom. The crier prayed silence for his Honour the Judge. The tipstaff walked stiffly as he had done for a generation. But there was nobody in the court, except, perhaps, an old woman resting.

When from the long list on his lordship's bench the cases were called, the Registrar gave some such answer as " Settled, my Lord," " Withdrawn, my Lord." The words rang hollow in the empty building, and must have sounded hollow in the judge's ears, for he knew, and all knew, that what the clerk was saying was : " Disposed of in the Courts of the Republic, my Lord,' " Settled by Republican Judges, my Lord."

In the first week of July 1920 that scene was enacted in every considerable town in four fifths of Ireland.

Judge Fleming entered his Quarter Sessions at Ballymote, and with a glance at the empty benches, said : " This does not look like a promising session," and the clerk made answer from below : "It may even become smaller, your Worship."

At Castlebar, Lord Justice Ronan came to try 92 important cases. The Assize was to last a week. The Registrar answered : "Settled, my lord," to eighty of them, which had been decided in the Republican Circuit Court just before his lordship came. Only the trivialities were left. Chief Justice Ronan made a speech about "lawlessness" in Ireland.

Mr. Justice Samuels, at Limerick, had two cases, and he, too, denounced the "lawlessness" of the Irish people.

Mr. Justice Moore, at Ennis, had no case at all, and his speech was fierce in its condemnation of this people who had no respect for law !

Mr. Justice Kenny at Athlone, Mr. Justice Dodd at Wexford, and so round the nation—empty courts and "lawless" people.

In Waterford City there was only a handful of Grand Jurors or any other kind of Jurors to hear this condemnation of Ireland, and Mr. Justice Gibson, saying that in all his experience in Ireland, England and Scotland, this was without parallel, fined the absent Grand Jurors £100 each. In 16 counties, not one case came for hearing before the crimsoned benches in the imposing courthouses over which flew the Union Jack.

But down the street, or often directly across the roadway, there was, in some undecorated hall, a table for a bench, and rough tweeds or glossy serges for ermine and crimson, and witnesses sat on kitchen chairs, and the public were gathered as at a concert. The judges did not need to lecture empty spaces on a nation's lawlessness.

The courts had no favourites, and if a man thought his Republicanism would help him, he was quickly taught otherwise. When in Ballinamuck an R.I.C. man's property had been stolen, the court punished the thief, while Republican police recovered and restored the property—to the R.I.C.

A British J.P. won his case in Longford. In Louth, two British ex-servicemen, tried for misappropriating £520, were set free because one link in a strong circumstantial chain was weak. The President of the Court told them : "As the Irish people demand justice for themselves they will give justice to others even though they have given their allegiance to an enemy nation." A big farmer, convicted of receiving cattle, knowing them to have been stolen, was fined £300 in North Kildare. The cattle belonged to the British Government, and were restored to that Government.

A Skibbereen court gave a decree for rent against a labourer. At Kilkenny, two men were sent to a makeshift prison for robbing the residence of a major in the British Army ; an Ulster Presbyterian won his land case against a Loughrea man at the Loughrea court ;

Messrs. Robertson, Ledlie and Ferguson, leading drapers of Belfast and Cork, won their case as defendants in a profiteering charge in Cork. At Annamoe, Co. Wicklow, men who had threatened Protestants with reprisals for the slaughter of Catholics in Belfast, were arrested, heavily fined, and made publicly apologise to their victims.

The courts dealt with everything, from a claim for damages for the sale of a kicking mare, to the fulfilment of a valuable contract made by a firm with the ex-Lord Mayor of Cork. It was all done with such a scrupulous regard for justice that the London *Daily News*, in an editorial on 5th July, could say:

> "The decisions of the judges and magistrates appear to be touched with considerable shrewdness and to be wanting neither in equity nor in wide human sympathy. Moreover, they have a distinguishing characteristic which is usually absent from our traditional temples of justice—they leave no bitterness behind them."

There was much wit in some of these judgments, and in the findings of the Land Courts, which were sitting at the same time.

Two brothers found themselves unable to agree as to how to divide land left to them by an uncle, and the court suggested that John, being the elder, should mark on a map the division he thought best. John was delighted, and carved two farms from the uncle's land—and then the court gave the younger brother his choice!

Whenever a Republican was charged before a British Court in those days, his first words were: "I refuse to recognise this court." A man charged with larceny before a Republican Court, in North Clare, told the President of it: "I refuse to recognise the authority of this court."

"That being so," replied the President, "kindly inform us which court do you recognise and we shall be pleased to hand you over immediately."

The man pleaded guilty and took his sentence cheerfully.

At Longford, a member of the Protestant community sued a neighbour for assault. His hat had been damaged by the blow of an ashplant. The court sent them both to a hatter's, the defendant to pay for a new hat to be chosen by the complainant.

At Loughrea, a young man, who had accused residents of being British spies, asked for a chance and he would undo the damage. The court gave him the fullest chance by ordering him to be taken outside churches on the following Sunday and there publicly withdraw his slanders.

But if the Republican Courts and police were making a new Ireland, Britain's anger was growing ever deeper. For here was the proof of what they most denied, Ireland's fitness for independence, and the Press of the world had taken notice of it. The propaganda that Sinn Féin was simply a murder-gang, who had terrorised a pro-British nation, was being answered unanswerably.

Professor Dicey, one of Britain's greatest constitutional lawyers, had once written of the " power of Great Britain " that:

> " If it should turn out that after every effort to enforce just laws by just methods, our justice itself, from whatever cause, remains hateful to the mass of the Irish people—then it will be clear that the Union must, for the sake of England no less than for Ireland, come to an end. The alternative policy will then be not Home Rule but Separation."

The hour for separation had clearly come. But Dublin Castle's decision was that, at all costs, it was the Republican Courts which must be destroyed, not the Union.

From the beginning of June, all through July and August, a hunt was carried out which must remain unique in modern history. It began with an incident which fixed the true character of what was happening. On 6th June, there escaped from Republican custody a thief named Connolly, who had raided many farmhouses in County Galway, and there, menacing the women with a dummy gun, forced them to hand over what money they had.

After escape, he went to the nearest R.I.C. barracks and offered to lead a party to his temporary prison. A large force was assembled, and the raid led to the capture of three Republican policemen, who were promptly sentenced to hard labour. This co-operation between criminal and Constabulary continued to the end.

Soon the raids had spread, and in one day, simultaneously in seven counties, scores of men and women, suspected of being associated with the courts, were arrested. Those on whom documents dealing with cases were found, were sent to summary trial and hard labour. Courts were surprised in session and sometimes merely dispersed, but, at others, the judges were arrested.

In Limerick, a raid led to the arrest of all the justices present, including Alderman Stephen O'Mara. Supreme Court Judge Diarmuid Crowley was seized when on Circuit and sentenced to 21 months' imprisonment. Mathew Joseph Smith, of Mill Street, Cavan, was tried and sentenced to six months by British Military Courtmartial for having in his possession the oath of office taken by Republican Judges.

It was on the orders of Dublin Castle that the British military took a hand. From the R.I.C. headquarters the following instruction was issued, dated 6th July, 1920:

" Referring to the recent assumption of police functions by Irish Volunteers, it has been decided that no unauthorised persons will be allowed to arrogate to themselves the duties of police.

" Any such gathering of Volunteers will be an illegal assembly, and the local police should take steps to disperse it and arrest the leaders. Military aid may be invoked where necessary. The troops have been instructed to assist the police in this matter.

" T. J. Smith,
Inspector General."

Republican Court officials and police were already being attacked when this circular was issued. At Youghal and at New Park, Kilmallock, on 17th June, fire was opened by the R.I.C. on Republican police escorting criminals to a temporary lock-up. At Charleville, in a similar incident, though three of the Republican police were wounded, they got their prisoner through to his " unknown destination," as was then the pseudonym for the jails of the Republic. Tralee Urban Council had asked Republican headquarters to take over police duties in the town. Eight times individual Volunteers on duty were seized, brought to the R.I.C. barracks, and beaten up.

This system of assault was adopted in many areas, and judges as well as police were made the victims of it. Joseph Cunningham, Republican Judge of Co. Westmeath, was taken, on 22nd August, by R.I.C. and beaten so mercilessly that he was found unconscious.

Death followed the police and judges. John O'Brien was shot dead while patrolling in Cork on 19th July. On 21st July, James Cogan, Chief of Republican police in Oldcastle district, was shot dead by military as he was escorting a notorious cattle stealer to trial. District Justice J. A. Lynch, as is described later, was murdered by British intelligence officers on 22nd September.

By the end of Steptember, hundreds of local justices, police, court officials, even witnesses and litigants were in prison. The rooting out of everybody associated with the courts became so intense that young men were seized and threatened with death if they would not name the local Republican police officer.

One such case from Masseytown, Co. Cork, was typical, where two men, taken on the night of 18th September, were asked to point out the house of the Republican police officer. When they refused, they were stripped, their eyes bandaged, and they were led out for execution. They were made to kneel, still blindfolded, and volleys were fired over their heads. But they kept their secret.

Though the administration of justice was dislocated everywhere, courts still met. The sessions had now to be in secret, but it was a secret so widely shared that everybody knew but the R.I.C. In one area in Co. Roscommon, thirty motor cars brought lawyers and litigants for the hearing of cases. In Co. Longford, the District Court sat all through the terror, and though all five judges were on the run, they came together for eight lengthy sessions from January to June, and 67 important cases were decided. In many other counties it was the same.

Though at the end of September, Sir Hamar Greenwood boasted that the Republican administration of justice had been broken up, even he could not say it had been destroyed. His boast was that he had driven the courts into the back rooms—he did not know that the courts, which were sitting everywhere as he spoke, were not concerned about the building in which they met, but about giving equal justice to all the citizens of the nation.

One incident illustrates the inherent power and dignity that rested in these courts, so plainly caparisoned. On 27th July, a Republican Land Court was in session in Claremorris, Co. Mayo. A strong body of Constabulary forced their way into the building with the intention of suppressing it. The court continued its hearing, and when the R.I.C., fully-armed, tramped into the room, the Republican judge rebuked them for the disturbance and ordered them to remove their hats at once. His voice had in it the authority of a people, and the caps came mutely off.

CHAPTER 15

UNDERGROUND NEWSPAPER

THROUGH almost the entire length of the War of Independence there was published in Dublin an underground newspaper whose adventures rivalled those of the famous *La Libre Belgique*.

There was nothing the British sought more vigorously than the offices and staff of *The Irish Bulletin*. They raided hundreds of houses in search of it. They held up great blocks of the capital, and for days and nights went from room to room. They had touts and G-men watching every likely building, and half-a-dozen agents dropping in casually to this or that shop or store or office on the chance of lighting on it.

They found those coveted offices once. It was at midnight, and they came across it by accident, but without a halt *The Irish Bulletin* was out again, never having missed an issue. They never even seized a whole edition in the post, although each evening it went into the letter boxes of Dublin, nearly a thousand copies of it, a few here, a few there, lest any unusual number would indicate the presence nearby of the long-sought-quarry.

Its publication was a triumph of organisation and discretion. It reflected the spirit of the times perfectly; the circumspect audacity of the movement. For *The Bulletin* office was not an easy thing to hide, especially in the heart of occupied Dublin. The workers on it had to come every morning to one building to which they could easily have been followed if they had been loose-tongued or had indicated the nature of their work to others. It never happened. And when that night the whole of the *Bulletin* organisation was discovered, and files, typewriters, duplicators, and all the paraphernalia of a small publishing house were carted off to Dublin Castle (with an astonishing sequel as will be told later), the workers were in new offices within a few hours, and the hunted paper was being written, duplicated, enveloped and despatched as usual.

The escapes the *Bulletin* had were extraordinary. One fine and sunny Saturday afternoon we were all busily at work, because though the *Bulletin* was not published on a Saturday (it would have to lie too long in the post), each issue required indexing, examination of records and sworn statements of the victims of the terror, as well as dealing with captured Castle mail, etc.

Breathlessly, one of the messengers burst in: " A hell of a raid has started," he said. " Half the British Army is in Kildare Street, and the cordons are across this street already." It was a crisis: the whole staff was there, and it looked as if, at last, we were caught. We decided to leave in ones and twos as the other office workers were leaving, and hope for the best.

These great raids had become a regular part of Dublin life. An area would be sealed off, and everybody and everything inside that area, when the final cordon was closed, would be interrogated and examined.

The *Bulletin* offices were then in Molesworth Street, a thoroughly good old Unionist street, with the Masonic Lodge at one end and an Episcopalian Hall at the other. In between were staid offices of family solicitors.

The particular building which housed the *Bulletin* offices had been chosen with a nice discrimination: the main suite of rooms were occupied by a Crown Solicitor, and his name and another brass plate announcing " The Church of Ireland Widows' and Orphans' Society " gave the tone of the whole place.

We, disguised as an insurance society, were the other tenants. For the chance visitor we had folders and typescripts on display, but behind this prosaic front, duplicating machines buzzed and whirred, pages of the *Bulletin* (it was mimeographed) shot into the waiting trays, there were sounds of typewriters and clipping machines, and piles of addressed envelopes waiting ready opened for the folded treason.

Now the troops were on our doorsteps and it seemed nothing could prevent discovery. So we stuffed our persons with the things that must be kept, burnt what might have given too many clues, and Anna Fitzsimons and myself, the last of the staff, locked up the offices and stepped out into the sunshine of Molesworth Street.

As we drew near that cordon, our eyes searched anxiously for the face of the G-man that was always on such occasions standing by. We did not know him and we prayed he would not know us. The Republicans of Dublin were by that time well trained in walking through cordons. The trick was never to hesitate: walk straight on into the cordon as one having the right to pass, nod to the officer in charge if he was looking, smile at the nearest Tommy and saunter on.

On this occasion it was more difficult for the cordon we first came up against—or rather which came up against us—was a line of Black-and-Tans. They bore right down on us, swinging their guns. It seemed the inescapable end.

Then, with her woman's wit, Anna Fitzsimons, innerly quaking but sweetly demure, walked up to the tallest man amongst them and as he bent down to hear her she explained that we two had to get through to buy some stamps. It sounds the very height of folly but it was so innocent-seeming that it worked! We were through.

Anna and I got around the corner with all our deadly cargo of papers (and I think she was carrying my gun): we were suffocated with the tension of it. Though now half out of danger, we did not dare to hasten our stroll lest any of the raiders might be staring doubtfully after us. At last we passed the foot of Dawson Street, and then the open door of Kidd's, which has since become Jammet's, was abreast of us with its smell of good cooking. Irresistible temptation! We had a hilarious lunch.

At least the staff was safe, and as the search parties in that great block between Dawson St. and Kildare St. worked like tunnelers from room to room, forcing doors, prizing open desks and presses, we planned new offices for the *Bulletin*.

The search went on that night and all through Sunday. It was Monday morning before the troops withdrew. In those tense days the disappearance of the raiding parties was no proof that the raid was over, as Republicans discovered to their cost. Inside the main entrance of the now innocent-looking building it was usual, when some secret office had been discovered, to station a group of armed detectives. One of those detectives would quietly open to any knock and, without showing himself, close the door carefully behind you; you were caught, and, worst of all, unable to warn those coming after.

Early that Monday morning I cycled past those precious offices. The house turned a blank gaze on me. The staff had started to arrive in Molesworth Street. A lad was on his way to school. A well-placed question or two showed that, like ninety per cent. of the youngsters of those days, he was a Republican.

Would he do a job for us? We did not know if the big raid was over, and wanted to visit a friend in that building over there. There might be a few G-men left behind. Could he go over and give a runaway knock? If there were any G-men waiting, the door would open at once and so he had better be nifty.

With shining eyes he crossed the road, looking back at us as Christopher Columbus must have looked back at the little harbour of Palos. That runaway knock barked through Molesworth Street with the sharpness of a midnight volley and the feet in flight tattooed after it. But the door never opened; the house never stirred.

When, after a noisy climb up the stairs, we came to the *Bulletin* offices, we found the door unopened and inside everything untouched. The explanation was easy in the end. That very building had been made the headquarters of the raid, chosen, no doubt, for the comfort

G

of the Crown Solicitor's big office immediately below ours. The officers directing the raid sat around the fine table there, and all day long, and the next day, the reports came in : no sign of the *Bulletin* office ; every party came back with the same story ; nothing even like it !

On Monday morning the raiders packed up and trekked away, and all the time, within a few feet of their heads in a building which they would not insult by searching, was the jewel they were after.

We sat with smiling incredulity in the office we had received back from Fate, and felt that all the care taken for months so that nobody, friend or foe, should learn what was being run off those whirring machines had been rewarded ten times over.

But I'm in the middle of the story without having begun it. . . .

There was no way by which the world could learn fully of what was happening in Ireland. The British were determined that only their side of the case would be heard. Not only was the Press censorship heavier than it had ever been, but care was taken that no Republican publications would get into print at all. No ordinary paper would venture to give the whole story of the Terror.

That became the function of *The Irish Bulletin*.

The idea of such a daily publication was Bob Brennan's, and it was he who, in the first months, gave the *Bulletin* its character and form. The first issue appeared on 11th November, 1919, and it never missed an issue until it ceased publication after the Treaty was signed. In between those dates it became the most effective of all weapons against Britain.

Day after day it set out, not in argument, but in cold, hard fact the reality of the horrors of British rule in Ireland. At first it went to a few people only—the Dublin newspaper offices, correspondents of outside papers in Dublin. Slowly its circulation widened—first by post to a few friendly British papers and M.P.'s, then to all important papers in Britain and the United States, to members of the British Opposition in the Commons and Lords, to the leading members of Senate and House of Representatives in Washington, then to leading men in all the English-speaking countries.

It went to India, Egypt and other nations asserting their right to freedom. It was translated by the Irish Republican delegations in Paris, Rome and Madrid, and went to leading personalities on the Continent and to every important newspaper.

Within a year, this mimeographed sheet, produced in hidden offices in Dublin, was being quoted over the world, and what it said was given a circulation of millions. It won this acceptance by a very simple rule—chapter and verse for everything. For every charge made against the British in the *Bulletin*, there was day and date and place.

The *Bulletin* not only reported the murder of Irish prisoners, but when it could, named those who committed the crime; it told the story of brutal raids on Irish homes and identified whoever was in charge; it published top-secret documents captured from the British which exposed the militaristic nature of the régime; it mercilessly uncovered the guilt of British Cabinet Ministers, the Viceroy, the Commanders of the Crown Forces and all other Senior Officers who were directing the Terror.

At first the *Bulletin* was not believed; it was put aside as war propaganda. Then there came into the ordinary news, from another source, reports of an outrage the *Bulletin* had already given in detail, and some of the more thoughtful recipients went back to its account to test its accuracy. They found it to be 100 per cent. true.

The *Bulletin* answered a lying official statement by citing fact after fact, and when some M.P. raised these facts in the Commons, he found the Government, from whom he demanded a denial, dumb. Soon it was appreciated that this was a new form of war propaganda —one based on actual happenings, observed and provable. Thus emboldened, more and more people in Britain and elsewhere, grounded their own statements on what they had read in this purple-inked sheet which reached them every morning. Even the London *Times* used material from it with devastating effect against the Government.

To provide material for the *Bulletin*, an elaborate organisation had to be set up in which all Departments of State co-operated. Volunteer Headquarters collected details of the murder and ill-treatment of its members, Republican police supplied well-vouched-for accounts of those raids where the British forces smashed everything, furniture, crockery, windows, pictures, mainly in the houses of the poor. The Department of Justice gave reports of the courts and their cases; the Department of Finance of the progress of the Dáil Loan, and the long list of collectors imprisoned and newspapers suppressed for advocating it; the Department of Local Government sent in the details of the working of public bodies which had transferred their allegiance to Dáil Éireann.

After Erskine Childers' appointment as Director of Propaganda, following Desmond Fitzgerald's arrest in February, 1921, a new section was added in which there was a weekly survey of the war, a record of all attacks and ambushes, with statistics of numbers engaged and of casualties on both sides.

These were compiled from the reports of the Republican O.C.'s in the field, and were so much fuller and more free from distortion than anything the British accounts gave that they added a new value to the *Bulletin* for Pressmen. From the prisons, through a hundred secret channels, came signed statements of the victims of interrogation. The *Bulletin* staff carefully sifted these, and published only what clearly could be proved.

From the first day of its life, the *Bulletin's* staff knew they were living on borrowed time, and had often at a moment's notice to disperse, carrying away what they could. On one occasion the warning came in the middle of running off that day's issue, and there was nothing for it but to pack the whole equipment, typewriters, stocks of paper, duplicators, etc., into a horse cab, which was then driven around Dublin's suburban streets until danger of the raid was over.

Everything had to be done under the shadow of death. If the staff of the *Bulletin* ever fell into the hands of the Black-and-Tans and Auxiliaries, or any branch of the Crown forces, they knew they would pay for their daily exposure of British methods. Yet though dangers hemmed them in from every side, those who edited, prepared, collected, typed, duplicated and distributed the *Bulletin* never in two years failed at their tasks.

The extraordinary importance of their work sustained them. The *Bulletin* had become almost the only direct channel between the Irish Government and the outside world. It had also become something of a shield for the oppressed people, since the fear of exposure in its pages was probably the only deterrent some of the leading terrorists felt.

CHAPTER 16

A FAMOUS EXPOSURE

THERE were many sensational issues of the *Bulletin*.

Several of them arose from the capture of documents from the British. It was a regular practice of the Volunteers to seize the Castle mails. By that means not only were the plans of British military and police discovered, but other material exposing the whole inner organisation of repression.

The mails were seized at railway stations, at the G.P.O. sorting offices, from post vans in the country and from trains. Constantly changing tactics had to be used in this form of warfare. As the G.P.O. in Dublin was still a hollow shell, the sorting office was in the roller-skating rink in the basement of the Rotunda. Into this the mail went from street level down a chute made glossy by the descent of many mail-bags. Down the chute came the mail one morning, and in a split second after it down the chute came Volunteer after Volunteer. While the staff were standing with hands up, the Castle mail-bags were picked out from the others.

On another occasion a strong guard of Auxiliaries, travelling in front and behind the mail car, saw the mails safely landed on to the platform outside the sorting office. Their task complete, they drove away, and again in the split-second before the guard at the G.P.O. took over, the Volunteers, who had trailed the Auxiliaries in a taxi, bundled the mail bags into their own car and were off.

Captured mails were brought to one of the secret Dáil offices and gone through swiftly and carefully. There was the inevitable sequel for me. A fat bundle would arrive in the evening of such a raid, just as the *Bulletin* office was closing. The job then was to bring that precious cargo home and work on it during the night, for it was a point of honour to use the documents within twenty-four hours if we could. It gave such an air of efficiency if we could publish in the *Bulletin* of the 6th the " very secret " report sent to the Viceroy on the 4th, or if a confidential Castle circular of the 9th could be got into the hands of the public through the *Bulletin* on the 11th.

The most sensational *Bulletin* of all, was of 10th September, 1920. The story of it has the quality of a first-class detective yarn. It begins on the day the first issue of the *Bulletin* appeared, 11th November, 1919. The British celebrated that first anniversary of Armistice

Day with a great raid on No. 76 Harcourt Street, then the Headquarters of Dáil Éireann. Everything movable was carried off.
While the staffs, under guard, stood by the walls, they saw the raiders
bundle up stacks of official Dáil notepaper and carry it out to the
waiting lorries. Nothing more was heard of the captured notepaper
until the following May.

In March and April, 1920, a number of leading Republicans were
assassinated in their homes. Before their murder, each had received
a death notice. Now, on 14th, 15th and 16th May the notepaper
reappeared. Every member of the Dáil, not yet in prison, received
through the post a death notice. Typed on official Dáil notepaper
in capital letters was the legend:

"AN EYE FOR AN EYE, A TOOTH FOR A TOOTH
THEREFORE A LIFE FOR A LIFE."

Arthur Griffith, who himself had got one of these notices, summoned a Press conference for 18th May. He showed the Pressmen
the letters and told them they were typed on the paper which the
Crown Forces had taken from No. 76 Harcourt Street on 11th November. He pointed out that all the death notices had been posted in
Dublin, and he accused the British Government in Ireland of being
a party to preparations for the assassination of the elected
representatives of the Irish people.

This accusation caused a flurry in the Castle, which lasted over
a week, and then, on 27th May, from the office of the Chief Commissioner of the D.M.P., came the following letter to the press:

"Sir,
"With reference to an article appearing in your issue of the
19th relative to threatening letters received by Sinn Féin Members
of Parliament and to the statement that paper similar to that
on which the threatening notices were written had been seized
by the authorities at 76 Harcourt Street, I am directed by Government to inform you that there is no foundation for your report
that notepaper or any writing paper was removed from 76 Harcourt Street or taken possession of by the police or by the military.

"W. E. Johnstone,
"Chief Commissioner.

Dublin Castle,
27th May, 1920."

Two days later, Griffith issued a brief statement:

"All Dáil Éireann notepaper was seized by detectives on the
occasion. No notepaper was left on the premises except some

that was in a place these detectives overlooked. New notepaper had to be printed to replace what was taken."

And there the matter rested for four months.

Then early in September there fell into the hands of the Volunteers rich treasure, indeed. Nothing was said until the correspondence had been photostated and copies placed in the hands of leading Americans and sent to the London *Times*. Then the *Bulletin* exploded its landmine.

The issue was that of 10th September, and all who worked on it will remember the thrill of that day. It contained the most damning series of letters that had ever fallen into the hands of the Republican forces.

The *Bulletin* recalled the raid of 11th November, the death notices on Dáil Éireann notepaper of 14th, 15th, 16th May, the Press conference when Griffith showed the newspaper men the notices, and, finally, the firm and categorical denial signed by the Chief Commissioner of the D.M.P. that any notepaper whatever was taken by British military or police.

Then the *Bulletin* went on: "Certain official correspondence of high-placed British Government officials in Ireland is now in the hands of the Irish Republican Authorities." It cited part of that correspondence—four reports and letters.

The first was a report by W. McFeely, an Inspector of the G-Division of the D.M.P., dated 15th January, 1920. It dealt with the arrival in Ireland of Dr. Chauviré, Professor of French, at University College, Dublin. "His movements on the 14th and 15th were watched and he was not observed to associate with extremists." The report bore the note:

"The I.G. transmitted. W. C. F. Redmond, Ass.-Comm. 16/1."

That is, it was seen by Mr. Redmond, Assistant to Chief Commissioner Johnstone, who had issued the denial about the notepaper.

The second document was a letter dated 8/4/20 from the North Dublin Union. On the face of it, it was a harmless document— a chatty letter to somebody named "Dear Ward" from "Yrs to the sticky end, P. Attwood." It told Ward that a ginger-haired typist had arrived in Attwood's office and that "Hyam is well away."

Now, these documents were important, because one had been written by an Inspector of the Detective Division of the Dublin Police and had been initialled by the Assistant Commissioner, and the other because P. Attwood and Hyam were both officers of the British General Staff then housed in the North Dublin Union. *And both letters were written on Dáil Éireann notepaper.*

So the heads of the police and the British General Staff not only knew, before the denial was issued, that paper had been taken from 76 Harcourt Street on 11th November, but they had that paper in Dublin Castle and were writing reports on it.

The third document of the four had nothing to do with Dáil Éireann notepaper. It was a report from F. Harper-Shove, Captain of the British General Staff, in charge of Intelligence in the Dublin district. This report dealt with the great hunger strike which had just ended in Mountjoy Jail. It was typical of the mists of self-deception which the British wreathed around themselves during the War of Independence.

It reported that of the 69 who hunger-struck, all but the leaders had been terrorised into participation! The leaders were fed by the warders on whiskey during the strike, but the rank and file got nothing, and " were in a bad way." In proof of this whiskey conspiracy, Staff-Captain Harper-Shove reported :

> " The leaders, i.e. Hunter, Clancy, Brennan, Gallagher, etc., *shook hands with each warder before leaving the prison.*"

But it was not this " evidence " that made Harper-Shove's report interesting—it was something much more significant. The report was typed, perhaps by that ginger-haired young lady, and *it was typed on the same machine on which the death notices had been typed.* The *Bulletin* had submitted the report to an expert in typescript. He showed that the flaws which every typewriter develops (unevenness in certain letters, inequalities in spacing, etc.) were to be found also in the addresses on the envelopes containing the death notices.

> " He (the expert) has reported that he is prepared to swear that the threatening letters, the envelopes and the above secret report were all typed on the same type-writing machine which is an Underwood."

Thus far, it had been proved that Dáil Éireann notepaper was in the hands of both the Military and Police when Col. Johnstone emphatically denied the fact, and that the death notices sent out on it had come from British Military headquarters. It needed one more link to make clear that this was not a boyish prank but the preliminary to murder. The *Bulletin*, in its fourth letter, provided that link.

In this case again, it was not a question of Dáil notepaper, nor were there any typing irregularities to be explained away. The fourth letter was written from " St. Andrew's Hotel, Exchequer Street, Dublin," and was dated " 2nd March, 1920." The important thing in this case was the signature " F. Harper-Shove." He was telling a " Dear Hardy " how things were with him :

" Have been given a free hand to carry on, and everyone has been very charming. Re our little stunt, I see no prospects until I have got things on a firmer basis, but still hope and believe there are possibilities."

The " little stunt " was the assassination of Irish leaders. He had things on a " firmer basis " soon after this letter was written. On 20th March, 1920, the great round of assassinations had begun: Alderman Tomás MacCurtain was murdered in his home in Cork on that date. Two days before his death he received a death notice. A week or so later, James McCarthy of Thurles, and Thomas O'Dwyer of Bouladuff, in the same county, were slain in their homes. The method, even the hour, of the assassinations was the same in all three cases. One hand was guiding them. James McCarthy and Thomas O'Dwyer had also received death notices. And when pressed for details of these crimes in the House of Commons, Sir Hamar Greenwood used these death notices as proof that the assassinations were planned by Sinn Féin itself, and the " extremists " were removing the " moderates."

Nothing could be a better proof of this, in the case of the next set of victims, than that they should have received their death notices from Dáil Éireann. When Captain Shove posted those letters he did not, of course, guess that it would ever be known whence they came.

He thought the members of the Dáil who received them would hide the fact that they were on Dáil notepaper. This, it was thought, would give the British—at the first enquiry into the murder of a T.D.—the opportunity of " discovering " and making sensational play of the " origin " of the threatening letters. Sincere people could not then have escaped the conclusion that there was much in Hamar Greenwood's explanation that the Irish were shooting one another. Griffith's prompt exposure of the letters, and their link with the raid on No. 76, threw the whole dread plot out of gear. The *Bulletin* of 10th September clinched the revelations.

It exposed the British General Staff in Ireland as caught red-handed in preparing for the murder of public representatives. The heads of the police by their denials, now shown to be completely and knowingly false, were involved also, and Col. Johnstone's phrase, " I am directed by Government," brought the whole machinery of Dublin Castle and the Irish Office in London into it.

The publication of this issue of the *Irish Bulletin* stunned the authorities, especially the announcement that proofs of their guilt had been placed in the hands of leading Americans and sent in full photostat

form to the principal London newspaper.   For five days there was
silence.

The London *Times* of 14th September reproduced most of the
Bulletin, and worse still for the Government, devoted an editorial
to its disclosures.   This asserted that the *Bulletin's* effort to combine
the death notices with an actual plot for assassination of public
representatives was far-fetched and unproven.

A few months, even a few days later, the *Times* might not so airily
have dismissed it, for it was on the night of 22nd September that
John Aloysius Lynch (Republican Judge and County Councillor)
was murdered in his bed by a group of British officers.

" In any case," the editorial said, " the matter is one which demands
either convincing denial or full explanation from the Government."

The Castle could no longer remain silent.

On 15th September, the Press Association were informed that the
statements by the *Bulletin* were " absolutely false," and that a detailed
refutation would follow.

It never came.   On the night of the 15th–16th September, there
was a series of raids in Dublin unlike in its thoroughness anything
experienced before.   Pictures were taken from their frames, books
were examined page by page, clothes were taken separately from
wardrobes, shaken and turned inside out, cycles were taken apart
and the hollow tubing searched, floor boards were lifted, pianos
were opened.   No receptacle was too small to be minutely searched,
no length of time too long to fine-comb the suspected house.   On
one premises the searchers sustained their meticulous examination
of bookcase, cupboards, presses, drawers, for seven hours.

Reporting these raids in the issue of 17th September, the *Bulletin*
said :

> " Some of the documents for which the British military authori-
> ties are looking are the originals of the letters upon which the
> ' absolutely false ' charges were made against them.   Could
> they recover and destroy these documents, the British Military
> Authorities would feel safer in issuing the detailed refutation
> they have promised."

They were never found, and the refutation was never issued.
But the *Bulletin* was now more eagerly and angrily sought than ever
by all forces of the Crown.

CHAPTER 17

MUTINY IN THE R.I.C.

AFTER nearly a year-and-a-half of the most intensive search an Army of Occupation ever made, the offices of the *Irish Bulletin* were found. On the night of Saturday-Sunday of 26–27th March, 1921, the British carried out what must have been to them a triumphant raid. Here was what they had looked for ever since November, 1919, with mounting anger and desperation. Yet they never mentioned the *Bulletin* in their official report of the raid. That report read:

> " *The headquarters of the Sinn Fein propaganda department was raided on Saturday night during curfew hours by ' C ' Company, Auxiliary Police, at 11 Molesworth Street, Dublin, resulting in the largest capture of seditious literature yet made in Ireland.*
>
> " *Several tons of files, books, literature, etc., were removed in Government lorries.*
>
> " *Office equipment of an elaborate character—including Roneo duplicators, typewriters and desks used by clerks—were seized.*
>
> " *There was a department dealing with propaganda in foreign countries —Italy, France, Spain—and files of letters, some being addressed to priests in these countries, were found.*
>
> " *There were files of the principal newspapers of Great Britain and large bundles of newspaper cuttings. Letters issued to M.P.'s were among the documents captured.*
>
> " *In the ' Parliamentary' section was captured the latest Order of Dáil Éireann, dated March 23, proclaiming a boycott of certain English goods.*
>
> " *Nobody was found on the premises.*"

Everything, plus a few inventions, was mentioned, except the one thing of importance. None of us could understand what was behind this strange omission. Their most secret military orders, their confidential reports, their private letters to one another, their sinister plans, set out in their own memos, had appeared in the *Bulletin's* pages and they were as silent as the grave when all the machinery that produced it fell into their hands by the same kind of mischance for us, as earlier for them, made them forget to search the room above their heads.

They had another reason for rejoicing. The *Bulletin* not only

exposed their régime. It did worse in the Castle's eyes : it helped
to break up their forces.

In its issue of 21st June, 1920, and subsequent issues, were published long lists of R.I.C men who, in protest against the tasks
being given it had resigned from the force : County Inspectors,
District Inspectors, Head Constables, Sergeants, Constables. The
Bulletin gave name, place, rank, length of service, everything. The
lists filled many pages.

The readers of the *Bulletin* were being prepared for one of the most
dramatic stories of the War of Independence—a mutiny in the R.I.C.
It was like a mutiny in a king's bodyguard.

The men allowed into the force were carefully chosen : they were
brought raw and young to the Depot in Dublin. There they were
not only trained and disciplined, but indoctrinated. There had been
for many years no open quarrel between the people and the Castle,
and no odium rested upon any who joined the force. It attracted
young lads of courage and intelligence in many areas.

These got a thorough grounding, which directed their minds
away from the national ideals, and against the interests of the common
people. In the Labour troubles of 1912–1913, in Dublin and elsewhere, the R.I.C. were thrown against their own brothers struggling
for social justice. But those brothers had first been represented
to them as godless Socialists and trouble-makers, and the young
police put a touch of hate into their batonings that pleased the
authorities well.

The Castle thought that the force had been tested, finally and
definitely, after 1916—anything else might break, but not the R.I.C.
And on 9th July, 1920, the *Bulletin* announced that the R.I.C. had
broken !

No paper in Ireland dared to be the first to publish the story, for
any mention of disturbance within the force would have brought
down the full rigour of a militarist régime.

The word came to the *Bulletin* office, and it, too, had to watch
that its reputation for accuracy, which had become a precious weapon,
was not injured. At last it was decided that the *Bulletin* would publish
the constables' own written and signed story, but omitting the
constables' names.

And what a story it was !

There had already been police difficulties in Listowel, when into
the barracks on 19th June, 1920, came a cavalcade of top-ranking
officers. Leading them was a top-ranking terrorist, not yet a month
appointed, Lieut.-Colonel Brice Ferguson Smyth, Divisional Commissioner for all Munster, a one-armed veteran of the World War.
With him was General Tudor, soon to make a black name for himself

as director of the Auxiliaries, County Inspector Poer O'Shee, Captain Chadwick, of the British Staff, Resident Magistrate Leatham, Assistant County Inspector Dobbyn, and a number of others. It was an imposing group for constables, who, through long days in the Depot, had had impressed on them the almost god-like importance of their superiors.

The constables, eighteen of them, were assembled in the day-room of the barracks, and Divisional Commissioner Smyth addressed them. He was no man for nonsense, and he cut like a knife to the point :

" Well, men, I have something of interest to tell you : something I am sure you would not wish your wives to hear."

The startled constables watched him :

" Sinn Féin has had all the sport up to the present and we are going to have the sport now. . . . I am promised as many troops from England as I require, thousands are coming daily. I am getting 7,000 police from England . . .

" Police and military will patrol the country at least five nights a week. They are not to confine themselves to the main roads but take across the country, lie in ambush, and when civilians are seen approaching shout ' Hands up.' Should the order not be immediately obeyed, shoot, and shoot with effect. If persons approaching carry their hands in their pockets and are in any way suspicious looking, shoot them down. . . . The more you shoot the better I will like it, and I assure you no policeman will get into trouble for shooting any man. . . . We want your assistance in carrying out this scheme and wiping out Sinn Féin."

The assembled constables were staring at him. Commissioner Smyth turned to the first man in the ranks : " Are you prepared to co-operate ? " But the men had already chosen a leader, Constable Jeremiah Mee, and it was indicated he would speak for all.

He did, in a speech that in this R.I.C barracks, in the heart of Kerry, suddenly became the voice of Ireland :

" By your accent," this simple constable said in one burning phrase, " I take it you are an Englishman ; and in your ignorance you forget you are addressing Irishmen."

The rows of startled officers faced the rows of determined men. Then in a gesture of contempt, the men's leader stripped from him his cap, his belt, and his arms, and laying them on the table, said :

" These too are English—— Take them . . . "

The Divisional Commissioner and the County Inspector shouted an order for the arrest of the leader. An angry murmur filled the day-room, and it was clear what any attempt to touch the spokesman would have meant. After a moment of bafflement, the high-ranking officers withdrew, and the constables held the Listowel barracks.

A little later, there was a similar scene in Killarney barracks. The one-armed Commissioner told the men of a new freedom. Hitherto, facilities had been given for an enquiry when the R.I.C. killed a man, he said. Those days were over.

> " Henceforward no such facilities would be provided and no such policemen would be held up to public odium by being pilloried before a Coroner's jury. Further, when a police patrol saw coming along a road a Sinn Féiner whom they *suspected* of intent to attack them they were to get in the first shot and there would be no further questions asked."

Here, Divisional Commissioner Smyth chalked a line on the floor of the day-room and asked any not prepared to carry out these instructions to step out and he would be paid off. Five men promptly stepped out, and after a pause the rest cheered them.

The *Bulletin*, with these accounts, was soon in the hands of members of the British House of Commons. There were awkward questions for the Chief Secretary, Sir Hamar Greenwood. He denied that Commissioner Smyth had ever used such words. What he said had been twisted entirely out of its true meaning.

T. P. O'Connor reminded him that many constables had sworn to the words. Had not hundreds of young men been sent to long terms of imprisonment on evidence consisting solely of " mental notes " by constables like these? Were constables not trained to report from memory the exact phrases used? The Government Front Bench wriggled.

T. P. O'Connor asked the Speaker's permission to raise the matter on the adjournment. But in those days the whole machinery of the British Parliament was turned against Ireland, and the Speaker was as deeply hostile as the Cabinet itself. The matter plainly was not urgent, he said. T.P. pleaded that the speech, if it were not straight-away disavowed, could lead to new horrors. The Speaker pooh-poohed the urgency and refused a debate.

That was on the afternoon of Wednesday, 14th July. By night-time on Saturday, July 17th, the Divisional Commissioner of the R.I.C. for all Munster, Lt.-Col. Gerald Brice Ferguson Smyth, D.S.O., King's Own Scottish Borderers, was dead.

Six Volunteers entered the exclusive County Club, Cork, where on the first floor, the Commissioner was sipping a glass with County

Inspector Craig. Three Volunteers guarded the entrance. Three went upstairs. They entered the room where Smyth was, and one, walking over to him, asked: " Were not your orders to shoot at sight ? Well, you are in sight now, so prepare." The Commissioner reached for his gun. He was dead as his hand closed on the butt.

That night T. P. O'Connor's appeal for a disavowal of the speech had another justification. The barrack gates were thrown open in Cork City, and through the streets raced armoured cars and lorries filled with yelling soldiers, Black-and-Tans and Auxiliaries, firing along the pavements and into houses. By morning, a Volunteer, who had been helping a wounded woman, was dead, and forty other Cork citizens had been shot. Even English newspapers raised an accusing finger, and pointed at the Speaker.

Facts soon proved that, despite Westminster denials, Commissioner Smyth had spoken merely what had already been agreed on in London. The 7,000 recruits began to arrive to make good the depleted ranks of the R.I.C.

Coroner's inquests on those shot by Crown Forces were suppressed. " The Restoration of Order in Ireland Bill," the most ferocious Coercion Act ever passed, was rushed into law, abolishing trials, giving Courts-martial new powers of imposing the death penalty and enabling them to sit in secret. Men and women could be brought forcibly before them, and if they refused to swear against their neigh-bours, be sent to prison. Martial Law became general. Troops as well as police could now shoot at sight.

The *Bulletin* earned the still deeper hatred of the Castle when in August it circulated the plans of Sinn Féin for looking after those who resigned from the R.I.C.. Local Cumainn were instructed to welcome them back to the national cause, see they took an honoured place in their localities, and to find employment for them. If employment could not be found, the resigned men were to avail themselves of a fund which Dáil Éireann had started for them. The local leaders of Sinn Féin were encouraged to approach constables still serving, and explain the people's welcome if they would leave the force. Of those who thus gave up their livelihood, and they were many hundreds, some joined the I.R.A., and were among those who fell gallantly for the liberty they had once repressed; others served Sinn Féin in its civil work. All were hunted, and if they fell into the hands of the Black-and-Tans, were mercilessly dealt with.

As the year advanced, and the repression became still more intense, the *Bulletin* went on naming the terrorists among the Crown forces, and giving their deeds. It shirked nothing. Through the Volunteer Intelligence Service it was able to get inside the Castle itself, and it described the cruelties that were being inflicted by high officers on the prisoners they were interrogating there.

Little over a month before its offices were found, it published Eamon de Valera's letter to the members of the British Cabinet and to every M.P. supporting it:

> "Lest by a plea of ignorance you should disclaim responsibility for what is being done here in your name——"

and he then gave a list of torturings, murders, floggings, looting, arson, and the slaying of hostages. The letter ended:

> "These things are done because it is your will they should be done. If you willed otherwise they would cease. It is you and not your troops who are primarily responsible."

Less than a week before the discovery of its offices, the *Bulletin* set out with names and full circumstances the forty-six murders committed by the Crown forces in the three weeks from 21st February to 14th March.

Yet when the hunt had ended, and the equipment was found, from which the ceaseless exposure of their tyranny had issued, Dublin Castle remained dumb about the chief thing they had discovered. Why?

CHAPTER 18

AN OFFICIAL FORGERY

T HE staff of the *Bulletin* had often wondered at their luck. They were lucky now because the raid on their offices took place on Holy Saturday night, 26th March. Had the offices been found a night or two earlier, the trick might have been worked of the innocent-looking door and the unsuspecting workers grabbed from the inside as they entered. They had the good fortune, too, that their own care told them that this time their offices had indeed been found.

Last duty before we left each evening was to make everything ship-shape so that a chance intruder would not find out our secret. The newspapers were stacked as unobtrusively as possible; the Gestetner stripped of its tell-tale stencil; blank sheets laid over piles of already printed pages, and anything that might cause suspicion drawn back from the windows. That care, practised day-in-day-out, paid dividends now in a way that nobody had anticipated. On Easter Sunday morning I cycled along Molesworth Street and as I looked up from my bike at No. 11, I saw newspapers tossed against the window-panes, and shadowy masses behind, speaking of obvious disorder. Within an hour the conference had begun as to where we would go now. The *Bulletin* was never issued on a Bank Holiday, and we had nearly two days in which to collect new equipment. I forget where we went, but it was, I think, out Harold's Cross way. There in Maureen Power's little front room of a little suburban house, with a pocket handkerchief of a garden separating its lace-curtained window from the street, the *Bulletin* took root again. With-out missing an issue, it was on its rounds on the evening of 29th March, and it was this issue which told its readers that the British had found the offices of their secret newspaper.

It was fortunate that it did. That issue was numbered No. 56, Volume IV, and was entitled, " The Raid on the *Irish Bulletin*." Next day, to all the readers of the *Bulletin*, two issues came. One was again numbered No. 56, Volume IV, but the date was Wednesday, 30th March. It was a forgery! That explained everything—the carting away of paper and ink, the absence of any shout of triumph. British Headquarters had decided to deceive the hundreds of inter-national journalists, M.P.'s, U.S. Senators and Congressmen and others by means of a counterfeit series. The numbering of the

H

first forgery showed they did not think the *Bulletin* could re-appear so soon.

The forgery in its outward appearance was perfect—the same typewriter, ink, watermaked paper, the same addresses from our addressograph, the same envelopes, the same arrangement of paragraphs. Nor, in content, did it arouse much suspicion that another hand was at work, and indeed, I have seen this first counterfeit copy bound with real issues as if it were one with them.

But there was a note in it that was absent from the genuine *Bulletin*, a note of exaggeration: "Thousands of murdered men, women and children," "millions of ruined homes." It could have been most damaging to the Republican movement had the crafty nature of some of its items not been spoiled by facetiousness. If there had been at the Castle in those days somebody whose capacity was equal to his intention, the real *Bulletin's* work could well have been undone.

For instance, a report of the Dáil Publicity Department had been captured in the raid. It was now faithfully reproduced in the Castle issue, with a sentence or two interpolated, so worded as to destroy the reputation for accuracy which statements published by the *Bulletin* had earned. This passage was slipped into the genuine report:

> "Where true statements (about British terrorism) can be secured, this should be done; but, if because of enemy aggression it is impossible for members of the Dáil to visit their constituencies, suitable statements can be prepared from any other sources at their disposal."

But this cleverness did not last, and the only effect in the end was to do still more damage to a prestige already grounded.

The real *Bulletin* quoted at length from its rival, showing its readers that here was a British publication, issued from military headquarters, saying such things as, "it has long been common knowledge that only the scum of the English entered her army," all in order to trap international writers into making false statements about Ireland. The forgery collapsed after a month.

Meanwhile, the real *Bulletin*, soon to bear on its front page a neat green circle enclosing the words "Official Copy," went on its way exposing the régime. It had a source of material which the forged issue dare not use—the intercepted secret reports of the administration. The aptness with which these were used became famous.

When Sir Hamar Greenwood boasted, early in November, 1920, that the Crown forces in Ireland were made up of honourable men, carefully chosen, the *Bulletin* published a long list of recent court cases and police reports:

" D. A. Richards, member of the Auxiliary Division of the R.I.C., sentenced on 26th September for deserting his wife and children.

" W. Charman, newly-recruited member of the R.I.C., arrested for felony on 28th September.

" Alfred Flint, of London, newly-recruited member of the R.I.C., dismissed on 29th September, for the theft of a comrade's trousers.

" Ernest Smith, newly-recruited member of the R.I.C., died in London from the effects of cocaine poisoning, on 4th October.

" Joseph Barclay, brought from London on 2nd October as a newly-recruited member of the R.I.C., certified a dangerous lunatic on 4th October.

" Thomas Landers, convicted of thefts in a hotel, asked to be let off with a fine as he wished to join the R.I.C. ; the court agreed.

" Laurie Dashington, newly-recruited member of the R.I.C., caught on 5th November stealing boots in the Angel Hotel in Liverpool, fired on the person who caught him and then committed suicide."

Nothing could have illustrated the character of the Black-and-Tans better than this simple list—every thief, drug addict, madman and murderer could come into this new force.

When Lord Robert Cecil quoted in the Commons a letter from Cardinal Logue, saying the Black-and-Tan camp at Gormanston was a " nest of bandits and homicides," there were angry protests from the Tory M.P.'s. The *Bulletin* promptly published a secret report from the Castle, showing that the Black-and-Tans in Gormanston camp had organised one of the largest series of frauds on the British Savings Bank ever uncovered.

After the destruction by Auxiliaries of Ballymote, on the night of 3rd–4th November, Sir Hamar Greenwood said in the House of Commons that the police " have been unsuccessful in their endeavours to find out who was responsible for the burnings." The *Bulletin* published a telegram sent on that date :

" To Head Constable, Constabulary, Ballaghadereen. Inform all available Auxiliary Force to proceed at once to Ballymote, where a sergeant has been shot. From D.I., Sligo."

When it was asserted by the British Government that the Republican movement was breaking up, and information against the Volunteers was now coming in freely, the *Bulletin* published a secret report from the Deputy-Inspector-General, Dublin Castle, to Cork R.I.C., questioning whether, " as no information from Cork is now being received," it was necessary to keep an office for the reception of information open at all.

When Sir Hamar Greenwood declared his desire for the widest publicity for all the doings of the Crown Forces, the *Bulletin* cited one of the most damning secret documents the Volunteers had ever captured. It was dated 16th November from Dublin Castle, and was signed by " L. Cheesman, County Inspector, for the Deputy Inspector-General."

Addressed to the County Inspector of the R.I.C. at Nenagh, it said :

" A man named Baker who is employed in the Dublin Tramways has just returned from Thurles and has furnished Griffiths (sic) with sworn statements of outrages committed by ' Black and Tans ' in Tipperary. He has relatives in Thurles and it is suggested that they should be ' looked up.' This should be done as discreetly as possible. Perhaps the police know something of these people and should act according to the best of their judgment and report the result of search, if search be made."

There was no mistaking the meaning of this directive in the Ireland of November, 1920. The force under the County Inspector at Nenagh were, as the Castle knew, mostly " Black-and-Tans " themselves. It can be imagined what they were intended to do to the relatives of those who reported their outrages.

The faked *Bulletin* could not draw on that other source of information we had—the sworn statements of the victims of British interrogation. Passionately it was denied in Parliament that any Irish prisoners were tortured. Week after week the *Bulletin* published statements smuggled out from the prisons which, on the face of them, were obviously true. Two famous cases were those of Commandant Thomas Hales and Quartermaster Patrick Harte who at Bandon Military Barracks were interrogated under circumstances of cruelty which in the end drove Harte insane.

They were stripped, flogged incessantly and their finger-tips squeezed in pincers. Their hands were tied behind their back, and when they refused to name a comrade they were punched in the face by several British officers, and in the end, after many hours of this, they were taken out to be shot. Tom Hales's statement, of over 2,500 words, was given by the *Bulletin* in full, and in it was this paragraph :

" We were then taken to Bandon into the military barracks yard, and were lined up to be shot. The soldiers were howling for our death and were anxious to shoot us. We had our backs to the wall, and Harte was on my left-hand side. Keogh (Lt. Keogh, of the Hants Regiment) said, 'Do you want to be blind-folded?' We said, 'No.' I asked to see a chaplain. Keogh said, 'Damn it, why do you want to see a chaplain?' I said, 'All right, go ahead.' We were still tied with our hands behind our backs and the soldiers hit us with their fists. . . . Kelly (Capt. Kelly, of the British Intelligence Staff) paced out 12 to 15 paces from me and then put five or six men with rifles at the end of the 15 paces. Harte was then very weak and could hardly see. He stuck a flag into Harte's hand (his wrists having been untied) and made him hold his hand up. I recognised that the flag Harte was holding up was the Union Jack, but Harte himself was too far gone to recognise it. A man came with a camera and took a snapshot. Kelly then said, 'We must get some information first before we shoot them.'"

Then the terrible interrogation began all over again. The *Bulletin* noticed that the date of their ill-treatment, 27th July, 1920, was the same day on which the Volunteers captured Brigadier General Lucas and treated him with all the courtesy due to his rank.

Prisoners all over Ireland were suffering as Hales and Harte suffered. It was done even to Kevin Barry. In a fight for his life, the *Bulletin* two days before they hanged him, on 1st November, 1920, published his statement of ill-usage by which they tried to force from him the names of his comrades.

"The same officer then said to me that if I persisted in my attitude he would turn me out to the men in the barrack square and he supposed I knew what that meant with the men in their present temper."

He was thrown to the floor:

"One of the sergeants knelt on the small of my back, the other two placed one foot each on my back and left shoulder and the man who knelt on me twisted my right arm, holding it by the wrist with one hand while he held my hair with the other to pull back my head. The arm was twisted from the elbow joint. This continued to the best of my judgment for five minutes. It was very painful."

The *Bulletin* published Griffith's appeal to the civilised world for Kevin Barry's life. It published Erskine Childers' letter to the British Press:

" I ask you, sir, to allow me to utter a vehement protest against the verdict and the sentence and to claim before British public opinion that the lad shall not be hanged. I make this protest and appeal both as a soldier who fought in the guerilla phase of the Boer War, as a historian and student of national struggles for freedom similar to the Irish struggle, and lastly as one living in the midst of the struggle and familiar with its incidents. . . . To hang Barry is to push to its logical extreme the hypocritical pretence that the national movement in Ireland, unflinchingly supported by the great mass of the Irish people, is the squalid conspiracy of a ' murder gang.' That is false, it is a national uprising, a collision between two Governments, one resting on consent, the other on force. The Irish are struggling against overwhelming odds to defend their own elected institutions against extinction. Kevin Barry should not be hanged. He should live as any British prisoner taken by his comrades would have lived."

They hanged Kevin Barry just the same.

His death, following so soon after Terence MacSwiney's, brought the younger generation and the older into a communion of sacrifice and the nation took fresh strength from the wasted body on the Brixton pallet and new gay courage from the boy who stood at the salute, smiling from the door of his death-cell, as he and his mother parted on the eve of his execution.

CHAPTER 19

NAILING THE LIES

IN the last year of its publication, the *Irish Bulletin* became the source from which many courageous British men and women, determined to redeem the name of their nation, drew their material.

Every second day on the Order Paper of the Commons, or interjected into debate, were facts taken from it. Lloyd George and Hamar Greenwood tried hard to blunt the effect of those deadly questions and quotations. Liberals and Labour M.P.'s, and indeed a few Conservatives also, who asked about the terror, were accused of associating themselves with murder. Sir Hamar Greenwood said in the Commons on 24th November, 1920 :

> " The murder gang in Ireland issues an illegal document known as the *Irish Republican Bulletin*. The murder gang sends that *Bulletin* to persons in England and to newspapers in England and some of them publish it (cries of ' shame ') . . . The murder gang's publication ought not to be the foundation for the literature of any member of this House. I consider it a loathsome alliance that men whose hands are red with the blood of gallant soldiers and policemen should come into the lobby of this House and be allowed to circulate their hideous documents of falsehood."

When we of the *Bulletin* staff read that speech, we knew how fearful the British Government had grown, and we bowed to our work with a new devotion. Some of the Commons' questioners shrank back from this charge of association with murder ; but the greater number were undaunted, and among them, to their credit let it now be said, were some who as Cabinet Ministers themselves had treated Ireland scurvily, including Asquith and Sir John Simon.

Early in the conflict, the British Government, to counter Sinn Féin, set up a publicity department in Dublin Castle. At first its official reports were factual, but they became more and more distorted, and soon were sheer propaganda, playing to the worst anti-Irish instincts of the British public.

It is hard to conceive in the quiet of to-day the anger that filled men's hearts in the years of the Irish struggle. For us it was a hard, cold anger that such bitter wrongs should be done to our people, and that in the twentieth century, immediately after a war for the liberation of nations, the very veterans of that war should be loosed on us, and because we, too, sought liberty, should repeat upon us the horrors of the Yeos.

In Britain it was a hot and savage anger, based on centuries of anti-Irish propaganda which made us out a base and murderous race, for whom any punishment was too lenient. As the Germans under Hitler were taught to think of the Jews, so the British under Lloyd George were taught to think of all in the Irish national movement. Hate filled every speech made about Sinn Féin, and this hate was passed down to the rank and file of the British Forces, who, thus infuriated, committed here unspeakable acts. As Ireland's resistance mounted, the official reports issuing from the Castle, used every trick to poison the minds of those who read them.

That is not too strong to say, as one illustration will show. A tragedy, inseparable from the kind of fight which any invaded people must make, occurred in Dublin on 17th December, 1920. A District Inspector of the R.I.C., working in the office of the Inspector-General, was walking in Henry Street with his fiancée when Volunteers approached, separated him from her, and shot him dead.

The British official report of the shooting represented the whole population of Dublin as acting without pity. It described the D.I.'s fiancée as left helpless beside the body where she

> " tried to render what assistance she could, no other help being available, for directly the rumour went round that the wounded man was a police officer the crowd melted away, none offering help to the distressed lady."

One can imagine with what disgust that official report was read in Britain, for, of course, except through the *Bulletin*, what did happen never reached the British people. It was a concoction, as the lady herself, in an interview with the Dublin Press, had the nobility to say :

> " Everyone in the street did all in their power to assist him Men, women and children gathered round, and prayers were recited, whilst dozens of people ran for the priest. . . . Men assembled and proceeded to bandage the wound and do every-thing possible to alleviate his sufferings. Persons in the crowd halted a military lorry which was passing and requested the occupants to take him to hospital."

This was done for a British officer in a city under the sternest repression, and every man who stayed by the wounded District

Inspector did so knowing that in a moment he might be shot out of hand in a frenzy of revenge by the Black-and-Tans this officer controlled.

These facts never reached the public in Britain. They were told only something that fed their illusion that this was a base people that must be struck down. It was from the Castle publicity office, which produced this " official report," that the vilest stories against Ireland's insurgents came—the mutilated bodies, the killing of wounded men with hatchets, and all the gross distortions which, by what they provoked, have left the period one of the meanest in English records. How can the mass of the English people be blamed for supporting the Terror in Ireland, when that was the only picture of it their " popular press " gave them ?

In these circumstances, the *Bulletin* strove more than ever to expose both the sources and the substance of these " official reports." By merciless analysis of their contents, they were shown to be false. An example was the case of Judge Lynch.

In fulfilment of Capt. Harper-Shove's " little stunt " assassins, who came apparently on foot from the near-by Castle, had slain John Aloysius Lynch. They had come stealthily to his hotel and had gone stealthily away. No sound of the murder was heard, for, it is presumed, they had wrapped the revolver in a blanket to deaden the noise. Fourteen hours after the assassination, the British issued an official report, saying that a

> " small military force, accompanied by police officers, visited the Exchange Hotel, Parliament Street, Dublin, in the early hours of this morning, for the purpose of arresting a man named Jack Lynch."

The *Irish Bulletin* next day replied :—

> " We assert that there was no intention to arrest Mr. Lynch, and that no attempt was made to arrest him."

It then went on to show that 500 arrests had been made at night in Dublin that year. In every one of them the procedure was the same. Troops carrying rifles and bayonets arrived in a military lorry. They knocked loudly at the door, which, if it was not opened quickly enough, was broken in. Guards were put at all the exits of the house. The prisoner was placed in the lorry and driven to jail. The *Bulletin* went on :—

> " In the case of John Aloysius Lynch the procedure was different from every other case of arrest which has occurred in Ireland. . . . The party of military was not conveyed to the

hotel in a motor lorry. A guard was not placed at the exits or around the hotel. No provision was made to convey the prisoner to jail. . . . When the military party withdrew they did not inform the night porter that they had shot a man who resisted arrest. They left the hotel without disclosing to any person in the hotel that they had killed Mr. John Aloysius Lynch. They did not even summon medical aid."

A similar exposure was made in the case of the triple murder in Dublin Castle on 22nd November, 1920. The British Government issued a long official report describing how Dick McKee, Peadar Clancy and Conor Clune had been killed in a desperate attempt to escape. It began by saying that the men had to be kept in the Guard-room of the Castle because there was a lack of prison accommodation. The *Bulletin* pointed out that for 150 men, arrested in Dublin a few hours later, plenty of room was found in the prisons.

The *Bulletin* then submitted the official report to a detailed analysis and showed it had been concoted by somebody who did not even understand the use of weapons. The three men (whom the Castle admitted they knew to be officers of the Volunteers) were, according to the report, put into a room with " boxes of bombs under a bed," rifles ready loaded lying handy, ammunition and piles of mattresses. The prisoners had four guards, said the report, but three of them were out, and one had his back turned when the three men made their " attempt to escape." They hurled two bombs at the one guard (a military man would have known that bombs bursting in a small room would have knocked out everybody). The bombs did not explode, and the prisoners then opened rifle fire at close range, but missed. When the guard and the others, rushing in, fired in return, those three Volunteer officers took cover from rifle bullets behind *mattresses* !

Everything in the report of the " fight " the *Bulletin* showed to be an obvious fabrication, and went on:

" During Sunday, McKee and Clancy were frequently tortured and threatened, and this torturing and threatening continued until Monday at 11 a.m., when they were done to death.

" In the guardroom in which these men were detained there were no rifles, no bombs, no mattresses, no beds. There were a table and a number of benches.

" They were adequately guarded and were given no opportunity to escape.

" The prisoners were defenceless when they were done to death. All evidence points to the fact that they were sitting by the fire when they were murdered."

With the same thoroughness, the *Bulletin* tore to pieces the two official reports of the massacre in Croke Park, pointing out that, in order to deceive those who had never been there, the Park was described as if it were open ground and as if those inside could see and fire on the troops surrounding it. No mention, said the *Bulletin*, was made of the twenty-foot wall which made it impossible for those standing in the park and those outside to see one another at all!

By this method, every official report which tried to screen an outrage or hide a murder was discredited, and towards the end of the struggle, few recipients of the *Bulletin*, in Britain or elsewhere, put trust in any statement issued from Dublin Castle.

In its last issue of 1920, the *Bulletin* reproduced a secret telegram sent a few days earlier by Major-General Strickland, Military Governor of Munster, to the officers of all the posts under his command :—

> " In future, a Sinn Féiner is to be taken *handcuffed* in front of every lorry which comes into or leaves their areas."

In the same issue, the *Bulletin* recorded the grim purpose of this order by citing the fate of James Looby and William Delaney. On the evening this telegram was sent, these two young Volunteers were taken from Cashel Jail and one placed in each of two lorries leaving for patrol work.

As there were no attacks, the manacled hostages should have come back alive, but only the bodies of Looby and Delaney came back. They had been murdered *en route*. The *Bulletin*, noting that the life of nobody in Ireland was now safe from attacks by troops and constabulary, added :

> " The lives of prisoners, whom it is the usage in all civilised warfare for their captors to protect with their own lives if necessary are now more unsafe than those of any others."

But the change was coming. On 17th June, 1921, the *Bulletin* published a VERY SECRET circular. Its appearance created a sensation, for it showed that the most rigorous repression had failed to break the will of the common people.

For months Lloyd George and Hamar Greenwood had been telling the Commons that the end was near. Lloyd George had said on 15th February, 1921, that only six months before :

> " The Irish Republican Organisation had all the symbols, and they had all the realities of a Government. The Courts of the Crown were superseded. They were deserted by witnesses, they were boycotted by jurors. . . . Sinn Féin Courts were held openly, attended by litigants, jurors, and advocates

and their decisions were respected. Sinn Féin soldiers patrolled the country; Sinn Féin police patrolled the towns."

As the *Bulletin* was not slow to point out, Lloyd George, at the date when he said this situation existed, was telling the world that Sinn Féin was really a tiny murder gang whom the Irish people hated. In this speech of 15th February, he went on:

"What is the condition now? The police (R.I.C.) have recovered their authority. The Courts of the Crown have recovered their authority. . . . We are beginning to get evidence. . . . Sinn Féin patrols, military and police, are gone. The Sinn Féin Courts have disappeared into cellars."

And he added triumphantly:

"The organisation (of the Volunteers) which was so perfect five or six months ago, is now shattered."

This optimism went on for a few weeks more, though a note of anxiety soon came back, and Lloyd George had to explain heavy British casualties by saying that the troops naturally suffered more when they were "chasing the murderers back into the hills."

And then the bottom fell out of British boasting!

The Very Secret Circular which the *Bulletin* published on 17th June was dated 12th May. The circular was an instruction to the Army of Occupation to change its tactics and change them quickly! It bore the signature of H. O. Hutchin, Lieut.-Colonel, General Staff, 6th Division, and addressed to troops and auxiliaries in several areas in Munster, said

"It must not be looked on as the normal procedure, for troops arriving in a village immediately to search it and see who they want interned. . . . They should adopt a friendly attitude towards the inhabitants and give no grounds for suspicion. . . . It is highly desirable on political grounds to endeavour to improve relations with the inhabitants."

This, the circular explained, was more than ever necessary now, as it was "impossible to supply sufficient troops."

It was all carefully worded, but it meant only one thing. For two years, Crown forces had murdered, looted, tortured, burned as they liked. Their victims included priests, old men and women, mothers, children, young girls, and prisoners by the hundred. Seventy Irish towns were shot-up, wrecked or fired. To punish the farmers, crops were burned and fifty creameries were destroyed. Fairs and markets were prohibited by martial law; the railways were paralysed.

In an effort to prevent shelter being given to the Volunteers, every house had to have nailed up inside the front door a list of all the occupants, so that if in a raid anybody extra was found, he must explain his presence convincingly or risk death there and then. Many a father in a raided house was told if he had not his sons there when the troops came back it would be worse for him; when they did come back, and the sons were still absent, they sacked the house, and on more than one occasion shot the father. In the cities, Auxiliaries would suddenly criss-cross the streets with cordons, and passers-by would be openly robbed of their valuables or flogged with whips. All day long, lorries sped through town and country with rows of men armed with rifles sitting back to back potting at people on the roads or in the fields as if they were wild game.

Yet, the ordinary men and women of Ireland held fast: it was the British who broke, and this Very Secret Circular was the first sign of cleavage in the walls of Dublin Castle.

CHAPTER 20

A SECRET CIRCULAR

THE work of the *Bulletin* did not end with the cessation of hostilities. It continued for more than six months after its publication of the Very Secret Circular showed that the Government in London was already, on 12th May, 1921, looking for a way out of the dishonour the Terror had brought.

In June the attacks on British forces by the Volunteers were greater and more deadly than in any similar period. Seven days after the "friendly attitude" Order had appeared in the *Bulletin* of 17th June, Lloyd George wrote to de Valera suggesting talks.

The truce came. There were a few days of rejoicing, then the Dáil staffs settled back to their work again. The whole story of this period is told later. Meanwhile, for the *Bulletin* staff there was as much work as ever. No sooner had the guns ceased to speak, than other hostile voices were directed against Ireland in an effort to weaken the Republican position, particularly by dividing the Irish people against themselves.

It became the *Bulletin's* main object to counter this new danger at home and to expound, in answer to British misrepresentation abroad, the real national position. It had also to fight the case of the thousands still in the prisons and internment camps, and to watch for British preparations for a resumption of war.

In this last regard a sensational *Bulletin* was published on 18th November, 1921. All through the struggle for independence, Britain had tried to turn the conflict into a religious war. She drove the Protestants frantic by representing to them, constantly and with whatever lurid details suggested themselves, that this was no fight for liberty, but an effort of the Catholic majority to exterminate the Protestants and their faith. Even acts of Britain's own forces were used for the purpose of inflaming Protestants against the Republican movement.

Thomas Hoggett, Protestant postmaster at Navan, was hustled from his home and marched off, though partially paralysed, in February, 1921. A month later his body, with a bullet wound through the head, was found in the Boyne, for he had been shot and thrown over the bridge. The crime was described by the Castle as a Sinn Féin outrage against the minority. The *Bulletin*, after an exhaustive inquiry, showed that Mr. Hoggett had, in fact, been murdered by a County Inspector of the R.I.C. and a notorious Sergeant from Dublin Castle who, with a civilian, masqueraded as the I.R.A. They were all known and named at the time. Mrs. Hoggett, who, like Hoggett himself, was a loyalist and Unionist, demanded first a coroner's inquest, then a public inquiry, and lastly even any tribunal which would hear her evidence. All were refused that the murder might stand as "proof" that Sinn Féin made war on Protestants.

An earlier case was that of Mr. G. W. Biggs, of Bantry, Co. Cork. On 24th July, 1920, he wrote a letter to the *Irish Times*, supporting what scores of other Protestant correspondents had already written in the same series of letters—that for the thirty-three years he was in business not one act of religious persecution by the majority was committed in the wide area with which he had commercial connections.

"In Munster," he went on, "where Catholics outnumber Protestants by 13 to 1, a large number of the leading traders are Protestants, who are being supported by Catholics and the greatest goodwill exists between them." Two nights later, in obvious revenge for his letter, his premises—one of the largest general stores in Bantry—was burned during curfew hours by Constabulary, who sprayed petrol on it and then set it alight.

When the struggle was rising to its height in midsummer, 1920, a London *Times* correspondent visited Derry, where for the first time there was a Nationalist majority on the Corporation. He found the Republican corporators and the Unionist officials working for the common good of the city, and he commented : "People who can do that for themselves might prove able to do something more for Ireland."

Britain, in her centuries of dominance in Ireland, had feared this most—Catholics and Protestants working together for the nation. Action to end their dreaded unity was prompt. Three days later, on 18th June, a pogrom was launched against the Catholics in Derry, and it soon spread, obviously as the result of careful organisation, to most of the North-East. It was fed by a fierce sectarian propaganda in the pro-British Press of the area.

The result was a series of wild disorders for more than two months, in which over sixty lives were lost, hundreds were wounded, whole streets were gutted and thousands driven from their work.

The provocation was so great and long-sustained that there were isolated incidents in which Protestants were slain outside the Six Counties, but these so horrified the mass of the Irish people that public indignation itself ended them almost as soon as they had begun. For the rest the effort to make the freedom war a religious war failed hopelessly from the British point of view, magnificently from the Irish. The Volunteers refused to be deflected from the assertion of the rights of all Irishmen to independence. They knew they were fighting as much for the minority as for the majority.

The British, in one of the most cynical acts of British statesmanship, took the sectarian Carsonite Volunteers, which had been set up expressly to defy the national will, converted them into a Special Constabulary, and used them to harry the Catholic minority of the North-East. The nation, nevertheless, kept its head and preserved scrupulously the national character of the struggle.

In the terms of the truce, Britain bound herself not to increase her armed forces in Ireland. During the truce, the British Press magnified every minor infringement of its terms by the I.R.A. into a national act of treachery. Then the *Bulletin* published a document which shook this hypocrisy to its foundations and carried the gravest implications as to Britain's honour.

It exposed the British as organising in truce time a new army against the Irish.

The capture of this particular document was certainly a *coup*, for it had been sent only to a few senior British officials. It was signed by Lt.-Col. Charles Wickham, Divisional Commissioner of the R.I.C., stationed in Belfast, and was addressed to other Commissioners and to County Commandants of the Special Constabulary. It was to be kept from the knowledge of everybody else.

In less than a week of issue it was in Republican hands. It ordered the British officers to whom it was sent to recruit an army of " regular military units " from among the " best elements " of the " loyalists," which simply meant the Orangemen.

The date of the document was of particular significance in view of the attempt made after disclosure to suggest that it was not the British but the Six County Government which was involved in Lt.-Col. Wickham's phrase, " the Government . . . have decided."

Sir James Craig visited London on 5th November at the height of the negotiations between the Irish and British delegations. On that same day, and again on 7th November, he saw Lloyd George. The circular bore the date, 9th November. The British Government alone controlled the R.I.C. on that date. The Act of 1920 expressly forbade the Six County Government from ever raising any form of military force.

The *Bulletin* introduced the publication of the captured order with these words :

" It would be invidious at such a moment to question the sincerity of the British Government in its search for peace.

A document has, however, come into our possession which will cause the gravest concern. The facts disclosed in it are of a sinister character and, if the interpretation we place upon them in the detailed analysis which follows is correct, it is difficult to avoid the conclusion that a step has been deliberately taken to wreck the possibility of peace. An Army is being secretly organised in North-East Ulster—organised as the document admits by the British Government—with the apparent object of taking the field at any given moment, and thus providing an excuse for its organisers to abandon any settlement that may be come to at the Conference."

The disclosure, of what was to have been one of the most closely-guarded secrets of the war, caused consternation. Day after day it remained front-page news. The British Government's own press was shaken by it, and the London *Daily Chronicle*, which had remained throughout a defender of that Government, commented on it gravely. Though it adopted the view that the Government referred to was the Belfast Government, it said :

" Sinn Féin was entitled to draw the inference that the circular was the British Government's and that while negotiating peace with one hand, they were organising a new North Irish army with the other. . . . It is necessary, if we are not to prejudice gravely the further progress of the negotiations, that the good faith of the British Government should be made perfectly clear."

It was never made clear. The London " Irish Office " did say it had no knowledge of the document, and did not even know if it were accurate.

To the question why none of the recipients of the circular, all officials of the force controlled by the Irish Office, reported its receipt, the Simple Simon answer was that they probably didn't because it it was marked " secret."

The *Bulletin* commented :

" The lame explanation by the official of the Irish Office makes it more incumbent than ever upon the British Government to state definitely and unequivocally whether it adopts or disowns the scandalous and sinister movement for the organisation of a secret and sectarian army in the Six Counties."

It referred to the pretended doubts of the Castle as to the authenticity of the circular :

" A telephone message to the Divisional Commissioner in Belfast would, it is presumed, have been the first step taken by

I

Dublin Castle if it doubted the accuracy of the circular. . . .
All that was needed was to ask for Commissioner Wickham
and put one question to him."

In issue after issue, the *Bulletin* pressed the British Government to
speak, saying the explanation that had been made, convinced

"many that what was most feared in Ireland is true, namely
that the British Government, while negotiations for 'peace'
are in progress, while a truce is in operation, have set about
organising the most horrible of all kinds of war in Ireland—
the fanatical religious wars of the 17th Century."

Still, the British remained silent, and the *Bulletin* of 25th November
said :

"Were the British Government proved guilty of this act,
the present Conference in London would seem to be a decoy
for keeping the attention of the Irish people fixed upon peace
while a treacherous war was being prepared against them."

The chill of foreboding in these words was soon felt by the whole
nation. For within a fortnight, the *Bulletin* was publishing its last
issue. The division Britain had so long been seeking, in the greater
part of Ireland, had been accomplished. In the North-East, the
sectarian army envisaged in the secret circular had been set up and
was in power. . . .

And now a few last words as to this gallant journal which weathered
all the storms but that last.

Before we went to the staid environment of Molesworth Street,
the *Bulletin* and its staff were housed for many months in 22 Upper
Mount Street. There the sterling Larry and Mrs Nugent, and their
family, were our protectors. There we had, again in discreet sur-
roundings—for it was an exclusive street—a fairly placid life, until
one night lorries poured raiding parties on to the pavement and
every house was diligently searched whose number had a two in it—
except ours. The British had got some tip near the mark. No. 2
was raided, No. 12, No. 32, No. 42. It was time to pack our bags
and move on. After a few temporary addresses, Molesworth Street
was our next stop.

The discovery of the Molesworth Street offices sent us on the road
again. For a little while we lived from pillar to post, but soon found
a home in a house out in Rathgar, standing in its own grounds. Into
it, through its flowered garden, we came each morning. We were
there when the Truce was signed. It was a large house and we occupied
all of one floor. In one room the statistics of the fight were compiled.
We kept regular archives, recording casualties, combats, courtsmartial,

everything, so that at any moment we could check official British reports or give accurate figures to our own Government. The figures were taken from the reports sent in by Commandants in the field in all parts of Ireland, from newspapers, and from eye-witnesses' accounts. In another room the newspapers were being indexed and filed, and the *Bulletin* was being drafted. When the " copy " was ready, or when he had not himself written that day's issue, I took the draft to Erskine Childers, then Director of Publicity. From him it got its final polish. Any exaggerations that remained from our pruning were cut out. All the too-eager statements were brought down to a calmer note, for he was a lover of unembellished truth. Thus, it was roneoed and sent on its international way, while British search parties stormed into buildings on the prowl for it.

Those who for these stern years devoted themselves to this dangerous work, deserve to have their names known.

There was the founder, Bob Brennan. There was the Director of Propaganda Desmond Fitzgerald, under whom the *Bulletin* grew to such importance, and his successor, Erskine Childers, under whom it came to full maturity. The staff whose daily task was to produce it were : Anna Kelly, Kathleen McGilligan, Sheila Murphy, and her sister, Honor, now a nun far away in the Philippines ; Kathleen McKenna, Michael Nunan, Seamus Hynes, our messenger, and myself. Desmond Fitzgerald and Erskine Childers are dead, but all the others are alive to recall those days of never-ending tension. It was a noble company who never failed under unbroken peril to fulfil this major task in the struggle for liberty.

CHAPTER 21

THE FIRST JAIL TERM

IT was in June, 1919, that I first saw the inside of a prison. I was to see many in the years that followed, but then it was all new and—frightening.

The preliminaries to this imprisonment were typical of the times. In an earlier Chapter I described how the young men poured out of Dublin each week-end to carry the latest arguments of Sinn Féin into the towns and villages. One of these trips took me to the little town of Myshall in Carlow on a May day when the green is lucent and the air itself has the quality of youth. The next Sunday I headed for Westmeath to speak at an aeridheacht at Fore, near Castlepollard.

It was Joe Kennedy's country—big, humorous, courageous Joe, who, through the sharing of a later imprisonment, was to become one of my best-loved friends. I remember now only an emerald hollow in which were gathered the young Gaels, and, on the lip of the hollow, troops in khaki, the sun on their bayonets.

The following Sunday I was off somewhere else. What it was I said on these wanderings, there is now no means of finding out, for it never appeared in print; but I suppose it was what we were all saying in those electric days—that the people's courage must in the end defeat an empire; that if they faced Britain fearlessly, and stood by their dead, all would be well.

Myshall and Fore were long forgotten when one day into the headquarters of the newly-founded Dáil Publicity Department came a man with a wonderful face. He was small and of slight build, and though he gave his name, I had not caught it. His gestures, and his quiet, musical voice, made me sure that he and I had met before, and that memory would name him for me.

As I listened, I was soon thinking of the South Armagh election of February, 1918. There we were a team—Ernest Blythe, Desmond Fitzgerald, Bob Barton, Nolan Whelan, myself and, I think, Pierce McCann. Using the village of Poyntzpass as a centre, we spoke in and canvassed the whole countryside. It was a great team, with humour brimming over every difficulty and dissolving it; with true eloquence, too, for Bob Barton and Desmond Fitzgerald were orators, and Ernest Blythe could talk to the people in his sharp dialect, using their homely metaphors. Nolan Whelan was a lawyer, and in measured phrases could beat the doctrine into reluctant minds. But I failed to see this slight man with the deep-set eyes now before me, and yet, even as he spoke, there were the Armagh Hills around Poyntzpass. I said:

> " Surely, sir, we have met before. I know your voice, your gestures, the way you hold your head."

He smiled. The smile which I was to see so often in the future had almost the effect of an inner light illuminating that fine head. " You are thinking of Robert Barton," he said. " I am his double first cousin, a relationship nearer even than brother, they say."

It was my first meeting with Erskine Childers.

He had come about a letter he was sending to the papers; I said I would deliver it as I passed through town, and we parted, not knowing that I was to vanish for a goodly spell—something I would always subsequently blame him for, and he, with indignant humour, would reject. In times of strain and trial in after years, I used to say: " Remember, Erskine, that time you gave me that spell in Mountjoy."

The appearance of most of the Dublin Castle detectives was known to us, and throughout that day I saw Sergeant Bruton haunting No. 6. But it was not unusual to have them everywhere around the building and across the street. Harry Boland used to confound them by calling out their names: " Hallo, Bruton; Hi, there, Wharton." Bruton was a thick-set, dark-visaged man, rather purple in complexion, not unlike a family coachman.

As I set off to the newspaper offices, I half-observed a movement near Harcourt Street as if a number of us were leaving at the same time; but I paid no heed to it. Opposite the clock on the College of Surgeons, Bruton suddenly stood before me: " I want you," he said.

And before I could do anything, there were three others standing around me, and in an instant my wrist was seized and I was handcuffed to a big lump of a plain-clothes man. If I had meant to do anything dramatic on the first occasion on which I was arrested—and I am sure I had day-dreamed a pretty noble scene with words that would pass into history—I was as dumb as an ox. All that I recall now is the revulsion I felt and a searing anger so sharp that even to-day I feel some of it still. It was a helpless, frustrated anger as I sat there in the cab into which they had bundled me and drove to the headquarters of the Detective Division in Townsend Street.

How can I convey what we thought of those G-men? We knew them for spies on our nation, who lurked meanly in the shadows, with the whole might of the British power behind them, to strike at individuals and to take liberty from whom they would, without thought of who wept or who hungered. To us they were the ugliest of all the wrongs we were resisting : this band of our own country-men, who had made themselves the tools of the tyrant; they were like the Belgians who spied against their brothers for German pay. They were like the Frenchmen who tracked down French patriots for the death-camps of Germany. We knew that these G-men had walked down the lines of the disarmed Volunteers after the Rising, picking out this one and that for execution. Seán MacDermott had been picked out that way by a G-man watching for a man with a limp. To him, and to many, they had ensured a cruel death. To be in their power was a loathsome thing.

In the police office at Townsend Street, Bruton put his hand in my pocket, and that seemed such an intrusion of my rights that I shouted : " How dare you do that." He only smiled, and as some-body else held me, went through all my pockets. When he pulled out the letters Erskine Childers had given me, addressed to each of the editors of the daily papers, I said : " These are the property of the Editors and must be delivered at once." That at last seemed to impress him, and the letters were duly delivered.

The next scene (all between is lost to memory) was in Green Street. I was in a dark hollow at the end of some stone steps down which light filtered, making a sharp pattern of grey squares set in ebony shadows. Into this grey and black world my friends came. She who is now my wife was there in that dark vaulted passage as I was being led through to what I did not know. With her was warm-hearted Mary Lynch, also from the South. There we stood, the three of us, and said a few stilted things to one another, for intimate con-versation is difficult in the umbrageous presence of constables in a half-light which increased their stature as it diminished mine. In later years we were all to become adepts at conversing in front of the law, and many an escape was so planned. Indeed, both my wife and I were to become wholly acclimatised to prison precincts, and in Mountjoy, civil prisoners, of a Christmas-time, would smuggle our letters of greeting to and fro.

But now in this crowded darkness it was all new, and there was even a relief when the mountainous and belted men moved forward at some summons I had not heard and said : " Up there, now."

I had no idea where the steps I mounted led to. There was silence above as my feet rang on the stone. · And then my head was above floor level, and in an instant I found myself in the dock of a court.

On the bench a few yards away from me sat Santa Claus—a bene-volent and ancient man with snow-white whiskers. His name, as I was to learn days later, was Swifte. He was the Chief Magistrate of the Dublin courts. He had his hand cupped to his right ear and was listening, leaning towards a scrawny long-necked parrot-headed man, who, the moment my head appeared over the dock rail began to read at top speed from a typewritten sheet.

I could not hear what was being read, and neither could Santa, to judge by his cupped hand and his bewildered eyes. But from a word here and there (I heard Pearse's name), both he and I knew it was a speech of some kind. I heard the old man say to the Parrot (alas for Ireland his name was O'Flaherty):

"It seems to me a dangerous kind of speech."

"Undoubtedly, your worship," said the Parrot.

The bench looked at me as if its sight as well as its hearing was not of the best, and in a voice that appeared to come through many persilled pillows, asked if I had anything to say in my defence; I asked him if he held his magistracy under the Constitution of the Irish Republic.

In reply, he mumbled something about months. I had no idea that I had been sentenced; I was still standing there, wondering what else would come from the recesses of that beard, when one of the constabulary bronzes, who had been grouped around me, tapped me on the shoulder and pointed downwards.

"Down you go."

It was days before I saw a copy of the paper which carried the report of the trial. I had been sentenced to four months' imprisonment—one paper said with hard labour, another said without hard labour, and I never found out which—for a seditious speech at Myshall, Co. Carlow, on the 25th day of May, in the year of Our Lord, Nineteen Hundred and Nineteen.

I was driven to Mountjoy in the black maria, and a receipt was given to those who brought me. I was passed through a series of tall iron gates to a man with bright red moustache and side-whiskers, an immense man with great keys hanging from a belt into which he seemed to have accommodated more weight than should rightly belong to a man. The deference of the others around him, the gold braid on his cap and, I think, on his shoulders, his air of being the Day after the General Judgment, made it unnecessary for him to tell me, which he did, that he was the Chief Warder. I was walking beside him, meditating on the folly of men with red hair wearing gold braid, when he said: "In here."

It was my first cell.

If my memory is not deceiving me, my feeling, as the great iron-studded door swung silently to behind me, and the bolts banged into position, was of an inflowing of peace. Suddenly it all became clear; I was locked in; I was powerless; there was nothing I could do, and I had no responsibility.

Like the others, I had been working day and night in 6 Harcourt Street for almost a year; more recently with lion-hearted old Larry Ginnell, first Dáil Director of Propaganda. I had seen one by one my friends and fellow-workers vanish. Some slipped away to work their passage to America to press the cause there. Others were taken as I was, some evening on the way home. The disappearance of each one left more work for the others, and so we toiled and spun far into the night. And now—nothing to do; no need any longer to hide away this document, to dodge that G-man, to go a long way round when calling on some friend on the run. All the responsibilities were gone, and there were no new ones. Life was free of burdens.

What did I do—rejoice? No, I slept. In that basement cell, into which I was first put, the light was so poor that it was hard to read. A tiny glazed window looked out on the foot of a wall. There was intense quiet. Then a warder came and took the folded bed clothes from the coffin-like bed-box that was leaning against the wall, and placing it on the floor, showed me how to make a prison bed. There was a regulation method of arranging blankets and coverlet and no other method would be tolerated.

It was June and warm. I drew the bedclothes around me and I slept for—thirty-six hours! I must have waked in between; and I supposed I may have eaten, too. But all that I remember was that tremendous sleep: the reward at last of years of living on one's nerves.

When finally I was awake again, my time of quarantine had passed and I began a new journey. Up from the semi-darkness I came, attended by three warders, the red-and-gold monster supervising from a distance, and we clanked our way through iron gates and up iron steps into a brighter light. It shone down from a partly glass roof into a barred circle like a great zoo cage. Out of that circle, as spokes out of a hub, stretched the wings of Mountjoy Jail—A Wing, B Wing, C Wing, D Wing—in time I was to sample them all. As I waited for whichever of the four gates in that barred circle would lead me to my new home, I was able to see how a warder, sitting in that central place, could see down every wing, and I thought of the first pictures from the air I had ever seen of Paris, where from L'Etoile the city's streets rayed out.

At the gate into B Wing the attendant warders stopped. There was not a soul about. Nothing but rows and rows of heavy, blank doors. Up the iron stairs we went to the second story. In single file we passed along the narrow stone-paved balcony, outside doors behind which men must have been listening. At B 29 we stopped.

The door was thrown wide open. This was to be my own—a clean, scrubbed floor, scrubbed table and stool, in the corner a pail, above it a red-edged Bible, an enamel plate and mug, a wooden bowl and a bone spoon, a peg for clothes, bed-boards and bed-clothes.

I sat on those bed-boards, and after a while heard a hollow, heart-sinking sound. It had an undertone of condemnation, of dire separation which it never lost; it was the warder on his evening rounds double-locking the cell-doors. It was a symphony in three movements, all allegro—the thrust of a key, the sharp noising of the lock into its receptive socket, then the shooting of the great bolt.

In the deep silence the sudden clanging had about it a cold horror, and that chill note became more penetrating as the sound came closer to me. And then I caught another sound! The warder was singing, and the beat of his song became the beat of his actions. And this, as my incredulous ears heard it that first evening in B Wing, was the song he was singing as he shot the bolts and turned the keys :

> " We love them yet (*bang*), we can't forget (*bang*)
> The felons of our land (*bang*)!"

CHAPTER 22

MATCH-MAKING

THERE were twenty other Republican prisoners in Mountjoy Jail the night the warder shot the bolts to the tune of a patriot song.

Later, I was to find out that he was unconscious of what it meant for him to sing it. At first every new independence movement seems, to its own time, to be out of place, to have no link with the past in the people's minds, as if all connection with tradition were broken. It must have been that way always, for down through our history there has been the same rhythm of unreason.

The Young Irelanders seemed mad to O'Connell; Parnell seemed mad to Butt; the Volunteers seemed mad to Redmond; and even in those 1919 days there were many still who loved Irish freedom and yet who looked on our movement with deep suspicion. Men who talked about Grattan, who referred endearingly to Lord Edward and Emmet, who quoted Mitchel, who boasted that a relative was a Fenian, or that their parents were Parnellites to the end, were for a long, long time hostile to Sinn Féin. They could sing the rebel songs of yesterday and never realise we were acting to-day what they sang.

This warder was like that. He hummed " The West's Awake " and " Clare's Dragoons " as he supervised our breakfasts in the morning, and he turned the double lock on us at night, keeping to the beat of " Wrap the Green Flag " and " Ireland Boys Hurrah ! " and was innocent of any feeling that he should not be locking us up at all.

They were not all so slow to come to us, these warders in Mountjoy, and as this tale unfolds, it will be seen how much to help us many of them did under cover.

But then. I knew nothing of what warders felt, and could just meet each day as it came. I was awakened at 5.30 a.m. by the clanging of the triangle. When one hears that strange sound for the first time, there is great urgency in it, for the notes are deep and resonant, and they echo through the long corridors with, as it were, a morning eagerness. I have never seen the triangle beaten as, of course, we were all inside our cells whenever it sounded. But it must have been a powerful instrument, for it had to percolate through doors and sleep, with strength enough to awaken us.

After it had clanged the prison awake, we had half an hour to dress and wash—there was no shaving, for they would not trust criminals with razors, and to them we were all criminals. We had no choice but to become bearded, and as we had no mirrors, we, mercifully, could not observe the process.

At six o'clock the cell doors were opened. A warder, with one of the civil prisoners, came to each door, and the night slops were collected in a great bucket, which, when disturbed, polluted all the air.

That first morning in B Wing, there was a message in the eyes of the prisoner with the bucket. I tried to understand it but could not; an urgent message, almost a hungry message. Half an hour later he came again, now with the breakfast—a dollop of delicious porridge, a little loaf with margarine sitting on its back like a howdah on an elephant, and a mug of sweetened tea, served out of a steaming dixie, all brought from door to door, and no door opened until the viands had reached it and all the other doors were shut.

Again in the prisoner's eyes there was this urgent message, and, to my shame, I could not read it. The man might be an agent of G.H.Q., and I seemed not to have the password. But just as he pulled the door to—he was in the grey prison shirt and the darker grey trousers—he whispered, " Any waistcoats ? " and vanished.

It was a strange and surprising request, and I first decided this was a code word to which I should have the right reply. Then, as he did not look like that kind of a man, I decided that he wanted what he said. He wanted a waistcoat. He probably had to work in the cold of the early morning, and as I, a political prisoner, would refuse to work either in the cold or the heat, and would be kept indoors for punishment, I parcelled up my waistcoat in a tight, round packet, handy for throwing.

When warder and prisoner came that day with dinner—potatoes in a net bag, soup in a tin mug, and meat on an iron plate—all to be eaten with a bone spoon—I flicked to him that tubular package just as the warder's back was turned to open the next cell door. He caught it with the dexterity of a long-term man. When he saw the size of the package flying through the air at him, he gave me a smlie of thanks so beatific that if I had had ten waistcoats it would have wheedled them all out of me.

Alas, for my innocence !

When tea came round—dark shell cocoa and two small loaves, one with margarine riding Indian-wise—that civil prisoner, as he was about to close my door, hurled my package into the cell at me with a lunge of disgust. It remained a mystery to me for many days, and then I learned that " waistcoat " is prison slang for a cigarette and that the beatific smile was given in the belief that he was getting a few hundred of them. I always admired that man for not sending my waistcoat back in shreds.

So the day went to the sounds of bolts and locks being drawn or shut—triangle, slops, breakfast, dinner, tea, double-locking, bed, triangle . . .

Outside each cell-door was a card with our names and misdemeanours. Me, " David Hogan : Seditious Speech : Four Months " ; the man on my right—" Wife-beating : Twelve Months " ; the man on my left—" Larceny : Three Months." But I never saw the wife-beater or the thief because no door opened until all the others were shut, and we would not work or exercise with the ordinary prisoners.

Once a week we scrubbed our cells : a bucket of warm foamy water, a chunk of red carbolic soap, a net-like rag. It was the nicest day of the week, and the floor and bed-boards and furniture were snowy after it all. The Governor came each morning, and the prisoner stood by his table and was asked what complaints he had. None of the political prisoners had at that time any but one : that our liberty had been taken from us. We scorned to make any lesser complaint ; and we asked for no amelioration but to be treated as prisoners-of-war if we must be held. These things only puzzled the little Governor, who had come from Accra, where the black men probably had no idea of what he was saying.

Because we would not work, we were allowed no communication with the world outside, no letters, no parcels, no visits. At exercise we were supposed to tramp around three stone circles inside a great open-air cage, to remain the while in complete silence, and just three paces, no more, no less, behind the man in front, with warders every few yards to shout and scold if we strayed or whispered. The political prisoners one day refused any longer to obey the rules at exercise and dared the powers that be to do as they liked. Other prisoners in other wings did the same, probably at some agreed signal which I have forgotten, and soon, because we were demoralising the civil prisoners, they put us all together on the landing in B Wing, with the criminals on the floors above us and below. So I lost my wife-beater and the man who loved petty larceny. But there were counter-balancing gains. Now we all took exercise together, and, like all Irish prisoners at all times, we began to organise.

Just about this time I had a stroke of luck. My warder became afraid of me—and then he dreamed of me as a son-in-law. It was a story that should be told dutifully.

Every prison door is made of a solid piece of iron riveted to a wooden base. There were two small apertures in this sweep of metal, one an eye-hole with a movable metal flap as if the door were a Cyclops with its single eye under an eye-shade. When the metal flap was lifted, the warder could gaze into the cell and spy on the prisoner by day. The other aperture was a wooden socket containing a circle of glass fitted into the centre of the door after it was made. Against that glass the warder pressed his lamp at night, filling the cell with light as he peeped through the eye-hole.

I did not mind the night surveillance, which seemed to me to be fair. The warders taking over from the day-men must make sure all the prisoners are there. But the day-peeping revolted me; its stealthiness added to its meanness. All one would hear was the click of the metal shade being lifted and then you knew an unseen eye was gazing at you. One evening, just after hearing the metal click, I rang my emergency bell.

The warder came in. He was a mild, ageing man whom we shall call Floyd, as he may still be living, and I must not hurt him. He had a facility for getting everything the wrong way round. My name was written in big script on my door : " David Hogan," and so he called me Dan Brogan.

" You rang," he said.

" I did, Mr. Floyd, just to tell you never again to spy on me in the daytime. You may have to do it when you are on night duty and you take over, just to make sure we're all there. But you know we are there in the daytime, and never again lift that eye-piece. Do you hear me ? "

" But," he began.

" Mr. Floyd," I said, " there will be no ' buts ' in this matter. I will not be spied upon and you will not spy on me from this day forth. Go now."

He went, and he never again lifted that metal flap.

From that day out he called me " Master Dan," and he told me his secret sorrow.

He should be Chief Warder now (indeed, he would have made a better one than the gold-and-red mountain) only for the man who was mad.

" What man, Mr. Floyd ? "

" Ah, Master Dan, do you remember the day you told me never to look through that spy-hole. I was nervous of you, Master Dan. It's a good few years now but there was a man in this very cell and whenever I looked in at him I saw strange sights, Master Dan. He was a long, thin, clothes-pole of a man and every time I looked at night, there he was on the floor without a stitch on him, saving your presence, Master Dan, and he wriggling his way in and out through the legs of the stool you're sitting on this blessed minute. I used to laugh at him, but the day came when I stopped my laughing. One night I shone my lamp into this cell, Master Dan, and he wasn't there, not a sound, or a sign, or a sight of him. He was gone, and I next in line for promotion."

He sighed deeply, and taking off his cap, he wiped his completely bald head, which shone with perspiration at the memory of that fell night.

"What had happened, Mr. Floyd?" I asked.

"Ah, Master Dan, he was no more mad than yourself. He had found out that the space underneath that stool was exactly the same as the opening in the ventilator up there on the wall." I shot my eyes to it expectantly, but it had been covered with a metal lattice.

"They put that on it after, but it was just an opening then. He practised his wriggling through the legs of the stool, and when he had made himself perfect he wriggled out through that ventilator, and that was why he had no clothes on. It was so tight a fit he could only do it in his pelt. He hauled his clothes up after him, got into the flues and travelled the whole length under the roof until he could drop down outside the walls. And my promotion dropped down with him, Master Dan."

He sighed again and went away.

We had many conversations after that. I noticed him eyeing me with particular attention for a few days, and then, in the course of conversation, he asked: "Are you pledged, Master Dan?"

"Pledged?"

"I mean are you engaged to be married?"

I became cautious at once.

"Well now, Mr. Floyd, who'd think of marrying a man who'd been in jail?"

"Ah, ye fellows aren't that sort at all. Sure there's no knowing where ye'll all end up. Listen now, Master Dan. I have a daughter, a lovely girl she is, and a teacher she's going to be. Herself is me second wife, you see, and she has a son, and she thinks the sun rises out of him. She has no use for my little one at all, and I'd love to see her settled; just turned eighteen she is, and she'd be a wonderful help to an educated man like yourself, Master Dan. What do you say now?"

"Arrah, Mr. Floyd, what can I say? I haven't even seen her, and she hasn't seen me; she doesn't even know I exist at all. Now if I only saw her . . ."

"Oh, God bless you, Master Dan; that's enough. I'll arrange it all when you get out. You'll be in love with her the first time you lay your eyes on her."

I never did lay my eyes on her, but, in his mind, the match was made there and then, and from that time forward, whenever Mr. Floyd was on duty he regarded me as, next to his promotion, his first concern. He brought me ink and paper and a pen. He even took out an odd letter for me, " but not about anything political, Master Dan."

One evening I rang my bell. " Mr Floyd," I said, " it's half-past five and I haven't seen the 6.30 *Mail* yet." We were supposed to see no newspapers.

" Oh, Mr. Dan," he said, " it's down with the Governor. But I'll have it up to you in a jiffy."

And he had. That was the way between us, and it was a useful way when the storm broke.

CHAPTER 23

WORK IN THE DARK

DURING those four years of struggle, the prisoners knew they could play a major part. If the greatest possible number of troops, warders, officials could be tied down to the jails, there would be less for the lads outside to fight. We knew what risks had to be taken. Thomas Ashe had set the standard. Lives must, if necessary, be lost in transferring the fight into the jails. Suffering of any kind was not to prevent the jailed Volunteer being on active service. The effect of this unity of action, which overleaped prison walls, was of great consequence. From 1917 to 1921 the prison struggles gave the people new fortitude. Ashe's swift death under forcible feeding, MacSwiney's prolonged fast, the capture of parts of Belfast Jail by the Republican prisoners, the great Mountjoy hunger-strike, became manifestations of the demand for independence which attracted attention far outside Ireland. That was particularly so about Terence MacSwiney's death. Few things—if indeed any one thing—in all the centuries of struggle had a wider influence. It brought the spirit of Ireland's resistance to the very ends of the earth : an unquenchable devotion to liberty pitted against the perfect war machine of a great Power. For a decade after that head fell suddenly limp on the Brixton pillow, men in distant countries, hearing someone say "I come from Ireland," would reply, "Ireland : ah, the country of brave MacSwiney."

The strike which, carefully planned, took place in Mountjoy Jail in the October of 1919, was not of that magnitude, but it, too, held the nation while it lasted. It was a new form of protest ; it was dramatic ; the turmoil sounding out through the night from those high dark walls, so long silent, stirred the sympathy of the ordinary man and woman of Dublin and of the nation.

We called it the " Racket Strike," and how well it justified that name ! Who first thought of and planned this elaborate outburst, I do not now remember. My part in it was that of a rank-and-filer. I think Maurice Crowe of Tipperary, had much to do with it, and a fiery Republican from Co. Mayo, Michael Kelly, if the front name remains correctly with me, and Séamus O'Doherty, who outwardly was so quiet. I remember, too, as valiant participants that giant of a man, Lar Brady of the Midlands ; Bob Slane, with his humorous eye under the great bald forehead, and the Tyrone inflections of his speech ; Eamon O'Kelly, a medical student, who was an I.R.B. man ; Páidín O'Keeffe, the Secretary of Sinn Féin, with his saturnine wit ; and Gearóid O'Sullivan, high up in the I.R.A.

There were two or three skirmishes with the Governor before the big engagement. One of them had a delicious, almost a shaggy-dog ending. As the summer wore on, we decided to protest against having only one suit of clothes. We were becoming ragged, we said, and as prisoners of war, we were entitled to have clothes sent in. The Governor refused, and the more we pressed, the more adamant he became.

Then one day a warder told us that a party of ladies, friends of the Governor, were coming to be shown around the prison, and they would be brought past the exercise cages at about 4.30. The Governor, he added, would like them to see us exercising happily. We decided to add to the thrill of the dear ladies' visit, and that afternoon we all went out in overcoats though the day was warm. We had asked the warder to signal the ladies' approach, and just as they turned the corner and came into full view, the little Governor pointed towards our cage. We threw off our coats and yelling : " He won't give us clothes," we raced around the ring in the least possible amount of clothing.

The Governor stood for one appalled moment in the midst of his flock of females, and then he hustled them around the corner again and was gone. Next day we got permission for our second suits.

Amidst minor clashes of this kind, the big plan was being worked out. As it neared its D-day, the co-operation of some of the civil prisoners, who worked near the tool-house, was needed, and one evening, when we thought the coast was clear, a thin, strong rope was lowered from one of our cell windows to that of a civil prisoner below. He tied some miscellaneous tools, smuggled from the workshops, to it, one a crowbar. As this strange bundle began to make its way up the blank outside wall, one of the Scottish troops, then guarding the prison, saw it. There was now enacted what we were so often to experience in those tense years—people whom we had never met, complete strangers to us and our movement, sympathising with and helping us.

To that Scottish lad, the jerky ascent of a bundle of tools up the walls of this prison must have been an unusual sight indeed. Instead of raising the alarm, he called out helpful directions in the sturdy dialect of Bobby Burns. " A wee bit to the recht," he called— " Swing awa' to the left "—until the crowbar, and its attendant

K

chisels and screwdrivers, had disappeared into Kelly's window. A word from him might have betrayed our plan, but that Scottish soldier held his peace, and soon, in the mattress of almost every prisoner, some tool was hidden. There was only one crowbar, but some had the smaller tools, others had awls and spokes, and I a long steel packing needle.

The night the struggle began we trooped in from the exercise yard after the last instructions had been given under cover of what seemed to the warders to be but an extra noisy game of rag-ball. Every man went meekly to his cell, but his heart was pounding at the thought of the night before him.

To understand that night's turmoil, the reader will need to keep in mind what a jail wing is like. Anybody who has been to a public swimming baths will know how the dressing cubicles run right round the pool. Imagine the same for thirty cells in three tiers, facing one another around a central hall. As in a baths, the passage outside the cell-door is narrow; two could not walk abreast there. The cells have foot-thick walls with heavily-barred windows high up on the back wall.

Our plan that night, in October, 1919, was that each prisoner should somehow get through the foot-thick wall to the next man— the task for which the tools were needed. It all had to be done in the greatest secrecy, for if the slightest noise disclosed what we were at, we would be clapped into irons without a moment's grace.

The instant the cell doors were locked at five-thirty, the work began. No man could hear his neighbour, who was now no wife-beater or expert in burglary, but a fellow Volunteer; the walls were too thick. But there was a method by which orders could be co - veyed. The prison hot-water pipes passed around the wing near the floor under the window. A tap on these pipes would be heard in every cell. While this plan was maturing, many of us learned Morse, and an order from our commandant could be given to all the cells simultaneously. This night a quick double-tap on the pipes was the most urgent signal of all.

Every half-an-hour after lock-up, warders were supposed to peep into every cell. Some of them, like my Mr. Floyd, could be scared off. Others were on our side. But the majority carried out this routine. At night they wore rubber-soled shoes, and the click of the lifted spy-hole cover would be the first warning the prisoner unbuilding his wall would get. So two men, one in the first cell of the warder's rounds, and one in the last, were given no task but to lie in bed, and as they heard the spy-hole cover move, to tap a signal "Warder coming" on the hot-water pipes, or "Inspection over."

At that first tap, every man leaped from his work at the wall and was sitting harmlessly reading at his cell table, or as the night went by, lay angelically sleeping while the cell suddenly filled with light and as suddenly became dark again. Lest he not have time to get under the blankets, each man wore his pyjamas over his day clothes.

That night was the most thrilling Mountjoy Jail can ever have seen. In the heavy silence of the prison—and prison silence is next to the silence of the tomb—the work of breaking through half a hundred walls went on noiselessly.

In my case, I hung my overcoat so that, when the warder's light flashed in, it threw a shadow over the hole I was making into the next cell. As I had only a long packing needle, it would take many hours picking at the mortar to loosen the first brick under its many coats of whitewash. The mortar was hard and resistant; it came away in tiny particles, and whenever the warning double-tap came I was angrily impatient for the all-clear, time meant everything now.

As evening changed to night, and the mortar still came out in tiny flakes, my arms ached and my fingers bled as the hard corners of the uncovered brick tore at them in the dark. Hour after hour I worked with my packing needle, and then at last it was possible to grip that stubborn brick, and, soon after, to shake it in its place. Whenever the tap came now, I leaped for bed and lay there till the " all clear," grateful in every fibre for those few minutes respite.

Often I paused and listened, and not one sound did I hear in that still jail of forty prisoners, who, like myself, were working furiously in their cells' blackness. Then, some time near midnight, there was a sudden thudding clang.

The man with the crowbar had dropped it; I could imagine his weariness if mine was such, who had only a packing needle to manipulate. The dull clanging sent us all hustling to bed, and the tap that followed immediately, showed that the night warder had also heard it. This round of his took longer than usual, and on my closed lids the light of his lantern remained for several seconds as his unseen eye examined every part of the cell. How could it miss the now gaping wall?

But it did miss it, not in my cell but in every other cell. For the " all clear " came after that slow round, and the jail settled down again to its outward calm and its hidden vigour.

I, and of a certainty the others, went back to their walls like men possessed. This could not last much longer. I wrung the brick free, and feeling rubble beyond it, clawed that out. I gripped another brick, and, holding it, swayed to and fro in the dark until, under my full weight, it, too, was about to come apart. Then the tap came, and I was barely back in bed when the light shone and was gone. The warder's suspicions were allayed; this was again a routine pilgrimage.

Now, if I listened with my ear against the wall, I could hear faint scrapings by the man in the next cell. The sense of victory that surged into me was suffocating. Here were a few dozen prisoners and they were destroying this dark jail from the inside. The prison authorities could not defeat us now; we had a long start of them. To-morrow—and then that crowbar fell from weary fingers again. The warder came hot foot upon the sound. His light remained in my cell for a long, long time. At last he passed on, obviously suspicious and puzzled. Luckily, I had not stirred for the light was back again, and again was gone. There was no other noise anywhere in that wing of pounding hearts, except the clicks of the raised eye-hole flaps.

Suddenly, higher up the ward, there was what I took to be a great shout, and then a long shrill blast on the warder's whistle, urgent, piercing, tremulous. It filled the whole wing for ten seconds. Then it was drowned by a very thunderclap of sound. The first stage of the prisoners' plan had been discovered; the second stage began with a rending and a smashing which filled the jail with pandemonium.

CHAPTER 24

THE RACKET STRIKE

THE whistle of the warder which, on that October night in 1919, brought as its echo an astonishing tempest of sound, recorded also that prisoners are insatiably curious. The long hours of confinement send thoughts like spies into every chink and hollow in a cell wall and floor, ceiling and door. The eye takes a thousand measurements, the mind multiplies, subtracts, meditates, conspires. Two important discoveries were made.

One was that if the prison table were taken asunder there would be nails enough to hammer its stout deal top into the wooden floor, so that it would prevent the door opening in the only way cell doors can open, which is inwards.

The other discovery was of the one chink in the prison armour. Someone found out that if the bracket, which holds the lamp glass, is struck a stout blow from the prison stool, in the right-hand upper corner, it flies out, glass, frame and all. The door then becomes, as it were, a medieval stock with an open space for the head.

With head out, the voice can travel, and one is free to sing and shout and order, and one can see, too, something of what is happening.

So when the whistle split the night, over forty prison tables were promptly torn to pieces, and a thundering of hammering showed that the tops were being driven into the floors. Then came a smashing of glass as the prison stools battered against the lamp-hole sockets, until at last the critical spot was struck, and out shot the piece, and one could bawl triumph into the echoing wing.

Many a late home-goer that night must have looked up startled as the sombre, high-walled, silent building suddenly became a great shadow of sound. It was after midnight and there was little light —a gas jet here and a gas jet there in the long dark wing. Along the balconies and stairways we could now hear running feet. The night warders were gathering. Shrill whistles still called hollowly along the lower passages, and there were excited voices. As each prisoner stood by his empty lamp socket and looked out into the shimmering darkness, he wondered what would be the end of this night.

The warders had gathered in the central hall. They mounted the iron stairs, and a hush came down as every prisoner stopped to follow the sound of that marching. Over the warders' footsteps came suddenly a booming Tipperary voice : " Get through your walls, quick ! "

It had not struck us that now, when secrecy and silence were no longer necessary, we might finish the job on the walls before the doors could be forced. Men turned in a flash from their doors to hack and thrust and claw at the wounded walls. The man with the crow-bar got through and, with a whoop, passed the weapon into the next cell. The prisoner, two-thirds through already, seized it with delight and drove it into his broken wall. He was soon through, and passed the bar on. It suddenly came through my cell wall, and, hearing the cry of my neighbour, I felt for it and soon I had those bricks flying which had ignored my packing needle.

On and on that crowbar went round the wing. But now there were other sounds. The counter-attack had begun. There was a blessed prison rule that no prisoner must be overpowered by less than three warders, and, if possible, in the presence of the Deputy Governor or the Head Warder. It was a rule designed in other days to spare both prisoners and warders, since the uneven odds ended the struggle in a few seconds. To-night the rule was insisted upon too, and it so delayed the attempt to force the cell doors that it gave us a glorious chance.

The warders had to run unusual risks, for, with the lamp hole out, the prisoner, standing just inside the door with a table leg or other weapon, could long frustrate the efforts to put the key in the lock.

One or other of the prisoners, whose cell-door was opposite the group of warders, relayed a commentary to all of us glued to the lamp holes, now that our walls were pierced. No moderns have ever sat by their radios with the rapture that we knelt beside that open space in our doors, listening to the excited voice of some youngster :

" They are at Paddy's door now ; they're using a crowbar. He's grabbing for it ; they have it under the door now and three of them are at it. They can't budge it. He's grabbing for it again—My God, he has it ; Paddy has the crowbar ; he's taken it from the warders. Oh, lawks, this is great——!"

And the rest of what he said was drowned by us in a shout that should have shattered the glass roof. The warders, dismayed, stood irresolutely for a while ; there was a whispered consultation on the landing above the iron stairs in that half-dark wing, and then the commentator began again :

" They're going ; they're going away down the stairs ; all except the three near here. They're on the way down." We cheered lustily.

" They are fetching the Tommies." We boohed that. A voice higher up the wing took up the description. " No; they are bringing a hose." We neither cheered nor boohed that. It silenced us. Up the stairs slithered the new weapon. Soon, as the warders toiled at the doors, the hose poured a resistless beam of water through the lamp hole, defeating every effort to attack them from within. Still the cells held out. Then came the ecstatic moment of that night's struggle.

Listening breathlessly above the descriptions of what was happening, we could hear all the sounds of the struggle : the drenched man, whose cell was being attacked, splashing through water, the noise of the crowbars on the steel door as they felt for the jamb to prise it open, forcing it inward on the wood ; the heavy breathing of the warders, shouts and answering muffled cries from within the cells. We could hear the tearing of wood as the prisoner sought for new weapons or some way to save himself from that glistening bar of water, or to prevent that heavy door wrenching his defences from the floor. Then a shriek came into the commentator's voice.

" He's got the nozzle ; he's torn the nozzle off the hose ; oh, glory ! "

Every man of us beat in triumph on his door and yelled our joy to the victor. It was marvellous. The hose, like a shorn Samson, lost all its strength. It fell from the warder's hand and lay coughing harmlessly on the passage outside the cell, the water sounding on the floor below as if we were beside some country cascade.

Again the battle ceased, and the warders withdrew for new consultations. But now the day staffs, as well as the night men, were hurried in, and when they came again, it was not only with a new nozzle for the old hose, but dragging a second hose with them.

The lights everywhere were turned on. The march of warders up the iron stairs had new purpose in it. On the landing they broke into several parties and attacked three cells at once. Whoever tried a commentary now, the hose was directed into that cell, and the voice soon died in a splashing and a gurgling. When, in a fury of noise, the first cell was forced, every listener determined that he would fight after that, too, and, as each barricaded door gave way, there were cries and shouts and finally an exhausted silence.

Hours after the first cell had fallen, they came to that beside mine. I could look in through the damaged wall and see my comrade, a huge man, standing aside from the purplish streak of water which darkly caught the golden light of the gas-jets outside. He had a slab of wood in his hand. Suddenly he clapped it over the lamp-hole, shutting out all light, and, putting his back to it, held it there. It sent the torrent from the hose back upon the warders themselves.

But the attacks were relentless. Crowbars splintered that wood, and soon the door was down, and my neighbour was in the midst of whirling warders. As I watched this battle of shadows, and heard the swish of water which was up to their ankles, and the panting as they overcame a savage resistance, I felt how little I could do by comparison. Then, with a sudden limpness, came the end, and one more prisoner was down handcuffed and exhausted.

I remember little of the struggle for my own cell except trying to keep that door from coming inwards, stamping on the table top to keep it nailed into the floor, lying down on it where the crowbars outside were nosing their way in. I forgot even whether I was hosed, but in the end here, as elsewhere, the door suddenly gave way. With the tearing of wood, and a moment's halt as somehow I closed it again, I found myself battling desperately as three warders simply, and it seems now, looking back, painlessly bowled me over. As they lay on top of me, searching for my wrists, one of them whispered, " This is great." In the mix-up I couldn't tell who had said it, but I felt triumphant as they left me lying on the cell floor with my hands handcuffed behind my back.

Dawn was coming through the high glass roof before the last of the cells was taken. Through the broken wall on each side of me I could chat with fellow-prisoners now lying manacled as I was. But our talk was desultory as sleep overcame us, and a great silence spread through the jail. Even the clanging of the triangle, though heard as if in a dream, did not mean anything now. It was evening before most of us awoke, and then the rest of the plan went into operation.

The ordinary prisoners run every jail; they are the bakers, the cooks, the tailors, the cleaners, the messengers. Probably hundreds were in Mountjoy in 1919, and our aim was so to disorganise the great institution as to make the Governor and, behind him, Dublin Castle pray to high heaven to be rid of us, and, when they were in that mood, to start a hunger-strike, of which we then knew they were mightily afraid.

One way of disorganising the jail was to keep the civil prisoners awake night after night. It was cruel, but in the task of liberating not a few prisoners, but the country, they, as well as we, had to share the suffering.

The cells were double locked at 5.30. Lights out came at 8.30. Thereafter the prison gradually fell asleep. But not in those days in 1919. At 8.30 each night we began a concert. Every man knelt at his door, and, by turning his head, was able to get it through the empty lamp hole bracket, and there he sang his song, or gave his recitation, or whistled his tune. I remember Lar Brady lamenting that he had not brought his violin! For applause, the warders had given us the means of making the sharpest noise of all.

After the first day, we protested; at not being handcuffed—for, after all, we had half-wrecked our wing—but at being handcuffed with our hands behind our backs; it left us so helpless. We asked that the handcuffs be left off at meals and that they then be fastened in front. It was so agreed, and a warder named Kelly came to change mine.

"What's coming next?" he asked. He was a friend and I told him. "Keep ye all awake," I said.

"How?" he asked.

"You'll know to-night."

And he did. When a song had ended or a recitation was complete, we saluted the artist with pounding the iron cuffs against the steel doors; it was a terrifying sound when they did it together in those echoing wings.

For the city man, jail concerts were a revelation. From each county came its ballads, its songs, given almost recitative, recounting the fate of some local patriot. These had an extraordinary hold over the men, and were listened to in tense silence, a burst of shouting, rather than applause, signalling the end. The national songs of the cities, and the ordinary music-hall hits, had their audiences, too, but it was the local songs, the fireside story in verse, that stirred the prisoners most deeply. Those, and the recitations, gripped them wholly; the speeches from the dock, so many of us had forgotten; and Pearse's oration at the grave of Rossa which even then had become a classic:

"... the fools—they have left us our Fenian dead and while Ireland holds these graves, Ireland unfree shall never be at peace."

The sentences, spoken in the strong dialect of Clare or Kerry, were heard in complete stillness. There was some strange, primitive strength in the cries after the last word died quietly away. When the concert was over, we could hear, through the floors, the civil prisoners settling down for the night. Alas, poor Yorick; thou shalt get no ease or sleep this night——

Half an hour after the concert ended the "Racket Strike" proper began. The sharp voice of our commandant sounded in the silent wing. "Company—'shun." Thereafter we were on parade, each head out of its studded door. The roll was called, and as the night grew on, if any man failed to answer, those on either side of him beat on the hot water pipes or shouted through the wall-opening, until at last his head came through his door and he gave answer to his name.

"Ready—present—fire!" These were the commands, and no rifles made a sharper or a more alarming noise than forty men banging suddenly and all together on iron doors with steel handcuffs, the whole cell acting as a sounding box. As suddenly, came the cease-fire whistle. It sounds childish. It was anything but that. All through the night, at every fifteen or twenty minutes (I cannot remember which), this appalling volume of sound filled the jail. As the night went on, we could hear the civil prisoners crying out in protest.

The triangle went at 5.30 a.m. and that relieved us from duty. The warders came before each meal to wake us and remove the hand-cuffs for half-an-hour. A friendly soul among them said one day to me :

"How do you make that awful racket ?"

I showed him. He watched me critically as quietly I beat my handcuffs against the iron door.

"It would be better this way," he said, fastening the handcuffs so that the flat circle for the key would be next the door as we beat it.

"Do it for the others," I asked him.

It was a wonderful improvement. That night the first volley deafened even ourselves, and, for the whole night, three or four times an hour, the first hurricane of sound kept on surprising us.

For a week we kept it up, and, at the end of that week, the poor civil prisoners were haggard and angry and incapable of work, the meals were late, the sick list grew, the shining, polished prison became a shabby, dirty place. We could imagine the despair of the Governor—and then we hunger-struck !

CHAPTER 25

" SOMETHING FOR SCIENCE "

IRELAND fought for her freedom with many weapons beside arms.

She used non-co-operation; she used passive resistance. Irishmen in the British civil service threw up their posts; others refused to join their forces. Some workers would not take jobs on army contracts. Taxis would not carry them. None would give them information. Few journalists would work for them. In many places shopkeepers would not serve them. Supporters of the Castle who openly sided with the British régime could not get farm labourers to gather their harvest. But the hardest weapon of all to use was the hunger-strike.

Men who launched themselves into these fasts had no idea what the fasts would do to them. It seemed impossible to live even a few days without food, and the extraordinary weakness, which came so quickly, was terrifying.

For refusal to work, political prisoners had to spend all but two hours of each day confined to cells. Jail life became bearable only because of the meals. The meals were not luscious. But they broke up the long day, and, as they were being served, one could see human faces and hear human voices. Hunger-striking took even that relief away at a time when the morbid fears that fasting induces magnified the tedium.

There was no physical excitement in hunger-striking. After a few days, one lay hour after hour on a bed with nothing to break the monotony except the gushes of panic following every half-faint which lack of food brought on. The men and women, boys and girls—for some of them were little more than that—who endured these fasts had no stirring tales to tell afterwards, no thrilling account of struggle and wild conflict. Their memories were of tense hours of silence in which, though there was no pain, there was unceasing fear and deep spiritual unrest as to the righteousness of so dying for liberty.

These hunger-strikes were not the most heroic things done in this mass struggle for freedom, but also they were not the least heroic, and those who participated in them should stand honoured wherever liberty is loved.

As for the enemy, one of the things he hated most were those clammy, shrinking bodies stretched out in cell after cell along a whole silent wing. The prison doctors so recently busy with exhausted thieves and pickpockets now stood before this mute protest undecided. Since the death of Ashe had finished forcible feeding, they just did not know what to do.

One day the head of the prison medical service came to my cell. He had been called to Mountjoy Jail on the second day, when already men had begun to collapse and were being rushed to the prison hospital. Day and night the emergency alarm bells were ringing, as either the men themselves felt they were going, or their neighbours took fright for them as no answers came to the calls through the broken walls.

Every morning, from the third day of this fast, there was a special medical inspection in which three doctors took part. When their arrival in the wing was whispered along the cells by friendly warders, some of the prisoners took time by the forelock and skipped and jumped wildly but noiselessly in their cells, to leap into bed when through the open lamp hole the voices of the doctors heralded their approach.

When these apparently resting prisoners' pulses were taken they were found to be racing and the befuddlement of the medical men was worse than ever. They simply could not understand the manifold effects of this mass fasting. There were other harmless ways of depressing the heart and quickening the breathing and many a sound man was raced to hospital after the three visitors had whispered in a corner about his inexplicable symptoms.

I practised none of these little deceits, and when the doctors came they found my pulse normal and my temperature steady. The result of this physical placidity was to convince them that I was the ideal subject for hunger-striking: no temperature, no excited pulse, no irregular heart, and one morning, I think it was on the last day of the six, the Chief Medical Adviser came into my cell and leaning against the wall looked down at me hesitantly,

"Hogan," he said slowly, "I want you to do something for science."

"Certainly, doctor; just tell me what."

"We don't understand much about this hunger-striking. It has so many different effects on the men. You will all be going out soon: that's settled I think. Now when you build up your strength I want you to carry out a fast for us, under ideal conditions," he added hurriedly, "no danger of course."

"Certainly, I will, doctor."

"Well, Hogan, I must say this is very sporting of you. I didn't expect you to be so co-operative in the kind of fight ye're in now. You'll really fast for us ? "

" Of course, doctor."

" That's fine : how long do you think it will take to build up your strength ? "

" Ah, a few weeks, doctor."

" Better make it two months. Could we fix a date some time after that ? "

" Certainly, doctor."

The dear man was in a grey topper : he was due at some race-course that afternoon and my acceptance of his offer evidently made the day seem a lucky one for him. He kept on thanking me, and then said :

" Fix the exact time yourself."

" I have already fixed it, doctor."

" Well, well, well, I'll certainly have a different impression of you fellows after this. What have you fixed ? "

" The first Thursday after the British Government recognises the Irish Republic, doctor."

He stood looking down at me, and at first the face under the grey topper grew dark, and then, despite himself, he laughed.

" I understand," he said, " and I certainly shall *not* have a different impression of you fellows after this."

" Doctor," said I, soothingly, " you couldn't surely expect me to solve this problem for you in the middle of an unfinished fight. We know the hunger-strike frightens ye : that is partly why we do it. If I fasted for you, neither you nor I nor the Castle would have any problem."

He went to his races mollified, I think. As for us, it was another kind of race. Our demand was for prisoner-of-war treatment, for special food, daily letters, parcels, papers and periodicals, visits when we wished them, five hours' exercise a day with the cell-doors left open, the right to dress as we liked, to smoke, to use razors and knives and forks.

That was what we asked for. But our secret objective was release. It did not matter to me and to many others, for our sentences were almost up and could not be added to. But amongst us there were men, some in under other names, and for them we must open the jail gates.

That was why this and several other hunger-strikes had to be a success, why we would accept no compromise. In this October strike they came near making us an offer which would have given us almost full political status. For a moment it was we who were nonplussed and we began discussions among ourselves how to get the endangered men out.

Fortunately the Castle hardened and withdrew its offer and the strike went on, with us rejoicing. They never found out what was strengthening us. They gave in at last after only five days. Late at night through the dark passages the word came dramatically. The cell doors began to be opened, the bolts to be banged back. Voices filled the passages. At first it seemed to confirm the dread of a general collapse, but as more and more doors swung open it began to dawn on us that something else had happened. Through the lampholes I heard the words :

" We're all going out."

It was a victory so swift and unexpected that it stunned us. Then somebody somewhere, started saying the Rosary, and in a flash men were on their knees and grateful prayer poured out in strong voices.

We went out in all our whiskers. Time came when I shaved mine off and in all the crises afterwards I was never again recognised. Twice I was in their hands and each time they let me go.

That beard was, indeed, worthy of the cause. It was a great flowing red beard, which certainly embarrassed my friends and me also, when at last I saw it in the glass. I could explain its colour only by that law of natural selection, which makes the caterpillar the same colour as the cabbage it eats, and the tiger have on his back stripes like shadows of the bamboo. My overcoat, which I brought into the cell following that day we danced as naiads for the Governor's ladies, was a foxy red, and the beard hit so exactly on the colour that when I put on that coat nobody knew where I ended and the coat began.

It was an epoch for beards, and the literati of Dublin, then as now, grew them, only then more luxuriantly. After my release I met at the corner of Grafton Street and Duke Street one windy day three other men—Darrell Figgis, Ernest Boyd and AE.

All of us were standing brilliantly bearded, when a great wit passed our way. He was Seumas O'Sullivan, the poet, who with Estella Solomons, the artist, afterwards to become his wife, were friends of us all and brave helpers in the movement. Seumas looked solemnly at me whom he had not seen since my arrest. Then he parodied :

" The wonder was that one small face
Could carry all he grew."

I brought the beard with me all through the months that separated the " Racket Strike " from the great Mountjoy hunger-strike. Men said I was mad to go around so, but as it proved, fate, if not myself, put method into this madness. One day in the office Desmond Fitzgerald handed me a note from Mick Collins. It went something like :

" Will you tell D.H. if he thinks his beard is a disguise to read this," and there followed on the sheet a clipping from a Castle intelligence report beginning with the words " Very Secret." It said : " Suspect Hogan was seen going into the Vegetarian Restaurant to-day at 12.45. An hour later he had not left." I had never been to the Vegetarian Restaurant. Some one else, some innocent poet or artist, was being tracked for me. Many years later I heard that the then Protestant Archbishop of Dublin, Dr. Gregg had on several occasions been brought to the Castle protesting to the soldiers who arrested him that he was *not* de Valera. Perhaps the scion of some stout, old Unionist family kept denying through his red beard that he was I.

I was still wearing that beard the evening Alan Bell was shot. I lived in lodgings kept by three sisters—good Unionists all—near Baggot Street Bridge. In time they learned my politics but we never quarrelled, though at hours of tension the strain was obvious. That night when I came home I knew at once something had happened. Not a word was spoken around that fire. Then one and another went to bed and the " good nights " to me were cold and formal. I had not seen an evening paper and had to wait till all were gone to dive for one.

Alan Bell had been taken from a Dun Laoghaire tram and shot dead by the roadside ! Two men beckoned to him as he sat in the tram and said " We want you." Death wanted him. He was a Resident Magistrate and the Castle had given him a special task. He was to discover where the Sinn Féin funds were hidden and confiscate them. He set up a court in Dublin Castle and summoned the officials of the various banks to him.

Several of them refused to go. Others went but proved dense fellows who, in all the ledgers which Alan Bell ordered them to bring, could find nothing. After a few sessions Bell had got nowhere, and then death tolled for him between Dublin and Dún Laoghaire. His shooting created one of the big sensations of that day, and had I known earlier, I might have slipped away to stay a few nights with friends. But it was too late

CHAPTER 26

" WE WANT YOU "

THOUSANDS of Irish men and women in the years of the struggle
were hunted in a way that is hard for the younger generation to-day
to understand. Many of us who so often stood in dark rooms at night,
listening over the house tops to distant lorries, trying to measure
the direction they were taking, did not understand it ourselves until
long afterwards.

The sense of being trapped grew on us more and more as the fight
deepened, as those we knew disappeared, swept away in some big
raid, to be heard of again only from some distant prison. With every
friend who vanished the anxiety to avoid capture deepened. Those
of us on the *Bulletin* staff knew better than most what a raid might
mean. We had published how troops had marched into a country
kitchen as the family were on their knees at the Rosary, to take out
the man of the house or a favourite son or a guest. As the others,
still kneeling, strained into the silence for sounds, poised like a
group of statuary, there would come a muffled noise through the
walls as their loved one was killed by the roadside. How often each
of us thought " that's me some time." And we said a wee prayer
that when that moment came we would go gamely.

When we published in full the affidavit of a young Volunteer
taken to the Castle and, if he would not speak, being loosed to a mob
of Auxiliaries in the Castle yard and battered as if he were a rat in a
barn—we then said *that* would be our fate, and we begged for the
courage of a closed mouth.

In these March days of 1920, when Alan Bell was slain, there
had come a new reason to wish not to be caught just now. It was
barely a week before this night that Tomás MacCurtain, Lord Mayor
of Cork, had been murdered in his home. Only a matter of hours
ago, James McCarthy, of Thurles, had been done to death in the same
way.

So that night when curfew came down—but that also needs
explanation, for the institution that went by this lovely name is
strange to these times, too. Curfew means the coming of quiet,
the settling down for the night, the covering of the fire. It had not
that meaning in the troubled times. It was like the closing of the doors
of a prison ; like the springing of a great trap. The Irish city councils

—Dublin and other Corporations—did, sensibly and bravely, give the word again something of its old meaning. As soon as the British imposed this new restraint, intending by it to lock up the whole people of a city in their homes that they might be the easier victims of the raiding parties, all public lighting went out. In those hours said the sturdy City Fathers, citizens cannot use the streets, then there is no need to light them. If the British forces, who alone use them, want light, let them bring their own. Thus Curfew came to mean that at 9 p.m. or 10 p.m., or whatever hour the British Military Governors decreed, everybody had to be in his home, and many will remember the universal sound that preceded the great silence : hundreds of hurrying feet upon the pavements as young and old ran for their homes before the hour struck and blackness fell. Trams, buses, bicycles, cars, the movements of pedestrians stopped not gradually, as in a normal city, but suddenly, as if at the turning of a switch. The streets became abandoned canyons of darkness and silence. And unless the moon was up, even the houses were swallowed up in the shadows.

There was a short period of noiselessness, then the sounds began again, but now quite differently, for they were dominated by one throbbing note : that of the running engines of the military patrols nosing their way out of barrack gates, racing through the city streets ; raiding lorries crowded with armed men, moving from house to house, trying to make out the street number some agent had given.

Even to this day you will know many men who lived long under the tension by the way they pause momentarily on a silent night at the sound of a distant lorry, the keen mind of the past trying to perceive where it is going. Then they recollect themselves and smile, and if the others with them are veterans, too, they will laugh. But then it was no laughing matter, and I have seen men—as the lorry came up the street, slowly moving searchlight beams blazing the house fronts into whiteness—I have seen men look for an instant like cornered rats, and it is not a pleasant thing to see. For myself, I could never get used to it, and when a lorry entered the street where I was " on the run," it took me all my time to pretend to my good hosts that it meant nothing to me—until I found they were listening fearfully, too.

This night as I sat by the fire looking at the great headlines which told that Alan Bell's hunt for the Republican funds was over, I heard the lorries coming from Beggars Bush Barracks near by. This would be a busy night. I tried to count them, but the intermingling of the engines baffled me. As I sat, one lorry came over the bridge and passed close to our house. When it had gone on, I found I was

L

on my feet, turning towards that humming engine. This was getting serious ; I decided it was better to sleep.

On the way upstairs, the youngest of my Unionist landladies, Louie Magee, came out to the hall to say good-night to me. She, too, paused and her face paled when the noise of yet another lorry sounded over the bridge. And though she did not share our ideal, in that moment she stood for countless women in Ireland who did. In tens of thousands of homes all over the nation there were, this night, women like that, pale-faced, silent, eyes looking far into space, a hand on the stair-rail, the knuckles white with the intensity of the grip that alone expressed the dread they felt. Ears on the distant sounds, they were ready if the noise grew closer to hurry to the bedrooms. The grown sons would be wakened, helped through some window, and the mother return to stand at the foot of the stairs, waiting for the thunder on the door at which the younger children screamed. For the men there was the bustle and excitement of the escape : for the women the tireless watch, the listening, the fear that it was too late, and then the secret triumph as their menfolk were away before the raiders burst in and sped armed to the empty rooms.

But then we never dwelt on these things. We developed some facility for putting tension aside and living each moment as it came. And so I said " good night " and continued on my way. Before I went into bed at the top of a high house, I looked out over the city. It was not as now, nearby roofs silhouetted against the steady glow of the city lights. It was a vast, dark prairie cut with the moving beams of hundreds of headlights which, as the lorries sloped up the canal bridges, shot in white lines to the sky. There was a mass raid in progress : the jails will be full to-morrow, I thought, as I turned from the dark scene.

Sleep came easily—and so did waking. The room was black as pitch. I heard the swish of a hand feeling for the switch. The walls blazed with light. At the door were half-a-dozen soldiers with fixed bayonets. There was a long silence and at last an officer came into the room :

" David Hogan ? "

" Yes."

There was again a pause and I watched the soldiers, wondering would they come suddenly towards me.

" Get up and dress——we want you."

The officer had spoken the last words Alan Bell had heard. In the chair beside which he was standing there was a Lee Enfield rifle, its parts distributed through the padding. If they searched now—but they did not search. . . .

The soldiers formed around me and at a sharp order we started down the stairs. I noticed that they had a kind of trot on staircases which kept their bearing straight. There was deep silence in the house, except for the trotting feet on the stairs, and thinking of the many other lodgers I tried to make up for it by stepping lightly! The youngest sister was in the hall. Our eyes met for a moment and my thought was that this raid would greatly damage that loyal " digs." As the hall door opened I heard her voice " Take care of him, officer," and his military-manual reply " yes, madam." The square bulk of the covered lorry stood outside. I smiled as I thought of it in this polite terrace where in every drawing-room the portrait of His Majesty King George V had place of honour.

All through the War of Independence humour kept us from taking ourselves too seriously. This night, marching as a prisoner between two files of troops, I had begun to feel of consequence, when an incident brought me back to earth with a bump. For months I had been avoiding a co-worker in the movement, one who was solid and brave, but could not stop talking. When I would see him come down Grafton Street I slipped hurriedly into the next shop or up a side street. I had become so practised at seeing him afar off that I had not fallen into his clutches for months and had thereby saved many an hour. Every week I missed him I counted as victory and realised that now I must dodge him more than ever for he would have that much more to talk about.

As I came to the rear of the lorry somebody shouted " Up." I looked for steps to the cavern above. I need not have minded. Well-practised soldiers' arms tossed me up to khaki arms which received me and pushed me to the far, dark end of the lorry. Out of the blackness rose a figure. " Well, well, David " he said. He was the talker—and he had me now !

Through that freezing night he talked as the lorry prowled from street to street. Here and there the officer would softly call " Halt," and a minute later we would hear the rattle of rifle butts on some door. Long afterwards the marching steps would sound again and our ears soon knew there was no prisoner's step among them. The talker and I would smile at one another in the dark, and he would rattle on once more. Again and again they drew blank. The word had gone out. To these houses some time before Curfew a girl from Cumann na mBan would have cycled and said to the wife or the mother : " He'd better not sleep here to-night." The warned men would vanish, and from raided houses the troops would come, as they came to-night, empty-handed. For the Fahys and the O'Connors and the Mulcahys had gone to some safe house as we called the places unlikely to be raided even on a night like this. " Safe houses " were everywhere in the cities and towns.

To look back on it is to be surprised at the way it became part of our lives : this sudden warning and the swift journey to another address. It was a bother—no more. Sometimes we were lucky, and I was lucky nearly all the time. Never again after that night and what followed was I in their hands for a spell of more than a day.

There was a little house near Upper Gardiner Street which used to take me. Simple folk, proud that they could shelter anybody. Burke was the name, a father, mother, daughters, and a son already in the Fianna. One of the girls was very ill and knew that she was soon to die. She, as so often happens in Ireland, " offered it up " for our protection, and the agony to her became a shield for us. The warmth of their welcome embarrassed me. It was as if I had done them a high honour, God help me. The little house was just outside the walls of a convent garden, and they would watch for us through the night and had an escape ready by a window underneath which the old man, who worked in the boiler-house, had turned the earth to take our jumping feet. The nuns, like ourselves, were marching in spirit with the nation. How many knew of the use to which the little house outside the walls was being put I do not know, but there would be delicacies at our meals whose origin we did know.

It was to that house one night that I brought Cathal Brugha. I had gone to him on some urgent message—I think it was from the Dáil Cabinet. In the surburban street in which he lived I noticed more men than usual sauntering unconcernedly along.

" Cathal," I said, " I wouldn't be surprised if this house were surrounded." Like a flash he was out of the room to stand looking out of the unlighted windows, watching the movements outside, He came back in ten minutes. " You're right. They're at the front and at the back." He paused for an instant in thought. " Have you a gun ? "

" No."

" Get one."

" Do you know a safe house ? "

" Yes, on the North side."

" If I can get out I'll be at Capel Street Bridge at 8.45 on a bicycle." He was there at the hour he said, though how he dodged the two G-men patrolling the lane at the back of his house was a miracle.

As soon as the Curfew came down, they raided his house, and when they found him gone, brought bloodhounds in a vain attempt to trail him.

The Burkes were a proud family that night. They were standing guard over the Minister for Defence of the Republic.

CHAPTER 27

DEATH LOOKS OUT

HAVE you ever seen death looking through a window? Volunteers saw it many times in those years of conflict. They saw it when dark figures in the shadows of an upper room peered out seeking to recognise men for the scaffold. They saw it in the guise of a tall, young detective walking superciliously along a line of newly-captured men.

It is curious how indefinite the memory becomes, not of the things that happened, but of their sequence. Try as I may I cannot put the events of the days immediately after my arrest in the order of their occurrence. But all that happened I can recall, the more easily because it became part of the history of the Four Glorious Years, part even of the history of Ireland, to withstand in the memory all the winnowing of time.

Dawn was tingeing the sky when, with but us two captives, the great lorry shouldered its way to the Bridewell, that place of horror, with its filthy beds and stinking open drains, where men dared not lie down lest they be eaten with vermin.

At first there were but the two of us, but each hour more were added and at last it looked as if the cells could hold no more. But the mass raids continued, and soon whenever a new prisoner arrived we must have looked to the warders like an over-crowded lift. As night fell, flanked on each side by police and troops, movement began again.

None of us knew where we were being taken but anywhere was better than that unclean place where the air became so foul that the cold wind that met us in the gray passages was delicious to breathe and gave back vitality in an instant. Somebody at the head of the procession started to sing:

> " *Left, right—left, right—*
> *Steady ! boys, and step together,*"

and in place of a shuffling swarm of dejected, unwashed men, conscious of lice crawling over them, there we were Volunteers again, filling the concrete alleyways of the Bridewell with the lilt of the song and the sharp beat of the march.

The British, thank God, were very dense. If they knew anything of Ireland they would have seen that they had thrown their net well that night and that in the tune and the swing of this column they had a fine catch of rebels. But they never did see that or much else.

They had three intelligence services—Army, R.I.C. and Auxiliaries —to comb the results of raids, to scrutinise documents, to interrogate prisoners, and yet they found little or nothing. They beat men to wring information from them, which, if they had used their brains, was already in their hands.

To give us comfort when some capture of theirs seemed to endanger many men, there was the classic case of Ernie O'Malley. The Auxiliaries caught him down Kilkenny way, guessed he was somebody important, but couldn't tell who. On him when he was taken were some notes in his indecipherable but distinctive handwriting. Almost simultaneously, the R.I.C. raided Eily McGrane's flat in Dublin, where Ernie had deposited some notebooks for safety. While in the Auxiliary section of the Castle, Ernie was maltreated to wrench from him his identity (he had given the name of Stewart), in the nearby R.I.C. office was proof of who he was, but never the twain did meet! Keys to many a Republican lock fell into enemy hands in those grim years, but they failed in most cases to bring lock and key together. Jealousy made the R.I.C. hide their finds from the Auxiliaries and both hid them from the military. Three blind mice was more than a fairy tale then.

When we swung along the dark alleys of the Bridewell that night, they might have said, " Well, we arrested the right people, anyhow," but they never said it, and because they never really knew whom they had, we beat them in the end.

We were packed into lorries at the gates of the Bridewell and brought to Mountjoy Jail handcuffed. I never got used to that. There was something hateful in these irons. They seemed to mutilate a man, cripple him in a mean way. We laughed at them as we laughed at everything, and we made comical gestures with our bound hands, but it stung to be spancelled thus, and as we were herded through the streets we used to hold up our hands so that the passers-by could see what they had done to us.

The Joy was crowded. Here I was back after a mere five months. But there was a spirit now which made it a different jail, just as the nation itself in that short time had become different too. There was a quicker temper, firmer jaws, less stressing of difficulties. Something had to be done—do it. That was becoming the motto. When I had come in here first there were fewer Republicans and they were scattered among the criminals all over the jail. It took a long time to organise them. Now, as that sudden march from the Bridewell showed, we were organised already.

Few of us knew the others. Dublin companies of the I.R.A. had to fight separately most of the time. It was the rarest thing at that early period for several companies to come together for joint action. Usually we struck at company strength and knew few of the rank and file outside our own. Yet here the bond of membership converted a haphazard bunch of prisoners into comrades at once.

There were dangers in this readiness to accept others as Volunteers, and the British exploited the situation. They started to " arrest," and place amongst us, specially selected agents. These would be the most talkative and fiery of us all advocates of a bloody solution for everything. After the first few sips of this stimulant it became easy to pick them out from the genuine out-and-outers. Their characters betrayed them.

There was at this time, and for the whole War of Independence, a keen sense of personal honour among the Volunteers. The willingness of the men of 1916 to accept death as full reward for their services to Ireland, the noble lives these men had lived, the spiritual quality in their writings, gave to the mass of the people an ideal which they did truly accept and serve. It governed and shaped the daily lives of the Volunteers,

> " *And righteous men must make our land*
> *A Nation Once Again.*"

Every time they sang them they felt these words were true, and, that without personal righteousness, their effort to free Ireland would fail. Unselfishness, readiness for sacrifice, stern self-discipline, were taken for granted. Few of the Volunteers drank liquor to excess, the majority drank none. To swear or use foulness in speech was looked upon as dishonouring the movement. The mystical conflict between good and evil which the Rising had become, projected itself into the years that followed. Deeply influenced, the bulk of the Volunteers acted as Christian patriots in the fullness of both words. Men and women sank all that was personal in a devotion to liberty, which spiritualised the whole nation. Against that bright background, defects in character showed clearly, and the words and actions of these planted agents quickly gave them away. Once recognised, they were so shunned that they became useless, and would be whipped away in the dead of night, perhaps to be put among some other column of prisoners marching into another jail. Taken all round, they did little harm.

The average Volunteer had been lectured often on how informers had frustrated efforts at freedom in the past, how these faithless

men had worked their way to the highest posts in the Fenian Brotherhood and the United Irishmen. The memory of it kept all our tongues
quiet, and with the ordinary seriousness of the movement made it
the least penetrated by informers of any in Irish history. The Castle
was baffled to an extraordinary degree by this muteness, and as
spies, when they were discovered, were promptly executed, many
British agents soon feared to show themselves openly at all. This
it was that led to a drama, now to be played out.

One day prisoners were assembled in two groups of six for baths.
Older hands who knew the way to the bath-house were surprised
that the men were led out past the corner of the main building and
in through a side door. The bath-house could be reached by a journey
through the interior of the jail.

On this day the first twelve men, picked out from particular cells,
myself amongst them, were marched around the corner and were
swinging along when something caused me to look up. I saw in a
window just above my head a sight, the memory of which still chills
me.

There behind the glass peered white-faced men and, I think, one
woman. There was something wolfish in their eagerness as, with
straining eyes, they pressed close to the glass staring down at us.
Peadar Clancy, who was to die in the Castle Yard before the year
was out, saw the sight at the same instant, and, unlike me, perceived
what it was.

" An identification parade," he shouted. " Don't look up ; turn
your faces to the wall and get right under that window."

We crowded in and when he had surveyed the remaining passages,
Peadar ordered us on again.

" Trying to find who executed Alan Bell," he whispered to me
as he strode along hugging the wall.

A day or two later there was a scene more tense, and it had a grim
ending. Nearly a hundred of us were in the exercise ring, some
of the lads playing with a rag ball ; others were at a sparring match.
A crowd at the far side were listening to a discussion of some kind.
At that moment around the corner, near the hospital, swung a company of troops. They were making for our ring.

As they came, first the sparring match stopped, then the game of
football, and a silence spread over us which caused the debate to
end, too. The troops were near the gate leading in to us. The officer
had a list in his hand. All the prisoners had involuntarily turned to
face him.

" Deportations," somebody said. For days there had been a

rumour that we were to be broken into groups and taken to Britain. This was obviously the beginning. The officer was in the ring. He called from the list twenty names. Peadar's was among them; mine was; among others, I think, were Andy McDonnell, Dick Humphreys, Liam Tobin. "Good-bye lads," called Peadar, as with troops on each side, we got the order to march. "Carry on: we'll do the same wherever we go."

"Van Diemen's Land," somebody jested, remembering Mitchel.

As we expected, we were first marched into our wing. We would get our clothes there. As the rhythm of our feet sounded through the empty hall, it emphasised our silence. A lad behind me started the "Soldier's Song," and we marched the rest of the way to the echoes of that song coming back from the high walls around us. Instead of mounting the stairs we swung away from them, then out past the Governor's office.

"They're taking us straight to the boat," somebody said. We came into the open: it was on the way to the wood shed. We were marching down a long open space when the cry of "Halt" brought us to a sudden stop. We were opposite some steps. On the steps were a group of men, their backs to us. Swiftly they turned and swiftly turned back again. Then one of them detached himself from the others and came slowly towards us.

He was a young man: tall and neatly dressed. His face was pale and his eyes were bright. He wore his hat jauntily, and on his lips there was what I then thought was a sneer but which was probably a challenge to us: for while those on the steps were fearful to face us, he knew he was doing a dangerous thing.

He was coming towards us at a leisurely pace and I watched those eyes as they travelled from face to face, a piercing look, almost avaricious. Suddenly it swept in on us that there was to be no deportation, that we had wandered, or blundered, into another identification parade, and that those on the steps were G-men, as this young man was; they reluctant, he eager.

All this which takes so long to write happened in not much more than a minute or two. It was Peadar Clancy's voice which again broke the spell. He had recognised that young detective. He called out: "Ah, Kells, so this is the work you're on. Look out," and an instant later: "Volunteers—about turn."

With a clatter of boots that jaunty G-man had but a long line of backs to gaze on. An effort to force us round led to some scuffling and tempers were rising, when it all ceased at some order we had not heard, and when we turned to march back the G-men were gone.

The hunger-strike came. It reached its crisis, and one day towards the end I was at a council-of-war in Peadar Clancy's cell, sitting as we always did on the low bed-board. Without a word he passed a letter to me. On it in a bold, round script I knew well, were the words :

"I am going to Kells to-morrow."

It was signed " M. C."

That was on a Monday. Kells was shot dead on Tuesday morning.

CHAPTER 28

FIRES IN THE NIGHT

THE first two weeks of April, 1920, were to be among the most notable days of the struggle.

Easter was early that year, 4th April was Easter Sunday. Every year since the Rising, the British had argued in the same way. There had been a Rising in Dublin on Easter Monday, 1916, they said. Therefore, it was likely that the Irish would rise again on Easter Monday. So over from Britain and into the cities reinforcements poured : barbed wire barricades were erected around Dublin. Troops fully armed stood ready to repulse " the hill tribes " if they tried to capture the Capital. The Irish wouldn't take the Castle by surprise this year.

The Irish smiled and took the Castle completely by surprise. On Easter Saturday night, before Curfew fell, little groups of men called, unnoticed, at the British tax collectors' offices everywhere. They were extremely polite, but determined. When they had been given the keys, they gathered together all the tax books and official documents of every kind and, having seen to the safety of any families in the house, they set the offices alight.

As promptly as these polite young men came, they went away. Each tax collector thought he had been the only victim and excitedly tried to inform headquarters. He found that scores of others were attempting the same thing : they had all been burnt out.

Not in Dublin only, but in every town from Belfast to Cork at the same hour the Volunteers had struck. Nearly a hundred tax offices were gutted that night. In the country, other buildings blazed : the hundreds of barracks which the R.I.C. abandoned when they were driven into the larger towns.

The R.I.C. were already being reinforced from England—the first of these English " recruits " had landed on 25th March, who, collectively, were to be known as the Black-and-Tans—and soon the British would try to come out again from the towns and re-occupy those evacuated buildings. That night the Volunteers decided that they would never come out. And as the smoke billowed up in the cities from the tax offices, great columns of it filled the country skies from hundreds of these empty buildings. It was a national operation, planned with great care and carried out simultaneously in every one of the 32 counties. Not a Castle agent had heard a whisper of it. This time there were no informers to run to the British with word of what was to happen. They filled up the towns and cities with troops to prevent the Volunteers rising on Easter Monday, but the Volunteers on Easter Saturday crippled their tax system and left a chain of charred barracks through Ireland to welcome a newcomer. The Press, in bold headlines, described his coming as " Military Dictator Appointed"—it was General Sir Nevil Macready, the new Commander-in-Chief. The bonfires were suitably for him. A hunger-strike would welcome him, too.

When the strike in October, 1919, ended, a face-saving pretence was made by the British that men were not being set free but merely let out on parole. As they shuffled down the iron stairs or were carried in stretchers out of the jail, all prisoners whose sentences had not been completed, had pressed into their hands a typewritten document which most of them read for the first time after a few days in hospital.

It was a revival of the " Cat and Mouse " Act, that brilliantly-named measure passed in 1913 to deal with suffragettes. The purpose of the Act was to set a dying prisoner free that by recovering he might become fit for rearrest and a new ordeal. I saw Maurice Crowe's copy, recently, and it read :

" PRISONERS (TEMPORARY DISCHARGE FOR ILL-HEALTH) ACT, 1913

NOTICE TO BE GIVEN TO PRISONERS

Maurice Crowe is this day discharged from Mountjoy Prison in pursuance of Lord Lieutenant's Order of 16th October, 1919, subject to the following conditions :

1. *The prisoner shall if this period of temporary discharge be not extended. return to above-mentioned prison on the 16th day of December, 1919.*
2. *The period of temporary discharge granted by this order may, if the Lord Lieutenant thinks fit, be extended.*
3. *The prisoner shall abstain from any violation of the law.*

If he fails to comply with any of the foregoing conditions the prisoner is liable to be arrested and taken back to prison. While he is at large under this order the currency of his sentence is suspended."

When the prisoners failed to return on 16th December, the hunt began for them again, and when I reached the Joy in the last days of March, there were in A wing many re-arrested men serving past sentences. In B Wing, where we were placed, the prisoners had not been charged with any offence, and it was this fact which at the end, brought ruin on the Castle plans. A prisoners' council had been formed among the sentenced men : Christy Lucey, of Cork ; Éamon Malone, of Athy ; and J. B. O'Driscoll, of Skibbereen, were the leaders under Maurice Crowe, Micky Carolan acting as adjutant. In our wing, the triumvirate was Tom Hunter, Peadar Clancy and myself.

In what, to the warders, seemed shouted greetings in Gaelic, between the A and B exercise rings, it was decided that the Governor be notified that unless we were given the status of war-prisoners, the jail would hunger-strike on Easter Monday, 5th April. When the day came there was a scene in our exercise ring which, for the emotion it stirred in us, must still haunt those high, cold buildings which gathered around us like a giant screen to shut out all else but our servitude.

The Governor had refused. Very well then. This day the strike would begin that must break open the iron cage in which we were crowded, or the cage would circle us for ever. Many felt that day as the first Volunteers felt at the Rotunda seven years before. In that round building, so close to Parnell's granite, Pearse and the others had laid the foundations of what we now were doing, and many who enrolled then felt that the step they were taking was one in which their lives were forfeit. So we felt now.

As it would be a fight needing every ounce of strength a man could give, we decided that men in delicate health would not be allowed to join the strike. I remember when we tried to order off Gerard Crofts, how angry he was, he who in many a country hall had sung the songs of challenge and now was paying for it by imprisonment. He refused to obey, and went through the strike with us. A few others we more successfully warned off.

To the rest we explained they were free to join or not, and if they did not join they would be accounted no less in our eyes. But if they did join they would be asked to take the most binding pledge—each to the other—never to yield. By these steps we hoped to ensure there would be no turning back and so it proved. Not one fell by the wayside.

When Peadar Clancy called quietly to us on that Easter Monday morning : " Now, lads," it is true that for an instant our hearts sank at the moment's coming ; but we gathered around him eagerly. Fifty or sixty men and youths then repeated slowly the words that were strength to us through many a dark night that followed :

> " *I pledge myself to the honour of Ireland and to the lives of my comrades not to eat food or drink anything except water, until all here have been given prisoner-of-war treatment or are released.*"

The circumstances in which that pledge was spoken must have been rare even among insurgent peoples. When we had come into the jail a week before each man found hanging over the table from which he ate his food, a notice:

"NOTICE"

"All persons committed to prison are informed that they will not be able by wilful injury to their bodily health, caused by refusal of food or in any other way, to procure their release before their discharge in the due course of law."

That notice was for the British Government, a burning of the boats. There would be no releases, not even a "Cat and Mouse" this time. They would stand and fight what they regarded as this mean weapon of the fast. That was our decision, too: we also would fight, putting our fast against all their power.

If they were determined, so were we. They could raid and cram the jails but we could walk through the nation and burn a hundred of their tax-offices, two hundred of their barracks. The flames would light up their silly barricades and silhouette their foolishness for the world to see. They on their part had decided in that same flame and smoke that there was only one way of meeting the rebels: break them. They had sent a military Dictator to do just that.

So the stage was set for the drama. The prisoners said to the Castle, we shall not eat again as prisoners: and the Castle said to the prisoners, either eat or die, for you will never force your way out. It was the elemental conflict.

Outside the cage as the pledge was being spoken were a circle of British troops. I marvelled at their immobility. If they listened to the words so distinctly spoken, how could they stand there without giving a sign? Did they not know that this must be the end, either for them or for us? Beyond them were the offices, where Governor Munro was sitting—a little dried man in perpetual agony at having prisoners who were not lags or pickpockets but men who would take foolish pledges and make his job more bothersome than ever!

That evening we marched gaily back to our cells, where we had earlier refused the dinners that were served to us. In the exercise ring we already felt the tremors of what was coming, but we who were old stagers, had prepared the others. The headaches meant nothing; the blinding weaknesses; the collapse, the gnawing emptiness. But we could not, without frightening them too much, speak so freely of the minds that would conjure up every terror, the lack of sleep, the darkness peopled by phantoms, the mounting temperature, the delirium, the sudden panic in which the bravest resolution would melt away and all one's being clamour for food. How could we explain to them that, after three or four days, they would lie abed with night and day one interminable twilight, with no borders and no beginning or end, and that the fast might go on for weeks as men slowly shrank away. All we said to them was that they must not expect an easy victory and that it wasn't something one could muster all one's courage to meet, such as a swift march to the gallows, or the moments waiting before a firing squad. It would go on for some time, was the most we said.

And it did go on. At first we were all handcuffed because we had to smash open our lamp holes and break the tough glass out of our windows, so that we could shout orders or encouragement to one another or to our other comrades in A Wing or C. At a time like this, when it was vital for the British to win, men must not be left completely alone. They would be told their comrades were eating, that the leaders were getting food while the duped rank and file had to die. They would be given names and dates and times so that lonely men might in anger give way, and that would be the beginning of the end. So we had to make it possible to call down the long, dark passages at night and give fortitude to any man who was shaken. But we had no wish that those who had never endured a hunger-strike should go through their first ordeal in irons, and after that first smash we did no further wrecking.

Prisons have moods like people, and wherever men be, however carefully isolated, these moods seem to seep through the walls and become part of the prisoners' own thinking. That happened now. Against all commonsense, an optimism came into the Joy towards the end of the first week. It was an overwhelming certainly of victory. Peadar Clancy felt it; I did also. Nobody encouraged it, but it spread through the jail like an incense. It filled the men's minds : they sang with it in their cells. What it was based on nobody knew, but we became convinced we'd be out before the jail closed down that Saturday night. The fact that we in B Wing were untried, seemed to set this universal feeling on solid ground. They daren't let men die against whom they could not even frame a charge.

Everything stressed the possibility of a swift ending. So many had already collapsed; the nation was becoming so moved at the grim tales coming out of the prison. The British and Continental Press had sent representatives to Dublin to watch this protest of men unjustly held—the weight of all that opinion would be too heavy for the stout walls of the Castle. It was not that we consciously convinced ourselves of this ; we felt it so strongly that it went unquestioned.

And when Mountjoy Jail closed down for the night that Saturday evening, the turning of locks sounded like the closing of a funeral vault, and the footfalls of the key-bearers dying away in the distance like the going of Hope itself. A silence came into the prison and spread from cell to cell until men, who on other nights as dusk changed into dark, came to their lamp-holes with a song or a shouted jest, remained in the cell's furthest shadows, fighting it out.

CHAPTER 29

NOISE IN THE CHAPEL

THERE were never shadows as deep as those in the B Wing of
Mountjoy Jail on that evening. The short, flat tongue of bluish
flame flickered from the gas jets into space, for there were no
incandescent mantles. These rare lights burned in a building filled
with a soft, velvety blackness, for the glass roof which let in the
daylight now reflected only the far, dark sky. There were no windows
to catch a street lamp or to let even the headlights of a car break the
darkness for a moment.

Normally we could never look into the vault which the wing
became at night. But now, with our lamp brackets out, each prisoner
could see the cell-doors opposite and the narrow passages outside.
So slender was the light that warders could pass our doors without
being seen except by the reflection of a distant gas jet on their polished
buttons. That darkness matched our hearts, and it was this con-
cordance of spirit and fact that gave Easter Saturday night, 1920,
an eeriness which even now—how many years afterwards?—can
be remembered only with a holding of the breath.

The sudden change from high hope to hopelessness was too
much for men who had never been on hunger-strike before. Men
who for the last six days had fought this thing on their feet now
went down like ninepins. We soon noticed that when one after
another the prisoners rang their alarm bells, the warders, who had
evidently been kept back in case this happened, came running,
noiselessly running in their night shoes.

Along the passage just outside my door and on the corridor on
the other side I saw, all through that long night, a procession of
grotesques. First the bell would sound, and a few moments later
flitting figures would hurry across my vision. Soon they would
come back, carrying the prisoner, whose head would loll from side
to side as the warders walked joltingly, due to the weight and the
narrow passages. Now and again the flickering light would shine
for an instant on the upturned face, and the gaunt skeleton lines
would make me grip the edge of the lamp-bracket.

I knew many of these men personally, and in some cases their
families : we who had been through it knew how terrifying a first
hunger-strike can be, and I felt as every leader of prisoners feels

at such a time, that we should not have declared this strike, that ordinary men's strength is not equal to what this asks of them.

Despite the trust we had in them as Volunteers, the haunting fear never left us that some would break under the strain. One surrender we knew, might mean the death of every one of us. That was the temper of the Castle just then. Our sole hope was to hold together through no matter what came. This need to forestall a yielding made it necessary for us to bring friendly warders into the conspiracy, and let it be said in tribute to them that they, too, ran this hunger-strike. They would come to us and say that this lad or that needed heartening. And secretly they would move back the bolts, one of them keeping watch into the circle lest the Governor appear. They would lead us to the troubled man's cell. In the scant light we would talk earnestly by that bedside to this comrade who had doubted if he could spend another night with his own wild thoughts, death at his elbow and around him in thought his wife and children, his mother and sisters.

These hunger-strikers were ordinary citizens who kept their homes by their weekly earnings. It was a grim thing for them to die with a family or loved ones unprovided for. They had joined the Volunteers for fighting: this was a manner of protest more suited to quieter men.

Perhaps I exaggerate it in recollection, but many times we paid those secret visits, and when dawn made the glass roof show itself faintly, we thanked God that another day had safely come. The mere brightening of the sky was indescribable relief.

Just at that dark hour the Castle did the one thing that could give us back the spirit of the first day. It was Sunday morning. The chapel in Mountjoy Jail was a large room on the second landing, approached from all the wings through special gates. Wainscotted walls and the many lights made it warm in colour and in fact. The altar standing out whitely against the dark shining wood seemed to draw all the light to it.

What was strangest about this chapel was the way the warders were placed. They knelt and sat on high seats which jutted up from the floor like turrets above a camp. To come from the shadowy landing and see these warders kneeling above the humped shoulders of lines of grey-clothed civil prisoners was to get the impression of a cowering people with the knout-men ready to strike.

On this Low Sunday, as we listened to the Last Gospel, we heard dully penetrating the double doors many muffled echoes. We knew these noises could only have reached us if there had been a tornado of sound. We glanced at one another, and then a look of triumph swept along our bench. Those few of us who had been able to shuffle to Mass, all read the same meaning into that sound.

The strike was won! The surging optimism of yesterday was justified after all. They had merely held us for the night in the hope that we might break. Now the men still in the cells were being let out. We thought we could hear in the rumble that came into us the sharp sound of the drawn bolts. Everyone had heard it: the warders, though in their high seats they faced the altar, had their heads leaning towards the sounds. The civil prisoners were openly whispering and nudging, and no rebuke came from above them. At last the Gospel was over, and some of the men were listening so intently that they remained standing. In the silence before the three Hail Marys we thought we heard cheering. We blessed ourselves and turned quickly to the door, almost shouting at the warder for being so long in opening it. At last he threw it back, and into the church flooded a storm of shouts and crashing doors and the sounds of warders running everywhere, now in their heavy boots. As we poured out we heard the Governor in the circle calling up: "Take it out: take it out."

It was *not* release. As it happened it was almost as great. When he thought he had the most weakened men alone, separated from those of us able to go to Mass, the Governor had placed food in every cell, and locked the men up with it.

The sequel must have astonished him. The meanness of the trick gave back those men their strength. In a few cases, when it was seen early enough what was afoot, there was a struggle with the warder. In the rest the food was hurled out through the broken lamp-holes, making puddles of porridge and milk all along the corridor, men yelling with an angry zest as they spooned it out, and it flopped like cow-dung on the stone floor. The jail by that one act was transmuted. From that instant to the end, something of that angry strength remained.

After a little while the singing began again, and they shouted jests from cell to cell. Prison regulations gave way, too. By medical orders, all cell doors were to be kept permanently open, so that collapsing men might be reached more quickly. Now when a man went under, a medical team came to bring him tenderly to hospital. The hospital, too, had become a place of chaos with half-conscious patients crowding every passage, refusing to eat. And the doctors stood by thinking of Tom Ashe, and wondering why none of these men were dead.

Some time after the pouring out of the porridge, the Governor came to the landing outside our cell-door with a long official envelope in his hand, and as he fixed his monocle to read, Peadar Clancy, Tom Hunter and myself had to make up for our weakness by gripping the wire-grating put there to prevent suicide among the ordinary prisoners, who might jump over into the lower wing. Looking at notes on the envelope (the message had, it seemed, been 'phoned to him), the Governor told us he had " good news." Our hearts leaped, but by now we were well-trained at wearing masks. It was well we were. His " good news " was that eight of us were to be deported to Wormwood Scrubbs prison : us three amongst them. We would be given full political treatment there. The strike, of course, must be called off. We waited for more, for word of the release of the other men. There was no more. The Governor put down his envelope and looked at us through his monocle, appealingly.

In reply, Peadar spoke with stinging contempt, hot, bitter words. Staring at him, the Governor's mouth opened and the eye-glass fell to the end of its long black cord. The torrent of Peadar's anger sounded along the silent corridor, engulfing everything, and the little crumpled man waited till the end, 'till the searing reference to his trick with the food. Then he turned, and without a word, hurried back the way he had come. Peadar called out to that retreating figure : " Tell them—all or none." But to us he whispered : " They're beginning to break."

We decided to draft an official reply, for we knew now this Governor would never understand how final our rejection was. He had lived his life ordering criminals about, reprimanding them, giving stern judgments against them, like a god. He still thought that somehow we would prove like them, and that an offer of preferential treatment to the leaders would get them to desert their comrades. Before the reply was sent, we went on a pilgrimage through the cells so that we could truly say we spoke for all the men. It was a painful journey.

A reaction had set in from the wild excitement of the morning, and men were lying on their pallets exhausted, making there a picture as out of some book of nightmares : the bright, sunken eyes ; the skin drawn tightly over the bones of the grey faces ; the moist, limp hands ; the thin necks ; and everywhere that smell like ether, which somebody told me was the body consuming its own tissues. When we came into some of the cells, the men, thinking that this was at last the announcement of release, sat up to relish the moment to the full. As we read, they eased themselves back and listened with closed eyes, nodding their assent at the end. One man, with a young family, said : " So that's their offer after seven days ; call me—if you can—when you get another," and he pulled the clothes over his head. But every man agreed that that must be the reply; the agreement was in most cases not enthusiastic or eager; but it was grim and deep.

Of the young lads amongst us who were still out of hospital, the youngest was Gabriel McGrath, seventeen. He was one of three brothers on strike, and he met our visit almost with a whoop. It was then that the phrase was in vogue: " That's the stuff to give the troops," and Gay said it with gleeful fervour when the reading was finished.

The Northerns, as usual, were sparing in their words, but the words were strong. This strike was the nation in revolt; every province was there. The accents of the West and the South puzzled the Dublin men, and the Northern accent puzzled the rest. There were many men from Newry. They came in a body one morning into the exercise ring, two days after the strike had begun, fresh and rosy from the open air and good eating. Peadar went towards them: " Boys," he began—

" Already on it," came the sturdy Northern reply; " we haven't eaten since we came in." And there was much hand-shaking. Now they responded to the rejection of the offer with the same prompt, terse speech.

We asked to see the Governor; he came hurriedly, thinking, perhaps, that we had changed our minds. " That's our answer," Peadar said, passing the paper to him. As he was searching for his monocle, we went back to our cells. It was our turn now, and we threw ourselves on our mattresses overcome with the horror of that procession through the cells. It was a long time before I took my head out of my hands.

But there was another procession under way—the procession of a people. The strike in Mountjoy had somehow, but perfectly, interpreted the spirit of the nation. The hundred fasting men became Ireland. The stories of exhaustion and collapse, of manacling and defiance were read in every home with fervent understanding. The union between people and prison was complete. And the people began to march.

First it was to the churches; all day long the file was unbroken of men, women and children paying visits for " the men." From the altars, Masses were offered that their lives might not be asked of them. Then, as the strike went on and the British Government made clear its will that the men must yield or die, the faces of the people turned to the jail itself, and there began that exaltation in which danger and fear had no part. The officials, looking out from the prison, saw a handful of watchers the first day, grow a little the second and the third, then increase noticeably on the fourth, while, on the fifth, all day long they came.

And on this Sunday, while we passed from cell to cell, they gathered from every part of the country, and crowded around that jail in one vast concourse. They filled the lanes and the streets, they covered the pavements with their comings and their goings. Nobody organised them; they just came.

As the multitude grew, the Castle decided to show what the Irish people were up against this time, and along the top of the high walls of the prison they mounted their machine-guns, and at the base of the walls they placed their tanks; and they trained their guns upon the people. But the people came and came, and they pressed up to the very mouths of those guns that they might be nearer to the doomed men inside, and by their prayers and their songs, might let them know that they were greatly loved.

CHAPTER 30

COME QUICKLY

IN those days of the great strike, stratagem was pitted against stratagem. The Castle was fighting with all its subtlety for a break among the prisoners. Had it come, had the men, or even a few of them, given way, it would have been a defeat that must have shaken the independence movement to its roots.

That was what inspired our enemies. What inspired us was that defeat for the Castle must have repercussions into all the subdivisions of that great machine of oppression. The stakes were high, and each contestant tried to anticipate the moves of the other; but the move now made against us was not anticipated by anybody.

Far and wide throughout the nation, the Castle sent frightening telegrams. The relatives were asked to come quickly as their men-folk were dying. From all over Ireland, fathers and mothers, brothers and sisters set out on a journey whose end terrified them.

What they feared most had now come. The Government itself had announced the imminence of death, not impersonally, as that some of the prisoners might die, but that " your son," " your brother," " your husband " was dying, come quickly.

That Sunday afternoon there began a procession that was to go on for three days. It was, perhaps, the most poignant that Mountjoy had yet seen. Through the great crowds outside the fathers and mothers pressed. Passing the Lewis guns at the street corners, they reached the cordons of helmeted troops. They passed on beside the tanks, from whose turrets some perky Cockney looked down at them. They came beneath the high wall, and there, cutting the sky over their heads, were the machine-gunners and their weapons. Then into the forbidding jail; the warders' keys jangling before them, iron gates opening and shutting with that noise so shattering for strained nerves. They entered the long, dark, silent wing with the all-pervading smell of the disintegration of the human body. They were led up the iron stairway, past open cell-doors, and if they glanced in, they saw a grey skull-like head on a frowsy pillow, or caught bright, tense eyes staring at them from the dimness. What could they do when they reached the cell of him for whom they searched so fearfully but break down ?

That was the hope behind this move; the chain of circumstances, begun by the telegram, was meant to end with fathers and mothers urging their sons to cease this horrible protest. And how, in fact, did it end?

Those parents travelled from far places in Ireland, in trains in which the talk was of the heroism of their sons. They arrived in a Dublin for which this was the greatest spiritual experience since the Rising. They found the people in endless procession to the churches, and if they disclosed that they were parents of men in jail, they were shown preference and honour; people were brought forward to meet them, children to shake their hands. When they set out on that part of the journey they shrank from most, they found all Dublin moving towards the jail with them, in the roads, along the pavements. Long before they reached the prison, they heard the singing; a few moments later, as they turned into the space outside the jail, there was a multitude answering, with deep-voiced fervour, some friar giving out the Rosary. A passage was made respectfully for them, the pressing crowds drawing aside as they came. And many a woman's voice blessed them, and many a man's voice called on them to strengthen their sons.

In contrast with the intimate affection of the people was the cold brutality of the tanks, the machine-guns, the khaki cordons topped with the white bayonets. The clanging gates, the dark passages, the unnatural quiet behind those rows of open doors gave them the measure of what was being endured, and even here they felt the respect of the nation, for the warders showed them deference, too. And just at that moment, when they perceived most clearly the nature of this struggle, there was the changed, haggard son himself looking at them from the floor. There were a few who broke down, but many who remembered those voices calling out to them from the crowd, and who did strengthen their sons.

All that Sunday afternoon the relatives came. The jail took on the air of a museum as warders with, as it were, conducted parties, filled the narrow passages with the pattering of feet as they went from cell to cell to see the exhibits. None of us resented it now; it could serve only to weaken them and strengthen us.

To my cell came my father, who had already lost one son in the struggle. Convinced we were dying, he came that long journey hiding as best he could his dread, as he hid it now, standing there above me in the cell with bantering words. To him it was an accepted thing that the fight must go on, without any wavering; but he knew, he need not speak of that. My brothers came also, one on the eve of ordination. Younger, they saw only the glorious defiance in it all. Erskine Childers came and sat at the end of my bed, saying little; whilst others, one an Australian priest, talked. I knew that all Erskine's energy, and his wife's, was being spent for us, but he did not mention that. He spoke for a moment on how strong a people can be who have no other strength but their will. To the young Australian, what was happening was merely out of its epoch, an incident from early Christian times, a scene in the catacombs. It was the hope of the world that it could happen at all.

As each group left the prison, the great crowd cheered them and called out their questions affectionately: " Is he all right, ma'am ? " " Hope you told him we're all praying for him, sir ? " Some came from the prison profoundly moved. No doubt, for the same purpose of unsettling the men, they had admitted many clergy. The result cannot have pleased them. The Bishop of Killaloe, Dr. Fogarty, said to the pressmen who gathered around him at the gate :

" It affected me profoundly . . . to look upon them stretched exhausted, calmly awaiting death should that be necessary for the sake of principle. They are absolutely inflexible in their resolution to die rather than submit to what they regard as the terrible outrage on common humanity and justice."

And with a gift for summary, he added :

" I doubt if there is a country in the world where you could have so much real heroism on the one hand and cruelty on the other."

Father Albert, the Capuchin, who had seen the men of 1916 die, came from the prison horrified.

" The scenes inside the prison are not good for one to witness," he said. " Wives saw their husbands, and mothers their sons, at death's door. The unflinching men lay cold on the mattresses on the floor. The clammy feel of their hands suggested something terrible, but the spirit to go on to the end remained the same."

Not only were these visitors to Mountjoy deeply moved. Over the prison doctors came a complete change. The chief medical officer of the prison service, Dr. McCormack, came into my cell that Monday morning.

" I can't keep some of your men alive another day," he said sharply to me. " What are you going to do about it ? "

" Nothing, doctor."

" You won't be the first to die ; it is easy for you to be strong."

" We are all ready to be the first, doctor."

His sharpness left him, and he said almost despairingly : " They won't give you what you want ; is there nothing even a little less that would make it easy for them ? "

" Nothing, doctor."

" We are fighting for release and have recommended it officially, but they have brushed it aside. Is there no stimulant the men might take while some settlement is being reached ? "

" No stimulant, doctor."

He was not long gone when the Governor came quietly in. He believed, he said, he could get his offer of yesterday extended. Twenty men would be deported to England and there given political status and meanwhile they would get " ameliorative treatment." Wouldn't even these twenty men—— ?

I stopped him by saying : " Mr. Clancy answered that yesterday," and remembering that scorching answer, he threw up his hands.

The head prison chaplain came a little afterwards and said that the Under-Secretary at the Castle was working might and main to get a settlement. If he had time he thought he could succeed.

" According to the doctors, he hasn't much time," I said, and said no more.

When he had gone, I went to see Peadar Clancy : " Boy, oh boy," he said : " Governor, head prison doctor, head prison chaplain. We're not shaken half as much as they are. See this."

He passed me a cutting, in which the Chairman of the Visiting Justices had his say. He was an old opponent of Sinn Féin, and went up as candidate in the 1918 election against us. He had been faithful to the régime all through the horrors since. Now he had wired Lord French :

" As Chairman of the Visiting Justices, I visited Mountjoy Prison to-day and found several of the men on hunger-strike in an almost dying condition. I beseech your Excellency to exercise your clemency and powers to save the lives of these men by granting them political treatment. Another day's delay may cause an appalling tragedy."

Coldly, almost tauntingly, came back the reply :

" His Excellency the Lord Lieutenant does not propose to modify the rules in the direction you suggest. All the prisoners on hunger-strike have been forewarned as to the consequences of perseverance in their conduct."

Visiting Justice Clarke's answer to this was simple. He sent in his resignation. He told the press :

" No man with a drop of Irish blood in his body could but resent it."

That was it. The sides had been taken, and all who had ever thought of Ireland as their nation, forgot all else now except that they and the prisoners were of one people. The kinship of nationality had over-leaped all barriers, and the resignations began.

But the Castle hardened its heart. It decided that the fight with Sinn Féin must come to its crisis now, and that the people must know there would be no compromise. New orders went out, and the military began to erect barbed wire entanglements around Mountjoy. They were expecting the first death at any moment, and feared that an angry people might tear the jail open with its bare hands. They cleared whole streets in its vicinity. They stationed machine-gun nests far out from the jail, and every gun had its cartridge belt inserted for instant use. Over the city in the daytime, aeroplanes watched every move of the citizens. At night, searchlights swung ceaselessly, lest the mass attack develop in the darkness. This time there would be no yielding.

Then an answering movement began among the people. The Workers took a hand. It started in the most nationally-conscious sections : the railwaymen, the dockers, the grocers' curates. Without warning, a thousand workers at Broadstone Railway Station downed tools, and leaving the outbound trains standing in the station, they went in a body to Mountjoy. From Inchicore the workers at the railway shops set out in a similar procession. Soon the processions became marches. Banners and bands and tricolours brought brightness and music to those striding columns.

This was the new Easter Rising that the British so dreaded and had now created ; the people were taking to the streets to show that tyranny would not be allowed to have its own way. The strike of a hundred men had become a city, a nation in revolt.

On to the Jail these workers marched, and there the crowds opened for them, and through the multitude they went, their banners flowing like a bright stream, right up to the cordons of troops. It was democracy against an army of occupation, the people against the powerful. Into the prison came the sounds of the singing of that vast crowd, songs of revolution, songs of patriotism. We heard them in our cells. The evening had come. The jail was still. The bustle of that strange day, with peering, frightened faces, was over. The prison officials, with their half-offers and their pleadings, were gone. Facing another night of fear, the fasting men heard far out from the prison, but clear from the stillness within, the voices of the singers, and sensed the fervour of their singing.

A sudden rattle of sound, and a friendly warder came hurrying along our passage. He came to where Peadar Clancy, Tom Hunter and I were reviewing the day. He pressed an evening paper into Peadar's hands.

In it was the proclamation of the General Strike.

CHAPTER 31

THE GENERAL STRIKE

BEFORE the warder came running, there had been rumours that the workers were coming out; not a group here or there in individual protest, not in single marches through one city, but all workers, everywhere.

We did not easily allow ourselves to believe it. The songs outside the jail, the words of the visitors, did give us inkling how this protest had grown. It had spread to other jails; it had gone across the sea to Wormwood Scrubbs; the Corporations and Councils in town and country had pledged themselves to us; but the rumour of a general strike surprised us. It was so ultimate a decision. It could then end only as national defeat or, a people'a victory; a triumph that would outspan anything that was local or sectional.

The scene in Peadar Clancy's cell, after the evening paper had been pressed into his hand, remains indelible. Peadar, wrapping his overcoat around him, stood up and moved directly under the blue flame of the gas-jet. He stood close to one of the lintels of the door, now shut. The light of the gas-tongue which, because of his closeness to it, threw great shadows over us seated on the floor below him and over the walls of the narrow space closing us in, shone brightly on the forehead and the upper face.

The bones, pressing through the drawn skin, the sunken eyes, gave, for the first few moments, the complete illusion of a skull—the black shadows making the eye-sockets appear empty, the hollows below the cheek bones deepened into ebony.

Peadar was more worn than most of us, for his energy, his eagerness, had made it impossible for him to rest. The sense of fighting, of having his opponents in a trap, was elixir to him, and though he was physically wasted, his stance, and the voice in which, without any preliminaries, he began to read, had the freshness of a boy's. After a few sentences, it is true, he had to rest against the door frame, but the voice did not change.

The words were brave words:

" To the Workers of Ireland:

" You are called upon to act swiftly and suddenly to save a hundred dauntless men. At this hour, their lives are hanging by a thread in a Bastille. These men—for the greater part our fellow workers and comrades in our Trades Unions—have been forcibly taken from their homes and their families and imprisoned without charge, or, if charged, tried under exceptional laws for alleged offences of a political character, in outrageous defiance of every canon of justice.

" They are suspected of loving Ireland and hating her oppressors—a heinous crime in the sight of tyrants, but one of which hundreds of thousands of Irish working men and women proudly acclaim their guilt.

" No one, therefore, is guaranteed his freedom ; no one dare be confident that he or she is safe from molestation, or can rely upon protection by law or justice.

" Our fellow workers now in Mountjoy, Wormwood Scrubbs and other prisons have adopted the only method remaining to them against the injustice of their imprisonment and against being treated as criminals. They have for eight days been on hunger-strike. To-day, though they are on the point of death, their titled jailers venomously shriek ' Let them die.'

" We, workers, dare not allow this tragedy to come to pass. Verbal protests are vain. Resolutions, votes, constitutional practices, have been worn to shreds. They are cast aside as useless.

" As trade unionists we have only one weapon left—a general strike—a weapon that may be used but seldom, and only in times of supreme crisis. Such an occasion has now arisen. The call is urgent. There is no time to gather your delegates into conference.

" Therefore, we, the undersigned, on behalf of the National Executive, hereby call for a general stoppage of all work throughout the country to-morrow, Tuesday, April 13th (with the exception of those employed on newspapers, telegraph service, baking of bread and essential food distribution, humanitarian services, and necessary work among horses and cattle), in protest against the barbarous treatment of the political prisoners, and demanding their release.

" Workers : Let your response to this sudden call be so unanimous as will impress the peoples of other lands with your determination to put an end to tyranny and oppression.

" Irish workers, in the name of humanity, give a lead in this, as you did in your fight against Conscription.

" Signed on behalf of the National Executive,

" 32 Lower Abbey   THOMAS FARREN, Chairman.
    Street, Dublin.   THOMAS JOHNSON, Acting Sec.
" April 12th, 1920."

When he had stopped reading, we rose and stood quiet for several minutes thinking it all out. It was he who broke the silence.

" That must be read to all the lads," he said triumphantly. How it was read to the men, I cannot now recall, but I think it must have been by one of us standing outside his cell speaking the tense words to the long rows of open doors, black openings in the greyness, now that evening had fallen. Afterwards the gas in the cells was lit, and individual men borrowed that paper until it was almost worn away by eager handling.

There was much else the prisoners had a chance of reading in those last days. With visitors, had come letters and papers. The inquest on Tomás MacCurtáin was being fully reported. Inexorably the evidence was being pieced together that pointed straight at the Crown forces. During Curfew, night workers had seen the assassins come from King Street Barracks into the empty streets ; later, others saw them stealing back and being admitted cautiously ; a passer-by heard one R.I.C. group tell another that they were going to " kill Curtin " ; a doctor had watched them taking the road to the Lord Mayor's home ; a night watchman had observed them pass close to the house unchallenged by the night-patrols, who obviously knew them for comrades ; a little later a postman heard one of them boast of the killing to another constable. An R.I.C. button was found on the landing where the Lord Mayor was done to death ; District Inspector Swanzy failed to produce records of the movements of his police " absent with arms " ; most damning of all, the officers of the barracks failed to record the murder, or even to send out investigating parties. The chain of evidence closed around the Castle's neck, establishing for all Ireland that it was a criminal régime, who had crimeless ones now fighting for life on a hundred prison pallets.

And from those worn papers we learned, too, that the British King's Viceroy had stepped on to the stage in a part that did him no honour. A *Daily Express* man asked to see Lord French. To his surprise, he was granted an interview immediately. He was brought to the Viceregal Lodge, and there the Viceroy told him many things : that " the best brains in Ireland are behind Sinn Féin " ; that the Volunteers, far from being a " murder gang," were a properly constituted army, " organised in regiments and brigades, led by disciplined officers " ; that Dublin Castle was inefficient, but that, nevertheless, he would break the rebels. He added that the Government had evidence that it was the Republicans who had murdered MacCurtain. Promptly, the Cork Coroners' Court ordered Lord French to appear before it and bring that evidence. The Viceroy replied, issuing a denial that he had given any interview or seen any *Daily Express* or other pressman.

The *Daily Express*, in its next issue, published not only the reassertion that everything attributed to Lord French had been spoken by him to their correspondent, but that Lord French had said many other indiscreet things which the *Daily Express* itself censored in the public interest. The Viceroy maintained an embarrassed silence, and every Irishman knew that the King's representative had been caught lying.

These things made it easier for us to go on, but that evening and night, the doctors and warders stood anxiously by, and many times the stretcher-bearers passed our cells with the angular bodies pressing out the canvas. As midnight struck, we reached the ninth day, longer than ever a mass hunger-strike had lasted. Sleep had left many of us, as, for some reason, the longer the fast the shorter the hours of sleep ; and through the night the delirium, which is inseparable from that kind of fasting, filled our cells with grim fantasies. It seemed impossible to get away from the physical presence of death. Death was there in the cell, looking out of the darkness, a motionless hunter waiting in the shadows. That cold presence made us yearn with a kind of frenzy for sleep, and the frenzy made sleep impossible. Hour after hour in that gaunt company we lay there in a city stilled by curfew, in a jail in which the only sound was the sudden hurrying of the stretcher-bearers. Through the brain was going a dark procession from our lives—the wrong-doings, the cruelties, the neglects, the unkindnesses : jack-booted memories that trampled down hope and peace and made spiritual fear the master. If sleep be the sister of death, then this unquenchable wakefulness was his base brother, chilling the heart before it stopped beating for ever.

At the first light of day men in their bare feet, strained, silent men, sought the cold landings, the stone passages, to be anywhere but in that cell where death sat in the corner.

As the day advanced, the noises of the crowds came in through the broken cell-windows. Soon we sensed their vastness expressed in a far-off but incessant murmuring, a constant vibration of the air. There was no work to go to now, and all could come.

Visitors again passed through the clanging gates. Among the first came the Governor excitedly up the stairs, stumbling, despite his military training. In his hand, once more, a piece of paper. He made for Peadar Clancy's cell and I followed him, and on my heels came Tom Hunter.

" Grand news," said the Governor : " the strike can end. Ameliorative treatment is to be given to everybody. You have got what you wished for : you will be treated as political prisoners, no exceptions."

He beamed. My own heart rose. They had yielded. Then I saw a wilfulness come into Peadar's face.

" We won't take it," he said intensely.

" You asked for it," the Governor answered bridling.

" We did on 1st April, we demanded that it be given us before 5th April. You forced us to go through this," and Peadar made a grimace of horror, " and we'll take nothing now but release."

The words were almost shot out. The Governor looked bewilderingly at me, at Tom Hunter. I dropped my eyes. Peadar had not consulted us about this. I felt he had taken a desperate risk : that men would not go through another night when one of their alternatives had been granted. Some men would break.

The Governor stood, and we stood, in complete silence for a long time. " And what will I tell them now ? " he asked gloomily. " Tell them what I have told you : that we'll take nothing now but release." The Governor looked towards Tom Hunter and towards me, and this time we met his eyes, lest he guess our disunity. He fumbled his way out of the cell, muttering what sounded like : " This is the end."

As soon as his steps died away, I turned on Peadar. Before I had a word out of me he held up his hand and the skin-tight face came forward towards mine :

" I know the risk I'm taking, and I mean to take it. There are men here who must get out before they are recognised. We must get out ourselves. This fight is only beginning. The Castle isn't done by a long chalk. But they're done for the moment. The general strike has them beaten. For all they know, and for all we know, either, the first death may mean the people themselves surging over them in sheer weight of numbers. They fear that, and they are in low ebb. Lord French has dragged their prestige into the mud ; nobody will stand by them if they let one of us die. The doctors will resign in a body. Now is the time to raise the stakes."

His words swept my objections aside. It was a gamble—our physical weakness against their political weakness : the British Government behind them ; the Irish workers behind us. I looked at Tom Hunter ; his face told me he had already gone over to Peadar's plan. I remained silent.

Peadar turned to me again. " Don't you see they'll only give in to what we force them to. They are weak to-day, but they'll be strong to-morrow, and how would we feel if, by taking political treatment now, we kept a few men back for them to hang when they thought

N

they had us down." I had no answer to make except " Let's put it
to the men."

The first few made clear what the dominant thought was : they
felt as Peadar felt—better have it all out at once. The general strike
had reacted powerfully on them. The days and nights they had been
through made this place hateful to them forever and release could be
won, they believed. The politically-minded recalled that the British
Government had not burnt its boats yet : there was a good chance.
It was so with nearly all : some voiced my fears, but they, too,
swung round to Peadar's certainty that this was the way to win.
Now it was freedom or death, with nothing in between.

All through that Tuesday we could hear the crowd outside growing.
The warders spoke in awe of its size : relatives coming in brought
news of the surging streets and beyond them the still city. No trams
or transport of any kind ; no shops open except the food shops ;
the publichouses closed ; the tobacconists, no cigarettes to be bought ;
even the street traders had trundled away their barrows ; the quays
were idle along the whole lower Liffey ; there were no letters, for the
post office workers were out, too ; some of the public clocks were
stopped, for the winders were on strike ; even Government workers
had left their jobs, the waiters had walked out of their hotels, the
teachers would not go to their schools. As the day went on the
Northern men got word that the strike was effective even in some
strong Unionist areas ; the postmen in Banbridge and Portadown
were out ; the dockers and coal carters in Belfast ; the railmen on
most of the G.N.R. system ; many workers and Corporation employees
in Derry, and in the smaller towns of the North-East many shops
were shut.

Then the blow fell.

It was announced from the British House of Commons that the
Government's decision had been taken—there would be no releases.

CHAPTER 32

FACING THE INEVITABLE

THE day had died out before the words Bonar Law had used in the Commons came into B Wing. But now they were not read in triumph, but recited quietly with a sense of awe at what they meant.

Bonar Law, Leader of the House, was speaking to a Commons, many of whose members were critical that untried men were being allowed to die. He replied sternly to all suggestions of release, and said :

> " The Government consider it their duty, as had been done over and over again when Ireland had been in a similar condition, to arrest men on suspicion in order to prevent crime. We have done so, and we feel it our duty to continue to do so, and it would be perfectly futile to do it if men are to be released because they choose to refuse food. . . . This decision has been taken by His Majesty's Government and I do not believe there is any chance of altering it."

Later that evening he said more decisively :   " There is no possibility of a change of attitude of the Government in the matter. The Government have counted the cost."

The change these words brought into the jail was complete. The certainty of victory on the heels of the General Strike was so obvious that this banging and bolting of the doors of mercy (as an English paper called it) seemed at first incomprehensible, like the sudden death of a friend.

It was not now a proposal of one or two more nights in the cells. It was that all those hopes that but an hour before looked so solidly based had already dissolved ; we had keyed ourselves for a struggle of days and now it might never end. I can still feel in my memory the inability to hold off any longer the personal dread of death, loosed by the phrase spoken with such emphasis after the General Strike had been in operation for a whole day—" The Government have counted the cost." To every man, I suppose, there came as there came to me, a shrinking from what we must now face. Like trapped animals we clawed with our minds for some way out. There was no way. We, too, had banged and bolted all doors but one and it was that which by this high authority was now so finally refused.

I do not know how long it took us to recover any kind of mental composure, but in the unpredictable way of human reactions it came from the manner in which Bonar Law had spoken, the truculent, the assured strength in the words he had used, with their implied conviction that, of course, we would yield. It was that note of surety, which, in the end, brought us to see how inevitable our own decision was.

We have counted the cost, said this British Vice-Premier. In the very phrase was the tolling of a bell for us and in imagination we could hear all over the land the slow, crushing beat of the death-bells, pausing, pounding down, filling all homes with   oration—and with tears. But the bell Bonar Law tolled raised an echo as we lay there, weak and silent, under its reverberations. His phrase shaped the tones of the echo. And it was: "We, too, have counted the cost."

Like the citing of a prayer in the hour of weakness, like the smile of a friend in the moment of danger, the words somehow gave us back first our courage and then, riding high over everything, an inner peace. It was not an acceptance of death, but a more conscious perception that its immediacy must be accepted. As the hours passed and we got used to the new situation, the tossed jig-saw fell into position again.

It became extraordinarily clear that it was not now ourselves who were involved. This was a challenge not to us but to our country. The challenge had come from Britain and we lost our own individual identities and became the challenged land: the Ireland of to-day and of that past with which our minds were so full, the suffering, defeated nation as well as the resurgent angry nation. I think I speak truly when I say that if the immediate effect of the British Government's decision that we would never be released created in me, and I suppose in others, an eagerness to escape what the words most clearly meant, their later effect was to impersonalise us, not in any heroic sense, but in making us see that what we, as persons, feared or suffered was of little account, but what we, as Irishmen now did, was decisive. Life or death became a secondary thing. And if this sudden descent from high hope to intractable certainty numbed us, and in its way unnerved us, I do not think there came into any mind the thought " Now, we must submit."

For a long time after the news became generally known throughout the Wing there was a silence in the prison so deep that every faraway sound came into us—most of all the faint singing from the thousands that had been pushed farther and farther from the jail walls. Rain was falling heavily, and a cold wind was blowing in gusts from the crowd to us and it carried the massed voices across the armoured gulf between.

The sign that the men were re-ordering their minds to face this new dark element in the contest came first in a curious and a moving way. Far out the multitude was singing that song with which—it seemed all so long ago !—the warder had first shot the bolts on me :

> " *We love them yet, we can't forget*
> *The felons of our land.*"

After a while a prisoner here and there responding to the fervour with which the words came to us took up the tune, first humming it and then singing the chorus quietly to himself and in the end, as if spontaneously, many men began to sing from their beds, strongly, keeping to the time of the far-away voices. It was extraordinary the way this bond with our own people leaped distance and despair and death and was a warmth and a strength about us in that moment when just that contact meant everything.

Before the night closed down and Curfew drove away that mighty crowd which in the pitiless rain had stood all day to be near us, the worst was over. We had come face to face with our fate and, no more than a young man with all his life before him will, we did not complain. Heigh-ho, we said, that's the part Ireland has given us to play in all this . . . .

When the long, long night had passed and the tenth day of the strike had come the warders, now more than ever on our side, brought the day's papers openly to us for there was good news as well as bad in them. There in the centre of the main pages was a new demand from a new and powerful ally. It was the Standing Committee of the Catholic Hierarchy who now spoke. The names at the foot of the statement included those of Cardinal Logue and of the other three Archbishops :

> " We feel it a solemn duty to call the attention of every one to the appalling tragedy that seems imminent in Mountjoy Prison. It is a very serious responsibility for any Government to arrest a man on suspicion and detain him in prison without charge or trial . . . in almost every civilised country political prisoners even after a fair trial receive the treatment of political prisoners and are not degraded to the level of the criminal class. But now to add to the miseries of this tortured country these canons of civilisation are trampled under foot and Irish political prisoners, tried and untried, are denied the consideration which is certainly their due, and which even last year they were allowed in Ireland. If a disaster which will do unspeakable damage for many a day ensues from this insensate course the responsibility must undoubtedly rest with the Government

that substitutes cruelty, vengeance and gross injustice for equity, moderation and fair-play. . . . The cry we utter to-day is the cry of humanity."

It meant much to us at a time like this when our lives at last were forfeit that the Hierarchy's statement accepted death for us without questioning the means we had chosen to assert our right to freedom. Those papers, too, had news of what visitors to the jail had seen and what they had said. Mrs. O'Reilly spoke of her only son :

"My son, Anthony, is very weak and ill. He is five weeks in prison without trial. He is my only boy and our only support, but I am willing for him to die for the cause."

Mrs. May said :

"My only son, Vincent, a mere boy, is worn almost to a skeleton. He looked strange to-day, and is lying in his clothes in his cell. He says he is determined to continue the hunger-strike to the finish."

The sister of Phil Shanahan, T.D., said :

"He is very weak but is full of determination."

The wife of Alec MacCabe, T.D., said :

"My husband could scarcely speak, but he will fight to the end."

The brother of Seán Byrne, T.C., said :

"He is completely exhausted, but no matter what the consequences he will hold out."

Thus spoke the fathers and mothers, brothers, wives and sisters coming from the half-light of the cells out to the crowds who swept around them to hear of the men themselves. The refrain rang through their horrified descriptions : "He will hold on" ; "He will not give in."

And now that day had come again the visitors were moving through the passages. Among them that morning was Father Sharkey from Roscommon, who with his sister Una, were old and ardent workers in Sinn Féin.

Father Sharkey's reaction to the grim scenes in the cells was typical of the dominant mood : a hopelessness, turning to anger and then to a determination somehow or other to shake those stone walls apart. That was what the Irish people felt that Wednesday morning, 14th April, 1920. They, like the prisoners, would not yield ; in some way, nobody knew how, they would get those men out. The workers expressed it by making the General Strike more complete. Those with influence, members of Sinn Féin and its opponents alike, stormed by telegram and interview anybody who could bring the facts to M.P.s, judges, mayors, prelates, labour leaders all through Britain. The Irish populations in every city in England, Wales and Scotland worked madly to save those lives that for them merged into Ireland itself.

The hero of those last hours in Dublin was the Lord Mayor, Larry O'Neill. A courteous and it seemed till then, a timid man, he came many times to the prison and after each visit he went or phoned or telegraphed to one or other of the Castle authorities, Viceroy, Chief Secretary, Under-Secretary, Commander-in-Chief, with a restless determination to make them see their folly in it all. As Chief Citizen he had free access to the jail and we saw him often in the passages or passing down below through the circle on his way to the Governor with a new argument. This last morning he did not come. The Government, having taken its decision that we must break or die, shut the Wing gates against him. The Lord Mayor used that denial of his civic right as a new weapon, and he began, in association with the High Sheriff, another series of telegrams to the Viceroy demanding to know what he meant to do with the prisoners who the doctors advised were on the point of death.

Lord French replied that the decision was now not his; that it rested solely with London. The Lord Mayor and Sheriff together wired London and London told them that the treatment of Irish prisoners was a matter for the Irish Executive, for, that is, the Viceroy and the Castle. Each side of the English Channel was trying to evade responsibility.

In fact the whole situation at the Castle had changed. The General Strike had not only paralysed all work: it had paralysed the official mind: they could not telephone, or post a letter; they could not call a taxi or board a train; they could not eat a meal in their exclusive clubs or be sure of to-morrow's dinner behind their castellated towers. They began to see that this was not for one day or for any measurable time. The workers, instead of tiring of this strike and of the loss of wages that it meant for them, were preparing for a long siege. In the greater towns they were setting up Food Committees to organise the feeding of the people. With the consent of the Local Councils they were installing themselves in Council offices, there the better to direct their challenge.

That afternoon three key visitors came along those stone passages outside our cells. The first was Arthur Griffith, Acting President of the Republic. As we saw him go from prisoner to prisoner there came on us a great pride. For in his thick-set body, in the determined set of his head, in his few words, and in that natural assumption of authority which made the warders stand back in respect as he went by, we saw the symbol of all that we were suffering for : the self-governing, independent Ireland of which he, now, was the acting head. His high office was the proof that this was not in its essence a protest *against* something but an assertion *of* something : of a free nation's right to have an army of her sons.

Soon after Griffith had gone, Tom Johnson came, that capable, quiet Labour leader. With him now was J. H. Thomas, British leader of the National Union of Railwaymen, who, coming on a routine visit the day before, now stared in wonder at men and a people who with hunger and bare hands were bringing his Empire's power to nought.

Something like a hush of waiting had come on the multitude outside and all that could be heard was the droning of the aeroplanes that watched the city. Then the warders came hurrying once more. An urgent message they told us had come for the Lord Mayor to go at once to the Viceregal Lodge where a conference had been sitting since midday and Larry O'Neill had ridden off in the first conveyance he found in this traffic-bound capital, a pony and trap. When he came back he waved in delight to the crowd. " They're coming out," he called, and a storm of cheering broke out such as has seldom stirred a city.

But they cheered too soon—these ever-faithful people—for even as the echo of the rejoicing beat upon the jail in waves, the three of us, Peadar Clancy, Tom Hunter and I were passing along the cells saying quietly but firmly :

" Get back to your beds, lads—the strike is not over."

CHAPTER 33

VICTORY

THE events of that last day of the Mountjoy hunger-strike are vivid in my memory still.

Evening was beginning to close in and the wing had grown noisy as men realised what the wild cheering outside meant. They said little, those spent men, but their joy was a mighty thing to watch. If an artist had only beheld it then : if even young Salkeld were there whom they sent out when they learned he was no more than fifteen, what a canvas it would be : the greyness of the darkening prison : the groups of men, their hands on one another's shoulders ; with transparent faces raised to the glass roof through which that cheering came. It would have been a grotesque of caged and famished men entitled " Victory."

At our urging, some went into their cells ; but to the others the far-away sounds were too precious, and they stood quite still, hearing it all in ecstasy. Then almost as quickly as it had come this intense emotion gave way to that sense of fun which saves Ireland from a lot of bathos. Some wag began to call to his pal across the corridor of what he would eat when he got out. Soon everybody was at it, piling the succulent dishes ever higher and there were meals spread in the air that evening which were never dreamt of even in the *Arabian Nights*.

It was in the midst of this imaginery banquetting that the first name was called. It was Patrick Shiels—of Derry. To all who heard it shouted in the strong voice of a warder, to all who heard it come echoing through prison shadows, it was the name of freedom itself. If Patrick Shiels of Derry went out, then, after him, one by one we would go out, too, free again—men who had not failed.

The name had dissolved in reverberations long before warders came carrying the stretcher, taking their burden down the iron stairs, along the central hall, through the great bars into the circle as we watched with burning hearts silently. It was all one piece, a tapestry. The day's conferences in the Viceregal Lodge, the representatives of empire who but yesterday evening had said most solemnly that we must eat or die, now decreeing our release. We had no weapons, the workers had no arms, the people who for days circled this jail in a vast living wreath, had only their songs and their prayers. As our lives ebbed the life of Dublin and of all cities and towns in Ireland died down with us.

That sight of an immobile nation which had made of its will an impenetrable cordon paralysed Field Marshal Lord French, the Victor of Ypres, and General Sir Nevil Macready, the new Military Dictator, and all the other Generals and high officials who had sat for hours this day in the palace of the King's Deputy arranging their own terms of surrender without any of the victors present. They had found a formula which gave them a way out. They allowed the doctors to decide. Any man in danger of death was to be set free. That was the decision the Lord Mayor of Dublin had brought back from the Park. It was that which he told that vast crowd standing for ever in the cold rain. And now it had all come to pass: the abasement of the Field Marshals and the Generals in their gold and their medals before Volunteer Patrick Shiels of Derry on a stretcher.

We waited to hear the shout that greeted the first man as he was carried to the taxis and the ambulances which had gathered at the great gates. The shout came, but was almost instantly hushed lest the man's slim grip on life be loosened. I forget whose name was called next. Perhaps it was that of Peter O'Hare of Newry, or Maurice Brennan the 1916 veteran, or Andrew Holt of Arklow, or Todd Andrews of Dublin, or one of the men from Camp, Co. Kerry. What happened now swept the name from my mind for good.

As we rummaged among our things, each man hoping he would soon be named, we perceived a silence coming over the jail. We came to the passages to listen. Then suddenly we heard shouting, angry words. A warder came up the stairs at the double. He went to Peadar Clancy's cell. I heard his words. The release was to be conditional. Every man must sign a pledge to return. Shiels had signed it thinking it a receipt for his returned valuables. The man now at the gate tore it up, flung it at the Governor, and turned to struggle back to his cell.

I saw Peadar's face over the warder's shoulder. Its present haggardness was consumed in a flame of anger. " Tell the Governor to come to me," he said in a voice of such command that the warder was gone almost at the word. While we were waiting for the Governor we went among the men saying : " They are demanding conditions. This strike may go on for a long time yet. Get back to bed."

While these men at our bidding turned and slowly made their way back to the mattresses on the floor there were no heroic gestures, no demonstrations of any eagerness to die, but all my memory is of a refusal to yield cost what it might.

The Governor came, a weary man, living, as we were, on his nerves. Peadar Clancy met him at the head of the iron stairs. Without any preliminaries he demanded the meaning of this " new trick " as he called it, in a voice whose sharpness rasped through the wing. The Governor answered sharply, too, that these were things he had nothing to do with. His job was to carry out his instructions. His orders were to release every man whom the doctors named but only after he had signed a form in which he agreed to return in six week's time to complete his sentence or to stand trial. He had done what he was bound to do.

Peadar replied with an angry question : Did he not know when he heard these terms that the prisoners would never accept them ? Why did he not tell his superiors that ? " Tell them now," he went on, " tell them that we would sooner rot here. I have informed these men," he made a gesture embracing the rows of open cell-doors, " and without one objection they have gone back to their beds to fight this thing to the end. They are as ready for a second ten days as they were for the first, and a third if need be." Speaking more slowly he said : " You know what the doctors say : that with what to-day has taken out of them they cannot all live through the night. They must go out before this day ends, or men will die and—I think you know that as well as I do—if men die now, nothing will hold in the people. Tell all that to those from whom you get your orders ; and it is your responsibility if they don't understand it this time, and that responsibility we shall hold you to." The Governor stood for a moment in silence and anger, and as silently turned away. His wordless opposition seemed another sign that the impassable gulf had been reached beyond which neither they nor we would go. As he, with the same automatic soldierly smartness, went back along the central hall, his feet echoing up to us who watched him, Peadar said : " I wonder if he will ever come back ? "

We need not have feared for though we did not know it, the Lord Mayor was already on his way to the Viceregal Lodge. He felt that he, too, had been tricked. I have never heard or seen described what happened at this new conference. But hours passed and in the end between the three parties to this tense drama : ourselves in this silent wing, the now voiceless multitude outside the gates, and that far-away conference, there seemed to come some kind of telepathic union. For towards seven o'clock there grew, every minute, more strongly, almost a knowledge that we had won it again. It came to the crowds, too. The singing started in the drenched streets and again one of our men sang in his cell and before he had finished more than a few lines a new storm of cheering swept the masses outside—and we knew that we were going home.

I came to my cell-door to listen. Peadar came to his at the self-same moment. He smiled over at me and held his two thumbs upwards.

My emotion was too overwhelming and I drew back but not before I saw down in the circle a warder run in and facing our Wing throw out his arms in the most intense gesture of congratulation I have ever seen.

Long before the official word had come men who could stand were up gathering their things. It was the Governor himself who told Peadar and he did so formally, conveying a decision he said "of the Government." And then there was one other moment of tension. Although the prisoners would be asked to sign nothing, said the Governor, it would be understood by their going that they accepted parole. "Then we'll stay," Peadar answered with a shout. "You cannot," said the Governor, "every man in danger of death must be sent out to-night." "There will be no parole accepted, given or understood," Peadar said. "My instructions are to release every man named by the doctors," the Governor replied.

So it ended, this great strike, in a fumbling effort by the Castle to cover its retreat.

The releases man by man began again, and in those voices calling them from below there was the note of triumph, too, for many of the warders were with us completely now. Of them, Warder John O'Brien of Limerick was the type. His had been the dangerous work of keeping communication between A Wing and Volunteer H.Q. during the strike. In the end when the trick was played to make us sign, his anger engulfed him and he stripped from him his warder's jacket and threw it on the ground. He had given up his livelihood for our sakes. Going out to the mighty crowd, he told them he had quit the service.

Some of us could still keep our feet, and several hours later standing at the grill I heard along the passages my own name resounding. I said good-bye to the few still left, for Peadar was going and Tom was gone and the night had closed in. With warders on either side ready at any stumble to bear me up, I walked through that flagstoned central hall. The once well-guarded gates swung back as I approached, for everywhere there were ready keys and a "Good luck now" or "God bless you." Out through the circle we went to the great doors. There, standing as he must have stood for hours, was the Governor, utterly wearied, muffled up in heavy overcoat and scarf, a friendless, woe-begone figure. As I came towards him he produced a paper and began to read. I listened for a moment and then, realising that this was the parole we were supposed to be accepting, I turned my back on him, feeling the twinge of this impoliteness at such an hour of victory over him. When he had stopped reading, I turned back and said: "I am giving no parole, and I am not coming back." There was a pause: then, feeling for the utter tiredness of him and for what he, too, must have gone through in those ten days, I held out my hand. " Good-bye," I said.

" Good-bye and good luck," his answer came as, surprised at himself, he shook hands.

The warders reached up for the bolts of the great door. It swung open. I saw a sea of faces ; I stepped over the threshold ; I was free—and then my strength gave out.

CHAPTER 34

FLICKERING GOLD

WHEN I stepped across the threshold of the main door of Mountjoy Prison all that had sustained me seemed suddenly to be withdrawn. What happened I did not then notice or afterwards remember. A series of disconnected pictures was all I could glean of that moment. Some of the great crowd had come in through those forbidding gates and stood now on the very steps of the gaol itself. When the doors opened there outside were dear friends waiting for me. Loving hands came up to receive me and then there is a memory of Anna Fitzsimons smoothing for my head a very white pillow ; of Frank Kelly, who had helped to bring Dev. out of Lincoln, sitting beside the driver of the taxi ; of my brother Dick, in his full clericals at my side, and a sense of fantasy over it all.

I had had a horror of being brought to hospital, and without telling him why, had won the doctor's consent to go home. Though the physical strain of the strike was mercifully less in some of our cases than in many others, the mental strain bedded in the fear of many deaths was all but insupportable. When I thought of the scene being merely changed, and those same gray-faced youths lying around me in an hospital, hearing their distress (for it is not an easy thing to come back from a hunger-strike), watching the nurses battling for their lives, I felt that that would be beyond my endurance. Anna Fitzsimons heard of this, and it was her nature not only to understand, but to act, and here she was in a taxi smoothing the pillows for me as we drove down, so slowly, the long passage between the door of the prison and the tall gates in its high dark wall. The tanks and troops were gone and now there were only the people, crowding close to the car on that dark night, peering in, murmuring their sympathy, especially when they saw the priest beside me. Here and there I heard the voices of my fellow Volunteers of K. Company. I wondered if Harry O'Farrell was there or Jim Brogan or Joe Sullivan or Jimmy Bird or Paddy Millar. There in the endless rain were thousands of watchers who had stood so long that their wet shoulders gleamed in the light of the street lamps. That line of faces just outside the window of the taxi was unbroken for a long long time.

I think it was in Lincoln Place that they stopped the taxi for brandy:

194

when the publican heard that it was one of the Mountjoy men he came himself with the glass as if he were serving some lord of another era.

And then at last a home, out in the Ballinteer Road at the foot of the Dublin Mountains. Sturdy Republicans lived there in a house called Hilton, Mr. and Mrs. Frank Golden, and it was there that I got back my strength. That first night was a leaping river of joyful things. Colour, whiteness, pure air. Last October I must have noticed how different outside life is from prison, but it is this hour that remains in my mind. Perhaps it was that I was coming not so much out of prison as out of death. Four hours ago we were returning to our mattresses on the floor. That grimness suited everything around us then—prison is grey, and coarse and foul, with stinking air and truculence everywhere and death the inseparable companion. Here was a bed with snowy sheets and a fire in the grate, and when they put out the light the flames danced in golden measures on the ceiling. I watched them dance as "Fitz" and Frank Kelly sat by the fire before they left me that night, and, though we probably spoke around it and about, I remember the light flowing over the ceiling most of all. And whenever through the night I opened my eyes there was the flickering gold as some kindly hand tended that fire till morning.

I shall not forget that morning. Sleep had been fitful. Some time during the night there came at last that exhaustion which the excitement and tension of that day and many days should have brought upon me in the jail, and I learned then and forever the full meaning of the word prostration. It was not till far into the night that sleep delivered me from this overwhelming fatigue.

As day came it seemed to me I was still in jail, and yet I could hear birds singing. Dimly, at first, and just a song now and a song then. And it struck me that it was a lovely thing that such music should come into prison. The singing grew louder and I could pick out the blackbird and the thrush in their rich, ever-changing glory, and behind their voices the chant of the finch. Always the same spray of notes ; and I perceived the cockiness of the wren, the throaty call of the missel-thrush and the song of birds I could not identify filling the world just beside me with, it seemed, anxious, caressing melody.

I was convinced I was dreaming and I lay there revelling in it, not knowing I could open my eyes, fearful to stir lest it should go and I wake to the horror of another day's beginning. How long I lay thus I cannot say but it was a long, long time and I thought I found a pattern in that singing, the liquid call of the blackbirds weaving in and out, under and over the other songs, making a shining tapestry of sound. The more intensely I listened, the more certain I sub-consciously became that it was all part of the hallucination that hunger brings and that I was immured forever in the stinking wing of Mountjoy Jail and that the strike was to go on and on. I felt with my hands along the sheets and was afraid to feel further lest I touch the floor of the cell and this blessed dream end. At last I had to pray for the fortitude to open my eyes. When I did and saw the great window with the dawn barely coming and beyond it a tree swaying slightly in a far wind—I thanked God and tears flowed from my eyes.

In this personal joy I was like the whole Irish nation that morning. There was no broadcasting in those days. But if there had been and it was used fairly what a story it would have meant. The people in every hamlet and village and town with faces of distress crowding around their radios and at last when it seemed hope itself was broken, hearing not of death but of triumph. They would have heard the Labour Proclamation asking the workers to return :

> " At four o'clock to-day (Wednesday) we were officially informed by the Lord Mayor of Dublin that the jailors who held the bodies of our comrades and vainly sought to break their spirit had bowed to the will of the Irish workers, proving once again in history that the dauntless spirit of a people will over-come armies.
>
> " To you, our comrades and fellow-workers, all the thanks are due ; to you and the wonderful fortitude and resolution of the heroic men of Mountjoy.
>
> " You have shown an example to the world of how Labour might make its will effective—an example of solidarity without parallel.
>
> " It is our duty now to declare the strike at an end, and work is to be resumed immediately. . . ."

And so the nation sprang to life again, and though there was no radio word travelled quickly that the hunger-strikers and workers together had won. Telegrams went to all the men's relatives and from these now honoured homes the news spread out. As night came down there was a peculiar charm in the people's expression of their joy. In thousands of windows in the country towns and villages candles were set upon the window sashes and bonfires blazed on the hills and in the main squares of the towns. The nation was illuminated not a place here and there, but everywhere, and through the streets poured the people toward the churches where special services of thanksgiving were held.

Here and there police and troops, angered at their defeat, batoned these joyful crowds, but they gathered again and went on with their jubilations, all except those at Miltown Malbay, for there the round of death began again. There, the bonfire was raised at Canada Cross in the town and men, women and children had just gathered around it and were singing the national songs when down the main street came a party of constabulary and troops. The officer in charge shouted to the crowd to disperse, but before anybody comprehended what was being said, the armed party poured a volley into those around the fire. The rejoicing crowd fled panic-stricken. Some did not move. Patrick Hennessy, Thomas O'Leary and John O'Loughlin were dead, and the many wounded lying around the blazing brushwood included two children, Tim Reidy and Nannie Donovan, and an American soldier, Michael J. O'Brien, home visiting his parents. His comment was : " Anything like it for sheer wantonness I have never seen." Yet it was typical of these days in Ireland that when Martin O'Loughlin held his brother who had been shot he said : " You are the second brother to die in my arms " ; the other had been shot in France fighting for the freedom of little nations ! It was one of his own ten children who found Tom O'Leary dead.

Much else we heard and read of in these days after the strike. Fitz and Frank and I ; of the text of what the Governor read to us in the great shadowy hall as we went out :

"I, George Munroe, Governor of His Majesty's Prison, Mountjoy, do hereby release the body of one David Hogan relying on his or her honour to return to His Majesty's Prison, Mountjoy, on or before 27th May, 1920."

We laughed at the " his or her " and the " on or before " with its suggestion of the prisoner's happy haste lest he be late back even by an hour.

Another of the things told then, or later, was of how the Proclamation of the General Strike went out. Tom Johnson called on Sunday evening, 11th April, at the offices of the *Freeman's Journal*. He wanted news of us. There he met Dr. Myles Keogh, then a visiting justice at Mountjoy. Dr. Keogh told him of Lord French's flint-like reply : the men would on no account be released, if they went on they must die. That was the final decision of the Government.

Tom Johnson went to that old Republican among the workers' leaders, Tom MacPartlin. MacPartlin had his home in Gloucester Street (now Cathal Brugha Street), on the upper floor of the Carpenters' Headquarters. Tom Johnson expressed his conviction that the only thing that could now bring the Castle to its knees was a general stoppage of work. MacPartlin after a long discussion as to details asked might he test the proposal on some of the rank and file

o

of the Carpenters' Union in the Hall below. The result was decisive. These Dublin craftsmen had no doubt; and telegrams went out that night at 11 o'clock calling a meeting of the National Executive for the next day. Tom Johnson went home, drafted the Manifesto, and when the Executive met the next morning it passed the great call.

Johnson had consulted Seán Lester, then in control of the *Evening Telegraph*, as to how soon after he received an important story could he have it on the streets, telling him what was afoot. Seán, wholly on our side and seeing the value of this startling decision as a weapon and as news, said he would have it in the newsboys' hands within an hour. And so he had and the greatest incident in the Mountjoy hunger-strike was being announced by running boys that afternoon through the streets of Dublin.

As soon as we were out the prisoners in Belfast made their demand. The note of command in their ultimatum was typical:

" On behalf of the 145 uncharged and untried men in Belfast prison we demand immediate and unconditional release. Failing this we go on hunger-strike to-night, Monday, 26th April, 1920.

DAN HEALY, Commandant.
OWEN O'DUFFY, Ulster and Connacht.
PHILIP LENNON, Leinster.
TOM CLIFFORD, Munster.

We all survived but one. In those days many men in the struggle bore more than one name. A young man went through the Mountjoy strike under the name of Aidan Redmond. It was a hard strike for him, and it was not until 3rd May that he left hospital. He was back again within three days with an acute appendicitis, and he did not survive the operation. The inquest disclosed how spent he was, and Ireland regarded him as a man who had laid down his life for his brothers. His real name was Frank Gleeson who had fought in the Rising, and his funeral became a demonstration of national gratitude. Twenty thousand marched behind that draped coffin; Dublin had a chance of saying how much her rebel sons meant to her and she took it as the proud mother-city of a nation.

CHAPTER 35

"WE FIND THAT—"

As a result of the Mountjoy hunger-strike the Irish people had its confidence in its own power deepened and strengthened, and it is my belief that the victory which opened the jail gates exercised an influence which persisted to the Truce and beyond it.

Britain was militarily in tremendous strength in Ireland at that hour. She was strong, too, in the number of influential individuals supporting her. Not a single Irish daily paper and only a handful of the weeklies or provincials supported independence. Only a minority of the Irish employers believed in Irish freedom; the majority were openly and even bitterly pro-British. Power, patronage, all social eminence belonged to the British.

All that was defeated by the hunger-strike and by the support given to it by every kind of worker from business-manager to news-boy. But Britain was not beaten by any means. The jails began to fill almost immediately again. The very night we came out, 150 young men and old were seized in the area of Cuffe Street, Camden Street, Harcourt Street, in Dublin and scores in other areas. "It reflects the chaotic state of affairs," said the English press, "that while one group of Castle officials was negotiating the release of prisoners another group was actually planning the capture of others." But it was not chaotic; it was inevitable. The prisoners had forced themselves out, but the British could not hold on in Ireland with empty prisons.

It was soon after we had been released that the Cork jury gave its findings on the murder of the Lord Mayor. Those jurors knew that after the verdict they must live in a city in which the R.I.C. had absolute power: power to kill or maim as well as imprison. Yet the Corkmen brought in this verdict:

"We find that the late Alderman Tomás MacCurtáin, Lord Mayor of Cork, died of shock and haemorrhage caused by bullet wounds, and that he was wilfully murdered under circumstances of the most callous brutality, and that the murder was organised and carried out by the R.I.C. officially directed by the British Government; and we return a verdict of wilful murder against David Lloyd George, Prime Minister of England; Lord French, Lord Lieutenant of Ireland; Ian Macpherson,

late Chief Secretary for Ireland; Acting Inspector-General
Smith of the R.I.C., Divisional Inspector Clayton of the R.I.C.,
District Inspector Swanzy, and some unknown members of the
R.I.C."

It was a daring verdict and the drama of the hearing was suitably
ended by it. Everything that the State machinery could do to prevent
a hostile finding had been done. Yet these ordinary people, plumbers,
painters, night watchmen, doctors, people of independent means,
shop-owners, volunteered to give their testimony. As they faced
the scorn of the Crown lawyers, they told a story which led the
search straight to senior officers of the R.I.C. who had planned it.
The exposure of it all was deadly.

A week afterwards the same strong voice of the people spoke out of
the rural areas. Thomas Dwyer, a young man, of the Ragg, in Tipperary, was murdered in his home. The murderers came at dead of
night, with blackened faces and masks and, battering their way
into his home, shot him dead in the presence of his sister. Then,
as in the Cork case, the agents of the Castle spread the rumour that
he had been killed by Sinn Féiners because he was less extreme than
they. This the British press took up avidly, thereby providing a
cloak for this kind of murder, a cloak that in the next year was to cover
many terrible deeds.

The people of the Ragg gathered for the inquest to which the
Castle sent one of its most famous lawyers. Again the verdict did not
mince words :

"We find that Thomas Dwyer was wilfully murdered by
unknown members of the R.I.C. . . . and in view of recent
murders we desire to say that arrests, searches and raids should
not be made later than 8 p.m. and earlier than 6 a.m."

A few days later when Thomas Mulholland was murdered in
Dundalk the jurors there did not hesitate either, naming the actual
R.I.C. killer. Soon all inquests were suppressed because the Castle
found that the people anywhere in Ireland could no longer be cowed.

Early in May the spirit that had triumphed in Mountjoy showed
itself in another way. The Irish railwaymen began a strike that was
to last many heart-breaking months. It arose simply. The British
dockers and railwaymen refused to arm the Poles against the Russians.
They would not transport the munitions Poland had bought from
British firms. The Irish workers promptly applied the idea much
nearer home. They would not transport the arms by which their
people were being murdered nor permit movements of armed British
forces. Thus begun a protracted struggle in which many an engine

driver and many a guard lost his employment. For it was not a strike in which any mass of workers withdrew their labour. It was decided that all trains would be driven except those on which British arms were loaded or British forces in war-kit sought to travel.

At first the interference with rail traffic was sporadic. A train would be ready with steam up at Kingsbridge or Cork or Tralee, all passengers seated, the green flag about to be waved, when on to the platform would come a posse of armed R.I.C. The moment they got into a carriage the driver of the train got out and so did the guard. The train remained on the platform as long as the R.I.C. men sat in the train. When they left the train chugged out. Drivers were dismissed ; guards were dismissed. Dockers who refused to handle ships were dismissed. But those who took their places did the same and for nearly a year no train was moved in Ireland which carried the armed enemies of the Irish people and no ship that brought them in was unloaded. There would have been more distress in the railwaymen's homes, but the Irish people subscribed over £100,000 to a special fund to ensure that these families did not suffer too keenly for the courage of their breadwinners.

In the end, the British regarded all railworkers as their special enemies, and when one of the British High Command was shot at Mallow, Co. Cork, the Auxiliaries marched into Mallow Junction after curfew that night and three of the railwaymen there were killed and several wounded in what was by then almost a universal sport of the Army of Occupation. The men were lined up, usually after having been beaten, and were told to run for it. As they ran, the Crown forces raised their rifles and tried to pick them off as if they were rabbits. Many an Irish man and boy fell in that foul game. Many of the railwaymen at Mallow were shot down that night in this new "sport." As was also typical of the times, the British N.U.R. leaders of the day, having first protested at the murder of their comrades, were cowed by Lloyd George's threats, and surrendered their demand for a public inquiry. A military "investigation" was held instead, which exonerated their fellow-servants of the Crown !

In these months immediately after the strike, the people's discipline and love of fair play stood the greatest test of all and saved the nation from collapse into mob law, for it was then as described earlier that the land seizures were dealt with. Those who led this taking over of estates did not hesitate to shoot owners who stood in their path. Captain Shawe Taylor was shot in the March of 1920. Other owners received death notices. Then the Dáil Cabinet acted swiftly.

A special Commissioner was sent to the disturbed areas and there he found turmoil. In April, May and June, 1920, the Republican Courts went to work on the problem. At first the landless men would not obey the decrees of the courts. But public opinion stood for no nonsense and the Volunteers for even less. If the court gave a decree protecting a landowner and it was ignored, those who had invaded that farm or estate, were moved off by force. Twelve of them would disappear " to an unknown destination," the synonym for a Republican Jail, and if that did not do any good, twelve more a few nights later until everybody learned that when a Republican Court came to a decision that decision must be accepted.

And so in the end it was. The judges who sat on plain wooden chairs in a farmer's kitchen or a draughty parish hall laid down the law and that law was obeyed or else—

A visiting British correspondent, Hugh Martin of the London *Daily News*, spoke of it in those months :

> " Sinn Féin has accomplished an amazing work in producing law and order in those parts of Ireland in which it is in power. Sinn Féin law has a sanction behind it such as no other law in Ireland has had for generations. . . . Even Unionists are astonished and pleased by it."

And one of the Unionists himself wrote to the *Irish Times* :

> " The Sinn Féin Courts are steadily extending their jurisdiction and disposing justice even-handed between man and man, Catholic and Protestant, farmer and shopkeeper, grazier and cattle-driver, landlord and tenant. . . . It shows the growing and remarkable capacity of the Irish people for self-government."

It was a time of reconstruction, of rebuilding Ireland at the very moment when the nation was worst beset.

After the Mountjoy releases the officials of the Castle and of the Irish Office in London fought among themselves, even in public. They issued contradictory statements, saying there should have been no releases of sentenced men, that the Governor had exceeded his powers, that Lord French had never consented to what happened, and that in any case the released men had all given parole. It was a quarrel as full of meanness as of vitriol. But behind it the terrorists both in London and in Dublin were fighting desperately for a free hand and in the end they got it. All who would not travel that road must step aside. Lloyd George, threatened with a Tory revolt which might cost him his office, yielded. It was full steam ahead for the Terror. The hour had struck for the ex-prisoners, too. The period for which the British said we had been released on parole was running out. One morning before the mirror in the lodge at Hilton I surveyed my great red beard. I had a scissors in my hand : I was about to go underground. To-morrow would be 27th May, 1920. "on or before" which date I was supposed to hurry back to the cell in B Wing. I had other appointments.

CHAPTER 36

THE RAID

FROM the early summer of 1920 to the end of the War of Independence most of the active Volunteers and political workers in the towns and in the country were " on the run." To the young people of to-day these three words convey little. But to us they signified one of the most general and enthralling of all the experiences of the struggle.

That day when I stood before the mirror at the lodge at Hilton I was beginning a pilgrimage that did not end until the Truce was signed. It was a pilgrimage to no set destination, but to anywhere away from those searching for me. They knew me now and where I was. To-morrow I would be gone and for the rest of the war would not use my own name. It proved a godsend that, despite my friends, I had kept that beard. I was known by it to the authorities and now I was so to change my appearance that none of their spies would ever find me after.

There was a momentary heartsinking when I began with the scissors : for of all humanity I most disliked those without chins and here was I about to expose my face to the harsh criticism of men and I had forgotten whether I myself had a chin. But it had to be done, and, after a pause to feel, that scissors began its work and my identity fell in fiery strands on the dressing table. I gathered all those strands into an empty tin of Three Castles cigarettes, labelled it " To be called for by the Police " and stood it on the mantelshelf. And in place of the patriarch there stood somebody remarkably like the champion of Fifth Form.

Where was I to go to ? The curious fact was that neither I nor many another cared. The struggle had become home, family, relations, everything to us young men. That we should vanish from our dearest friends was part of it all ; that we should change our mode of life, forego the things that pleased us meant nothing. Because we had to live in furtive addresses under other names cut us off so much that we heard little of our families. I had close kin in this fight in other parts of Ireland and did not know it till long afterwards. Now my one idea was to become lost to those who sought me most. I mounted my bicycle and rode out of kindly Hilton, away from the care of the Goldens and of Fitz and Frank Kelly, out into the Ballinteer

Road, through Dundrum, and in by the back road to Rathfarnham and thence to Rathmines and beyond.

In that short trip my name had become Henry O'Neill, and I was now a commercial traveller in soaps. I had business letters to myself and an occasional sample scattered around the room so that any chance raid would " prove " my story. Old Margaret Foley, one of those faithful women whose love of God and of Ireland expressed itself in the quiet care of " rebels," had a little house at the foot of Charleston Road, and she let me the front room on the ground floor. There I set up my books and my bed and there I stayed with occasional disappearances until the fighting ended. I was raided twice in that room, and on both occasions the raiders went away suspicious still, but uncertain.

At times of great tension I had to find some other hiding place such as on Bloody Sunday in November, 1920. On that night, Dublin and many of the neighbouring counties became places of wandering men looking for shelter. It was so after any big blow and though each of us knew a " safe " house where people would take both us and the risk happily, we might learn that just on that night somebody much more important than ourselves was hiding there and we turned to look elsewhere.

As curfew came on some place had to be found, so we chanced the house of a friend or an address that we had heard another Volunteer speak of. I remember several places. One was in Beechwood Avenue, Ranelagh. Séamus Moore and his sisters lived there. Bride Moore was housekeeper and the younger sister, Mary, was a government servant—a supervisor in the telephone Exchange—and she took the risk not only of shielding us but of instant dismissal. There, also, Josephine Ahern, now our Minister at The Hague, and Maureen McGavock lodged. One night Ernie O'Malley after his escape from Kilmainham was with me at Charleston Road when some warning came not to remain where we were that night. Ernie was determined not to be taken alive again and as he would fight if a raid came we needed a house where there were no children and where our hosts were ready for every danger. We headed for Beechwood Avenue. I remember there was great laughter when we appeared on the doorstep for the house had already two others " on the run," Desmond Fitzgerald, a member of the Government, and some other whose name slips me. But in the upper room where they put the men the single bed was still further widened by chairs and pillows and somehow or other we all got some sleep. The Moore sisters and these two young girl graduates were typical of the Irishwomen of that day. There was no peril they would not face to shield men wanted for their part in the war. It was not only that they gave them a room; they watched for them through the night; they acted as couriers and helpers for them. Departments of State at that time had to be run at least partly in private houses. The Cabinet when it met, the army chiefs when they planned, gathered in somebody's drawing-room. It had all to be done quietly and with much discretion. The neighbours, no matter how friendly, must not know and concealment was difficult for the house was often in a terrace or was one of a score of small homes in a suburban street.

One of the safest houses at this time was in the highly-respectable district of Wellington Road. It became a refuge for me through some of the tensest nights of the struggle. It was the home of Mrs. Louise Murphy, widow of a Dublin doctor. Of her family one son left the British Navy, where he held the rank of Lieut.-Commander, because after the war for " small nations " his ship was to be used to bring Irish prisoners to Britain; another son was a Volunteer, and afterwards became a priest on the Chinese Mission. Her two daughters were to come on to the staff of the *Irish Bulletin*. She herself was a sturdy Protestant Republican from the Six Counties, and she opened her house to hunted men in the crisis of the war. I directed many an army chief and more than one member of the Republican Government to it, and I went there myself when the hunt became too eager.

Whether it was this luxurious house on the South side or Burke's little cottage on the North side or Margaret Foley's room in Charleston Road or that expanding bed in Beechwood Avenue; the welcome was the same. Though it must have meant many a night of peril and anxious watching, no door I ever knocked at with curfew on my heels, but opened and gladly. Thousands in Dublin and in the country experienced that, and there was no lessening of the welcome when the British made clear that the penalty for sheltering " rebels " was death. That penalty was exacted when Dan Breen and Seán Treacy were tracked to Fernside, Professor Carolan's house in Drumcondra. In one of the most dramatic combats of the war, they shot their way out of a ring of British raiders, both wounded, Dan Breen many times. The British lost five dead, including one of their key intelligence men, Major Smyth. In revenge for the escape they murdered Professor Carolan who had given Breen and Treacy shelter.

As I think back on those days when summer deepened into autumn and autumn into winter and recall the ever-heightening terror and the death or capture of many a friend, I remember these faithful houses where a quiet knock late at night brought a mother or a daughter instantly to the door where without showing any light— for that was part of the ritual lest somebody see a wanted man go in—the door was opened and the caller slipped into safety. At that

time I fear few of us realised the heroism behind it all but now thirty
years later one still thinks of it with emotion.

Not only did we who worked on the *Bulletin* know by experience
of the fate given to shelterers, we knew of it also from the reports
sent to H.Q. by Volunteer units throughout the country and frequently passed on to us, and from the Castle mails which were so often
seized. Many a night I worked at these captured documents under
my shrouded table light and behind my heavily curtained window in
Charleston Road.

Only a few feet from me, across a tiny garden plot, was the street.
I could hear the footsteps of people hurrying home before curfew.
This was the ideal time to work. From outside no chink of light
showed, nothing to draw the attention of passing patrols to the
house. Beside the window I sat at a little table and went through
what the day had brought. The city was stilled and even if I worked
far into the night the only sound would be the occasional lorry
speeding to somebody else's arrest.

On one particular night there was a rich harvest of R.I.C. documents. One of them was the report already referred to, signed by
County Inspector Cheesman for the Deputy Inspector General of
the R.I.C., ordering that relatives of a trade unionist who had exposed
Black-and-Tan methods be " looked up." Another, which I remember
well but have been unable to trace, dealt with a proposed raid for a
Republican Councillor. The raiding-party were advised to wear
rubber-soled shoes as these would conceal their approach to the
house. I was to remember that report for many a long day afterwards.

The stillness everywhere as I went through these documents was
complete, not a sound from without or within. Then the silence
was broken by a curious noise. It came suddenly from somewhere
near and was like the rattle of iron on stone. Before I paid it much
heed it had sounded at least twice. Then it came regularly, with a
pause of a second or two between, and after many times I noticed
that the pause was always about the same duration. It ceased and no
other sound followed it ; the whole world was intensely quiet again.
I tried to put it out of my mind, to go on writing, but it came back
again and again—the regular pause, the rattle of iron on stone, the
pause, the rattle, perhaps as many as 12 times. I had no idea of what
it could mean ; I sat there a long time by the table, my pen in my
hand, the papers all around me, trying to fathom it. Then I switched
off the light and cautiously and slowly lifted the blind. It was moonlight and I could see through railings on to the road and the houses
opposite. It was a completely deserted street and there was no sign
of movement of any kind. I was about to let the blind back carefully
when a glint of reflected brightness caught my eye from the road

itself. I gazed at it for a second or two, and, letting down the blind, I resettled the curtains about the window so that no light would shine out.

With a pounding heart, I gathered together the Castle mails, went to my door and called "Margaret." Mrs. Foley came quickly.

"Margaret," I said, "did you make that secret pocket in your skirt for me?"

"Yes," she said.

"Thanks," I answered. "Put those in it," passing her the captured documents. "I think there may be a raid fairly soon."

She took them without excitement or alarm and brought them out into the kitchen. I do not remember talking to her any more that night, but I suppose she was there watching just the same. What I had seen glinting from the road in the moonlight was only a manhole cover. But it told me clearly enough what had happened. Men, many men, had passed over it; they had passed as troops pass, in rows or in a file. They were somewhere near, surrounding a house or terrace up the street, maybe. They wished to raid without warning. They were in rubber-soled shoes.

It was a crisis for me; but nothing could be done about it now. If I tried the way out at the back which I had inspected as soon as I moved in, I might blunder into their arms, for somewhere near me there was a cordon drawn across the night. Besides, my alibi was good and there was a chance of brazening it out. I had often thought of what should be the first move in such a case as had now befallen me, and I had decided that the most deceptive for them would be for me to go forward to meet them. I made up my mind that when the thunder of the rifles beat upon the door I would go out and open that door myself. I now went about the room making sure there were no tell-tale papers lying around. My book shelves were themselves a betrayal, for all the Separatist books were there. But there were also many others and those who raided were unlikely to be bright on that topic, and so with a little luck—

CHAPTER 37

THE DARK MAN

THE raid that took place later that night was not exceptional. Just this was happening in hundreds of Irish homes every night, in city parlours, in country kitchens. In another part of Dublin within a few hours of my questioning another young man whose answers displeased the raiders was shot dead. Those who raided were either the British military, the Auxiliaries or the Black-and-Tans. Every Republican house took its susceptibility to raids for granted. But raids were not gentle things. It was not a case as at first of officers and men sincerely questioning and politely searching. It had become very different, and fear deepened as the lorries turned into your street or came on to the country road where your house was. At that time all sections of the British forces were being spurred on to terrible acts by a special Dublin Castle publication which drove them into a frenzy against the people. They had only to be told, or to see for themselves, that those who were being raided were in the movement—and they knew they had a free hand.

To make things worse for whoever crossed their path, many of the regular British officers had imbibed a fanatical hatred of the insurgents, and British regiments with noble names dishonoured them in Ireland by what they did. In Co. Cork the Essex Regiment and in Co. Wexford the Devon Regiment were guilty of many brutalities. They murdered out of hand Volunteers whom they captured and they treated Republican prisoners shamefully. Yet, all in all, because discipline was better, there was more hope of fair dealing if the raiders were British troops. The other two groups were specially recruited to terrorise. The Auxiliaries and Black-and-Tans, though called by different names, were similarly fashioned. When Irishmen refused any longer to enlist in the R.I.C., it became a predominantly British force, recruited from among out-of-work ex-service men in the English and Scottish cities. No questions were asked about character or anything else but whether the recruit was able and ready to handle a gun against the Irish rebels ? If he was, the pay was good and the questions few.

The Auxiliaries differed from the Black-and-Tans by being ex-officers who were unable to settle down to orderly life. They were wild and unmanageable in civil organisation. They formed a wild and unmanageable terrorist corps. They had over them some of the toughest officers a bloody and unsparing war had produced. Every Auxiliary knew he had nothing to fear if he killed a " Sinn Féiner," or if he wrecked the houses he raided, stole, looted, fired the cities of the " mere Irish." It was all part of the contract. If he did not catch on in the beginning the individual Black-and-Tan or Auxiliary soon learned that there were no limits and no punishments.

After the looting cases in Trim, when a platoon of Auxiliaries in broad daylight filled their lorries with stolen stock from the shop, and jewellery and bedding from the home, of a Unionist couple in Co. Meath, there was an effort to stop the rot. Brigadier General Crozier, one of its commanders, set about restoring discipline in the force. He had the thieves arrested and was preparing to have them tried when London intervened, and the incident ended with the looters returning to their company with flags flying, while it was General Crozier who was dismissed. Every crime was palliated and covered up like this by the Castle in Dublin, the Cabinet in London, and the Press in England. The Premier himself, Lloyd George, and the leaders of the Conservatives, Bonar Law and Churchill, made it quite clear that they were behind it all. " Rough justice " it was officially called. And the Auxiliaries took the hint, until their Glengarry caps became a badge of murder and outrage.

Men, women and children looked on them with horror as they went by on their raids night and day, and many a mother who looked out when the rifle-butts fell upon her door, felt her heart grow cold when the tassels of those caps swung in the light. So that night when I gave Margaret Foley my Castle documents and waited for the raiding party which had passed over the manhole-cover, I hoped that at least it would not be the Auxiliaries. I had long dreaded such a raid as this : now that it was upon me I experienced what many men felt all through the struggle—that at the moment of crisis fear vanishes. As it grew late I undressed and got into bed. I must have fallen asleep because when the battering at the door came I could not at first understand it. The sound of running feet upon the path and the rumble of a lorry on the roadway, brought it all back suddenly and in fulfilment of my plan I leapt out of bed and not waiting for my overcoat I ran in my pyjamas to the door.

I opened it—and saw nothing. For there, a few inches from my face, was a powerful portable searchlight blazing in on me. There was a second's pause as eyes I did not see must have surveyed me. Then a voice somewhere behind that light said in a Glasgow accent :

" Who lives here ? "

I said : " I do, Henry O'Neill."

Instead of a verbal reply I felt myself struck in the ribs by something heavy that threw me back along the hall and as I fell I heard the same voice say angrily, " Doesn't Mrs. Foley live here ? " Before I could answer, a group of men rushed up the stairs with revolvers in their hands, carrying the portable searchlight with them. I could hear the murmur of the flex as it ran past me after them. I gathered myself up and angrily went back to my room. There followed me a tall, dark man with a handsome olive face and that blue-black hair that could be either Welsh or Irish. He, too, had a revolver in his hand. He said from behind me :

" Don't judge us by the fellow who struck you : we are not all like that."

He walked over to my books, which were facing the door, and stood looking at them as he spoke over his shoulder :

" You are in a for a tough time to-night : the man in charge of this raid is drunk."

A silence came into the room. He stood in front of the books and began to comment on them :

" That's a nice edition of *Young Ireland*." . . . " I see you have the whole set of Pearse." . . . " There's Professor Henry's *Evolution of Sinn Fein* : a good book that." . . . " Mitchel : too angry always." I looked towards that tall back and wondered who on earth this might be. He sensed the silence and again, without looking round, he shot a question at me, the first of many I was to hear that night. There was a challenge in his voice :

" Do you believe in shooting policemen in the back ? " The change in his attitude was as ominous as the question. But an answer came to me in the same challenging spirit as his own.

I said : " That's an unfair question in a situation like this. If I say ' Yes,' you take me out and shoot me ; if I say ' No,' it looks like letting down my own side."

He faced around suddenly and we stood thus looking at one another in complete silence for a second or two as, without speaking, he put his gun into his bright leather holster and in the quiet of the room the noise was sharp as he snapped the button-fastener over it. " Yes, it wasn't a very fair question," he said meditatively.

A second later he said sharply : " Here they come," and with his voice came the sound of tramping footsteps on the stairs. " Be careful with your answers," he said, just before they came trouping into the room.

There were seven or eight of them : a scraggy, tough lot. Every man swung a gun in his hand. All of them as they passed through the door swept their eyes over the room as if looking for some tell-tale picture or emblem. Then they looked at me, a long look, and in more than one face I thought I saw the anticipation of " sport."

Those already in the room made way for a thickset, muddy complexioned man, who was obviously the leader. He spoke with the Glasgow accent I had heard behind the light. He had drink taken, but was not drunk.

I forget how it came about that way, but before the questioning began I was standing with my back to the mantelpiece and could just feel the heat of the dying fire through my pyjamas. The Glasgow man drew towards him my small table and, sitting on the bed, placed on it his Glengarry and his gun. He drew from the breast pocket of his jacket a bundle of papers and called to somebody behind him for a pencil. The others placed themselves around the room : some sat on my trunk, one on the chair, two at the end of the bed, and the rest below me on the floor. One who had more drink than the leader kept twirling his gun in his hand, with his eyes fixed vacantly on me. The tall dark man was in the corner by the books. I could not see him without turning.

The leader, whose thick glasses made it difficult for me to see his eyes from my standing position, began by warning me curtly but without anger that I would be shot if I did not answer promptly and clearly what I was asked. He began at my baptism. My name ?—Henry O'Neill. My age ?—twenty-seven. My job now ?—traveller for Crean's soaps. How long had I held the job ?—two years. Before that ?

I had long ago decided that I would dovetail my ordinary life into this fictitious one wherever there was no essential conflict, so in answer I said that I used to write for the papers, that I had been in London ; that I had once been Parliamentary correspondent for a paper, but that night-work was too much of a strain. Out of all my answers came many other questions from here, there and everywhere. I noticed that no two questioned me together. These sudden questions would come from a corner near the door, from the floor under the window, from the end of the bed. Many of the queries were ordinary ones, provoked by what I was saying ; but many times questions were thrown out, sharply, suddenly, in the obvious hope of trapping me. Sometimes three or four questions came quickly on the heels of one another. A question from the leader, my answer, one from the man near the door, my answer, one from the trunk, my answer. All the time there was the sense of a co-ordinating mind following the story keenly, carefully, watching for a discrepancy. The leader took notes.

Suddenly, probably because a long run of easy questions had put me off my guard, I was caught. To this day I cannot remember what the exact question was : but I know it was important. I think it was a question of dates. What astonished me was that the apparently thick-skulled and insensitive leader saw it at once. His reaction was momentarily terrifying. He stood up and leaning over the table between us he hit me across the face with his open hand, and with full force. It was a savage blow and threw me off my feet for a moment. I can never remember whether it hurt greatly, but from what followed I conclude it must have, for after it I showed no more concern for my safety or for ordinary caution. In blazing anger, I said to him :

" You have eight men, all armed, in this room and yet you strike a blow like that. It was a coward's blow." Snatching his gun from it, he pushed the table away from between us and came close to me. As I waited for another blow, I saw men in various parts of the room rise, too. The leader did not strike but carefully he put his gun almost over my heart and pressed the nozzle against my pyjamas until I could feel the cold ring of it. Then he said in a deep angry voice :

" You have called me a coward. Take that back or I'll let the bloody daylight into you."

He fastened his eyes on mine and waited.

I had no father and mother standing outside the door trying to hear what was happening in this grim room : no sisters and brothers pressing their ears against the walls in hope of hearing if I might get through without death. But in other homes where just this was going on there were mothers and fathers, a wife and children, sisters and brothers outside the ring of armed questioners praying that they would not hear the dread words—" Come outside."

CHAPTER 38

DEATH DIDN'T MATTER

No illustration of the War of Independence could be more effective or dramatic than that night scene in Charleston Road. In this great city hushed under curfew, with its streets deserted, but its dark windows filled with watching eyes, there was here and there a house like mine where some one stood in the centre of his armed enemies, who knew they had the power to kill him. They, ruthless in their strength, sought only an excuse; he, powerless, had but his wits to save him. When individual soldiers were caught, as I was now, they would not, if it became a necessity to assert their national faith, deny that they were Volunteers, but outside of that denial they would parry every attempt to establish their connection with the movement. They would mislead their captors somehow and get back into the fighting as quickly as possible. That was what was happening in that room in Charleston Road, and I am sure that, as I write of my quandary, I am reminding many others of just such a crisis in which either they themselves, or someone dear to them, was but a word from death. It was my intention, too, to bluff my way out of their hands, but the blow across my face knocked the importance of all that out of my head. If I survived it was not my doing. With that blow the whole nature of this immediate contest changed for me. From a battle of wits it became a battle of wills, with an added element that I could not rightly understand, and have never since understood. Though I was looking into two eyes staring into mine, and though I was conscious of the cold muzzle of a gun pressed against my chest, I saw also the shadowy presence of all the others, leaning forward now at the tension of it. But I could not see, without turning my head, the strange dark man who had apologised for the roughness of his comrades, who had spoken with knowledge of the books of the movement, who had warned me to watch my words this night, and who now stood in the corner by my shelves completely out of my sight. To glance at him would have meant taking my eyes from those of the leader, and somehow I felt that to do that meant defeat.

"You called me a coward: are you going to take it back?" the Glasgow voice said in tones which rose to a shout.

"I said the man who struck that blow was a coward."

" Take it back while I count three, or I'll leave your bloody carcase like a sieve."

" The man who struck that blow was a coward," I heard myself repeating.

He began : " One . . ."

We stared at one another. The thought going through my mind was not of death or of wounding but simply that if I could get that man to drop his eyes he would be beaten, he would not fire.

" Two . . ."

Everything in the room vanished but those two eyes into which I was staring, grey, bloodshot eyes.

I thought I saw the trigger rise faintly under the pressure of his finger. Still it meant nothing more than that I must somehow force down those grey eyes that held mine from behind the thick spectacles. They would not drop and I sensed defeat, more as a disappointed spectator than as a participant, disappointed not because a shot was to be fired, but because it was the Auxiliary who would have won this contest of wills.

The " three " was never spoken. Just after my seeming to see that trigger move, I suddenly lost the grip of those eyes. They swung a glance to where my dark-faced friend was standing by the books. They swung back to me and were now hesitant and uncertain. At last they dropped and the leader threw his gun on the table, letting out a string of bitter and filthy names at me. As his eyes left mine I tried to see what was happening in that corner. All I saw was the tall man replacing his gun in his holster. When later that night I put it all together, I concluded that he must have covered the leader before the word " three " was spoken, for I recalled how at the start of the raid he had put away his gun fastening the button over it.

I was tense and circumspect now in the moment of my escape for I knew that any other slip would bring everything down. The investigation went on and I watched for every question to meet it swiftly and without apparent anxiety. At one point in the recital of my past the leader, who had been quiet for a long while, shot out in vicious eagerness :

" And you joined the I.R.A. when ? "

All through that night, I suppose because I was standing there among men in uniform, I had been conscious of how poor an appearance I must have cut. My hair was very long and my pyjamas short. My hair was long because a hair-cut meant sitting in a barber's shop for twenty minutes. If any tout had seen you go in, you might bring your neatly-trimmed head within the hour to Dublin Castle. My pyjamas were short through shrinkage and I was so concerned as to how I looked that an answer came to me which proved the most effective of any I gave that night. To his " And you joined the I.R.A. when ? " I replied :

" Anybody looking at me would know I wasn't a soldier."

Every head was raised and every pair of eyes fixed themselves on me. There was a long silence in the room and the heads nodded unconsciously in unison. When the questions were resumed I knew I had now a chance of getting through.

For another twenty minutes the queries came from here, from there, from everywhere. But it seemed that there was no vigour in them, that they had become formal, something to get finished with. The questioners had become convinced, or almost convinced, that they had blundered into the wrong house. At last the leader stood up :

" We're going to search the room, now," he said, " and if we find anything, I suppose you know what'll happen to you."

They dragged the clothes from the bed, they tumbled the books, but without looking at the titles, they lifted the carpet at the edges, they looked behind the pictures. They searched the pockets of my coats. And here they found a sample of soap, and there a letter giving an order for six dozen tablets.

Suddenly the Glasgow voice said : " What's in there ? " pointing to my trunk. " Clothes, I suppose," I said.

" Open it." I did and stood back. A painful tap of a revolver nose on the shoulder came with the words : " Do you expect me to handle that filthy mess ? Pull them out."

Somebody was praying hard for me that night, for, as I started to take out the shirts and flannel trousers the trunk contained, there looking up at me was the First Aid packet so many Volunteer officers carried when their company went into action. I swept it into a bundle of woollens and dumped it hard on the floor, hoping that it would not roll out. My head was happily down at the searching, or they would have seen the whiteness the shock of that package brought to my face. Soon the trunk was empty, and the leader said : " Put them all back now." Nobody ever closed a trunk with such devotion as I did a minute later.

They were going. The leader stood in front of me and said : " I'm in two minds about you : and if we don't take you now, we'll come back for you and if the door is not opened more quickly the next time we'll open it with a bomb."

He went out. The others followed, slowly. The last to go was the tall, dark man. He turned at the door, stared at me for a second or two, and then said with a half-smile on his face : " Good-night, now." The door closed. There was talk still in the hall. I had reported too many raids to know that there is no certainty of their end until the lorry has driven away. I remained standing with my back to the dead fire when, as I thought might happen, the door shot wide open again. I braced myself for the order to come outside. Instead, an Auxie with a sharp Cockney accent thrust his head in and said :

" Anyhow, we ain't got no use for fellers as won't get their 'air cut."

He was gone almost with the last word. I heard the hall door open and the Glasgow voice calling the Christian names to make sure they were all there. I wished I could hear even the front name of that stranger who for no reason that I could see, or have since seen, defended me that night. He was deeply interested in the movement ; and must have been of some standing in the Auxiliaries or his drawing on his leader would not have checked that angry man. How he got into such a force and, stranger still, how he remained in it, was one of the surprises with which that time was full. I forget how I learned it, but I have a vague memory that either I heard or he himself told me in that interval before the raiders came tumbling down from the upper rooms, that he was in Queens University, Belfast, but could not study and, under the influence of the Belfast press, joined up.

In the remaining months of the struggle though I quested for word of him everywhere, he vanished completely. He may have been shot by his comrades as any who stood in their path was likely to be, but somehow he showed himself more careful than to permit a situation like that to arise or if it did to be the victim of it.

Perhaps if he reads this he will write to me, as did one of the four clerks in Banbridge Post Office who joined in the General Strike. In the letter that brave man said :

" Some time later we strikers were forced at the point of the gun to leave the town by an Orange mob who broke into the office, maltreating some of us. The police stood idly by."

And he quoted the British Postmaster-General, Illingworth :

" I regret I cannot dismiss these officers for if I did I am sure the bulk of the service would cease work in sympathy."

When I got back to the office with my summary of Castle documents next day there on the office table were recent issues of the *Bulletin*. One told of the raid on the Turners' home at Coolderragh, Scarriff, Co. Clare, when the family were rough-handled, the windows smashed in, the rooms and beds sprinkled with petrol and the outhouses and hay set on fire. Another was of incessant raiding of the home of Miss A. McDonnell, M.A., at Kielta, Tuamgraney, a few miles away. She described in a formal statement six raids between the previous

October and December. The raiders were Auxiliaries under a Colonel Andrews. The statement said:

> "During the search Colonel Andrews ordered his men to 'bayonet every bloody thing in the house.' They filled sacks with valuable books. They also took with them my bicycle, the servant's watch, a number of fowl. . . . The Colonel's parting salute to my mother was, 'Madame, give my compliments to your son and tell him I will shoot him when I see him.'"

They were back within a week and the statement describes the final raid:

> "They broke open everything, looted all valuables, silver, jewellery, cutlery, linen, etc. I met one with my dressing-gown under his arm, another with my suitcase full of blouses, a third with everything portable out of my brother's room. A cousin who was with us that night was dragged from his bed, knocked, kicked and beaten with revolver butts. They took his money, a gold watch and other belongings. After five or six minutes we heard the order : 'Take those women out of the house.' We were escorted to a neighbour's house and there left in darkness under lock and key while our home was being burned down."

Another recent copy of the *Bulletin* had the sworn statement of Mary Harrington, of 30 O'Connell Street, Tipperary. It too described a raid :

> "One of the men . . . asked my sister-in-law, who was in bed, 'Who is that inside you ?' She said, 'My husband.' They asked her what was his name. She said 'Michael Edmonds.' Then the man in the frieze coat said, 'That's the bloody fellow we want.' He made a grasp at him and pulled him out of the bed. They scarcely gave him time to put on his clothes and told him he would do as he was."

The *Bulletin* went on :

> "The dead body of Michael Edmonds was found in a spot in the hills. His face was covered with blood, his head was cut at the top, his left jaw-bone was broken ; his left eye was a black mass ; over the right eye was a cut of some sharp weapon. There was a bullet wound in the right temple. Both shoulders were dislocated, and from the throat to the bottom of his stomach was one black mass as from kicking. His hands were clasped. It seemed he must have been on one knee praying with the other leg stretched out when the shot was fired that killed him."

I bowed my head in thanks at my sparing.

CHAPTER 39

A CORK MEETING

IN all the cities of Ireland and in many a country town and village the halls were busy places in the year after the Rising. The Volunteers were being reorganised. To describe the life of a Volunteer at the height of the struggle I must go back to put it all in the right setting.

All the main outlines are known—the foundation of the Volunteers in 1913. Redmond's capture of the executive in 1914, the consequent division into Irish Volunteers who stayed faithful to the Republican cause, and the more easily influenced National Volunteers, thousands of whom under Redmond's persuasion and the propaganda of the time joined the British armies.

In Cork during November, 1913, I was attached to a committee organised to establish the Volunteers in that city. The arrangement was to bring Roger Casement and Eóin MacNéill down to launch the movement at a great meeting in the City Hall on 14th December. As it is nearly forty years ago, I cannot recall the whole Committee nor my own status on it, which was probably minor. But I do know that J. J. Walsh, who later took a leading part in Irish affairs, was the chairman of the meeting and that other Committee-men included Diarmuid Fawsitt, now a Judge; Liam de Róiste, afterwards T.D.; J. C. Saunders, now City Medical Officer of Health; Maurice O'Connor, now State Solicitor, and others whose faces I dimly see but whose names I have forgotten. No doubt, as did the leaders in Dublin, Terence MacSwiney, Tomás MacCurtáin, and other well-known Cork Republicans stood in the background.

At any rate, Casement and MacNeill came and I was to see the first of many of the tense scenes which filled the succeeding years. The members of the Committee had varying political views, for the Volunteer movement was to be above ordinary political divisions, wide enough for all to join and its pledge was worded to that end:

"I, the undersigned, desire to be enrolled in the Irish Volunteers founded to secure and maintain the rights and liberties common to all the people of Ireland without distinction of creed, class or politics."

At that time the views of the Republicans (or Sinn Féiners, as we used to call ourselves), and of the Parliamentarians were poles apart, even on this new question. For us, the Volunteers were founded to achieve independence; the Redmondites thought they should be used to defeat Carson. But Carson had an entirely different aspect for us, and one that would, no doubt, have surprised that gentleman. To us he was an Irishman in revolt against a British law—Asquith's Home Rule Bill—which we did not think highly of, anyhow.

It was on this difference of view that our first frail craft seemed to founder. The gross discrimination against the Nationalists of the Six Counties had driven them to seek protection in a new organisation. It was known as the A.O.H., or, to give it its full title, the Ancient Order of Hibernians (Board of Erin). Under Joe Devlin's forceful leadership the Board of Erin became a Northern spearhead of the Redmondite movement, and it was strongly sectarian. To them anything that Carson was concerned with was anathema.

The meeting filled the City Hall, floors and gallery alike, and I was for some reason in the gallery close above the platform, Jack Saunders and I sitting together. J. J. Walsh presided and Fawsitt read the Manifesto first read at the foundation meeting at the Rotunda in Dublin three weeks earlier.

Here, as we in the crowded hall heard it, are some of its passages:

"If ever in history a people could say that an opportunity was given them by God's will to make an honest and manly stand for their rights, that opportunity is given us to-day. . . . From time immemorial it has been held by every race of mankind to be the right and duty of a free man to defend his freedom with all his resources and with his life itself. The exercise of that right distinguishes the free man from the serf, the discharge of that duty distinguishes him from the coward.

"To drill, to learn the use of arms, to acquire the habit of concerted and disciplined action, to form a citizen army from a population now at the mercy of almost any organised aggression —this beyond all doubt is a programme that appeals to all Ireland, but especially to young Ireland."

And after a tribute to the enthusiasm for freedom of the " women of Ireland, true to their record " it ended with these words which, as Diarmuid Fawsitt spoke them moved many:

"In the name of National Unity, of National dignity, of National and individual Liberty, of manly citizenship, we appeal to our countrymen to recognise and accept without hesitation, the opportunity that has been granted to them to join the ranks of the Irish Volunteers and to make the movement now begun not unworthy of the historic title which it has adopted."

Then Eoin MacNeill came forward. I remember his tall spare figure standing by the table and his voice with the sharp Northern inflection, for he was an Antrim man. That he was unwise in his way of saying what he said, even his associates on the platform admitted that night. But that nationally he was merely before his time we can all now see.

Eoin MacNeill told that crowded hall that he and Roger Casement had just come from the West and went on:

> "A few nights ago I addressed a great meeting in Galway to establish a corps of Irish Volunteers there and the building rang with cheers for Sir Edward Carson's Ulster Volunteers. The action of these men in taking steps to preserve what they considered their freedom was action which deserved the commendation of every Irishman."

A voice presaged the storm:

The voice said: "If they come down here they will be met half way." Eoin MacNeill went on:

> "Yes, if they are met half-way by us they will be met with an open hand. It is they who have set the model and the standard of public duty for us. We stand in no fear of them and they stand in no fear of us, and there is no reason why either of us should fear the other. Our own way in our own country is what we want and we shall be content with nothing less. The North began, the North held on, God bless the Northern land, and now I ask you to do as the young men of Galway did—Catholics and Nationalists alike—I ask you to give three cheers for Sir Edward Carson's Volunteers."

What in fact that call summoned was chaos. Scores of men, obviously placed there for the purpose of wrecking this project which the old leaders feared, rose from the front seats and stormed the platform. They carried their chairs with them and I recall seeing that spare man who had just spoken standing above the rushing tide facing the audience still.

And the tall, bearded Casement was on his feet, his dark, intelligent face looking out on that turbulent scene as those who had rushed the platform laid about them with their chairs. J. J. Walsh was struck down and lay bleeding near the organ and others fell beneath the blows. Then the lights went out, and in a less serious meeting there would have been panic and perhaps many deaths. When they came on again, many were leaving and the turmoil slowly died down.

Those on the platform stood there still and in the end the meeting was resumed, and instead of angry words from Casement there were understanding words without a murmur of complaint at what had happened. And before the meeting ended, five hundred names had been handed in. The Volunteer movement in Cork had been founded.

In those years it was all part of the day's work to meet violent antagonism such as this and we took that day's turbulence in our stride. Soon here, as in so many other places in Ireland, the drill halls resounded to the " Left," " Right " and " About Turn," to the " March," " Halt," and " Stand Easy." All I remember of it now is a long narrow room with Tomás MacCurtáin taking the drill parade and Terence MacSwiney standing by, watching it all. It would have been a hardy prophet then who said that in little more than half a decade these two men would have succeeded one another as Lords Mayor of the City, and have laid down their lives for freedom in a way that resounded throughout the world.

Some time, either earlier or later, I was admitted a member of another A.O.H., whose full title was Ancient Order of Hibernians (Irish-American Alliance), whose head-centre at that time was Frank Healy, a solicitor, of Cove. It was an organisation established among the exiles in the U.S.A., with the object of winning independence for Ireland. Its meetings were grave affairs. When we assembled under the guise of some social club, a Sergeant-at-Arms took over the door and was, I think, armed.

But the great Home Rule debates were on in London and I was chosen by the owner of the paper I worked on, the *Cork Free Press*, to go there to report them. Old William O'Brien, the centenary of whose birth has just passed, was then the nearest of the National leaders to Sinn Féin. He had kept much of his Fenian spirit and when Redmond made his Woodenbridge speech, recruiting for Britain, O'Brien became the hope of those who looked for a voice for freedom.

When the war began William, like countless other Irishmen, took the view that this was a struggle of Great Powers and, perhaps, before it was over the little nations would get their chance, too. But he was a great lover of France and of Paris, his wife's beautiful city, and when, in the first six weeks or so, the Germans swept towards the French capital, William O'Brien was troubled. At the same time, the British propaganda machine got to work, and the horror stories pouring out of Belgium and France were overwhelming. In the end, through a mixture of pity and propaganda, William O'Brien decided that a world without French civilisation would be a poor place. From that it was an easy step to the end of the road.

One evening he sent me a note to come to him. I was then in the press gallery, and we often had such meetings. A relationship had developed between us almost of father and son. When we met he would lead me to one of the further wings of the library, where his favourite place of conversation was a long, red-carpeted passage between twelve-foot-high shelves laden with law books. Up and down that passage we walked many a night, putting the world through our hands. He talked of people and books, of movements and memories ; he told me of his party troubles, he sketched his plans and invited my views. He was then sixty-one years of age, and I had just turned twenty.

CHAPTER 40

A JOURNEY TO LONDON

THAT night William O'Brien told me he was going to declare for Britain in the war. I had seen signs of that decision peeping out of his conversation in the last few days and was surprised only by its suddenness. Its firmness was to be a surprise, too.

There abides with me a recollection of a conversation, entirely placid, which is strange. For William O'Brien was a volatile man who threw into his talk the whole vividness of his personality. He could become suddenly like a 100-mile-an-hour tornado when he reacted to some criticism. But now there was a quiet earnestness about his stating his views. We argued for hours as we strode that red carpet between the walls of leather-bound books in this quiet backway of the " Mother of Parliaments."

I urged on him the wisdom of not committing himself : there was no need for that. Ireland had a right to a policy of her own. The Independence movement was already strong, and was growing. It had as yet no voice from among the elected leaders. He had the record of the land wars, of imprisonments, of his association with Parnell in the early years. His movement, the All-for-Ireland League was, I told him, capable of becoming an important section of the freedom movement, many of its members were already in the Volunteers.

After Redmond's recruiting speech, thousands of young men were looking for a leader to speak from Ireland's point of view. He agreed with much I had to say, but it soon became evident that his mind was made up. He summed it all up in the phrase, in which, to me, there seemed to be the strong accent of regret : " We must either be the open enemy or the open friend of England in this war—and we are not strong enough to be the open enemy." I turned to the practical effect of what he was going to do. If he made a recruiting speech, the life of his paper would be over : its circulation would fall at least by half ; his All-for-Ireland clubs would swing away and become branches of Sinn Féin.

" I don't believe a word of it," he said.

He made his speech—and his leadership was over. The circulation of his daily paper fell, not by half, but by three-quarters, and it had soon to become a weekly. His All-for-Ireland movement melted away and its place was taken by Volunteer companies and Sinn Féin clubs. Later, I was called back to Ireland to run the paper, and I found that the staff was Sinn Féin, too. Tadhg Barry, who was our G.A.A. specialist, was later shot dead by troops in Ballykinlar Camp. Others I remember with strong national convictions were: Seán Ó Tuama, Paddy Reilly, old Ned Lane, and, of course, many of the printers.

On Easter Monday, 1916, came the Rising and at once the deluge of propaganda. We had some corrective against it in Ireland and from our knowledge of the men who were in the movement. In London, William O'Brien, exposed unprotected to the whole blast of the anti-Sinn Féin hurricane, wired an editorial which deplored this " heart-breaking folly." The executions started and just when the horror was deepest the staff and I talked it over and it was decided that I must go to London to see William. Only scrappy remembrances remain—the visit to that King Street R.I.C. barracks from which four years later the slayers of MacCurtáin stole out. As I see it now, I was darkly received, and was granted an exit permit grudgingly, as if they were afraid to have a refusal raised by William O'Brien in the House. Other memories are of the sea journey on the blacked-out ship, the careful talk in the crowded railway carriage on the other side.

It was Saturday night when I left, and on Sunday morning I was at the Victoria Mansions, near the House, where the All-For-Ireland leader had a suite of rooms. It was a stormy meeting. William had received only the anti-Irish story of the Rising. He believed from it that this was a Socialist revolt and that only those behind it were the *sans-culottes* and the down-and-outs. We can be superior about that view to-day, but with all the Irish papers which could give the true picture suppressed, and all the others hostile, it was a usual view enough in these first weeks after the Rising.

It took a long, long time to convince him of the quality of the men who had made the Rising: Pearse, Tom MacDonagh, Joe Plunkett. The men in his own city who were in the same movement— MacSwiney, MacCurtáin, J. J. Walsh. I recalled for him his own past and convinced him the men of the Rising were as the Land League leaders were and, like them, were now being maligned by every instrument the British had.

" And was it only to tell me this that you came from Ireland ? " he asked.

" No," I said, " the staff and I think the paper should not be used to attack Sinn Féin."

He was an explosive man and he exploded. Whose paper was it ? What did men who attacked England in the midst of a war think they were going to get for Ireland ? How long could the paper live under military rule with such a policy, anyhow ? " I have worked all my life for Ireland," he said, " and whenever it seemed we were getting anywhere this kind of thing has happened. I know the Irish people and believe me there won't be a Sinn Féiner in Ireland in three months."

" Mr. O'Brien," I answered with a young man's dogmatism, " there won't be any but Sinn Féiners in Ireland in three months!"

He made a sweeping gesture of dissent and refused to yield control of the paper. Quietly I told him that I had the resignation of the editorial staff in my pocket. His response was electric. All his Irishism resented this attempt at what he regarded almost as blackmail : and I left him, a very angry man. As I went through the outer room Mrs. O'Brien, in her courteous, friendly way, asked me if I had succeeded. I said, " No, indeed," and she suggested in the same undisturbed voice that I should come back in the afternoon.

When I returned the storm of its very violence was over and we talked of ways and means. On our side it was agreed that the paper was not to become Sinn Féin or conduct itself so as to be suppressed ; and on his side that it was not itself to attack Sinn Féin or to publish letters attacking it which were not fully signed. With just time for me to catch the night train home we said good-bye.

For nearly six months, when the voice of insurgency was throttled, the *Cork Free Press*, though it could not openly support Sinn Féin, spoke out of a background of Ireland's right to be free and to have her own policy even in war. It was condemned in the Commons as being a paper that might be published in neutral Holland or Denmark and when it ceased its career by a sudden decision to close it down, there was pleasure in London.

Before that happened Lloyd George was given his task to settle the Irish question and proceeded to do so on a basis of partition. This threat of dismemberment horrified the nation and none reacted more violently against it than William O'Brien. He summoned a meeting of protest for June in the same City Hall which had seen the foundation of the Volunteers. On those great occasions, he would come without script or even notes and make a speech beautifully rounded, full of detailed argument, often with quotations and statistics. The secret about this extraordinary fluency was a unique memory. William would speak his speech to Mrs. O'Brien, who took it in shorthand and transcribed it. The script would be read over by William himself, before a mirror, From that moment it remained in his mind so fixedly that he could speak it word for word days after he had given the only copy in Mrs. O'Brien's handwriting to me. On the night of the great meeting in the City Hall that practice stood him in good stead.

I wanted to hear that speech delivered with all the orator's vigour and colourfulness, and before he spoke I wrote for our first edition a description of what had not yet happened. It was easy. I had the text of the speech and I knew where the people would break in with their cheers and their clapping, and stamping with the feet. I had the enthusiastic scene in print before he had risen to speak.

Alas for man's expectations! I arrived in the City Hall just as the speech introducing William was concluding. As I anticipated, the building was crowded to the doors and the roof. O'Brien came forward, the great figure slightly stooped now but lithe still, the handsome, leonine head thrust forward, the slender hands free of any impedimenta like notes or script, ready for those whirling and expressive gestures that lit so many passages and made the words they embroidered so impressive.

The story is told that Gladstone, hearing his daughters refer at second hand to William O'Brien as a poor orator, advised them to go that very night and hear him, for he was speaking to the exiles in London. When they came back, he asked them what did they now think: " We wanted to break every window on the way home," they said. That was William's way. He could rouse a crowd to flaming passion, move it to tears, rock it with laughter, drive it to angry contempt, sweep it off its feet with enthusiasm.

But to-night the voice did none of these things: to-night was the closing of an era. William O'Brien made that speech, every word of it with all the gestures and all the apparent nonchalance he would normally have shown, but hardly a word of it reached even the press table where we sat just below him.

For the galleries had begun to sing as he began to speak, and they sang the songs of the Rising all through that address—great choruses, rollicking melodies, rapid humorous songs, and when they were not singing they were cheering the names of the 1916 men. William, without any sign of impatience or any hurry, turned back to the chairman's table only when he had spoken the last memorised sentence. The body of the Hall rose to cheer him for his courage, but the galleries sang on.

That William O'Brien should have been denied a hearing in the city he had represented for so long meant more than a political change. It was a national turning away from even the kindlier phases of " Constitutionalism." After the meeting I went to see him for a moment before I hurried back to change the rapturous reception we had described in the Bandon edition. He was seated in his rooms in Turner's Hotel, his friends and colleagues about him, and looking up quizzically as I came through the door he said: " So this is what you and your Sinn Féiners have done to me." " Not the Sinn

Féiners," I answered, " because you remember, Mr. O'Brien that in three months——" and as I vanished I heard his burst of laughter.

Two years afterwards I was in Tyrone at a bye election, staying in the happy home of Pat Campbell and his wife at The Rock near Dungannon. Pat had marched to take part in the Rising and he was the natural Republican leader of that area. Other parts of this Nationalist county were strongly Devlinite, and the canvassers used to concentrate on these hostile areas, content even with crumbs. In one of them I found a wide pocket of farm houses strongly Sinn Féin. " How did that come about ? " I asked my philosopher and guide. " Ah," he said, " there used to be a Cork teacher there and he got a paper—what happened it at all ? "

Some months after the close down I came to Dublin and found a job on P. J. Little's *New Ireland* printed by the Wood Printing Works in Fleet Street. The big office up the narrow stairs on the first floor had become the meeting-place of the writers and artists who stood beside Sinn Féin. Fred Higgins used to come shyly into the room and after talking and banter would take from his inside pocket a poem specially written for us. Pádraic Ó Conaire with his pipe and his short story in Irish, came as frequently. It was there, or through that group, I first met Andrew E. Malone, Austin Clarke, and Stephen MacKenna, the translator of Plotinus. I met there Mario Esposito, son of the composer, and now living again in his native Florence ; and Liam Slattery, Kevin O'Sheil, Liam Ó Briain of Galway and, I think, Rory O'Connor. There, too, I met Seumas MacManus, Jack Morrow, Jack B. Yeats and Kathleen Goodfellow, who wrote stirring ballads and stories of the period under the name of Michael Scot. Each of those poets, writers and artists, in his or her own way, added to the strength and the beauty of the hour.

But there was another group in the movement, more ordinary men and women, and these the writers and the artists fortified and inspired. Of them, I was soon the comrade, too. They were the Volunteers. How it was I came to join " K " Company, of the Third Battalion of the Dublin Brigade, I cannot now remember. Tom Cullen, the architect, was its Captain ; Larry Nugent, its Adjutant ; Seán McCluskey, its instructor. Late in the autumn of 1917, I think, we enrolled, my brother and I, and there began a life in the Volunteers that did not end for over seven years.

CHAPTER 41

THE VOLUNTEERS PREPARE

I THINK nothing while we live will take from us the thrill of those early days of the Volunteer reorganisation.

The best illustration I know of an underground movement was the Dublin of late 1917. The life of the city went on outwardly as in any other city. Day and night (for Curfew had not yet come), there was the uninterrupted coming and going of the citizens, many shops were open in the late evening, the theatres and social gatherings drew their crowds, and that new invention, the cinema, was building up its great following. The capital was still under some form of military rule, but the people had got used to the troops and nobody gave them more than a passing glance. Although O'Connell Street was still a ruin and the G.P.O. roofless to the sky, a visitor to Dublin would have observed nothing much else than a great city busy at its own tasks.

Yet, beneath that placid surface, there was an activity unbelievable in its intensity. Through the streets, with their sauntering couples, went a young lad here and there who, at some unpretentious doorway, melted away from the scene. That was usually around seven-thirty or eight in the evening; and these young men did not come back on to the streets again until ten o'clock or after. Without hurry or apparent secretiveness, they rejoined the saunterers and went home on the late trams.

Perhaps a careful watcher, told beforehand what to look for, might have found the secret. For if he had seen one young man or two pass through that inconspicuous doorway, he would see another and another every half-minute or so until he had counted fifty or sixty.

Where were they going, these young men? It could have been to a billiard rooms, or a bar, or to a " smoker," that concert for men only which was so popular in Dublin in those days. But if the watcher got inside that door, he would have seen a man leaning lazily against the wall, nodding as men came through. If a stranger blundered in, that lounging man came quickly to life and asked awkward questions. Those who nodded and passed him by went through a long passage. Towards the end of it was a large hall, well back from the street, fronted by shops, without any chance of sound coming to the people outside. There were a group of men chatting and laughing, a group growing in numbers every minute. When the hour fixed for the parade came, from that seeming careless mass a company of Volunteers would spring into being, and soon that hall would ring with sharp commands and tramping feet, with rapid turns and quick directions.

There were other nights when the men would stand easy while, from a table, the company captain read of de Wet's campaigns in the veldt or the operations of the famous German-led Askaris of East Africa. These were typical guerilla campaigns, such as we were being prepared for. Another night, an officer, who had been out in the Rising, came and, with chalk and blackboard, gave lectures on some action in that fight. The men would ask questions, and this elementary military science would supplement the handbooks on training, mainly British, which circulated amonst us.

With most of these listeners in the ranks, it wasn't that they wanted to be soldiers as such, or yearned for a life in arms. It was that somehow they saw coming a struggle in which, if they were trained, they could be of some use. That drilling had been declared illegal had something to do with it, and that it was already being punished with imprisonment had even more. The more the right to serve our own nation was condemned, the more we felt that right must be asserted.

How did these men live? Had they professions or trades or any special skills of their own? Well, I was a newspaper man, my brother and our friend, David Saunders, who joined with us, were bank officials, our captain was Tom Cullen, the celebrated architect, our first lieutenant a tailor, our section commanders and squad leader, were, one, a corporation inspector, another a dental mechanic, a third a labourer, a fourth a clerk. There were blacksmiths, painters, salesmen, chauffeurs, carters, electricians, barbers, shoemakers, railway men, shop assistants, bar tenders in this company. In fact, we were just a cross-section of the people who had been drawn together by each man's feeling that Ireland needed him. The pace of the national movement was quickening again, and to delay it, the British had set up the Plunkett Convention. But as the Convention talked, only to discover another trick of Lloyd George's and to collapse, the young men, without any outward show, slipped into the drill halls and slowly grew to be a disciplined army. The halls my company drilled in were: 6 Harcourt Street, 41 York Street, 44 Parnell Square, and a long room at 34 Lower Camden Street.

Among the lectures we got was a series on the mechanism and handling of arms. I remember the excitement of the first lesson in the workings of a rifle. The expert brought a Lee-Enfield, cut in sections, so that it could be opened like a book, and we could see the process that went to its loading and its firing. Other weapons followed, and the one that intrigued us most was the Peter the Painter, an automatic, self-loading, repeating pistol, compact and powerful.

The men provided their own arms. If they had no contact with somebody who could get weapons from the British forces, they paid whatever the ruling price of rifles was. This equipment came out of the nearest barracks, and I knew of some of our men who brought away material slipped to them from, it must have been, Wellington Barracks, by swimming hither and thither across the canal with it, in the depth of night, with blackened faces. When the way of purchases was closed to us, we raided.

The humour of one of these raids still bubbles in my recollection. The ordinary people had become the eyes and ears of the movement, and when somebody passed the word that the British Provost-Marshal had, in his private house in Haddington Road, a small museum of rifles and revolvers, Captain Cullen decided to get them. To disarm one of the military Governors of Dublin would be a delicious coup, and the whole thing was planned in great detail. The officers and N.C.O.'s of " K " Company were to become a plain-clothes squad of the Dublin Metropolitan Police. Tom Cullen, tall and soldierly, fitted perfectly the part of an ultra-responsible Sergeant O'Riordan, whom the Commissioner had charged with a special mission. Lieut. Harry O'Farrell, and others of us, were his aides. Sergeant O'Riordan and his squad would enter the house openly and explain to the Provost that it had got around that he had these arms. As the D.M.P. would be held to blame if they were taken by the I.R.A., we had come to fetch them for safe-keeping. He would get a receipt for them, and Tom had a police note-book for the purpose.

It was no trouble to enter the house, a large one in its own grounds. Tom asked at once for the Provost-Marshal, instructing others in the house to stay where they were and light no lights in the hall or on the stairs. This was necessary, as we feared that any close inspection of the rest of us would show how different we were from what the average D.M.P. man looked like. The Provost-Marshal was at first very stubborn in his refusal to allow any arms to be taken. The courteous sergeant patiently explained to him that he, the Marshal, would feel it very much if the I.R.A. did get them, and there was wind of the word that they might try. And any way, in times like these, a policeman had to do his duty, if necessary by force.

As we, in the hall, waited while the conference was on below in the armoury, a young lady came from the dining-room to talk to us, and to such loyal men she did not hide what she thought of that fellow de Valera and his gunmen. She certainly did not like them or him ; and in the next few days I often imagined, with delight, her horror as she recalled that conversation. Her eloquence was interrupted by the Provost-Marshal and Sergeant O'Riordan coming up from below with rifles under each arm. The sergeant gave them to us to bring to the car, and there followed several revolvers, a few hand-grenades and, I think a couple of bayonets. But the crowning joy was when the Provost-Marshal at last ran back into the armoury to take down a great German helmet hanging there and present it to Sergeant O'Riordan as a mark of appreciation of "Your courtesy, my man," adding "Good-bye, Sergeant, and I won't forget to write to the Commissioner about you." "Ah, you needn't do that, sir, we're only doing our duty."

There were no happier six men in the world than the carload that drove from the Provost's house to the company dump through the dusk of that evening. There, on Captain Cullen's lap, was the great helmet, and the glorious absurdity of it all, and the vision of that poor Provost-Marshal next morning, set us into laughter that has hardly died away since.

These rifles, and the weapons we bought and the guns we stole, were used for rifle practice and small arms drill on many a Sunday in the Dublin mountains. For the whole range of hills, behind the city, was the nursery of the new army. Young Dubliners were then, as now, great walkers. From the early Spring they crowded on to the roads leading to the Pine Forest and around Ticknock and over the Featherbed. The trams to Rathfarnham, and other termini for the hills, were thronged after early Masses, and among them were many a company going to its field manœuvres. In the valleys between the hills there were scores of places where, over rough ground, a company could be made adept and hardy. Aeroplanes were few and far between in those days, but if it had ever struck the British to send an observer plane low-flying over these crests and hollows, they would have had a better idea of what the next few years was to bring them.

Wherever noises of grenade practice might betray us, we had to move deeper into the hills and do our training with a curtain of scouts around the edge of the hollow. More than once we had to vanish behind the next shoulder of land as a raiding party would sweep past on the roads, searching, as they thought, the hills. On every side of them, in the brown heather and behind the clumps of the long mountain grass, the companies of the Volunteers would be waiting, only to be up again at their manœuvring as soon as the scouts had signalled the all-clear, and till evening came, they would be advancing, retreating, taking cover, out-flanking, moving silently to hand signals.

There was the spice of danger in it always, but as the months went by, and the elections came, and the Dáil was set up, the element of recreation gave way to the sternness of the deadly struggle.

CHAPTER 42

THE COMPANY COUNCIL

In 1920, all Ireland was an embattled citadel. The British had learned by then that they had against them a well-organised, closely-knit force, the strength of which they could not measure, the members of which they could not identify among the general population.

The parades in the drill halls, the mountain manœuvres were less frequent now, for that stage had passed. When we gathered, our purpose was not to drill, but to attack.

Day after day, the Volunteers delivered ambush and assault on the British regiments and convoys. These were no haphazard blows, but were planned with care and carried out with precision.

In Dublin, as 1920 changed into 1921, attack and ambush were incessant. In many cases it was not a few men, but fifty and a hundred, who struck. These men had to be mobilised from a hundred homes; they had to be armed, equipped, positioned without awakening the suspicions of the Power who held their city. The pretence that it was only a " gang " who were making war on them was blown to pieces every week in Dublin by this constant triumph of organisation, and by the full-scale operations that it led to. It forced from the British military chiefs themselves, admissions which have gone into history. They were being attacked, General Macready, the British Commander-in-Chief, said, " by a trained disciplined military force. . . . The chiefs of the rebel organisation issued military orders, had general headquarters and were continuously engaged in levying guerilla warfare against the Crown Forces."

Lord French, the Viceroy, had said of the Volunteers: " They are a formidable army."

Not only had the Volunteers become a well-organised military force, but its members shared an ideal which brought them readily into the heart of a thousand dangers.

Another English general, Lt.-General Sir Henry Lawson, wrote of the Volunteer officers as being " transparently sincere and single-minded idealists, highly religious for the most part, and often with an almost mystical sense of duty to their country. These men gave to the task of organising their Volunteers their best in mind and spirit. They fought against drunkenness and self-indulgence, and it is no exaggeration to say that, as a class, they represented all that was best

234

in the countryside. They and their Volunteers were trained to discipline, they imbibed the military spirit, the sense of military honour, etc. . . . . Behind their organisation there is the spirit of a nation."

That was true of every district—and of Dublin it was especially true. Each Dublin company was in charge of a clearly delimited area, and, as far as its resources permitted, made that area perilous for any British force that used it or passed through it.

Daylight attacks could not be frequent, because the Volunteers were workers by day. A permanent squad, called later the Active Service Unit, stood ready for action at all times, and brought off some great coups. But the war of attrition proper had to be carried out after the factories, workshops, shops and business places had closed, and the mass of the fighting men were free.

The actual fighting filled our daily thoughts then, but, as time passes, it all melts into a vague background to our lives. One action is remembered, another forgotten. Of the winter of 1920-21 there comes back a scene that was duplicated in many parts of the insurgent capital and, indeed, all over the land. There was the meeting of the Company Council. This particular one took place in the house in Capel Street of our new Captain, Harry O'Farrell, for Tom Cullen had been moved up.

The officers of the company were summoned by the usual chit handed to each member of the Council by a messenger who had to dare the holds-up and the cordons to fulfil his round of mobilisation. The order would read something like:

"K" COMPANY III

"You will attend a Company Council at 8 p.m. to-night. Usual place. Arms will be carried."

Busy as we were, such an order took precedence over everything, and somehow or other we found our way across an occupied city to the rendezvous. A Volunteer who knew us would be in the shadows by the slightly open door, and as we came towards it would stand aside. We mounted the stairs to the front drawing-room, and there, with all the noise of the city around us, some operation would be planned. There would be an adjournment for some days while the site was inspected, and a description of the proposal sent to Headquarters for approval. When approval came, the Council would work out every detail and try to foresee and provide for every eventuality. The captain sat at the head of the table, and insisted that every session would be as brief and as business-like as efficiency required.

One night in January, 1921, as we sat, to put the finishing touches to an important plan, a scout reported that a raiding party had entered the street and was coming up towards us, using a portable searchlight on the houses on this side.   There were eight or nine of us there, for the section commanders were taking part too.

We sat around a table, on which there was a map of the area, under a heavily-shaded lamp, when, through the blinds, the room was filled with a golden light—the searchlight was full on the windows. Captain O'Farrell told us, in that phlegmatic way of his, to go on with the discussion.   But, I am afraid, my mind wandered on to the luck we'd have if this were the house to be raided and we had to fight our way downstairs and out.   Slowly the blazing light outside moved on, and that night, before we dismissed, preparations had been completed for an attack on a British motor convoy, as elaborate as anything done by any other Dublin company.

We had been taught the rudiments of tactics.   Lessons for company officers were given in one of the big houses in Parnell Square, I forget which now.   There, in what was once the reception-room of an aristocratic pro-British family, the mere Irish sat now, a hundred junior officers.   At a large blackboard stood Commandant General J. J. O'Connell, known as " Ginger," for his hair was not black. He gave us a series of talks on street fighting, and excellent talks they were.   Some recent engagement would be taken, and we would learn how it might have been done otherwise with greater effect. We came armed to these lectures, and as the raiding lorries passed nearby, there was always some one to make the whispered comment as to *their* surprise if they came upon *us*.   But Ginger O'Connell's Northern accent would go nonchalantly on, and soon the tactics of the fight would have obliterated all other thought.   The principles we learned in that Parnell Square room we applied now.   Two things stand out, in memory, of what he said : That we do not ever underrate our enemy or fail to see to it there was a way of retreat from whatever position we occupied.

In every Volunteer Company, two of the most important officers were men in charge of intelligence, the " I.O." as we knew him, and the man in charge of arms, the Quartermaster.   They were usually not combatants at all.   I knew several with physical defects which put them outside the sphere of enemy suspicion.   The " I.O. " in his own time noted the coming and the going of every enemy convoy through his company's area, its composition, its strength, its destination.   He produced our " target for to-night."   He had observed that, every Friday evening at 7.40, a strong party of Auxiliaries, in two Crossleys, left Beggars' Bush Barracks to collect the mails at Westland Row.   They crossed Mount Street Bridge about

7.45, and, passing Holles Street a minute later, turned off towards the Station at Merrion Place.

It was decided to mobilise the whole company, and dividing them into three attacking parties, ambush that convoy, first at Holles Street, then, when the whole length of Merrion Square had made them feel secure again, at Leinster Street, and if the cars raced for the Castle, as they would if there were casualties, to come at them again at Lincoln Place. If the fight bogged down, or the Auxiliaries disembarked at any of the three points, the others would come effectively in as a rear attack. We brought riflemen to deal with a fight at long range.

For operations of this kind, the quartermaster would bring the arms to a nearby cache. This was necessary, as some of the arms might be " out " in the hands of another company on the previous night. The men, as they arrived for duty, got their small arms and their grenades. The rifles were ready for the special squad.

I remember the little room in a laneway off Holles Street—a tiny shop it seemed to be—and the scene could stand as a memorial to the gay gallantry of the young men of Dublin and, by extension, of all Ireland.

These Volunteers came from their work benches, after a hurried meal, still in their working clothes, to meet in battle the troops of the victorious British armies, in a battle not sought by the British but by them. They had no steel-sided protective vehicles to bring them to the conflict and safeguard them in it. They must use the shadows. They had no choice of perfect weapons with great firepower, and so must use the home-made grenade, the small calibre revolver, the out-of-date rifle. They had no vast military machine barracked all over the city, and ready, at a Verey light, to swoop down and surround the fighting area. They had no long training under perfect conditions, but night drill and Sunday marching, with a day or two of rifle practice. They had no hardening in the field of battle to accustom them to being under fire. Yet, to see them outside that little store off Holles Street, with the light shining on their faces as they took their weapons from Quartermaster Harding, was to see smiling lips and eager hands, and to hear the constant quip and jest which, as Irishmen and Dublinmen, they could not resist, no matter how serious the work they were bent on.

The trouble in all these conflicts was the uncertainty of the enemy being there at all. Any incident during that day might cause a change of plans and the target vanish. So it was that night. That convoy of Auxiliaries never came. We armed, and took our places as inconspicuously as possible around the railings of the Square at one side, and outside the big houses on the other. Somebody in the lighting department of the Corporation arranged for us that two of the street lights would be off, and so give us better cover. Eight o'clock passed, twenty past. It was decided we would hold on till something did come, and towards nine o'clock, over the Bridge came a convoy. I remember herding the passers-by into the hotel, where the National Maternity Hospital now stands. Then, with the street to ourselves, we waited.

It proved to be a military motor force of strength. The troops held their rifles as if they did not expect attack. As it entered our position, the sauntering, idling couples sprang to life, and, with a shout, the battle was on. I suppose it went on for only a few minutes, but it was fierce while it lasted, and the training up the mountain made it effective. When the convoy had passed beyond the range of grenade and revolver, it slowed down and stopped. But we had the riflemen up in an instant, and after an exchange of volleys, the engines roared again. The troops replied with rifle and machine-gun fire, and soon after the fight began to slacken, I remember thinking how suddenly the heavy rain had come, and, subconsciously, I turned up my coat collar against it. There was no rain; what I heard was machine-gun bullets spattering on the pavements around me. Happily the gunner's aim was low. At last the convoy moved out of range towards the other end of the Square, and we, by our plan, doubled back to act as a reserve to the other groups. As we ran, I remember a cry that showed how the people felt about it all. A woman ran out from a house and held out her apron to one of our men, whose revolver she had seen. " If you're caught with that, they'll kill you, ducky," she said. " Drop it in here and I'll keep it for you." But it was needed still, and we thanked her and sped on. A few minutes later we came up with the other sections. They were dispersing. The convoy had been hammered at Merrion Place, and again, as it raced for the Castle, at Lincoln Place. Some time later, we learned that twelve of the troops had been wounded.

What we did that night, other companies of the battalions of the Dublin Brigade did the next night, and the next. Only Headquarters, and the particular company officers, knew what was planned, and together they spaced the attacks and arranged which company would strike. By this co-ordination they kept too much enemy pressure from being used against any one area, and weakened the whole strength of the British forces by pinning them down to a score of scattered points. All through that winter and spring the Volunteers held the initiative. They had losses, heavy losses. In addition to those who fell in battle, some of their captured men and officers were basely hanged and many sent to penal servitude. But they struck blows which in the end brought the Occupying Power into a very accommodating mind indeed.

All through the latter part of the struggle, and, indeed, from the beginning, the British never knew where the next blow was coming from. Their great spy system was countered and defeated, too.

CHAPTER 43

THE WRONG LABEL

IN the War of Independence there were cases where bodies were found by the roadside with a placard attached to them bearing the legend " Spies and Informers Beware." Some of these were the bodies of faithful Republicans taken prisoner by the Crown Forces, murdered while in custody, and then labelled as if the Volunteers had shot them.

But the greater number were of men who in this local area or that had given information to those waging war on the nation, information which led to the capture or death of Ireland's defenders. The number was few when the length of the struggle and its penetration through the whole country is considered. In Ireland, as in France and other countries in enemy occupation, there were spotters and touts that always hang around tyranny, but the most singular thing about the struggle for liberty thirty years ago, compared with the previous uprisings, was that there were no national traitors. The British knew less of the insurgent army of 1917–1921 than of any revolutionary force in Ireland's history.

As the fight progressed, hundreds of Volunteers would be in the one secret, and not a little of it would be known outside the ranks. Often the very nation knew, and the British never heard of it. The burning of the tax-offices and vacated police barracks, on the one night, marked the ineffectiveness of the British secret service everywhere. A tradition that shielded the Volunteers greatly was their attitude to drink. Because there were few drinkers, and no drunkenness, one of the easiest ways to information was lost to the British.

The lines of political division helped in this keeping of secrets. In the Home Rule struggle, the " gentry," all but a handful, had massed themselves against the nation, and thus cut themselves mentally off from the whole Nationalist population. The Great War had at first obliterated that separation as thousands of Nationalists flocked into the British forces. But the scurvy treatment Nationalism got, the denial to Irish soldiers of any national symbol or separateness, dried up the enlistments and estranged those already in. The sympathy which " little Belgium " had created slowly evaporated as the brutality with which the Rising was suppressed became known.

All this was capped by the new effort to partition Ireland before the dead of 1916 had properly settled in their graves. Thus, it happened that when the War of Independence began in earnest the men in the actual fighting, and the deciders of policy above them, were united in one body with the mass of the people, and that unit differed so deeply from those who were against independence, that exchange of thought and information had ceased between them. The wall had grown too high for the neighbours to gossip or even to peep over.

There were other reasons. The R.I.C. had been invaluable to the British, spying in every little townland, sending a constant stream of information to the Castle. In the towns and cities, to which they had been driven, they knew few and could observe little. The " G " Division, who were the spies of Dublin, were bitterly regarded by the people, and as soon as the big fight began, several were shot dead in daylight in the streets, one on the very steps of the Headquarters of the Division in Brunswick Street. And though there were a few men with enough misplaced courage to go on to the end, and a few others who, believing in a free Ireland, daily risked their lives by acting for the Volunteers inside the Castle itself, the majority of the remainder did their civil detective duty, but looked the other way when the Volunteers were concerned.

Their ordinary intelligence forces having failed them, the British began to send agents to Ireland to infiltrate into the higher ranks of the Volunteers. Two famous cases were those of Jameson and Quinlisk. Jameson was the more successful, and came near achieving something real. He posed as a person able to secure arms through international agents and also through British acquaintances.

He was extraordinarily clever and came to Dublin with an introduction from Republicans in London. He saw Michael Collins several times, and might have brought off his capture if the R.I.C. Command itself had not blundered. Volunteer headquarters became suspicious of him, but Jameson was able to reassure them, and having visited England, came back to try again. A trap was laid for him. He was told a document which he wanted returned was in Collins's files in an address in Iona Drive, then occupied by a strongly pro-British family. The house was promptly raided, and Jameson, at his next request for an interview, was given an appointment. But the messengers he met this time were the messengers of death, and he was shot dead on the Ballymun Road half an hour later.

Quinlisk had been a British N.C.O., was captured by the Germans, and later joined Casement's Brigade. On his return to Ireland, he was helped for a long time out of national funds, and then decided to go to the Castle. He played the double role—the spy for the British and pretended spy for the Volunteers, seeing Collins himself, and reporting to him on his own visits to the British. But a trap was set for him, too. Next time he asked to see Collins, he was told he was in Cork, staying at Wren's Hotel, Winthrop Street, and a little later a code message to the Cork R.I.C. gave the information. Quinlisk went to Cork to be in at the kill. He was executed there within the week, on 18th February, 1920.

Baulked again and again of getting inside the Irish lines, the British, with great care and secrecy, prepared a net of espionage in and around Dublin. Highly-trained intelligence officers were sent over. Under assumed names, they took lodgings in various areas of the city, and began to establish social and business connections. Their wives came with them, and under the cover of ordinary residence, they began to organise a system of runners and touts who would be their agents in the rough and tumble of city life. They were mainly officers, some with high rank, but to the neighbours they were just Mr. This and Mr. That and it was only at later trials of those charged with slaying them, that their real names and their military ranks appeared.

They had a purpose other than spying. London had the fatuous belief that they could break this movement by removing the leaders. In the country, the local leader was arrested if he could be easily taken alive, and was shot dead if he could not be. Arrests were the main method. But those whom Britain most wanted could not be found to be arrested, and towards the end of 1920 the plan to assassinate high Volunteer officers, wherever they could be discovered, was being worked out between the Castle and the chain of military Secret Service men planted around Dublin.

It was later to succeed momentarily in Limerick, where, on one night, forces of the Crown shot dead in their homes some of the most prominent Republican leaders in the city, and the number would have been greater if all the plans had worked. In Dublin the same idea was being entertained—in one night to raid the houses of the leaders and kill them.

Those who planned this " settlement " did not know that if the British were not inside our lines, we were inside theirs, and that all through October, and the early weeks of November, 1920, the identity of the secret agents was being established. The Minister for Defence and General Headquarters had to be satisfied that every man believed to be an agent, was, in fact, one. When the final list was being compiled, Cathal Brugha removed from it the names of fifteen men as the evidence against them was not beyond doubt.

Photographs of many of the others had been secured and were carried into the houses on the morning of Sunday, 21st November, 1920, in order that the wrong men would not be shot. And yet one was. It was the most widespread operation the Dublin Brigade had carried out. At nine o'clock that Sunday morning, at many scattered points around the city, Volunteers, in twos and threes, entered the private houses and small hotels in which the agents lived. At the same hour the rest of the particular company took up positions outside, so that when the men came back they would be saved from arrest, if necessary by a full-scale action. Until the men had got away, the guarding force was not withdrawn.

There was but one fight that morning. In Upper Mount Street a passing party of Auxiliaries heard the shots, and a battle opened at once. Elsewhere, the marked men were shot out of hand. In two or three instances, men on the list had gone away for the week-end.

The British intelligence service never recovered from that blow. Though hundreds of Dublin men knew it—for each company, the night before, had been mobilised and given directions—it came as a thunderbolt upon the Castle. The revenge they took was typical of the character of the whole repression. Early that afternoon it was learned from inside the Castle that an armed attack on the players and spectators at the match in Croke Park had been organised. Though word was rushed to the Park, it was too late, and many were killed and wounded in that pitiless onslaught. Next morning, Dick McKee and Peadar Clancy, arrested the night before, and knowing their own fate from the secret of what the day was to bring, died by murder, and with them a young Clare Volunteer, Conor Clune. But the effect of the operation was that the whole British spy system collapsed and was never restored.

In the next few days, Dublin saw one of the strangest sights that old city had ever witnessed. From all corners of the capital there began a trek of minor spies and spotters and touts into the Castle, which was the size of a small town. They brought their families, their personal belongings. They crowded in behind those high walls in full admission that their day was done. Already the " G " Division of the D.M.P. had been driven in; then the heads of the R.I.C., and now a motley gathering of undesirables of all kinds and sorts who had looked for blood-money, and in this day of doom wanted nothing so much as protection. They trundled through the gates of the Castle, themselves the embodiment of what alien rule had become in Ireland, corrupt, furtive, down-at-heel. And the heads of the régime who met them, and took them in, must have sensed that their own day was over. By hiding the real quality of those who had been shot, they made vast propaganda of the deaths of the secret service officers. They represented it as the wilful slaying by the murderous Irish of innocent men. But the massacre at Croke Park blunted the pretence, and the well-informed, even in Britain, guessed that there was much more in the story than was being told in the fantastic official reports.

CHAPTER 44

THE ARMY DECIDES

THE flight of the spotters and the touts into the Castle was the outward sign of a fundamental change in the war against insurgent Ireland. From that point forward, the British concentrated on force alone. The month after Bloody Sunday saw direct military rule clamped down on whole counties, and the institution of such practices as carrying hostages with every raiding convoy. All the executions, except that of Kevin Barry, took place after 21st November, and some of the worst of the systematic destruction by troops and police, such as the burning of the heart of Cork City, on 11th December, 1920. From 1st January to 20th November, 1920, there had been 116 murders by the Crown forces, counting none of the Republican casualties in the struggle. In the month after 21st November, there were sixty-nine, and in the six months to May, 1921, there were 258.

The refusal of the people to help them, convinced the Castle that all Ireland was their enemy, and that they could now strike where they liked without much fear of injuring a friend.

All these things convinced those of us who were not by nature soldiers that only by force could this wild beast be cornered and driven out. Every democrat knew that force could be a Frankenstein. Unless the Volunteers were to be the servants of the people, they might well become the masters of the people. The perception of this peril came to many minds at the foundation of the movement, and they tried to counter it by making the whole scheme an elective one.

Each company elected its own officers. Tom Cullen was elected our captain, Harry O'Farrell and I its lieutenants, and so it was with every company. Through the battalion and the brigade this election system ran, and it was crowned by the convention of Volunteer delegates, who chose the supreme body of the movement, the Executive. So in the early days, before Ireland's independence was proclaimed in National Parliament, the control rested in its own membership.

The elective system had a remarkable effect on the character of this armed movement. It brought men to the top more as citizens than as soldiers. The efficient military man was less likely to appeal to his fellows, and to be commissioned by vote, than the man who

believed most deeply in Ireland's independence.   No doubt, it lessened
the professional efficiency of the force, but it gave it something
much more important in the years immediately after the Rising,
namely, a leadership that believed fully in the ideals of the 1916 men,
and had a fundamental bias towards democracy.   This was a safeguard against the danger that the great machine would be used to
any lesser end than full freedom.   It was something of a safeguard
also against the possibility of a secret society getting control of the
movement.   There was not then the example the world later provided
of the private armies of Nazism and Communism, fastening these
creeds on great peoples and bringing powerful nations to ruin.   But
the danger was there, and it was felt, particularly by those of us who
had been in prison, and had there met some of the more extreme
I.R.B. men.   That organisation plainly had plans of its own which
were not those of an elected Government.   The I.R.B. regarded
as the primary authority in Ireland the Supreme Council of their own
Secret Society.   There were the seeds of calamity in that kind of
attitude.   The creation of a Government with a Parliament and a
Minister for Defence, responsible to it, prevented any immediate
germination of those seeds.   Dual control was, we hoped, gone.
The secret I.R.B., and the open Volunteer Executive, had been
replaced by the elected Government of the Republic of Ireland.

There was opposition to the control of the Volunteers by the Dáil.
It came partly from the prior claims of the I.R.B., partly from many
who feared all political influences.   The difficulty was resolved by
letting the Volunteers themselves discuss and determine the issue.
At least, I suppose that was the meaning of the delegate conferences
which met in the Autumn of 1919 and considered the proposal
that each Volunteer should take the same oath as was taken by the
elected deputies.   More than one of those soldier-delegates raised
the question of what would happen if Dáil Éireann itself deserted
the Republic.   The answer was given that in that case the Army
would automatically be freed of its allegiance to the Dáil and would
return to its former method of governance, an elected Executive.

I recall these discussions as deep and grave, for I was a delegate to
at least one convention.   The delegates were little swayed by the
platform, and expressed their own views freely.   The feeling was
general that this submission to the Government of the Republic
was the right thing to do, and the decision to take the oath was
unanimous.   The Volunteers thus became constitutionally what, in
fact, they were already in spirit, the servants of the civil power.
They were not openly acknowledged to be the Army of the Republic,
but they themselves knew that was their status.   What was to prove a
tragedy later for the Volunteers, and for Ireland, was that a section

of the I.R.B. continued its secret existence, and its struggle for control both of the Dáil and of the Army.

To those of us in the companies, the establishment of the Volunteers as the military arm of the elected Government, solved many a moral difficulty. We, who had to take life, were now soldiers of a democratically-established State, to whom the people, in open election, had given all the rights and authority of a sovereign power. Our duty became the simple one, expressed in the terms of the oath, to " support and defend the Irish Republic and the Government of the Irish Republic, which is Dáil Éireann."

It was in virtue of that pledge of allegiance that, to save the Dáil, the great spy-ring was broken.

The days that followed Bloody Sunday were hectic days. In the cities the great raids began by which whole areas, embracing many streets, were cordoned off and sealed by barbed wire. Inside the cordons, groups of Auxiliaries and military intelligence officers visited every room and shop, every office and house, examining every cupboard and scrap of paper. The cordon was sometimes not lifted for three days, and the search went on inside it through day and night. Many were taken in these huge raids. So many, that the jails and prisons could no longer hold them, and there were established those great prison camps, in which neglect and ill-usage and sometimes death was the fate of many. Two of the most notorious were Ballykinler in Co. Down and the Curragh. Untried and uncharged men lived hard and bitter lives in these camps for more than a year.

The greatest care to prevent escapes was taken, and each camp was surrounded by well-manned towers, equipped with searchlights and machine-guns. Yet, hundreds found their way back into the struggle. By countless strange devices, through tunnels, dressed as workmen, wearing a copy of some uniform, sneaking under the body of a bread-van or garbage cart, using night and fog and snowstorms as screens, men slipped out week after week, to be hidden away by the people until they could get in touch with their own units. Several were shot in these attempts, but the risk of that they thought better than to be broken in health in these festering camps which to the end held over 4,000 boys and men.

The military dictatorship was intensified in other ways after the elimination of the spy-ring. Curfew was extended immediately. A Proclamation was issued on 10th December, putting all Cork and Cork County, Limerick City and Limerick County, Tipperary and Kerry under Martial Law, and the area thus placed in complete military power was extended to nearly half the nation in the following months. On 14th December, Courts of British Officers were set up to which were given power of the death penalty almost without limit.

It was not any longer a question of whether one bore arms, it was giving aid in any way to the struggle. Three-fourths of Ireland was at that hour guilty of this capital crime and because they remained undeterred and kept their doors open for the hunted, the Volunteers, in the cities particularly were able to carry on.

The savagery of the Auxiliaries and Black-and-Tans passed all bounds. The case of the Brothers Loughnane, of Gort, Co. Galway, and of Canon Magner, of Dunmanway, Co. Cork, became typical of the treatment of any who stood against tyranny. The Loughnanes were arrested at the end of November and were not seen again until, on 6th December, their bodies were found in a pond. From their fearful injuries it could only be concluded that they had been tied to the tail of a lorry and drawn over the roads until the bouncing had killed them. On 15th December, Canon Magner, an old priest of 73, had seen a young parishioner, Volunteer Timothy Crowley, murdered in his presence at the roadside by a convoy of twenty Auxiliaries. His shocked and stern protest brought fire upon himself and he, too, was murdered. On St. Stephen's night the Black-and-Tans burst into a dance hall at Bruff, Co. Limerick, and there killed and wounded twenty-two young men.

From all over Ireland the tales of these sufferings came in a flood, but with them came reports of the answer—ambush, attack, stratagem and surprise.   Ceaselessly the insurgents harried the forces of oppression. The struggle was reaching its blazing zenith.

In America the President learned on the 27th November of the arrest of Arthur Griffith and of Eoin MacNeill. There was much still to do for Ireland, for her safety and her victory, but with the acting head of the Republic in jail, the President's place now was in Ireland.

CHAPTER 45

THE AMERICAN MISSION

BECAUSE of the rush and tumble of the times, the mission of the President of the Republic to the United States never became widely known in the Ireland of that day.

A few of us, then workers at No. 6, knew that he had gone, and later came to understand the importance of what was happening on "the other side." The Cabinet and Dáil Éireann when it met got regular reports, and occasional messengers from beyond would tell us of meetings, the size and spirit of which they had never seen before. But the mass of the people never got the chance to understand the vital need for that mission and the fruitful consequences of it.

Before any hint at all came to the people that de Valera was out of Ireland, Arthur Griffith told a meeting of Dáil Éireann on 17th June, 1919:

> "The President has, by and with the advice of the Ministry, gone on a mission abroad."

He was to speak of it again at a session, held now in secret, in October, 1919, when Griffith referred the Dáil to the growing list of British military aggressions and added:

> "All these acts which succeed each other in regular procession are of the greatest assistance to our efforts in the United States and it is there that the centre of gravity of the political situation is for the present fixed."

That was the new fact of the situation. The centre of gravity had swung to America and that land had become of primary importance in the struggle for Irish freedom.

World War I had ended less than a year before Griffith's October speech. The American President, Woodrow Wilson, had made many speeches describing the United State's war aims, and if they were implemented, it must mean freedom for Ireland. Immediately after the United States' entry into the war Wilson said (May, 1917) that America:

> "is fighting for no advantage or selfish object of her own, but for the liberation of peoples everywhere from the aggressions of autocratic force."

In August he said :

> " The American people believe that peace should rest upon the rights of peoples, not the rights of governments—the rights of peoples, great or small, weak or powerful—their equal right to security and freedom and self-government."

And, in February, 1919 :

> " We set this Nation up to make men free . . . and now we will make them free."

On 4th March he spoke in New York and seemed to identify our nation in his pledge :

> " The nations that have long been under the heel have called out to the world, generation after generation, for justice, liberation and succour and no Cabinet in the world has heard them. Private organisations, philanthropic men and women, have poured out their treasure in order to relieve their sufferings but no nation has said to the nations responsible : ' You must stop ; this thing is intolerable and we will not permit it.' "

To the Irish people the promise was so clear ; the description so fitted their own nation, that the United States they felt would now surely come to their aid.

The leaders were less sanguine, but they did feel that this was the ideal moment for a mission to America. No other great power was likely to give international recognition to the Republic, and the smaller nations friendly to us held back on that account. If America could be got to recognise us, the other nations would follow. From America, too, would come the sinews of war, and if the American citizens on Ireland's side could only be properly organised that very weight of their opinion might do much that was vital. Britain might even be forced to accept the independence which the nation had so recently declared, and which filled the requirements for self-deter-mination laid down in the victors' speeches.

All this had become clear to de Valera in Lincoln prison and to others in other jails. Within a week or so of his escape in February, the national leader slipped back to Ireland, and the proposed journey was discussed with leading members of Dáil Éireann who were still at liberty.

It was not easy to fix details for this secret voyage, but early in March there seemed a chance, and de Valera crossed back to Liverpool to be ready to board the first liner to take him through the British lines. The arrangements fell through at the last moment, but while he waited in hiding he who had drafted the Constitution under which

the new Sinn Féin had become the greatest mass movement since
O'Connell's day, now drafted the Constitution of the Self-Determination League of Great Britain, through which the Irish across the
Channel, and later those in Canada, Australia and New Zealand,
helped so substantially the struggle of their motherland.

At the second session of the Dáil which chose him President,
de Valera nominated a broadly-based Cabinet which, as we commented
at the time, embraced every facet of the movement : Griffith at one
end of the Republican scale, Cathal Brugha at the other, with Collins,
Cosgrave, MacNeill, Count Plunkett and Countess Markievicz in
between.

All the groups in the insurgency had been provided for. For
then, and all through the War of Independence, the demon of disunity
was mortally feared by de Valera and Griffith. They had seen so many
bright hopes for Ireland brought to the dust by it ! And they were
now warned again of the danger by news of a split among the leaders
of the Friends of Irish Freedom, founded in the United States after
the Rising and led by members of the American I.R.B., or, as it was
called there, the Clann na Gael. De Valera commissioned Harry
Boland, who then held high office in the I.R.B. at home, to go to
America and bring those warring sections into unity.

Anybody who worked in 6 Harcourt Street at that time will
remember Harry's going. It took from our Headquarters the gayest
spirit of us all. He combined his work for Ireland with such joy in
life and delight in the struggle, that he became an impersonation of
that exalted time ; boyish, indomitable, full of laughter and at the
core of it all a hidden toughness. I see again the scenes of the day he
left. Anna Fitzsimons had typed for him a copy of the Declaration
of Independence on thin, durable paper and Fintan Murphy had
arranged with a Republican shoemaker in Cross Kevin Street, Dublin,
to have it secreted in the heel of one of Harry's heavy sea boots
together with a copy of the prospectus of the Dáil Loan which Fintan
himself typed. The copy of the Declaration bore, I think, the signatures of the Speaker of the Dáil and members of the Ministry
He was to make the crossing as a furnace hand and we pitied him
in the days that followed. " Fitz " and I fled from the gloom that
came down on No. 6 on the day of his going, and at a sad lunch at
Kidd's, we mourned for him and for ourselves. For all his authority
in the I.R.B. and his gift for bringing men together, Harry did not
succeed in closing the divide in the Friends of Irish Freedom.

About this time, early in May, 1919, there came to Dublin an
American Mission which had gone to Paris to press Ireland's claim
to be heard at the Peace Conference. The mission was composed of a
former Governor of Illinois, Edward Dunne, a former Presidential

candidate and one of Ireland's staunchest friends, Frank P. Walsh, and a high official of Pennsylvania, M. J. Ryan.

With these de Valera discussed what could be done to secure American recognition of the Republic and to float a loan there. Ryan was a banker and replied that a loan would be too difficult, the laws governing flotation by other countries were too comprehensive and the banks would refuse to handle it. Then, catching something of de Valera's intentness, he added : " Unless you yourself were to come and do it." The search for a boat was straightway speeded up.

In the first days of June, the President left Ireland. He bought a return ticket to Manchester, where Austin Stack was in prison, and openly boarded the mail boat. But at Holyhead he changed direction and eventually reached Birkenhead, where late one night, he slipped aboard the *S.S. Lapland*, and was hidden deep down in the hold where rats were his only companions. When the vessel had made the open sea he was brought up to the tiny lamp-room in the prow. There he could hear through the long voyage—for the *Lapland* went first to Halifax—the Atlantic storms smashing against the ship and the talk of returning Canadian soldiers as they sat a few feet from him. It was a rough voyage and the leader concealed in the stuffy den suffered grievously from sea-sickness.

There were three Irish sailors through whose courage and care the President made that voyage safely : Barney Downes, of Wexford, the bosun; Paddy McMahon, of Clare, the lamptender; and Dick O'Neill, able seaman. We shall meet them again.

It was a relieved stowaway who in the quiet of the night came down the crews' gang-plank into the New York docks. There Harry Boland and, I think, Joe McGarrity met him. He was safely through the British lines. When news came secretly home that he had arrived, Arthur Griffith told the Dáil of the Cabinet's advice to de Valera that he go " on a mission abroad."

On 23rd June de Valera made his presence in the United States public in an announcement at the first of many press conferences :

> " From to-day I am in America as the official head of the
> Republic established by the will of the Irish people in accordance
> with the principles of self-determination."

Thus there began one of the most powerful and fruitful movements in the history of the Irish in America. It was not now only a political leader who had come out to them, but the President of that independent Ireland for which they had so long yearned and worked. Much was already being done by many groups, it was to unify that work, to intensify it, to give it agreed direction that he had come, not to change. Both he and Harry Boland tried again to close the division in the leadership of The Friends of Irish Freedom, and it was patched up, though only for a time. Eventually, a year later the President had to seek other means to fulfil his task if the enthusiasm and all the energy were not to founder in frustration. He launched the organisation that was numerically to surpass even Sinn Féin and the Self-Determination League.

This latest body went by an alphabetical title, the A.A.R.I.R., but its extended name contained its purpose : The American Association for the Recognition of the Irish Republic. The major task which the Cabinet had committed to the President was to secure from the American Government acceptance of Ireland's declared independence. If that could be accomplished Ireland's fight would at least be more even—there could be no executions, no midnight assassinations, no breaking of men in the prisons, no dragooning of the civil population, no carrying of hostages, no blazing towns. The Irish Volunteers would be a belligerent force entitled on capture to the status of belligerents and entitled to purchase, too, wherever they could, proper armaments. In a word, the rules of war would apply and the people be saved incalculable suffering. It was something to work oneself to the bone to achieve, and de Valera's whole company out from Ireland (for some had come before and others were to follow), so worked—Harry Boland, James O'Mara, and Stephen O'Mara who succeeded him, Liam Mellows, Kathleen O'Connell, Seán Nunan, Annie Ryan of Grenanstown, afterwards to become Mrs. Nunan ; Dr. McCartan, Diarmuid Lynch, Joe Begley, Liam Pedlar, Gilbert Ward, Garth Healy, and a host of the Irish in America. Tirelessly, day after day, the work went on. The way was prepared for the floating of the Dáil Éireann Loan by a series of meetings and the establishing of committees in every city, town, and state. Thanks to lawyer friends, like Martin Conboy and Frank P. Walsh, the legal difficulties were got over by the issue of bond certificates, which became known as the Dáil Bonds. Beautifully designed and printed they bore the inscription :

" I, Eamon de Valera, President of the Elected Government of the Republic of Ireland, acting in the name of and by the authority of the elected representatives of the Irish Nation, issue this certificate in acknowledgment of your subscription of .... dollars to the First National Loan of the Republic of Ireland. This certificate is not negotiable, but it is exchangeable if presented at the Treasury of the Republic of Ireland one month after the international recognition of the said Republic for one............... Gold Bond of the Republic of Ireland. Said Bond to bear interest at five per cent., per annum, from the first day of the seventh month after the freeing of the territory of the Republic of Ireland from Britain's military control, and said Bond to be redeemable at par within one year thereafter."

The bonds were issued at values from $10 to $10,000 and they were bought in every state of the Union. The F.O.I.F. and other Irish organisations, and later the A.A.R.I.R., which was to reach an active membership of almost 800,000, organised their sale through a vast network of clubs and branches covering the States, east to west, north to south.

The President had been authorised by the Cabinet at home to raise $1,250,000, but with the work of mission and helpers together, that total was soon passed, and in the end over six million dollars worth of bonds were sold. The Republic was being provided with the funds to fight on and, at the same time, the people of America were being enabled to see the facts of Ireland's struggle in their true light.

CHAPTER 46

THE IRISH MOVE UP

THE British sent lecturers and propagandists to America and organised pro-British writers and speakers to counter the effect of de Valera's mission and to turn away from herself the rising anger at the conditions in Ireland.

Yet, much though those agents did, they could not stop the surge in Ireland's favour.

Their attack was a multiple one. The External Loan was jibed at as taking dollars from servant girls for murder in Ireland. It is true that many a young woman emigrant and many a young lad, too, poured every cent. they could spare into the loan. But the second generation of the Irish, and the third and the fourth, were buying the bonds, too. And so were young men and women who had no drop of Irish blood in their veins, but felt angry that the American war-aims should have been abandoned in the case of Ireland.

The sectarian argument was used to the full, suggesting to the predominantly Protestant population of America that this was purely a papist affair and that the Irish Catholics wanted to get power to persecute the Protestant minority. Whereat many of those who were speaking and working for the Loan disclosed that they were Protestants. Three of the most eloquent and active workers for it were Protestant clergymen, a Baptist, a Methodist, and a Presbyterian. And from Ireland had come Rev. Dr. J. A. Hamilton Irwin, who toured every State in the Union. These and a score of others put on record the innumerable tributes by the minority in Ireland to their generous treatment by the Catholic majority.

It was then suggested that the money that was being raised would never reach Ireland, but would be squandered in riotous living by a group of leaders in America. That had been foreseen, too, and from the reception of the first dollar the Irish President had insisted that the accounts should be kept with the same care as the Treasury of any free nation would keep them. They were fully audited by firms of high standing, and so presented that the expenditure of each cent. could be traced.

I myself sat in the Supreme Court of New York State in 1927, after disagreement at home had led to a lawsuit about the residue of the loan. I heard Judge Peters of that court speak with respect of the protection given to these moneys and the care with which they were husbanded and allocated for the purposes for which they were subscribed.

The Irish in the States were greatly strengthened by this kind of integrity and those who were not Irish at all watched and were impressed. The President of the Irish Republic was officially invited to visit their cities and their States, to address their legislatures, to speak of Ireland's hopes and of the unequal war she was fighting. When he came to many of their State capitals, they gave him the salute reserved for rulers, the 21 guns. Governors officially welcomed him, State troops were detailed to escort him, great cities were decorated at public cost in his honour, and everywhere there were such gatherings as had not been seen in the United States even in the days of Parnell.

There were places where the old anti-Irish feeling was whipped into fury, halls were refused and official welcomes denied. That spurred the friends of Ireland to supreme efforts, and if the hall remained empty, the greatest open space in the city was filled and overflowing, and if there was no official welcome, then the citizens themselves seemed to tidal-wave out far from the city boundary to meet the incoming President and escort him with their bands, their banners, and their songs, in an imposing march through the main streets.

Years later, I was at 29th Street, a down-town section of New York, and I was guest of that magnificent fighter for Ireland, the Very Rev. Father Larry Flanagan, of the Carmelite Priory there. I asked him if there were many Irish in his parish. " There were nearly all Irish five or six years ago," he answered, " but there are now practically none, thanks to you fellows in Ireland and to de Valera here." He paused and said : " The fight that was made here and in Ireland put such spirit and such pride into the Irish emigrants that they quit their menial jobs and moved uptown, and you find them now at better work, and in finer homes everywhere."

In March, 1920, came the first major fruit of the effort by the President to get recognition. The Senate at Washington, one of the most conservative bodies in the world, ratified the Peace Treaty, with a reservation which declared :

> " The United States adheres to the principle of self-determina-
> tion and to the resolution of sympathy with the aspiration of the
> Irish people for a Government of their own choice adopted
> by the Senate, 6th June, 1919, and declares that when such
> Government is attained by Ireland—a consummation which
> it is hoped is at hand—it should promptly be admitted as a
> member of the League of Nations."

It was not recognition by any means, but coming from the intensely cautious Senate of the United States, it measured how far the case for Irish independence had won sympathy up to the top. If the American people could be convinced that, in fact, Ireland had *now* the Government of her choice, the rest might follow.

All this time the struggle in Ireland was growing in intensity, the great prison strikes came, the assassination of leaders, the destruction of towns, the suppression of Dáil Éireann. News of these things could not now be hidden in back pages. There was an eager public for the truth.

It was in this atmosphere that the President undertook his nation-wide tours, which are declared to be the sternest test of stamina in American political life. I have myself witnessed a little of what they entail, this rail journey of upwards of ten thousand miles, a meeting almost every day, some days two, occasionally three. Few breaks, and these filled with conferences, receptions, speeches at dinners, Press interviews, visits to universities, State and Mayoral receptions, addresses to legislatures, and the long chain of calls that must be carried out in every city and State capital. Many times the only chance for sleep came in the trains.

The President travelled that vast territory several times in steaming heat, in freezing cold. (I remember one day, in this land of many climates, reading on the ice-covered hoardings in Chicago, advertisements to " Bathe at Bimini Beach " away on the Pacific coast.) Many times the early morning sleeps on the trains would be broken by welcoming committees coming aboard many miles below the city to be next visited, and often at midnight, when he took the last train out, he could not lie down because a group would board it with him to discuss problems to the next big station an hour or two away.

Behind him de Valera would leave groups, committees, branches of the A.A.R.I.R., more determined than ever to have Ireland's voice heard, divergencies would be smoothed out, splits healed, and with the maximum of unity the drive would go on.

The greatest chance came with the political conventions of the summer of 1920, for this was a Presidential year. At these conventions, the platforms of the great parties, Republican and Democrat, were compiled on which the candidates would seek the support of the voters. To get a plank into these programmes pledging the candidates specifically to recognise the Republic was of first importance. But it was here, at the very climax of the mission, that the conflict in the leadership of the Friends of Irish Freedom proved fatal to Ireland. Some of these leaders thought to save embarrassment to American politicians by suggesting that less than what the mission from Ireland sought would be enough. Though de Valera and all his closest and

wisest Irish and American friends fought like tigers for the forthright
pledge of recognition, the drafting committees were glad to take
advantage of the weaker counsel and proposed only the same resolutions of friendliness and sympathy, of which there were already so
many. But the time for these, with the Irish people now under a dire
tyranny, had passed, and de Valera would not accept them.

All the time—as anybody who understands political rivalry will
appreciate—the section of Clann na Gael who from the first had
disliked the President's coming, was watching him like a lynx. It
was counted that some major mistake would be made on the basis
of which a campaign could be launched to drive him home. No such
mistake was made, de Valera had insisted that his mission not interfere
in American internal politics and though this resolution required
phenomenal care in the keeping—it was kept.

Some breach of behaviour or conduct would have served as well,
and that, too, was waited for. But, says Dr. McCartan, himself
deeply critical, " he had conducted himself in public with so much
circumspection and dignity as to bring him universal respect."

In the end an issue had to be manufactured, and it was found in an
interview which in February, 1920, de Valera gave to the United
States representative of the *Westminster Gazette*, and out of it arose
the now forgotten storm over the " Cuban settlement."

In this interview, de Valera dealt with the British fear—a natural
one even then from the British point of view, and one it was wise
for Ireland to meet—that a free Ireland might allow herself to be
used by another power to attack Britain in time of war. De Valera's
answer was a simple one, and was a forerunner of the unanimous
policy of Dáil and people in the Second World War. A free Ireland,
said de Valera, and her neighbour Britain could enter into an agreement in which both would undertake to respect the inviolability of
the other. He instanced, as an example, of what he had in mind—
the Platt Amendment to the American settlement with Cuba. In
that, Cuba pledged herself to preserve her own integrity and
independence and

> " never enter into any treaty or other compact with any
> foreign power or powers which will impair or tend to impair the
> independence of Cuba, nor in any manner authorize or permit
> any foreign power or powers to obtain colonization or for
> military or naval purposes or otherwise, lodgment in or control
> over any portion of the said Island."

An undertaking to permit no foreign power to take over any part
of the liberated territory of Ireland was not only in consonance with
full independence, but was, in fact, an exercise of it. To the watching

group, however, more anti-British than pro-Irish, it seemed ideal as the long-sought grounds for an attack on the Irish mission. It was made the basis of a fierce campaign and a long one.

De Valera was accused of yielding to Britain, of lessening the demand for independence, of letting down the Republic, of wanting only Cuban status for Ireland. All the hidden antagonism to him burst into a searing denunciation. Efforts were made to spread the hostility to Ireland, but the Cabinet and the Dáil had been kept fully informed, and at its secret meeting of 29th June, 1920, Arthur Griffith tabled a motion that the following message be sent to the President :

> " Dáil Éireann, assembled in full session to-day, unanimously reaffirms the allegiance of the citizens of Ireland to your policy, expresses complete satisfaction with the work you have performed, and relies with confidence upon the great American nation to accord recognition to the Republic of Ireland now in fact and in law established."

Speaking of what had been achieved, Griffith said :

> " In America, the work accomplished by the President has been extraordinary ; he has welded the Irish race into a united force ; he has raised the Irish question there into the position of an international issue."

Dáil and Cabinet together begged him to continue his work, and empowered him to spend a million dollars to secure recognition of the Republic.

The tours, the organisation of the A.A.R.I.R., the great meetings went on. Events at home lit up those platforms from which Ireland's case was being stated : the success of the Dáil courts, the mutiny in the R.I.C., the coming of the Black-and-Tans, the arrest of Dr. Mannix, the heroism and death of Terence MacSwiney, the bravery of Kevin Barry.

CHAPTER 47

THE C.I.D. AND BUSY MEN

IN that turmoil into which Ireland was thrown after Bloody Sunday, I was one evening with Arthur Griffith.

We were in the big front room of the Sinn Féin headquarters, and he told me of the certainty of his arrest, of which he seemed to have had word from inside the Castle. He scorned to go on the run, and might now be taken at any time. We talked of the effect of his being jailed, and of the fact that, with the President in the United States, there would then be no experienced political leadership at the top.

He did not make much of the immediate danger of that, and I agreed with him, for it was a time simply for standing fast. Yet, in a very little while, we were to see—he in prison and I on the run— how swiftly things can change. But he agreed that if he was taken, it would be well to have a statement published from him, calling on the nation not to lose heart, to hold on to its great purpose whatever came.

He sat by a table in that long room and wrote his message. His way was the journalist's way. He seized a pad and started writing at once. If the sentences did not flow easily, he turned the pad over and began again, and this went on until the right phrase came, and then swiftly the job was done.

I remember his signing it "Arthur Griffith," and then, after a moment's conversation, "Acting President of the Irish Republic." That message he gave to me with the instruction that it be released immediately he was taken.

On the night of Friday–Saturday, 26th–27th November, 1920, Griffith's home in Clontarf Road was surrounded. Without warning, the door was smashed in; troops and constabulary spread over the house. They were crude those raiders, and in reply to Mrs. Griffith's appeal to tell her where they were taking her husband, she was told he was being brought out to be shot. As the lorry drove away, a more kindly voice called out that he was being taken to the Bridewell. That same night, Eóin MacNéill, another member of the Government, Éamonn Duggan, T.D., and many others were captured.

The arrest of Griffith removed a wise and cautious man, and within

CROWDS ON WESTLAND ROW TO MEET RELEASED PRISONERS, 1917.
(Courtesy of National Library of Ireland, KE125)

EAST CLARE ELECTION, 1917.
(Courtesy of National Library of Ireland, KE144)

EAST CLARE ELECTION: DE VALERA ADDRESSING HIS CONSTITUENTS ON THE RESULT, 1917.
(Courtesy of National Library of Ireland, KE132)

DÁIL ÉIREANN, 22 JANUARY 1919.
(Courtesy of National Library of Ireland, R26340)

S. J. O. Swiney
(Donegal)

Kevin O'Higgins
(Queen's Co.)

J. Doherty
(N. Donegal)

John Hayes
(W. Cork)

R. Barton
(W. Wicklow)

D. Buckley
(N. Kildare)

J.J. O'Kelly
(Louth)

D. Mulcahy
(Clontarf)

E. Duggan
(S. Meath)

Count Plunkett
(Roscommon)

Con. Collins
(W. Limerick)

P. Beasley
(E. Kerry)

Cathal Brugha
(Waterford)

P. Shanahan
(Harbour)

Dr. J. Ryan
(S. Wexford)

J. T. O'Kelly
(College Green)

Dr. Crowley
(N. Mayo)

J. Ward
(S. Donegal)

P. O'Malley
(Galway)

J. Bourke
(M. Tipperary)

P. J. Molony
(S. Tipperary)

J.J. Walsh
(Cork)

R. Sweetman
(N. Wexford)

Ald. Thos. Kelly
(Stephen's Green)

HARRY BOLAND, MICHAEL COLLINS AND EAMON DE VALERA AT THE FIRST MEETING OF DÁIL ÉIREANN,
MANSION HOUSE, 1919.
(Courtesy of National Library of Ireland, INDH54)

Dáil Éireann Meeting in the Mansion House, August 1919.
(Courtesy of National Library of Ireland, KE219)

MILITARY CARRYING OUT OFFICIAL REPRISAL FOLLOWING AN AMBUSH IN MEELIN, CO. CORK,
1 FEBRUARY 1921.
(Courtesy of National Library of Ireland, HOG156)

CUSTOM HOUSE ON FIRE, MAY 1921.
(Courtesy of National Library of Ireland, INDH81)

MILITARY AND VICTIMS' FRIENDS IN THE GROUNDS OF JERVIS STREET HOSPITAL DURING THE
MILITARY ENQUIRY INTO THE CROKE PARK SHOOTINGS, 24TH NOVEMBER 1920.
(Courtesy of National Library of Ireland, HOG161)

PRISONERS OUTSIDE BURNING CUSTOM HOUSE, MAY 1921.
(Courtesy of National Library of Ireland, INDH82)

Treaty Plenipotentiaries including Arthur Griffith and De Valera on Board the Boat to England, c. 1921.
(Courtesy of National Library of Ireland, INDH97)

Men, Women and Children outside Mountjoy Prison, July 1921.
(Courtesy of National Library of Ireland, HOG165)

a few weeks a "peace" move was begun which had harsh consequences.

Meanwhile, just as the President was setting out on a new speaking tour to the West the news reached Washington that the Acting President had been taken. Before he left, he told Harry Boland and Seán Nunan that the time had come for him to go back. They were to find a ship and tell him when all was ready. He was beyond the Great Lakes and at Minneapolis, one of the Twin Cities of Minnesota, when word came to him in the midst of an enthusiastic meeting that there might be a chance on the s.s. *Celtic*.

Some infection in his food laid the President low for a day or two, and, using the illness as an excuse to cancel his tour, he returned to New York. There it was given out that he needed complete rest, and would go into the country over the Christmas, attending to no public business.

On 10th December, he left his hotel late in the evening and made for the docks, where the liner was getting ready to put to sea. Barney Downes and Dick O'Neill were among her crew, and soon de Valera was aboard. It was in the hours of waiting for the *Celtic* to draw out that the President composed his moving valedictory message to the American nation. From the cubby-hole in the prow of the ship, he looked back in memory at the great scenes of which he had been the centre ; the innumerable marches past of the Irish-Americans, the crowds that had filled the great open commons or the vast high-tiered auditoriums ; the questioning glances of the rows of members of some State legislature as he endeavoured to win them to Ireland's cause ; the pomp and panoply of the Governors' welcomes ; the State banquets ; the military parades ; the flag of the Republic, banned at home, but flying officially on many a State capitol. He remembered, too, the rank and file, the warm-hearted citizens of America who could not understand why the war ideals should be abandoned now, and who worked in these passionate years for a liberty for Ireland which the great and the powerful denied.

De Valera knew that these things were not done for him personally, or for any merit in him, but that they had been all poured out around him for love of his motherland, and in respect for the courage of a little nation brave enough to strike for her rights against an Empire. So as the waters swirled almost silently around the still-moored ship, he wrote :

"I came to you on a holy mission, a mission of freedom. I return to my people who sent me, not indeed, as I had dreamed, with the mission accomplished, but, withal, with a message that will cheer in the dark days that have come upon them, and that will inspire the acceptance of

*such sacrifices as must yet be made. So farewell—young, mighty,
fortunate land. No wish that I can express can measure the depth of
my esteem for you, or my desire for your welfare and your glory.*

*" And, farewell the many dear friends I have made and the tens of
thousands who for the reason that I was the representative of a noble
nation and a storied, appealing cause, gave me honours they denied to
princes—you will not need the assurance that Ireland will not forget and
that Ireland will not be ungrateful."*

A little later, as the tugs came close and the engines began to throb,
the message was brought ashore, and so ended the mission to which
Griffith had paid such grateful tribute, and of which another man,
who saw it at close quarters for all its time, also spoke.   Liam Mellows,
a short while before his death in Mountjoy Jail, told of how de Valera
had come to America, and there

*" changed an ignorant and either apathetic or hostile people into genuine
sympathisers in two years. He made the name of Ireland respected
where it was despised, and the Irish Cause an ideal where it had been
regarded as political humbug."*

The voyage home was speedier than that of eighteen months ago,
but the danger of discovery grew with every day out from New York.

For in Ireland, things had taken a new turn.   Lloyd George was
being secretly beseeched by British representatives in America to
end the oppression.   The joint effect of Black-and-Tan outrages
in Ireland and the President's mission were, the Premier was told,
proving disastrous for Britain's prestige.   He asked the Archbishop
of Perth (Australia), Dr. Clune, who was in London, to be his emissary
for peace, telling His Grace to seek out the leaders and arrange a truce,
as the preliminary to discussion.

Dr. Clune saw Griffith and MacNeill in Mountjoy Jail, and Collins
at a secret rendezvous, and eventually a truce was arranged.   But
at that moment a foolish resolution, seeking peace, was reported—
wrongly, some say—as having been passed by six members of the
Galway County Council (the other 25 were on the run), and a telegram
from Father O'Flanagan, in the same sense, were thought by the
British premier to show a break in the morale of the Republicans.

When Archbishop Clune came back to London, he found, as
Chamberlain did, nearly two decades later at Godesberg, that the
terms of peace had been changed in his absence.   Lloyd George,
on the very day the *Celtic* drew out from New York, announced in
the Commons that the Irish were breaking, and that the troops and
soldiers had been instructed to finish the job.   He would now accept
no truce unless the Irish first surrendered their arms.

These events filled the transatlantic cables of the time, and set the journalists in America anxious to get de Valera's reaction to them.

They besieged the National Headquarters in Washington, where Harry Boland and Kathleen O'Connell had to use sublime diplomatic tact not to disclose what was happening. In New York, the other members of the mission, and Diarmuid Fawsitt, then the Republic's first Consul in the U.S.A., battled with the same situation successfully.

For a day or two, suspicions were lulled, but then, as no message came from the President, it was concluded that there was more to this silence than illness, or rest. It was felt that he might not be in America at all, and from that it was easy to conclude that he was on the high seas. Acting on this, the British Government ordered the searching of all ships recently out from any American port.

Passenger liners publish a daily news sheet, and one day, near the end of the voyage, Barney Downes saw in the *Celtic's White Star News* that British ships at Cherbourg were being searched for de Valera. The crisis had come. It was certain the *Celtic* would be searched at Liverpool, and there were hurried discussions as to where de Valera had better go.

The sailors had no doubt. The safest place on the ship, the President was told, was in one of the ballast tanks. Closely questioning the members of the crew, who were in the secret, de Valera was assured that that tank had never been filled for at least two years, and was not likely ever to be. He thought it over for a long time, and then announced: " I am not going into the ballast tank."

And then it happened—the C.I.D. came down the Mersey and boarded the *Celtic* from a launch. Word came racing down to O'Neill and Barney. An English sailor, Billie Humphries, who had learned what was afoot, suggested a certain storage room several decks up, where the potatoes for the voyage were kept.

The danger was that it had no doorway, being but a long, low-roofed space, and that men passing on the companion way could see into it. But de Valera decided that that was the place, and it was Billie Humphries who got him a seaman's jersey, and together he, and Billie and Dick O'Neill, carrying bundles on their shoulders, started up from the lower decks.

Before they came to the potato loft, they met the searchers on their way down and trotted on. The C.I.D. stood aside to allow such busy men get on with their job. Soon, de Valera was in that long, low loft and had taken cover, as a soldier in the field would, behind one of the farthest back of the dark potato heaps.

The search went on, and was soon to become more eager. For in Dick O'Neill's cabin they found a new suit, and on a tailor's tab inside one pocket was the name " H. Boland." Harry had given Dick the suit. O'Neill was sent for and asked to explain the name. He had no trouble, being that kind of a man. His real name, he told the C.I.D. men, was Murphy, but he usually went by the name he now used, Dick O'Neill; at other times he went by the name Boland.

Put on that suit, the C.I.D. men ordered. Dick put it on and it fitted : " Now you see," he said, as if that explained it all, and the searchers thought it did for they were badly instructed and did not know who " H. Boland " was. A few minutes later, in a search of Barney Downes's bunk, they found de Valera's overcoat.

CHAPTER 48

THE SAILOR EXPLAINS

THE C.I.D. men saw the importance of this find, for the overcoat was for a man of more than usual height. They got Barney to put the coat on. It reached almost to his toes. But sailors are simple and plausible men, and when Barney was asked to explain, he had had time to prepare a yarn. It was given him by a chum in New York, and he named the chum, the place, the date and the hour of day he got that coat. He was to bring it to his brother, who was out of a job, and he named the brother, and the kind of job he had, and how tall he was, and he hoped the C.I.D. men didn't think he pinched that coat. Barney was so open and frank about it all that, again, the searchers' suspicions were allayed. They still had doubts, but they never dreamt that the man they were looking for was, at most, twenty or thirty yards from them. Before the *Celtic* docked, the seamen learned, with scared faces, that the ballast tank had been filled for the first time in years. Had de Valera responded to their urgings, he would have been drowned.

When the great vessel berthed, everyone who left her was scrutinised, crew and passengers alike. As night came down, watchers from the crew's quarters saw at the foot of their gangway two plain-clothes men. The hour grew late, and the air grew colder, and to keep up their circulation, the two men below began to pace the dockside, soldier-like.

Each, on his own side of the gangway, made a sentry beat parallel to the ship, but outward from the gangway. There were thus several moments when both had their backs to that one way of escape. After midnight, as soon as the sentries about-turned at the gangway's foot, two figures came swiftly down, and, before the guards faced around again, had vanished into the dockland shadows. One was the English sailor, Billie Humphries, and other the Irish leader, Éamon de Valera.

That night de Valera stayed at Humphries's home, Billie telling his wife that this was Barney Downes, of whom he had often talked but whom she had never seen. Barney, he told her, was ill and must not be disturbed by anyone at all. Next day an old pal, hearing that Downes was sick, called at Billie's house. Happily, Mrs. Humphries remembered that nobody must be allowed near the sick man—and so again the secret was preserved.

But if de Valera was safely across the Atlantic, he was only in Britain. And it was just then a Britain worked into white-heat fury against the Irish. The pretence that the intelligence officers, shot on Bloody Sunday, were innocent men had caught on. Lloyd George capitalised on it with an elaborate public funeral, and a service at Westminster Abbey, which the Cabinet attended. Ten days later, another spectacle to harrow the public was staged. The coffins of some of the Auxiliaries who fell in the Kilmichael Ambush were brought to London amid descriptions of mutilation and hatchetings by the I.R.A. These libels fouled not only the gutter Press, but such papers as the London *Times*, which, all through the British terror in Ireland, played in its news columns an ignoble part.

It was in that Britain that de Valera had now landed, and he must step with a double caution if he were to get back to his own land. Leaving a large sum of money with Billie Humphries, which that true man kept safely for Ireland, he slipped on board a cargo boat heading next night out of Liverpool to Dublin. He stowed away in the upper bunk of " Johnny Moore's " cabin. There, after the boat had put to sea, he heard, with consternation, Johnny being called for through the ship—and no answer coming. The door of his cabin was tried by the callers, and found to be locked. It was shaken and pounded on. At last the mate, accompanied by the captain, brought a master-key, and the door was opened. Lying in the upper bunk was a man who apparently could not be awakened, and in the midst of this scene, Johnny turned up. Alas, he had been celebrating !

He stood unsteadily by the door, and the mate bawled at him : " Who the hell is up there ? " Johnny rose to the occasion with one of the most triumphant pieces of fiction in Irish annals. That, why that was his poor sister's unfortunate husband. A divil for drink he was, and at Christmastime he was worst of all ; he went on a mad tear altogether, and wasn't the better of it for months. His sister, out of her mind almost, had asked him to look after the unfortunate man over the Christmas, and the only way he could do that was to bring him along in his cabin. Johnny apologised to the captain, mate and everybody, but appealed to them to let the poor fellow be, as they knew how it was with men who were slaves to drink. And they knew, and though they lectured Johnny on the utter wrong of bringing unauthorised persons on to a ship, they told him they would overlook it this time. Next morning—and it was Christmas Eve, 1920—when all was quiet on the quays of Dublin, Johnny Moore's erring brother-in-law came ashore.

De Valera was safely back in Ireland.

The weeks before his arrival had been the period of great raids. Day after day, night after night, they went on. Among the buildings forced and searched, from ceiling to cellar, were the Jesuit Mother-house at Milltown Park Dublin, the Carmelite Priory in Clarendon Street, Dublin, and the Capuchin Friary in Church Street. Every priest's room was visited and ransacked. From Church Street the two heroic priests, Father Albert and Father Dominic, were taken. Father Albert, who had attended the 1916 men; Father Dominic who, as Chaplain to the Lord Mayor of Cork, had consoled Terence MacSwiney in his long agony. Now he was brought away to be courtmartialled and sent to penal servitude for possessing a "seditious" letter.

As well as religious houses, Trade Union halls were entered—Liberty Hall, the Builders' and Carpenters' Unions, the I.T.G.W.U. branches, the Irish National House Painters' Union, and many others. There were arrests of Labour organisers all over the country. Among the leaders taken were : Tom Farren, Tom Johnson, and the indomitable William O'Brien, who, in the previous spring, had all but lost his life on hunger-strike.

Twelve days before the President's return, the British Military Government in Ireland issued a proclamation in which all Irish men and women were told :

" NOTE WELL ;

" That a state of armed rebellion exists, that any person taking part therein or harbouring any person who has taken part therein or procuring, inviting, aiding or abetting any person to take part therein, is guilty of levying war against His Majesty the King and is liable on conviction to suffer DEATH."

To give shelter to hunted men was now a capital offence. Into this tense world, de Valera stepped.

The British had known that the President had left New York, and that he could not be found in Washington; but they had no idea where he was. They searched the *Aquitania* at Cherbourg, the *Celtic* at Liverpool; several ships arriving in Southampton were boarded and examined.

After he was safely in Dublin, speculation filled the British Press. The London *Daily Chronicle* declared that: "The Sinn Féin leader will probably be arrested at the first opportunity." But apparently, as he was not in Ireland, it could not be there. "It is definitely stated in well-informed circles " (which meant Dublin Castle), said the Dublin correspondent of the *Chronicle*, " that Mr. de Valera has not landed in Ireland." The date of that announcement was 1st January, 1921.

On that day, on the other side of the Atlantic, Harry Boland asked the pressmen in New York to come and see him. They came flying.

He told them he had a bit of news for them ; he had had a telegram from over the sea, and he would like them to know that the President was in Ireland !

" We wanted to show that we could put President de Valera back in Ireland just as easily as we could bring him to the United States. To-day's message from him shows that we can do it."

He added his thanks :

> " On behalf of President de Valera and myself, I wish to thank the newspapers and the newspaper men who have been assigned to find Mr. de Valera for the courteous way that they have treated us. It was a hard job to keep the thing secret, but we managed it."

The British were too wise to be taken in by a bluff of this kind, and now they seized the United States ship *Portia* as she berthed on the Dublin quays. On the morning of 2nd January, they waited for her with troops, armoured cars and armed coastguards—a proud display. They boarded her and held her incommunicado. This went on for days, and the captain could not land his cargo. The dockers were there and ready, but they would not come aboard while British troops were on the ship. At last the military agreed to withdraw in favour of the unarmed D.M.P., so that she could be unloaded, and the dockers came and hoisted the cargo out of her with a will—but the British found no stowaway.

And then the head of the British Secret Service gave John Steele, of the *Chicago Tribune*, a scoop :

> " Sir Basil Thomson, chief of the British Secret Service," wrote John Steele on 4th January, " told me that he does not believe the report from New York, but added that if de Valera has actually come to Europe he must have landed in France."

A French journalist had interviewed the President after his return, but to protect him, wrote on his own volition as if he had seen de Valera in Paris. The interview convinced the British Government that he was actually in France, and a statement was issued saying that Mr. de Valera had gone to Paris with the British Government's consent !

Harold Spender, one of the big writers on the London *Daily News*, had himself just returned from America, and he had something to say of the effects of de Valera's work there, which must have fallen sombrely on ears in Downing Street and in Dublin Castle :

" Six weeks just spent in America," Spender wrote in his paper, " has taught me the immense urgency of an Irish settlement if the United States is not to drift into a condition of permanent alienation from Great Britain.   Now I hear around me in England a great clamour and wonder about the new American Navy, the American hostility to the League of Nations, and about the American attitude in the Near and Far East. There is great perplexity on these matters, but the solution is quite simple.   All these phases of American policy begin and end with the Irish question.   Fail to settle the Irish question and we shall continue to have a hostile America."

Meanwhile, in Ireland, the President took his place at the head of the Government and resumed his chairmanship of the Army Council.

CHAPTER 49

OFFICIAL REPRISALS

THE British Government celebrated New Year's Day, 1921, by an innovation which was to create a whirlwind of protest in Britain itself. That was the launching of " official reprisals."

Hitherto, when an attack on British forces had been carried out by the Volunteers, the answer came from the nearest military or constabulary barracks. With the connivance, and often the participation, of the officers, a procession of crowded lorries took the road. These were well stocked with bombs and petrol tins, and when night had fallen they made a shambles of the first town they met, blew up the local creamery, destroyed farmhouses and crops, killed, looted, burned at their will. Reluctant to punish their forces for these actions, which were so tarnishing Britain's name throughout the world, the British Government sought to restrain them. The method was simple. They would take on the job themselves.

An order was issued that, after every attack by the Volunteers, homes of Republicans in the neighbourhood would be dynamited.

Midleton, Co. Cork, saw the first operation of this new scheme for the better government of Ireland. General Strickland, who had just presided over the burning of Cork City, issued this statement on 2nd January, 1921 :

" As a result of the ambush and attack on police in Midleton and Glebe House, it was decided by the Military Governor that certain houses in the vicinity of the outrages were to be destroyed, as the inhabitants were bound to have known of the ambush and attack, and that they neglected to give any information either to the military or the police authorities.

" The houses of the following were duly destroyed between 3 p.m. and 6 p.m. on 1st January :

Mr. John O'Shea, Midleton.
Mr. Paul McCarthy, Midleton.
Mr. Edward Carey, Midleton.
Mr. Cotter, Ballyadam.
Mr. Donovan, Ballyadam.
Mr. McDorgan, Knockgriffin.
Mr. Ahearn, Knockgriffin.

" Previous to the burnings, notice was served on the persons affected giving them one hour to clear out valuables, but not furniture. No foodstuffs, corn or hay were destroyed."

Official reprisals did not restrain the Crown forces, but encouraged them, and Ireland now saw a grim competition—whether the official burners or the unofficial would get there first. In the two weeks after 1st January, apart from houses destroyed by order, Ballina, Co. Mayo, Nenagh, Co. Tipperary ; Cork City, and Carrickmacross, Co. Monaghan, were " shot up." Shops and houses were burnt in Scarriff, Co. Clare ; Elphin and Carrowkeel, Co. Roscommon ; Camlough, Co. Armagh ; Falcarragh, Co. Donegal ; Ballinalee, Co Longford ; Garrybawn and Ballybay, Co. Monaghan ; Kilbeggan, Co. Meath, and Innishannon, Co. Cork. Halls were destroyed in Tramore, Co. Waterford ; at Crossan, Co. Westmeath, and at Limerick Junction.

The method by which the Government of the Republic met this new terror was essentially simple, too. They got on with the job.

The British picture (and it was an hallucination that served the Republic well) was of leaders—dark, saturnine, wild-eyed fellows—hidden away in some fastness from which they seldom emerged. The fact was that the Government and General Headquarters of the army took terrorism for granted and went on with their work. Where they worked was within sight of the British barracks, within sight, indeed, of Dublin Castle. The State Departments were in the heart of the city, as was the *Bulletin* office. Regular hours were kept, and the staffs came and went as to any other employment. Care was taken against too much talk, against being followed easily. Nothing was left lying around to disclose what any office was doing. For the rest, it was " business as usual."

This careful openness, running counter, as it did, to the whole British idea, proved a great protection. Members of the Government and high army officers went wherever it was necessary to go. They did not court arrest, but they did not let the chance of it immobilise them.

As I cycled to some tryst late in the evening to gather captured mail for the next day's *Bulletin*, I knew that Ministers and staff officers were doing just this as they, too, went about this occupied city.

The President travelled to meetings and conferences, to interviews and Dáil sessions on a bicycle through crowded streets without protection of any kind, as did Cathal Brugha, Michael Collins, Dick Mulcahy, Erskine Childers and the rest.

I remember a Cabinet meeting held in March, 1921, in the home of Mrs. Humphreys at 36 Ailesbury Road. When the Cabinet or

Army Council was summoned the notice would bear no place but a number. The number was either " 36 " or " 40," for No. 40 Herbert Park was the home of Madame O'Rahilly. Why these houses were never suspected is extraordinary, one was that of the widow of The O'Rahilly, who had fallen in the Rising, and the other was that of his sisters. Their being overlooked can only be explained by the British inability to rise above their own propaganda. They could not imagine that a Sinn Féin supporter could live in a fashionable suburb. But Tone's dictum did not hold just then. Merchants, as well as sailormen, made very good revolutionaries.

It was at such a house that I watched the Ministry assembling in the height of the terror that March. These hunted men rode up, a few minutes between each arrival, and their greetings to one another were laughing accounts of cordons scouted and hold-ups dodged. The house rang with heartiness, and certainly no by-stander would dream that guns were out for every one of them. I had brought some papers for Erskine Childers, and was in the room near the door as the Ministers left, as close to curfew as was safe. There was just enough time for each to get to his hiding-place for the night before the British took over the city, but there was no melodrama or mock heroics.

They took care not to leave together, that was all, bidding one another good-night with a jest, as if one piece of ill-luck in that journey home might not have meant the end of that life.

It was after one of the first of these meetings, after his return, that the President commemorated the second anniversary of the Declaration of Independence by a statement to the nation announcing his arrival, and paying tribute to the people for their courage :

" The faithfulness with which through two terrible years you have stood firm in the face of a ruthless repression, will," the statement said, " make our Nation shine out as long as human records endure, a glorious exception in this sad period of abandonment of ideals and conscienceless betrayals. . . .

" Thank God, that splendid morale which has made you the wonder of the nations remains unbroken and the enemy is once more learning that though with brute force brave men and brave women may be murdered, brute force can never reach the spirit which inspires them . . . every drop of patriot blood that he sheds will but make for us more sacred the duty of perseverance and more certain its fulfilment.

" No one can be base enough now to barter away that for which our noblest have given up their lives and so though the moment is dark and the world unheeding, confident of final success, with calm deliberation, let us face the new year of the Republic, ready to endure whatever yet may be necessary . . ."

At one of the meetings of the Army leaders at which he presided, the President put forward the views that had come from his experience in the United States. The Volunteers' actions had been given to the American public by the British-controlled newsagencies as street brawls, terroristic acts, attacks by hundreds against handfuls. He suggested that the best counter to this would be engagements on so large a scale that their true nature could not be concealed. Thus there came to be discussed the capture of the Auxiliary Headquarters at Beggars' Bush Barracks, or the taking and destruction of the seat of the British civil administration, the Custom House.

Oscar Traynor had succeeded Dick McKee as Commandant of the Dublin Brigade, and those proposals were examined by him in detail. It was found that Beggars' Bush Barracks were too carefully sited and designed to permit of capture, but that there was a chance of taking the Custom House. Brigadier Traynor himself visited the great building, and, carrying an envelope marked " On His Majesty's Service," he went to every floor, taking note of passage-ways, sections, exits, staircases.

As the plan was maturing, the operations of the Volunteers assumed a broader character generally ; and typical of this was the raid on the Railway Works at Inchicore.

Just as curfew fell, members of F Company converged from all sides on the works, where steel plates had been delivered a few days before for the making of armoured cars. They captured the extensive area without firing a shot, and, locking up watchman and night staff, proceeded to load the steel plates on to lorries.

As dawn came and the curfew was lifted, the lorries drove out from the great yards and vanished into the unknown, carrying with them the precious steel.

The Government had up to this never publicly assumed responsibility for the acts of the Volunteers. The Volunteers were, of course, recognised as the Army of the Republic, were under the ultimate control of the Minister for Defence, and had sworn allegiance to the Dáil. From the Dáil the moneys came to maintain and arm them. But neither Government nor Dáil had yet professed this connection openly. The President felt that that situation should not continue, and the Dáil gave him authority publicly to assume responsibility for the Army at whatever moment seemed suitable. The chance came at the end of March. On 30th March, de Valera gave an interview to an American newsagency and said :

" Those who question the moral validity of the Republic now must challenge the foundations of democracy and the constitutional right of peoples everywhere. . . . We took office knowing that the people wanted us to be the government . . . one of our first governmental acts was to take control of the voluntary armed forces of the nation. From the Irish Volunteers we fashioned the Irish Republican Army to be the military arm of the Government. This army is, therefore, a regular State force, under the civil control of the elected representatives, under organisation and a discipline imposed by these representatives, and under officers who hold their commissions under warrant from these representatives. The Government is, therefore, responsible for the actions of this army. . . . It is the national army of defence."

It was in the same interview that he was asked if he thought ambushing the British forces was justified. His answer was vigorous and left no room for doubt:

" If the Irish nation and the Irish Republic, as a State directly founded upon the consent and the will of the people, is not entitled to use force to defend itself, then no nation and no State is entitled to use force. The English forces are in our country as invaders . . . actually waging upon us, not only an unjust, but a barbarous war. Protected by the most modern war appliances, they swoop down upon us and kill and burn and loot and outrage—why should it be wrong for us to see that they will not do these things with impunity ? If they may use their tanks and steel-armoured cars, why should we hesitate to use the cover of stone walls and ditches ? Why should the element of surprise be denied to us ? . . . If German forces had landed in England during the recent war, would it have been wrong for Englishmen to surprise them . . . to harass the invader by every means in their powe ? If not wrong for Englishmen, why wrong for us ? "

Statements like this strengthened the morale both of the nation and of the Volunteers everywhere, and events moved on towards the close of the War of Independence, with Ireland striking back vigorously and uncowed.

CHAPTER 50

THE CRIMSON COWL

EVERY struggle for freedom has some one occurrence which shows forth the whole character of the conflict. The capture and destruction of the Custom House had that distinction in the Ireland of 1921. Its initiation no less than its fulfilment spoke out the courage of the times.

The decisive meeting at which it was initiated was held in 40 Herbert Park, Madame O'Rahilly's home. To it came some of the most sought-after men in Ireland. Cathal Brugha was there, Michael Collins, Austin Stack, Dick Mulcahy, Seán Russell, Liam Mellows, Diarmuid O'Hegarty, Gearóid O'Sullivan, "Ginger" O'Connell, Seán MacMahon, Piaras Béaslaí, and Oscar Traynor.

As these officers, who were nearly all members of General Head-quarters staff, waited for the President, word was brought to them that a British military cordon had been thrown across the entrance of the street. It might mean a great raid or that those military leaders had been seen gathering. The leaders, whose lives were lived in this proximity to danger, took the situation half-humorously and were discussing a way of retreat when, to the surprise of everybody, the President came in. "I was held up," he said, smiling. "They questioned me and finally passed me through." Nearly every man in the room recalled in his own case a similar situation in which all seemed lost when a stout heart and a ready tongue did the trick.

De Valera reminded that keen audience, so ready to rise to a daring lead, that Dublin was known throughout the world as widely as London or Paris, and that news of an operation there by the Volunteers organised on a great scale would travel far. Above all else it would convey to the people of the world the true character of the struggle.

It was a long step from this birth of the idea to its fulfilment more than four months afterward. Its success had to be based on a secret which in the end thousands shared, on plans meticulously worked out, on superb daring in carrying out those plans, and finally on the completely preserved element of surprise.

After Oscar Traynor's visit, previously mentioned, Commandant Tom Ennis of the Second Battalion, in whose area the Custom House was, went through the building with the detailed operation in mind.

Then the Commandant of the Fifth Battalion, Liam O'Doherty, was asked for and got the architectural plans, and these were studied from every angle, distances measured, timings re-arranged.

The telephones presented a special problem, for not only had every office one, but there was a direct line to the Castle. These had all to be made ineffective, but a moment too soon would be as perilous as a moment too late. Eventually at zero hour, the engineers did the job, which included an open climbing of a telegraph pole and a descent into a manhole.

Day after day at a score of meetings the coup was worked out. The fundamentals were : a last-minute mobilisation, for which the many streets leading to the Custom House were excellent ; then an unostentatious entry ; the calming and assemblage of the clerks in the main hall ; the preparation of the offices for burning ; finally, the torch and the evacuation of the staffs, after which the raiders themselves would disperse and leave the British headquarters beyond saving. It was timed to take exactly twenty-five minutes. Through a mishap that could not have been foreseen, it lasted thirty, and in that five extra minutes death swooped down.

One of the most dangerous periods were the hours before the actual attack. There had to be preliminary operations and if one of these got to the Castle's ears the enemy would have been alerted. It had, for instance, been decided to use, not petrol which would endanger the staff, but paraffin. Therefore, it was necessary that morning to raid an oil company's premises and hold it for long enough to fill scores of petrol tins with paraffin. Then a lorry had to be commandeered and loaded with the tins, be driven to the gates of the Custom House grounds, arriving exactly at 12.55 p.m. At that moment, precisely, the building became the centre of a wonderful activity. Workers in dungarees appeared at the three entrances : not too many at any one. Many carried cans. On the heels of the paraffin carriers came other Volunteers who, without hesitancy or gaping, spread over the whole building, for each knew his landing and his corridor. Each of the captains of the 2nd Battalion took charge of a floor, and each had his company, every man of whom he knew, under him. It was 2nd Battalion men who did all the inside work, for this was their territory and to give the honour to any others would have been unfair. The whole movement roused no suspicion, for it was like good workmen coming on a job, trotting upstairs, walking confidently along corridors.

Then, when the selected teams were ready on each floor, the visits to the offices began simultaneously all over the house. The leader told the staffs not to be disturbed. They were being evacuated from the building and would they collect their personal belongings.

At the same moment the 'phones were disconnected. As the staffs began to assemble in the main hall, two or three men visited each empty office, piled files and presses, chairs and desks into a neat pyre and soaked the whole with paraffin. Office after office was done swiftly efficiently. In all, it should have taken about 15 minutes. But it is here that the mistake, so costly in the end, was made.

A wrong signal was given. It had been arranged that one blast of a whistle meant that the fires be begun; that two meant the work complete and that the movement out of the Custom House could start. This double blast was given too early and officers came running to explain that they had not all their offices ready yet. There were some moments of confusion and then the Volunteers returned to complete the job. Five vital minutes had been lost. The carefully-fixed hour—1.20 p.m. came when the building should have been evacuated. Had there been no delay the operation could have been carried out without loss. But at that minute an enemy patrol passed by the Custom House and becoming suspicious for some reason, nosed nearer. It halted and was immediately engaged.

The screen of armed men which had been thrown around the building to protect the Volunteers inside dropped the pose of workers and sprang to very angry life indeed. These opening volleys started one of the biggest engagements in Dublin. From all parts of the city British forces, hearing the fighting, converged on the Custom House. The guards outside the grounds fought each new party as it came.

Soon they were joined by the men coming from inside and a way of escape had to be cut through the British circle. It was done but at a heavy cost. Before the scores of linked actions were over five volunteers were dead, many were wounded, and nearly a hundred of Dublin's best fighting men had been captured.

While this major operation was being accomplished minor ones were carried out all over the city. A fire was no good until it got such a grip that it could not be extinguished and the plan which took nothing for granted included the city fire stations. Every company in whose area was a fire station was ordered to occupy it and allow no fire engines out between one o'clock and 1.50 p.m.

The adventures of my company K of the Third Battalion were typical of these supplementary actions. To Captain Jim Brogan, our Adjutant Joe Sullivan, brought sealed orders on the night of 24th May. The Company was to take over the Central Fire Station at Tara Street at 1 o'clock. They were around the fire station armed at 12.55, just as the squads were moving into the Custom House. Five minutes later they marched in on the surprised Fire Brigade and took over. Two quietly spoken "K" men, Fred Lawlor and Johnny Kiernan,

T

were posted to the telephone room and nobody was ever so court-
eously answered and so readily promised help as those who rang
during the next fifty minutes. The Brigade, all callers were told,
would be on its way in a split second. Then just at 1.30 when the
Custom House fire gave outward sign the calls became frantic.

A policeman ran to the building from the blaze itself only two
hundred yards away. He was admitted and held prisoner. Two other
enquirers came : one turned out to be an American and the other
an English Pressman. The English journalist was interned ; the
American was given the freedom of the place including the commentary on the fire coming down from the tower of the station in
which K Company had posted a look-out.

Eventually the Black-and-Tans becoming suspicious arrived in
force and pounded on the side doors for admission. It was 1.50.
The Custom House was blazing beyond saving. Captain Brogan
saw the ambulance standing there idle and with that wit which
showed itself all through the struggle packed the company into it,
got the reluctant driver to take the wheel in his red fireman's shirt
and swinging open the great central doors rode his men to safety
as the Black-and-Tans burst in the other door and saw their quarry
gone.

Other fire stations in the city were held in the same way and every
'phone call for the Brigades was answered with the same quiet,
re-assuring voices. When at last their help was useless the Brigades
came clanging and hooting through the streets. By then the great
building was an inferno and it burned not for an hour or day but for a
week and over Dublin hung a pall of black smoke by day and a
crimson cowl by night. It was a conflagration which consumed
Britain's power and prestige together.

Only a little while before Sir Hamar Greenwood had been telling
the House of Commons that the policy of reprisals had succeeded
and that Sinn Féin was everywhere broken. And now had come an
operation of such magnitude as could only be explained by the
existence of a great organisation having the firm support of the
people. It could not be concealed that the burning had been planned
over a long period and involved hundreds of participants. Not a
whisper of it had come to the Castle.

British propaganda tried to cover this defeat by starring the baseness
of the Irish in destroying so beautiful a building. The *Bulletin* came
out with a swift answer, in which the Government of the Republic
took full responsibility. The issue on 27th May said :

" In accordance with a decision arrived at after due deliberation by the Ministry of Dáil Éireann, a detachment of the Dublin

Brigade of the Irish Army was ordered to carry out the destruction of the Dublin Custom House. The operation, a most hazardous one, was carried out with complete success at 1 p.m. on 25th May."

The *Bulletin* went on :

" An outcry, repulsive in its hypocrisy, is being raised in the English Press and the pro-British Press in Ireland against the destruction by Irishmen of an historic and beautiful edifice. We, in common with the rest of the nation, regret the destruction of historic buildings. But the lives of four million people are a more sacred charge than any architectural masterpiece. The Custom House was one of the seats of an alien tyranny. If it had been possible to strike as effectively at the tyranny it represented without injury to the structure the Custom House would have been spared. But it was not possible. The destruction was an unavoidable military necessity. The Press which cries out against it is the same Press which remained callously silent while fifteen city and town halls were being destroyed in various parts of Ireland, and while whole streets of shops and hundreds of residences and farmsteads were being wiped out of existence by British soldiers and ' police.' "

The *Bulletin*, speaking for the nation, went on :

" We are resolved to make British Government in this country impossible, and we claim and shall continue to exercise the right to attack that Government irrespective of the buildings in which it is housed. . . . Until the nation itself is protected against destruction, the question of preserving this or that building does not arise. Freedom comes by sacrifice, and in property as well as in life Ireland is willing to make that sacrifice."

I see the hand of Erskine Childers in this proud utterance. The British immediate reply to the ɔurning of the Custom House, was to intensify the Terror. Winston Churchill urged " the most unlimited exercise of rough-handed justice." At a Cabinet meeting in Downing Street on 26th May, while the Custom House was still burning, a decision was taken to put the whole Twenty-Six Counties under full Martial Law. The Cabinet hoped that one " tremendous onslaught " would give them victory—the gambler's extra throw !

CHAPTER 51

" WE'RE TAKING YOU "

ERSKINE CHILDERS was appointed Minister for Propaganda on the arrest of Desmond Fitzgerald in February, 1921. He was in charge, therefore, at this time of high tension and he used to work from a house in Victoria Terrace, Rathgar, where Lily O'Brennan and Moira O'Byrne were his staff. The house was owned by May Langan (later Mrs. Kilbride) who, like so many others, would take any risk or make any sacrifice for the movement. A secret room was built in it so that if there were a raid all publicity material could be swept into it and the staff, if necessary, saved too.

Neither I nor any other of the *Bulletin* workers ever called at that house lest we might have become known to some spotter and so lead to the Headquarters of one of our Ministries. Our consultations took place at Erskine's own house in Bushy Park Road—an easy house to visit in daylight as there were several ways to it and one could look down the whole length of the road before turning into it.

Erskine was one of the most extraordinary workers I have ever met. He had, as will be seen later, a study upstairs in which there was order and quiet for his writing. But he loved to have family and friends around him and so would often bring his work to the drawing-room at night and write at the mahogany table as callers sat around the fire and put the world through their hands. He had developed in himself such powers of concentration that he would soon be writing there oblivious of all else and when tea was ready he had to be shaken, as calling was of no avail, and at times Mrs. Childers had to tell his young son to take the pen out of his hand. This control of mind made him able to compose the statement of a long and intricate argument so that when it was taken down from his dictation it needed practically no alteration.

It was either in Bushy Park Road or in Maureen Power's front room in Harold's Cross Road—that I remember a feat of memory which was typical of him.

He decided to devote a *Bulletin* to answering criticism that Volunteers did not wear uniform. This the British made the excuse for executions as the Germans had made it in Belgium in the case of the *francs-tireurs*.

The argument could best be used, he thought, in relation to the hanging a few days before of Thomas Traynor, father of ten children.

An auxiliary Cadet fell in a long and hard fought engagement in Brunswick Street, Dublin, in which the Volunteers had heavy losses. Thomas Traynor was captured, armed, near the scene of the battle. Tried by courtmartial and sentenced to death for " murder," he was hanged on 25th April.

" Give me about twenty minutes," Erskine said three days afterwards, and then sat by the fire staring into it without moving, still in his raincoat just as he had come in.

" I'm ready now," he said suddenly, and he dictated without pausing for the better part of an hour. When I had finished taking him in shorthand he said : " Go back to the third paragraph where I said ' the names of the officers making up the court,' change it to ' officers composing the court.'

" In the fifth paragraph change ' certain requirements of Article 1 of the Hague Convention ' to ' certain requirements laid down by Article 1.' " After that, what he dictated was typed and no more alteration was necessary,

I was in his study at Bushy Park Road one morning discussing the next issue of the *Bulletin*. Mrs. Childers was there, for she used to help him in his work, and as she was invalided, she was lying on a specially-made couch beside the bookshelves.

The Dáil was soon to meet, and for it we had prepared a Report of the Publicity Department's work. I had done a draft for the section dealing with the printing and distribution of the *Bulletin* and, though I did not, I think, name the publication, it was clearly a report on publicity.

It was a May day and through the study window beside Erskine's desk the late spring flowers could be seen giving colour to the trim dark earth. Without a second's warning came the thunder at the door—a raid ! Erskine's first thought was of me, and he was about to open the window from which I could have reached the garden when an Auxiliary's glengarry cap appeared by the wall below. The house was surrounded.

Between the thunder on the door and the raiders bursting into the room, there were a few merciful seconds in which the carpet was lifted and valuable papers crammed underneath a loose board.

With the main secret papers gone, Erskine then turned in his chair to face a motley crowd of Auxiliaries, Black-and-Tans and Army officers as they flung the door in. The raid was led by a man in plain clothes, with the mean look of a ferret. He had gone straight to Erskine's desk and shuffling through the papers he found the section of our Report in my handwriting. At his call the others hunched around the desk. While they were there Erskine moved over to comfort his wife and, as was his way, took her hand in his. In the palm of his own he had placed a wee book of addresses which he was carrying and with that gone he came back to the desk.

The ferrety man told him he had found a seditious document and asked him whose the handwriting was. Erskine said quite simply : " I cannot tell you that." They began to threaten. " We shall take you to the Castle," he said, " you will remember what happened to Clune and Clancy there and you will know what to expect."

When Erskine remained silent they turned to Mrs. Childers and questioned her. She answered quietly that she would not reply to their queries either.

I remember the look of detachment with which she made this reply, her indifference to their threats. It was in Erskine, too, and, they told me later, it was also in me, which made me proud. How this sense of separateness, almost of unconcern for life or death came to us at such crises I cannot tell. But it was, I think, the outward sign of our certainty that though they could raid and kill they could not reach the spirit which held us up and carried the nation on.

They warned Mrs. Childers that she must answer or she might not see her husband again and waited for her reply. None came and the silence was filled with a denial of their right to ask, and the baffled look came into their faces that so many of us saw in those years.

It was at this moment that young Bobby Childers, still a mere lad, arriving from school saw the lorries and troops outside his house. He ran in and hurried to where his parents were and stood close to his mother; and he, too, turned to that crowd of enemy officers that look of outward imperturbability. The silence became oppressive and to break it the man in civvies asked who I was. Erskine said I was a friend, a journalist. My name ? Henry O'Neill. What was I doing there—interviewing him.

One of the officers suddenly tapped me on the shoulder. He wanted me to follow him. There were troops on the landing outside, on the stairs, in the hall. He led me to the long drawingroom with its dominant colour, cardinal red, and beyond the porch, the bright garden. He sat on the sofa and asked me to explain my work. I had come to question Major Childers for the *Daily News* : no, I was not on the *Daily News* staff, but worked free-lance, sending interviews to any paper likely to take them.

" Interviews about us, I suppose," he said sourly.

" Perhaps, but not necessarily," I said. There was much more questioning and I felt it was absurd trying to bluff them on this occasion. Suddenly he said " We're taking you."

" On what charge ? " I asked.

" Oh, no charge : we just think you're not what you pretend to be."

" There'll be a row about this," I had the sense to say, but inside I felt that he had pronounced sentence over me.

I was marched to a waiting lorry and put into the front seat between the driver and an officer who sat with a gun on his knees.

He let me understand that if there was an attack I would be shot and so would Erskine Childers, who was in a car behind ours. I knew that this was a convoy which the Active Service unit would be delighted to strike at, and I must confess I scanned, with none too eager eyes, those corners of what we called The Dardanelles, a favourite place of attack, where Wexford Street and Redmond's Hill narrowed into Aungier Street.

None of us in that car spoke : just looked ahead and, once or twice, I thought they stiffened as if expecting an assault. The sun was shining : the streets were crowded ; our cavalcade drew attention from many, for we were an imposing force : two lorries, two smaller cars, in one of which Erskine was and, I think, some kind of escort car in the rear. We took the corners at fairly high speed, for these were the danger points for them, and at last we swung into Dame Street and raced for the Castle gates.

It is hard to get people of to-day to realise what Dublin Castle then meant to us. It was the seat of the tyranny we had vowed to destroy and it was a place of many horrors. It was from there the orders to misuse the Irish people daily went out, there the discarded spies and touts crowded for safety. The notorious trio, Captains Hardy, King and Price, leaders of the British Intelligence operated there and had prisoners brought to them from the various jails in the dead of night. As Ernie O'Malley has described, there was no limit to the brutality used on these defenceless men.

It was in the Castle that many of the murders that shocked the nation were planned, and those at this centre of oppression knew that whatever was done to their unhappy victims would be covered up by the highest in the land—Viceroy and all. To be discovered, now to be associated with the *Bulletin* would not add any pleasure to my visit. I remember sitting in some spacious place—I think it must have been the hall of the main entrance. Wherever it was, Staff Captains, R.I.C. officers and the heads of the Auxiliaries, were continually hurrying through on their avocations. Of more concern to me were the plain-clothes men, for Bruton was still alive and Wharton had recovered from his wound. They and several others knew my appearance before I had grown that beard, and one glance at this new prisoner sitting there under guard would end my innocent story of interviewing for the *Daily News*.

I had extraordinary luck that day. Many plain-clothes men came in and studied me, but none of the old hands, and after a while I was put into one of the cells near the Lower Castle Gate. As the cell-door closed, I leant against the tarnished wall in an ecstasy of relief, which told me how tensely I had watched those who came through the swinging door in the Castle vestibule. An hour later I was handed over to the Auxiliaries and taken by them in a steel-sided, wire-netted Crossley tender to the Royal Barracks near Kingsbridge Station.

I was put into a great day-room and sat by the fire with Auxiliaries around me who were waiting for their dinner. I said many a fervent prayer that none of those I had bluffed a few months earlier would come in and find their traveller in soaps now become, as one of the Auxiliaries called me with deference, a " writing Johnny."

One young cadet suddenly burst in :—

" You're Mr. Childers' secretary, I believe ? " he said.

" No, a journalist friend of his," I said.

" Same thing," he said inconsequently, waving my correction aside with his gun, and went on :

" Read any books ? "

" Some," I said.

" Read any of A. E. W. Mason ? "

" I have," I said.

" *The Four Feathers* ? "

" Yes."

" *Running Water* ? "

" Yes."

" Jolly good books, aren't they ?"

" They are good," I was fortunate enough to say.

" My uncle !" he announced with infinite pride, and beaming at me hurried on his way with a parting wave of his weapon. It was like that all the afternoon. They talked about themselves to impress the secretary of Erskine Childers.

Suddenly a group of men came to the door at the end of the room, guns in their hands :

" We've come for the corpse," one of them boomed in a deep funereal voice. I looked around. " You're the corpse," said an Auxie sitting beside me. " They're taking you away. God knows where."

CHAPTER 52

WAITING FOR THE VOLLEY

A S through the great room of the Auxiliaries Headquarters in the Royal Barracks that afternoon in May, 1921, the voice called for the corpse I doubt if I hid my feelings.

I had often braced myself that day to meet the worst and it had not happened. But this call sounded as if it was truly introducing the last chapter. That certainty made it like walking towards an open grave to go down the long room to the open door now filled with dark-faced, dark-uniformed men, their guns picked out in sullen light. A chilly silence put its hand over every other noise. My footfalls on the resounding wood echoed loud and clear through the room. Every eye was raised to watch my progress, and I had the sense that the moment the door closed behind me the men at the table would bet among themselves on the chances of my survival.

I was taken only a little distance, and when I jumped down from the lorry there were military policemen waiting for me. I had been handed over to the army, and it was with the army that the notorious captains of the Intelligence worked!

There was no furniture whatever in the cell into which I was locked, and but a tiny tightly-barred window. It was dark and smelly. I began to speculate what the next step might be, and then it suddenly dawned on me. I was to be brought to the Castle for interrogation some time in the middle of the night. King and Price and Hardy would be waiting for me. The thought of such an encounter unnerved me, and then, slowly, I realised I could do nothing about it except to try to have a quiet mind with which to meet their queries. But my mind went back to the *Bulletin* of 22nd April, 1921, which said:

> "Captains King and Hardy have been notorious in Ireland for six months. There is abundant evidence to prove that in their capacity as Intelligence Officers at Dublin Castle they have been primarily responsible for abominable cruelties perpetrated on Irish prisoners in order to extract information. The cases include those of Christopher Carbery, assaulted in the Intelligence Office at Dublin Castle and whose treatment was detailed in the *Irish Bulletin* of 13th April [in that issue it was described how Carbery was made to drink his own blood] and of Bernard Stewart who escaped from Kilmainham Gaol on

21st February, 1921, and who in the third week of December, 1920, was for over an hour buffeted and punched about the Intelligence Office at Dublin Castle by King and Hardy until his blood was spattered over the floor. King then heated a poker and threatened to brand Stewart with it if he would not give information. He held a revolver to Stewart's forehead and slowly drew back the trigger. Many prisoners who have passed through the Intelligence Room at Dublin Castle have described at their courtsmartial similar treatment given them by Hardy and King, but the Courts have invariably announced that the Press representatives will publish at their peril these declarations. King is a degenerate, Hardy is a drunkard; both men are inhuman brutes. Both were concerned with the murders, after brutal ill-usage, of Richard McKee, Peadar Clancy and Conor Clune. . . ."

In the cell that night I wondered would I last out as gallantly as the Carberys and Stewarts (Stewart was, as we knew at the time, Ernie O'Malley, but they had not guessed who it was they had tortured).

At that time all of us carried hidden somewhere in our clothes some paper money and I found use for it now. A sergeant of a Liverpool regiment came into the cell with a blanket. He was careful in his talk, but I noticed at the back of the English accent just a trace of an Irish inflection. I asked his name: it was an Irish one which I now forget, and we spoke of the Irish in Liverpool where I had been once or twice. Suddenly he spilled over: how he hated this work he was put to; and those Auxies; and what they were doing. It was I who had to warn him to be quiet.

I gave him the money and told him to get me cigarettes and a few extra blankets, and that I expected callers during the night. I would like him to tell any friends or relatives who called next day where I was taken and who took me. It sounds cold-blooded and so it was. If I was taken to the Castle I might never come back and I was determined that somebody would know in whose hands I had last been. It would at least make good copy for the *Bulletin*.

Above all, I wanted to sleep, because the one chance I had now was to be able to parry the questions of Hardy and Price and King. Wrapped in the many blankets the Liverpool sergeant brought me, I prepared quick answers to every conceivable question and, at last, I fell asleep. The next thing I remembered was a tap of a boot on the back. I was lying on the floor of the cell. An English voice said: " Get up and get your things." This was the midnight call and, lying there, I tried to brace myself so that I would show nothing in my face.

But when I opened my eyes there was the grey light of day in the cell. It was morning—but that was funny : what about the interrogation ? The boot gave me a harder, though not a rough, kick.

"Are you going to lie there all day : get up and get your things in the office. You are going out."

I unwrapped myself and got to my feet. It was a military officer who stood beside me and said again the words : "You are going out." I began to grasp that I was being freed, and then I remembered that Erskine Childers had been taken because he would not answer their questions or tell whose handwriting it was on that Report. I would now have to sign for the return of what had been taken from me. It was a trick to put me at my ease and get my handwriting.

I hesitated and then, fearing that I was showing I had guessed their plan, I gathered my overcoat and hat and turned towards the door. Impatiently, the officer said : "Follow me." I went after him and halfway down that long passage I tried to think how to spell O'Neill. Was it "ie" or "ei"? I stopped in dismay, and then calling, "I forgot something," I raced back to the cell, and with the stub of a pencil the Liverpool sergeant had given me I wrote "Henry O'Neill" on the wall and went back to where the officer was standing, glad at least that I could spell my name !

There was an air of disinterest in the office as they took from a pigeonhole marked "O" my watch and pen, and whatever other trifles I had left. Then the clerk pulled down a large ledger and pointed to where I should sign : an instant of inner panic, and then, in as different a hand to my usual one as I could invent, I wrote boldly my pseudonym. The officer led me to a small wicket door and said "Good-bye." I stood there, thinking. After a while he said, petulantly : "Aren't you going out?"

I said : "Oh, yes, I am," and stood for a moment or two more. I saw his eyes on me, but I could not explain to him what was passing through my mind.

It seemed impossible that through all the peregrinations yesterday, from Bushy Park Road to the Castle, from the Castle to the barracks, and from the barracks to these cells, nobody had recognised me. Why had they not questioned me ? Why was I not confronted with anybody ? As I stood there on that step waiting to go down that brick-walled path to the barracks entrance and freedom, one thought singled itself out from all the others that went pounding through my mind, and at last I felt sure I had the secret of it all.

The *Bulletin* again and again had exposed the murder of suspected men shot while "attempting to escape." The victims had usually been slain in lorries or inside the prisons, or sometimes near the jail gates to give more colour to the story. Over a hundred men had been killed thus. I felt that if I walked down that narrow way rifles would speak behind me.

"What the hell is up with you?" roared the exasperated officer. "Are you going to stay there forever."

"I'm going now," I said, and I started down that long passage. I felt that the only way I might defeat them was to show I didn't care, and though my heart beat hard, my feet went slowly on, while my ears waited for the volley which did not come. I turned at the end of that narrow way out into the open space leading to the main gate. I was still in the sight of sentries, and plodded on as if I had nowhere else in the world to go. In seconds that seemed an hour I reached the quays at last. Then, when I should have known I was safe, I panicked and ran and ran.

When I was normal again I jumped on a tram going towards the city: the conductor came for my fare and I found that I had no money. I told him I had just got out of jail, and with infinite concern I was passed from tram to tram through the city, until I came within sight of Margaret Foley's door. And the first thing I heard was that a raiding party had come and gone, early though the day was.

"Yes, they've searched everywhere and everything," Margaret said. "But Mr. Childers was here as soon as ever curfew was lifted. He took away whatever was likely to be noticed. He told me you were caught, but would be released if nothing 'incriminating' was found. I went over it all again, after he left, but there was nothing he had forgotten."

Looking back, I think it curious now that all that previous day I felt no nervousness for Erskine's safety. Perhaps it was because we took every danger and calamity for granted and, in imagination, had already endured the fears that should assail us now. To all of us who worked with Erskine Childers, it seemed in those days that none would dare to harm him. He had the air of a man so bent on truth, and so fearless in uttering it, that it awed men and overbore them.

How much the British knew of his work we could not guess. They must have appreciated that he was one of the sternest opponents of their tyranny, they probably knew nothing of his work on the *Bulletin*, or that he was in close touch with General Headquarters. He was trusted with the most secret information and papers, as the heads of the Army responded to his determination to place the official organ fully behind the Volunteers in their defence of liberty.

In a little while, Erskine himself was telling me that, as soon as he reached the Castle, there was much hugger-mugger and runnings to and fro. Then he was brought to Alfred Cope, the Assistant Under-Secretary. Cope made to him proposals for an Anglo-Irish settlement, Dominion home rule, and what not. Erskine's reply was that the President and the Cabinet alone could deal with these things. When they tired of getting any other reaction from him they told him he would be released.

"But I cannot go until I know that the guest whom you took from my house is to be freed, too," he said.

They would give him no such undertaking. But they were clearly embarrassed at having arrested this man who in Britain was known as one of the most accurate writers of the time, friend to scores of men high in British politics whose voices were still respected. The political heads at the Castle felt that to hold him meant yet another kind of discredit and they wished heartily now he would go. Nothing could shake his determination that he would stay until the release of his guest had been guaranteed.

At last, late at night, Cope himself promised that if after a search of my lodgings nothing was found, I, too, would be set free. Even then he went with an anxious heart, for none knew better the value-lessness of such promises.

When in the quiet of the night his wife heard the familiar key in the lock, the day's strain of waiting for word of his death broke in such joy that she, who till then had held high her heart, fainted.

Although both of us were in British hands all that day the *Bulletin* came out just the same. When Erskine failed to arrive at Victoria Terrace, Lily O'Brennan and Moira O'Byrne came to Bushy Park Road and learned of the arrests. Mrs. Childers sent word through them to Mick Collins that the *Bulletin* would be compiled as usual until new arrangements could be made. She prepared the issue and passed it to the staff in the house at Rathgar and it was on its way to its readers as Erskine in the Castle and I in the Royal Barracks tried to guess our fate.

Next day I said to him : " Wasn't it well we were not ambushed on the way to the Castle ? "

" I thought it was a pity," he said, simply and earnestly, " a pity that they should be free to travel any journey without being attacked, and to tell the truth I looked out for our lads expectantly at every corner."

" My heavens," said I, " and what do you think would have happened to yourself ? "

He hadn't thought of that and he answered me with a jest : " Well, wouldn't it have been wonderful to be blown up by one of our own land-mines—and come down in some dear old Unionist lady's lap ? "

CHAPTER 53

AN OFFICIAL JOURNAL

DURING the War of Independence it was a difficulty to get well-meaning English men and women to realise the savagery which the Black-and-Tans used against the Irish people.

British journalists who came to Ireland remained incredulous until they became eye-witnesses to what was happening. Then they could not understand it, the terror was so universal, and official restraint so absent. They would have understood it better if they had seen even one number of an official British publication of that time, the *Weekly Summary*.

On 24th November, 1920, Sir Hamar Greenwood, the member of the British Cabinet responsible for Ireland, stated in the House of Commons:

> " When I came to Ireland, my first duty was to revive the morale of the force (the constabulary). . . . One of the methods adopted for heartening this force was to issue this *Weekly Summary* . . . I took it upon myself to issue this *Weekly Summary*."

When, some weeks later, Joe Devlin asked him if he intended to continue this publication, " every copy of which is an incitement to assassinate civilians," Sir Hamar replied:

> " I do intend to continue the *Summary*. . . . I am convinced it serves a useful purpose to sorely tried forces."

The paper was never intended to get into the hands of the public. It was printed in the Castle and was circulated only to Constabulary Barracks and other British posts in Ireland. It devoted itself to the incessant slander of the Independence movement and to traducing the leaders. Other activities were the invention of " atrocities " on the part of the Irish people and open incitement to the Crown Forces to take the law into their own hands and settle scores with this vile nation.

It was the *Irish Bulletin* which exposed this organ to the public quoting again and again from its columns and saying what it thought of those quotations:

> " This is probably the first occasion in the record of civilised governments," it said on 30th November, 1920, " upon which

an official State publication has defended the murders committed by a constabulary whose duties are supposed to be the protection of civilian life."

The *Bulletin* quoted from the references in the *Weekly Summary* of 12th November, 1920, to the Sinn Féin movement which at that time had either in its membership or openly supporting it 75 per cent. of the Irish people.

" Sinn Féin," the official British paper told its constabulary, " has organised outrage. It has systematised murder. It has pig-ringed Irishwomen and defiled their beauty."

That was from one of its editorials. Its "news" columns were filled with selected passages from the wildest speeches and the bitterest things written against the Irish. Here are two typical passages from it :

> " The Sinn Féiner is a rebel, a criminal, an assassin. He glories in his crime. . . . He cannot complain if sometimes he is paid back in the same coin. These are the legitimate and defensible acts of retaliation."

The sacking of towns was known as "reprisals." The *Weekly Summary* included this from the London *Globe* :

> " Reprisals may be right or wrong in themselves. For our part we say quite plainly that we hope they will go on until their purpose has been accomplished."

The paper containing these quotations reached the Black-and-Tans with the full approval of the Chief Secretary, and bore bitter fruit almost every night. The British forces were mainly Protestant and to them and their Irish co-religionists, with whom they mixed, the *Summary* represented the movement for freedom as murderously anti-Protestant.

It reproduced as " taken from a Sinn Féin prisoner " one of the oldest anti-Catholic fakes known to the English-speaking world, now distorted to rouse new fears. It was this oath :

> " In the presence of Almighty God and this my brother I do swear that I will suffer my right hand to be cut off from my body and laid at the jail door before I will waylay and betray a brother and I will . . . not spare from the cradle to the crutch and from the crutch to the cradle and that I will not hear the moans of infancy or old age but that I will wade deep in Orangemen's blood and do as King James did.
>
> " By virtue of the oath I have taken I will aid and assist with all my might and strength when called upon to massacre Protestants

and cut away heretics, burn British churches, abolish all Protestant Kings and princes and all others except the Church of Rome and its system, and by virtue of the oath I have taken I will think no sin to kill and massacre a Protestant whenever an opportunity occurs."

This savage anti-Catholic propaganda became a constant part of the British Chief Secretary's paper. A letter purporting to have been written to the *Summary* by " An Irish Catholic " said :

> " Sinn Féin is using the Catholic clergy as its tools but it is decidedly anti-Christian. I have heard Sinn Féiners give blasphemous travesties of the Mass. This is not surprising. For years the Catholic clergy have degraded the Mass into a political instrument—"

which showed how much this " Irish Catholic " knew about the Mass.

Later it was an unnamed shipowner in Liverpool, referred to as a Catholic, who repeated for the *Summary's* readers another stock-in-trade of British propaganda :

> " I tell you that the root of the trouble in Ireland lies in the teaching of the young priests."

Catholicism was described as the friend of suicides and murderers. The Pope was taunted for not checking " rebellious priests like Dr. Mannix," the Church for giving absolution and Christian burial to Terence MacSwiney " who clearly committed suicide."

The Protestant view of Spain was exploited in one of the many attacks on the President :

> " de Valera belongs to a race of treacherous murderers and he has inducted Ireland into the murderous treachery of his race—"

which was promptly sent by the President's Secretary to the Spanish Ambassador in London, H.E. Señor Don Merry del Val, with this comment:

> " Your Excellency,
>
> " President de Valera thinks you may be interested in the marked passage of the accompanying British Government's official publication, as it affects the honour of the Spanish race and nation.
>
> " I have the honour to be, etc."

The forces among whom these libels circulated, were, many of them, drawn from Orange and other anti-Catholic groups. For in 1920-21 the traditional British policy was as sedulously carried out as in the seventeenth and eighteenth centuries—the use of people of one faith to oppress the people of another, to incite Protestants against Catholics and fill them with a frenzy of hatred.

The results we know. Father Michael Griffin was taken from his home in Galway by Black-and-Tans on a pretended sick-call and he was later found in a bog-hole murdered.

That was in November, 1920. In December old Canon Magner, of Dunmanway, Co. Cork, was murdered by the roadside by an Auxiliary cadet, watched placidly by twenty of his comrades. In March, 1921, Father James O'Callaghan was shot dead deliberately in Cork City in the course of a raid on the house of Alderman Liam de Róiste. Several priests were courtmartialled, some were sentenced to hard labour and one to penal servitude. Many were interned like Father T. Burbage of Geashill, Offaly. Priests were seized at night in the streets and beaten up by Black-and-Tans. Priests were carried as hostages in British raiding lorries. The great religious houses were raided, the Dominicans in Dominick Street, Dublin; the Redemptorists at Dundalk, the Augustinians in Galway, the Jesuit Fathers in Gardiner Street, Dublin; the Carmelites in Whitefriar Street, the Sisters of Charity in Temple Street, and many, many others. Members of the Orders were arrested and priests' houses were forcibly entered in town and country. Many presbyteries were raided and in some cases burned and bombed. It became noticeable that in the raids on ordinary houses religious emblems were attacked. Windows of churches were broken by Crown Forces. On 2nd February, 1921, Cardinal Logue in his Lenten Pastoral said :

> " Latterly even religion is not spared. Churches and sacristies are raided, and sometimes at least, little respect is shown to sacred vessels, vestments and other requisites for divine worship. A new phase has been introduced which savours strongly of insult to the Faith and contempt for the feelings of our Catholic people. Churches are surrounded by armed men while the people discharge the sacred duty of hearing Mass. . . . Even the convents of our religious Sisters, who are not likely to commit or participate in outrages, are raided by armed men. . . . Two of these convents were broken into : one at least at the dead of night, every part of the place ransacked, including the garden, even the new-made grave of a poor Sister lain to rest in their little cemetery was dug up."

On 1st March, 1921, the *Bulletin*, reporting the effects of the sectarianism of the *Weekly Summary*, recorded thirty-two attacks on religious—imprisonments, raids, assaults and arrests—all in the previous eight weeks.

As the war went on, the incitements in the *Summary* against the

v

whole people became wilder still. One of the issues quoted with approval this Proclamation issued by General Paine in the American Civil War:

> " A loyal citizen is the only one left with rights at this time. . . . I shall shoot every guerilla taken in my district, and if you Southern brethren retaliate by shooting a federal soldier I will walk out five of your rich bankers, brokers and cotton men and make you kneel down and shoot them. I will do it, so help me God."

And in quoting a pretended resolution of the Anti-Sinn Féin Society, which everyone knew was simply another name for the Black-and-Tans, it applied that sinister Proclamation to Ireland:

> " If in future any member of His Majesty's Forces be murdered two members of the Sinn Féin party in the County of Cork will be killed. And in the event of a member of the Sinn Féin party not being available, three sympathisers will be killed. This applies equally to laity and clergy of all denominations."

On 11th February, 1921, the *Summary* reported under the headings:

" STOUT ROPE AND A SIX-FOOT DROP "

" REBELS HAVE NO RIGHTS "

—a speech in which the axiom was laid down that: " When a man became a rebel he forfeited his right to live." When William Sears, T.D., was carried round on a military lorry as a hostage, to be shot if any attack were made on the convoy, the *Summary* published the fact under the heading " New Use for Members of Parliament."

One of the most widespread efforts of the terror was the destruction by British forces of the co-operative creameries founded as the result of the movement led by Sir Horace Plunkett. The burnings and sackings went on for months and Lloyd George answering some protest by Sir Horace once convulsed the House of Commons with the quip: " He cannot claim to speak for anybody: he cannot even speak for his own creameries."

The *Weekly Summary* lost no opportunity of speeding on the good work:

> " It is notorious," it said, " that the Irish creameries had fallen into the hands of rebels and were centres of conspiracy and crime. What has happened them? Some have already been destroyed and all are in danger."

Within a few days of this condonation, two other creameries were destroyed: one at Inver, Co. Donegal, the other at Ballylongford, Co. Kerry. More reason than ever was given to AE (George Russell) to lament that

> " In these attacks creameries and mills have been burned to the ground, the machinery wrecked ; agricultural stores have also been burned, property looted, employees have been killed, wounded, beaten, threatened and otherwise ill-treated."

The *Summary* constantly carried reports of cruelties likely to stir the Constabulary to fierce anger. That these " atrocities " were invented was of no account. They appeared in this official organ under headings such as :

" SHINNERS' WAR ON WOMEN "

" WOMAN'S FACE TARRED "

A story followed of horrible indignity visited on an " elderly woman " because " she was seen speaking to a policeman." It was false. This gross publication had regular editorials. One of them, printed on the second anniversary of the Declaration of Independence, 21st January, 1921, had this passage :

> " Sinn Féin always was—and still is—a movement based on a murder policy.
> " Shinnerea is a blight and a pestilence.
> " Shinnerea is crime incarnate and for its propagators the rope and the bullet are all too good."

Among the British forces to whom went every week this publication instituted by a British Cabinet Minister and printed at the Headquarters of the British Government in Ireland, there were some who had restraint and lived and acted honourably. But the vast majority were, as acts proved, men of low calibre. Many were out of the jails of Britain, many were men who, after World War I, were unable to accept normal living and the order of civil society. Many were heavy drinkers, others blackmailers or men of unassuagable violence as shown by the high percentage of prosecutions among them already quoted.

That each week there should have been distributed to them a paper of this kind led to acts which have made the name Black-and-Tans an international synonym for bestial deeds. Robert Lynd, the kindly essayist was moved by what he saw in Ireland to write in the London *Daily News* of 26th January, 1921 :

> " Various incidents have shown that the incitements of the *Weekly Summary* have had their natural result in making the Black-and-Tans feel towards their Irish ' enemies ' as men feel towards wild beasts."

During the publication of this book in instalments I received many letters from all parts of Ireland. One of these dated 6th March, 1952, came from Edinburgh Villa, New Castle, Galway. It was signed (Mrs.) C. T. O'Hanlon Fallon and could well bring this chapter to a close so typical is its story of what the *Weekly Summary* produced :

"You may print the following if you wish. On 2nd October, 1920, my brother, John O'Hanlon, R.I.P., was taken out of his home by Black-and-Tans and cruelly murdered in the presence of his parents, wife and two babies for, they said, being the leader of the Rebels in that area, Lackagh, Turloughmore, Co. Galway. At his funeral afterwards the Tans arrived in lorries and fired into the crowd, wounding several. They shot at cattle and sheep, killing several on their way into Tuam, where they had come from that day.

"I think it is only right to show up their cruel deeds."

Similar letters have been written from a hundred other places in Ireland through which these wild forces rode, striking at a people against whom they had been incited by the basest arts of propaganda emanating from the British Cabinet itself.

CHAPTER 54

THE PRESIDENT IS TAKEN

ALTHOUGH at the beginning of the summer of 1921, the British acted as if they were more determined than ever to break the Independence movement, the core of the apple was rotten. The flames of the Custom House consumed more than paper and wood, furniture and files. It burnt up the morale of the whole régime.

To the Volunteers, the loss of fighting men in and around the Custom House was a stiff reverse. To conceal it, the Dublin Commandants, immediately after 25th May, increased the number of attacks. Hardly an evening went by in which invaders and insurgents did not clash in the streets of the capital as they were clashing all over the nation.

Three major actions were fought in Kerry, Mayo and Tipperary within the next week, and in June there were 266 attacks on British forces and positions, higher by far than in any previous months. The gamblers in the Castle were calling for just a little more time, just another month of cudgelling, and all would be well. But the volatile Lloyd George had, even before the Custom House, sensed the need for a second string to his bow.

As in the case of Archbishop Clune of Perth, he used the strategy of indirect approach. At the end of April, 1921, he sent over Mr. Edwards. The first Irish hotel porter who met Mr. Edwards knew he was Lord Derby, and knew he came from Lloyd George to spy out the land, but the pretence was kept up to the end.

Mr. Edwards saw the President, and the President said the Irish people had declared for independence and would not surrender their right to determine their own destiny no matter what the cost was. The President immediately wrote to others outside the Republican ranks whom Lord Derby was to see, and he urged them to reply nationally to this emissary. If they were not ready to declare that Ireland must have independence, they could take the attitude that questions of policy could only be decided by the elected representatives of the people.

So that Mr. Edwards should not go back under any misapprehension, or the Irish people pay more attention than they need to these furtive peace manœuvres, an official statement defining national policy was issued to the daily press. It was forthright:

" The public," it said, " should be accustomed by this time to this ' peace move ' device of the British Government. Whenever a special difficulty is to be got over or an infamous act to be covered up, a fresh peace move is set in motion."

It then defined the response of the head of the government to these efforts :

" His attitude is the same in public as in private, quite simple and plain. . . . Once the aggression is removed there can be peace. . . . The Irish people must be recognised as an independent nation with the right to determine freely its own destiny."

Michael Collins spoke as directly in his address to the electors of Armagh on 10th May :

" Ireland is one and indivisible, not to be torn asunder by any Act of an English assembly. We stand, further, to reassert the principle fought for in 1916, confirmed by the votes of all Ireland in 1918, and being fought for at the present moment throughout the length and breadth of Ireland."

In several press interviews at this time, de Valera stressed that the only negotiations in which Ireland could take part would be those in which she could participate without surrendering any right.

Asked what guarantees a free Ireland would give Britain concerning her military security, de Valera said : " We are ready to give guarantees of our neutrality—a neutrality we would spend our last man in preserving."

Mr. Edwards went home, and though he had stated that he came merely to see things for himself, he was soon in conference with Lloyd George.

De Valera told Michael Collins in a note :

" This particular peace move business has been on for some time. The reply I have sent through other channels is that if they send a written communication to me directly, and not through intermediaries, they will get a reply."

The repression went on.

On 30th May, Lloyd George announced in the Commons : " It was proposed to take sterner measures."

Great raids in Munster and Connacht enclosed mountains in their scope, but when the net closed, it was nearly always empty. The shooting down of civilians, men and women, at their doors or in the fields continued. The British Press began to turn against the "smother-them-in-blood " group. The London *Times* and *Daily Mail* were calling for peace.

Parliamentary elections were held in Ireland in May, and they emphasised that all the military excesses had secured just nothing. Of the 128 seats in the Twenty-Six Counties, the Republicans won 124 without a fight. Owing to British repression, John Dillon, though fundamentally opposed to the Republic, would not put forward a single candidate, and every other political section of the people felt the same way. Sinn Féin had come to represent everybody in its non-submission to British violence. Only the four seats of Trinity College stood by the dishonoured Crown.

In the Six Counties there was widespread interference with Republican candidates, agents, canvassers, committee rooms, and voters, in which the Crown forces took a lusty part. Yet, twelve of the fifty-two seats were won there by the Nationalist-Republican nominees, so that out of 180 seats in all Ireland, 136, or more than 75 per cent, went to those who stood for Irish freedom and against Partition.

The British King, too, seemed to tire of his name being dragged in the mud. Having been advised to go to Belfast and there open one of the two unwanted Parliaments set up by Lloyd George's Partition Act, he had a speech submitted to him. It was drafted partly by Dublin Castle, and, not surprisingly, George V did not like it. He had it redrafted and it was re-submitted to the British Cabinet. They agreed to its expression of hope that there might be peace, but reluctantly, for they had just been preparing for an all-out assault on Ireland.

The speech was made on 22nd June, 1921, and immediately afterwards the British Cabinet broke; Chamberlain and Birkenhead wanted negotiations; Lloyd George and Churchill more ruthless war. In the end, after much pressure, the war-makers were overborne.

But in Ireland, another kind of drama was being played. On the evening of the same day, 22nd June, a house named Glenvar, at Blackrock, Co. Dublin, was raided. The raiders were a company of the Worcestershire Regiment. The house was not an ordinary residence. Glenvar was in fact the President's office.

When de Valera came back from America, he went first to Dr. Farnan's house at 5 Merrion Square. It was there that the President greeted the Ministers and resumed control. But for any long period some place less central was necessary, and so in January, 1921, Loughnavale, Strand Road, Merrion, owned by Mrs. MacGarry, was taken. It survived inviolate for three months. Then on 16th April, another MacGarry house in Fitzwilliam Square, also being used to shelter a Department, was raided, and in a desk was found a receipt for the rent of Loughnavale.

The President had just had a long conference with some of the officers of the Southern Divisions, and was later with Liam Mellows, when word of the receipt being found, an hour or so before, was brought to him.

There was only one thing to do. Papers that had been dealt with, or could be done without, went into the grates and were burned. Others were packed into suitcases and were brought later that evening by Liam Mellows and Kathleen O'Connell to an address in Leinster Road, one of the many houses that the British thought were Unionist, but which were always ready to shelter Republicans.

Meanwhile, de Valera had cycled his way back to Dr. Farnan's, which was used until a new house could be secured. Happily, the British were slow to appreciate what they had found, and it was not until 19th April that Loughnavale was raided. They ransacked it as seldom a building had been searched, and when they found there a pair of gloves, with the initials E. de V. inside them, Kathleen O'Connell had much to do to put them off the real scent.

And now in the bright light of the evening of 22nd June, here they were riding up the avenue of Glenvar, which, since 18th May, had been the new office of the President.

The raiders were seen from one of the long front windows by Kathleen O'Connell, who had just time to race to the back and wave a warning to de Valera. He was walking along a path running by the outside of a high-walled garden. In a few strides he reached a gateway in the wall—but, alas, the gardener had locked it.

All he could do now, for the lorries were close to him, was walk with apparent unconcern into the house by a side door. He made his way to his room. Then the troops were over the house and he was under arrest.

The raiders could soon see that this was no ordinary residence— the typewriter, the files, the routine documents, showed it as one of the Departments of the Republic, though which they did not yet know.

All at Glenvar were arrested except Maeve MacGarry, who kept house, and was out. Miss O'Connell, Miss Margaret Macken, Dr. Farnan's sister-in-law, who was on a visit, and the tall man were put in armoured lorries and driven away.

At the Castle, Miss Macken was released, and Miss O'Connell sent to the Bridewell. De Valera was taken away separately and brought to Portobello Barracks. There he was put into the detention cells, and some time later that night he was identified as the President.

The whoop of triumph that must have been wired to London was not received in the same spirit, though nothing was yet known of the sudden change of heart. Having been held for one night, the President, to his own and his colleagues bewilderment, was released. It was de Valera himself who instructed the Department of Publicity to announce his arrest. He knew his enemies, and this might be a manœuvre to create the appearance of a deal, and so divide the movement and the leaders who had held together through the great storm.

On 24th June, therefore, this was sent out:

> "In an investigation raid on a house in the Blackrock district on the evening of the 22nd June, President de Valera was discovered by the British Crown Forces. He was taken to Portobello Barracks and detained there until 2 p.m. on 23rd June, when he was released.
>
> "The motive of the British authorities in ordering the release is unknown, but the position remains unchanged."

For two days the mystery continued, and then, on 25th June, the President received from Lloyd George the written communication he had said he would deal with when it was addressed directly to him. It was an invitation to London to "explore to the utmost the possibility of a settlement" by conference, and de Valera was to bring "any colleagues whom you may select."

The letter was characteristic of Lloyd George, and the reply was no less characteristic of the movement whose leader he was addressing. Without boldly putting it into words, the British Premier sought to commit the Irish President to accept Partition and British supremacy by referring to his desire to confer with "representatives of Southern and Northern Ireland."

He implied also that the real troubles were "in Ireland," not international but internal. It was the first of many such efforts.

De Valera, now and always met the British efforts to commit him by asserting the contrary. He would, he said, discuss the letter with "such of the principal representatives of our nation as are available," and would seek also the views "of the political minority in this country" before replying more fully. But he wished Lloyd George to know at once that in this international matter:

> "We most earnestly desire to help in bringing about a lasting peace between the peoples of these two lands, but see no avenue by which it can be reached if you deny Ireland's essential unity and set aside the principle of national self-determination."

The British would have preferred not to have released any of those they held in their prisons, for they regarded them as hostages. But the Press Association, by a false statement, gave the opportunity, and on 30th June the President issued this denial:

" The statement of the Press Association, that President de Valera visited and conferred with Mr. Arthur Griffith in Mountjoy Prison, is untrue. No such indignity would be offered to Mr. Griffith by the President as to seek a conference with him within the walls of a British prison."

Next day, Arthur Griffith was free, and was sitting at the preliminary conference in the Mansion House, which was held on 4th July. The President had invited the Unionist leaders to meet him there. Five were asked, four accepted. Sir James Craig declined. Over the Mansion House, on the day of this historic meeting of Irishmen, flew the Stars and Stripes. They were raised by the President's order, in gratitude, he said, for the support the people of America had given to the struggle for liberty, and as the symbol (he quoted Wilson's war aims) " of the principle for which we are fighting— namely, ' Governments derive their just powers from the consent of the governed.' "

At that first meeting, Griffith stood firmly by de Valera when he insisted on a truce. Lloyd George refused, only to yield when he realised there would be no talks without a cessation of hostilities.

CHAPTER 55

PEACE AT NOON

THE terms of the truce were agreed to on 9th July, when the British and Irish Commanders met in the Dublin Mansion House. Outside, a vast crowd cheered the Chief of Staff of the I.R.A., General Mulcahy; cheered the British Commander, Macready; cheered all who came. The Volunteers among them remained silent, for this was not the end. But as the people saw it, the Terror would be lifted; for the first time for over five years, mothers need not go in daily dread for their sons. The darkness of the night, and the silence of it, would no longer be broken by the lights and the purr of the raiding lorries. Doors would not echo to rifle butts, nor the deserted streets to the shots which murdered son or brother. Curfew would be lifted, and people could go freely, day or night, to where among their friends there was rejoicing or sorrow or illness. The city lights would come up again, and, in the country, men and women could till the fields or meet in the streets without being shot from some speeding Crossley tender. No wonder that the ordinary people of Ireland expressed their joy on the day the Truce came into force, 11th July, by going out to collect materials for bonfires, which that night dotted the nation with the fires of rejoicing.

Those last weeks, the War had flamed to a new intensity, a troop train was derailed in Armagh with heavy losses, Auxiliaries were shot dead in Grafton Street, Dublin, three barracks were attacked in Cork City, a deadly ambush was carried out at Rosscarbery, coastguard stations were burned, and all Ireland was in the grip of the great conflict.

Almost up to the very stroke of mid-day, the attacks continued, the last two at Castlepollard, Co. Westmeath and at Kingscourt, Co. Cavan. Then suddenly, as at a knife stroke, there was peace. At noon, a silence came over the greater part of the nation. News from the country was of actions broken off at the minute of mid-day, of men in ambush rising up and marching away, of British convoys which missed death by seconds. Discipline was perfect; the fighting had ended, and the people danced around the bonfires in the streets and at the crossroads at the mere strangeness of it all.

But there was one constant reminder, that a Truce was not peace. In parts of Ireland the Terror went on—in the North-East. There the Orange leaders closed their ears to the King they had so often named and sung to. In his opening of the Six-County Parliament, he specifically called on them for "forbearance and conciliation, to forgive and forget, to join in making for the land they love a new era of peace, contentment and goodwill." The response was the torch, the cudgel, the bomb through the window.

When the British realised that Ireland was slipping from their grasp, the Black-and-Tans were recruited to deal with the Twenty-Six Counties, and in the Six Counties the Ascendancy was given a free hand to organise a war on the Catholic minority. While elsewhere the Crown forces burned Sinn Féin halls and the farmhouses and residences of Republican supporters, in the North-East, the houses of Catholics were gutted by fire, their shops and business places destroyed, and their leaders slain in their homes. Month after month it went on for two years, and the dead were in the end, numbered in hundreds and the wounded in thousands.

Under searing inflammatory speeches, the Orange workmen forgot the " brotherhood of man," and set upon their Catholic fellow-workers at the same factory bench, at the next slip in the shipyards. They drove them from their employment, and then swept into the streets they lived in and burned their little houses wholesale. In the Catholics' desperate resistance, Protestants were killed, too, and these casualties were then displayed as proof that Sinn Féin wished to exterminate all Protestants.

Within forty-eight hours of the signing of the Truce, the Belfast pogroms reached a new fury. Seventeen people, thirteen Catholics and four Protestants, were shot dead; 68, nearly all Catholics, were seriously wounded, and 161 houses (every one of them Catholic) were given to the flames. The head of the American Committee for Relief in Ireland was in Belfast city, and, as he gazed on the ruins of this Catholic district, he said : " As an American citizen, I cannot comprehend how such a thing could occur." He did not know his Lloyd George or his Dublin Castle !

These things were very much in the hearts of the Volunteers, and they did not throw their hats in the air. There was rejoicing, of course, as when men, who had been unable to come back to their homes for many months, marched down, gaunt, bronzed men from " our allies the hills."

There were many who did not come back, and now began all through Ireland scenes of the most moving kind. The bodies of men who had fallen in action had been hastily buried, lest the knowledge of their deaths fortify the British. Now, they were exhumed and given the honours of a soldier's funeral. The opportunity had come to pay tribute, and from many a lonely moor or stoney hill the fallen soldier was taken from the earth, and, all the countryside gathering around him, was brought to the cemetery where his father slept. Often the journey was long, for many had fallen far from home, and as the draped coffin passed through the villages, hundreds from the neighbouring townlands walked the three steps of mercy with it, and each local company of Volunteers became its guard of honour. The shops were shut and blinds were drawn, and only the slow marching of men sounded in the quiet streets. The emotion of the people, their gratitude to those men who died for their freedom, was immense.

These scenes constantly reminded the nation that this was a cessation only, and the Volunteers used the period to perfect their training, and members of the Republican Cabinet and General Headquarters carried out frequent rounds of inspection.

Sir James Craig, as we have seen, would not come to the discussions in the Mansion House. De Valera, when he received this reply, telegraphed to him his regret, saying :

> " Irish political differences ought to be adjusted and can, I believe, be adjusted on Irish soil. But it is obvious that in negotiating peace with Great Britain the Irish delegation ought not to be divided . . . "

After his conference with the other Unionist leaders, everything was ready for the preliminary talks in London, and de Valera accepted the British Premier's invitation. When the Truce was announced, the President issued a Proclamation warning the nation against seeing in the Truce any victory for freedom :

> " An unbending determination to endure all that may still be necessary, and fortitude such as you have shown in all your recent sufferings—these alone will lead you to the peace you desire.
>
> " Should force be resumed against our nation, you must be ready on your part once more to resist."

On 12th July, the Irish leaders left Ireland for London. As well as the President, there were the Vice-President, Arthur Griffith ; the Minister for Home Affairs, Austin Stack ; the Minister for Economic Affairs, Robert Barton, and the Director of Propaganda, Erskine Childers.

The nation acclaimed them as they set out ; the exiles welcomed them passionately and with pride as they went through Britain. These were some of the men who had directed the greatest of all struggles for Irish liberty, who had shared with their people prison, deportation, exile, sentence of death.

As the Ministers looked back at Dun Laoghaire they saw its piers and its esplanades thronged with cheering people; as they came into Holyhead, they heard the same songs, the same cries, saw the same eager devotion. After many such scenes along the route, they reached Euston, and there was Ireland again, more tense in the pride of its exiles because they had lived in the heart of the enemy country, by many reviled and hated.

On 14th July, in the afternoon, accompanied by Art O'Brien, who, through the War of Independence, had filled in London the difficult and dangerous post of Ambassador of the Republic, President de Valera went to Downing Street to meet alone the man who had loosed the most savage repression since 1798.

Many stories have been told of that meeting, true stories and false. Lloyd George's descriptions were false and Churchill's were filled with that venom he cherished against all who withstood Britain's will. Frank Pakenham, in his *Peace by Ordeal*, gives more accurate detail, and time has added a little.

Lloyd George, like many gifted, shallow men, was an artist in pretence, in assumed concern, in well-planned showmanship. In the first moments he was full of camaraderie. This was a great meeting, one Celtic leader meeting another. It was extraordinary what the English would put up with: they did not mind who ruled them so long as the work was well done. So they had Scotsmen as well as Englishmen as Premiers, and here he, a Welshman, was now at the head of the British Empire.

The guest did not respond to these digs at the English, and a new line was attempted, a thrust at the Irish Parliamentary Party; they were de Valera's opponents; he would surely rise to that. The moment was unpropitious for, the evening before, among the papers de Valera used to prepare himself for this interview had been some pages from the June, 1919, issue of *Studies*.

They contained an article by John J. Horgan, of Cork, entitled "Precepts and Practice in Ireland, 1914–19," and contrasted the British leaders' emphatic war-aims of liberty to all, with their steady betrayal of Ireland, and of the Irish Party, who had trusted them so much. When the Premier began to criticise to the President the party opposed to him in Ireland, instead of agreement there was what every Irishman must feel in such circumstances—that, at least, it was not the business of the Britisher to attack one group of Irishmen to the leader of another.

De Valera said sharply: "You broke your pledges to them, didn't you?"

Taken aback for a moment, Lloyd George soon recovered : " Oh, circumstances altered, of course," he said.

De Valera's comment was that changing circumstances could never justify betrayal. There were no more derogatory remarks about the Irish Party !

CHAPTER 56

THE EMPTY CHAIR

WHEN silenced at his criticism of the movement Sinn Féin replaced, Lloyd George then fell back upon a piece of showmanship that had been well thought out. The talks were held in the British Cabinet room, and across the end wall there had been stretched a great map of the world. De Valera noticed how much red there was on it.

Lloyd George pointed to it now, telling his visitor about the morning's meeting of the Imperial Conference in that same room, and he began to point out the chairs in which each of the Premiers had sat: there Hughes of Australia; in this chair, Smuts of South Africa; in that, Meighen of Canada; there, Sastri of India; in the chair beside it Massey of New Zealand, and in this chair, himself as Premier of England. There was one chair immediately opposite Lloyd George; he waved towards it, but said nothing. He waited expectantly. De Valera also said nothing. Lloyd George began again: there Australia, there South Africa, there Canada, there India, there New Zealand, there England; again the empty chair, again the outstretched arm, and again the unspoken pause.

It was obvious that the Premier wanted to be asked whose chair that was; he would have answered: " That is Ireland's chair . . . waiting for her First Premier." It would have been a triumphant opening if this were a play; but it was something much more grave than theatricals to one of those present, and chairs at a conference of the British Empire had nothing to do with it. The carefully rehearsed charade had ended limply.

Lloyd George was a mercurial man. He recovered quickly, and when he turned to de Valera after these few false starts, it was with a seriousness that matched the occasion, and on that first day they discussed the question of Partition.

The two met again the next day, 15th July, and again on 18th July. It was at the end of that meeting that, on a proposal of Lloyd George's, the first clash of wills over a decision came. As they were about to part, Lloyd George said that when they got together for the next and last meeting, arranged for 21st July, he would hand de Valera the British terms. De Valera said "No," he must see the terms before they met. He must have time to consider them with his colleagues in London.

Lloyd George airily waved the suggestion aside. It could not be done. De Valera said: "I must see the terms before we meet." Impossible, said Lloyd George; they could not be ready; he had not expected this demand. "I must see the proposals before we meet again," de Valera said with a finality that silenced the excuses of the little man. Late on the night of 20th July they were brought to the Grosvenor Hotel, where the Irish delegation were staying, and where, after each day's conference, de Valera recited the details of the talks to Griffith, Stack, Barton and Childers, and they discussed together the points the Prime Minister had put forward.

The British proposals were drafted with all the art of diplomacy. Couched in generous words, full of sympathy for Ireland's claims, regretful of the long and bitter struggle, radiant with the liberality of what was being offered, the document proposed that "Ireland shall assume forthwith the status of a Dominion with all the powers and privileges set forth in this document." But what followed were not more gifts, but the taking back of what was—for propaganda sake—described as being given. Only a partitioned Ireland could get this Dominion status; only an Ireland which abandoned her independence and crept back under the Crown, only an Ireland which took on her back part of the vast public debt of Britain, which bound herself never to protect her industries, which agreed that all Ireland should be an air base in peace and war, which concurred in Britain occupying six Irish counties and, in addition, Ireland's strategic ports, to use them in war against Britain's enemies.

When de Valera went to Downing Street on the afternoon of 21st July, it was to hand back to Lloyd George this British document, and to tell him that he and his colleagues rejected the terms so completely that they would not even bring them to Ireland. They stood facing one another, Irish leader and British Premier. De Valera cold and hard; the British Prime Minister dark and angry. He blazed now, and, like the bully in the street fight, he produced the cosh.

"You realise this means war," he said.

The Irish leader eyed him sharply.

"Don't you realise," repeated Lloyd George, his voice rising, "that by rejecting those terms, the responsibility for war rests on your shoulders and yours only?"

De Valera replied quietly: "No, Mr. Lloyd George, if you insist on attacking us, it is you, not I, who alone will be responsible."

There was a long pause. The silence showed the ultimatum had gone astray. Lloyd George tried another stratagem. "I will

w

publish the terms at once for the Irish people to see ; I must give the Irish people the chance of knowing what is being offered to them."

De Valera saw the danger in that procedure. The proposals had been worded for just that, to deceive the unwary, but if he showed the concern he felt at what the British Premier proposed, it would be done more quickly. He answered :

" Go ahead—but I thought nothing was to be published unless we both agreed ? " Lloyd George, with a gesture, waived the reminder aside. " That was a little matter. We are dealing with big things now."

De Valera replied : " So that is how you keep your promises. Have your way. You publish your terms and I will publish my refusal of them."

They walked from the room together, the document still lying on the Cabinet table. As they reached the door, Lloyd George's mood again changed.

" Won't you give me a considered answer ? " he asked, as if there had never been a harsh word in his mouth.

" Yes, certainly," de Valera answered, " if you give me time for consultation with my colleagues and refrain from publishing in the meanwhile."

" Very well," said Lloyd George.

The two never met again, but, even this last promise, Lloyd George found a way of breaking.

While the terms were being considered in Ireland, General Smuts was used to bring pressure on the Irish leaders. He saw de Valera, and wrote extolling the, as yet unpublished, British terms, representing them as full Dominion status, " not in doles or instalments, but at once and completely." That letter Lloyd George himself gave to the press. It was a piece of sharp practice typical of the man, and it wrung from Tim Healy, no lover of Sinn Féin, one of the sharpest rebukes in political writing :

> " To enlist the great Boer statesman to string the Government proposals into nursery rhymes set to African lullabies for Irish ears was crudely inartistic," wrote Tim with his mordant wit. " To publish the letters in advance of the text of the Cabinet offer and thereby give the world a false and unwarranted idea of its generosity, was sheer mischief. It injured the prospect of acceptance as anything wearing the air of trickiness must."

Tim Healy ended his protest with a phrase which answered Smuts's meanness in calling the Irish leaders " small men " :

" No man is small who braves death for his country, or who is ready to go back to the death-in-life endured by these men for years."

To Smuts, de Valera himself replied :

" An Ireland in fragments nobody cares about. A unified Ireland alone can be happy and prosperous."

The Republican Cabinet met, and the proposals were examined in full detail. The letter replying to them was drafted and re-drafted until it expressed the mind of all. It was brought to London by two officers of the I.R.A., Commandant Robert Barton, T.D., and Commandant Joseph McGrath, T.D. It contained the formal rejection of the terms, and in it was the following assertion :

" Ireland's right to choose for herself the path she shall take to realise her own destiny must be accepted as indefeasible. It is a right that has been maintained through centuries of oppression and at the cost of unparalleled sacrifice and untold suffering, and it will not be surrendered . . . it is our deep conviction that true friendship with England, which military coercion has frustrated for centuries, can be obtained most readily now through amicable but absolute separation."

As soon as the reply was delivered at 10 Downing Street, it was flown by special plane to Paris, where Lloyd George was attending a meeting of the Allied Supreme Council. He glanced through it, told M. Briand, who was presiding, that a crisis had arisen and took a plane to London. From the plane he summoned a special meeting of the Cabinet.

It was all done in the whitest glare of publicity. When the Cabinet met, General Macready was called into consultation, and it was announced that the British army in Ireland was to be strengthened. The British press warned the people of Ireland what would happen them if they did not accept this " freedom," and accept it quickly.

The *Daily Mail* announced that a refusal would mean that " the dragooning of villages " would start again ; the *Daily Telegraph* that the " conditions which preceded the truce " were the alternative to acceptance ; the *Daily Sketch* that a rejection would mean " military action on an unprecedented scale " ; the London *Times* that refusal would " commit Ireland to the terror from which the truce freed her." Day after day, through every vehicle of propaganda, the inconsistent duality of British policy was repeated, that Ireland was being offered full freedom, and that if her people did not take it, hell itself would be loosed upon them.

This blare of propaganda, this whirlwind of deception, swept itself into every newspaper in the world, the Irish papers no less than others, and in the midst of it, de Valera summoned all deputies to attend a meeting of Dáil Éireann.

On the evening of 6th August, Dublin Castle responded with the following statement :—

> "In keeping with the public undertaking given by the Prime Minister that his Majesty's Government would facilitate in every practicable way the steps now being taken to promote peace in Ireland, it has been decided to release forthwith, and without conditions, all members of Dáil Éireann who are at present interned, or who are undergoing sentence of penal servitude or imprisonment, to enable them to attend a meeting of Dáil Éireann, which has been summoned for 16th August.
>
> "His Majesty's Government have decided that one member, J. J. McKeown, who has been convicted of murder, cannot be released."

The response of the President of the Republic was immediate and electric. He announced that unless Commandant Mac Eóin was released, the talks were over : "I cannot accept responsibility for proceeding further with the negotiations." De Valera's statement went on :

> "Commandant Mac Eóin typifies in his person everything that we have been fighting for. The whole Irish people are proud of him for in him they see the patriot soldier that their history has taught them to love. He is the ideal citizen whose dauntless courage and readiness to sacrifice himself for his country is matched only in his chivalry as a soldier. We, the Irish Government and the Headquarters Staff of the Irish Army are proud of him as a splendid representative of the type of Irish soldier this fight has developed and as a living model of what we want our Army officers to be. His conduct in the field as borne testimony to at the British courtmartial and his speech and conduct at the trial itself prove to the whole world the manner of man he is. In British legal phraseology he is termed a murderer; but for us, and I believe for the world, he is a heroic Irishman."

That night, Seán Mac Eóin walked out from the condemned cell a free man. It was an hour in which Ireland's prestige touched new heights. Even the London *Times* saw the portent in what had happened, that a people and its leaders were ready to go under the harrow again rather than that one brave comrade's life should be taken.

"For good or evil," said *The Times*, " the old Ireland is gone. Instead of it there is a young people with new qualities and also with new defects. Though tested sternly, as undoubtedly it has been, it has given proof of nationhood. None of the efforts that have been made to divide the people . . . have succeeded. On the contrary, they have vindicated the strength of the national ideal."

In those days of 1921 the Republic lived nobly, earning even the admiration of its enemies.

CHAPTER 57

THE ACTOR

ON 16th August, the Second Dáil, elected in May, met for the first time.

Next to the day on which the Declaration of Independence was made, no assembly met in Ireland so charged with destiny.

They had come from all parts those deputies. Nearly forty of them were back from that death-in-life which British imprisonment then meant: from the convict prison, from the hard-labour yards of the British jails, from the solitary confinement cells, from the insanitary, overcrowded camps. They were the elected of the people, and so from the beginning were marked out as the special victims of the tyranny. Many had escaped arrest by living in disguise under assumed names. Others had been military leaders in the field, and came now from the hills to the Dáil.

To that Session came also deputies who, as Ambassadors and Ministers of the Republic, had slipped out to Europe and America to keep the facts of Ireland's struggle before the world: Seán T. O'Kelly from Paris; Harry Boland from Washington; George Gavan Duffy from Rome; Dr. McCartan from the U.S.A.; these and others, who were not T.D.'s, had relentlessly fought British influence and propaganda which everywhere were distorting Ireland's aims: L. H. Kerney in France; Michael MacWhite in Geneva; Donal Hales in Northern Italy; Diarmuid Fawsitt in New York; Máire O'Brien in Spain; Lindsay Crawford in Canada; P. J. Little in South Africa; Osmond Grattan Esmonde in Australasia; Larry Ginnell and Éamonn Bulfin in South America—a gallant band, of whose work little was then known at home, but by whom Ireland's voice was sent echoing through the nations.

As on Independence Day, the Dáil met in the Round Room of the Mansion House. Three hundred Republican police had taken over that section of the city and regulated the traffic and controlled the vast crowds. Only a fraction of those seeking admission could get into the Round Room, where, under the dais, were reserved seats for the Deputies—and several rows of empty chairs.

These chairs were for the wives and mothers, the fathers and children, the sisters and brothers of some who had given their lives n the contest. Later still, many white-faced men, maimed in the defence of the Republic, were carried in. That great chattering room fell into silence as the dark-clad figures, and then the wounded Volunteers, were brought to the spaces kept for them. For this meeting of Dáil Éireann was not a spectacle only but a symbol.

The welcome to the Deputies was tumultuous, again to be quenched as voices rose in unison while phrase by phrase, with uplifted hands, the T.D.'s, in the now wholly still Room, swore to God to maintain the Republic at all costs. There were two occasions in that Session of several days when the Speaker could not control the crowd, otherwise so co-operative and obedient to his command. One was when the President, addressing the House on the British proposals, said :

> " We cannot, and we will not, on behalf of this nation, accept these terms."

The audience approved with a great shout, coming with such suddenness, that the Speaker could just look on powerless. It was re-échoed at the end of the address, when, having said how ready the Irish Government were to make a just peace, de Valera referred to London's new threats, and added :

> " I feel that as the Irish people in the past have not flinched when force was brought against them to deprive them of their rights, the Irish people will not flinch now because more arms are being sent for."

The cry of determination that rushed through the hall on the heels of those words was the voice of Ireland's unbroken will after centuries of endurance.

The Ministry having resigned at this opening of a new Parliament, Seán Mac Eóin rose to name his leader for the first position in the land :

> " The honour has fallen to me to put before the Dáil the name of Éamon de Valera as President of the Irish Republic. You know, and the people of Ireland know, what he has done for Irish freedom. Our hope and our belief now are that he will bring our cause to success. In no generation for more than a century has any Irish leader equalled his achievements. No one has shown himself more fitted to deal with our traditional foe. He has not been deceived by promises nor intimidated by threats. Éamon de Valera first met the English as a soldier and he beat them as a soldier. He has been meeting them now as a statesman, and he will beat them as a statesman. The honour and the interests of our nation are alike safe in his hands."

General Mulcahy seconded, and when the Speaker had declared Éamon de Valera re-elected, the President thanked the House with emotion :

" My comrades and colleagues have conferred upon me what
I believe is the highest honour that can be conferred at this
moment on any human being."

From that Dáil the newly-elected President then asked approval
for a letter which contained an answer to the British threats.   One
passage read :

" If our refusal to betray our nation's honour and the trust
that has been reposed in us is to be made an issue of war by Great
Britain we deplore it.   We are as conscious of our responsibilities
to the living as we are mindful of principle or of our obligations
to the heroic dead.   We have not sought war, nor do we seek
war, but if war be made upon us we must defend ourselves and
shall do so, confident that whether our defence be successful or
unsuccessful, no body of representative Irishmen or Irishwomen
will ever propose to the nation the surrender of its birthright."

The ensuing correspondence is famous.   The British sought a
conference at which, even before she entered it, Ireland must accept
Crown, Empire and Partition.   De Valera sought a conference in
which the Irish delegation would be free to take part without abate-
ment of Ireland's assertion of Independence and free to propose and
secure separation.

In every letter, Britain demanded that Ireland agree to come on
her terms ;   in every reply, de Valera re-stated that Ireland must
have full right to self-determination, and that Britain must not try
to impose conditions before the negotiators met.

Eventually, Lloyd George fixed the Conference for Inverness on
20th September.   De Valera felt it should not be left in any doubt
the precise capacity in which the plenipotentiaries met the British
delegates.   So into the letter of 12th September, accepting date and
place of Conference, de Valera put this formal statement :

" In this final note we deem it our duty to re-affirm that our
position is and can only be as we have defined it throughout this
correspondence.   Our nation has formally declared its independence and recognises itself as a Sovereign State.   It is only as
the representatives of that State and as its chosen guardians
that we have any authority or powers to act on behalf of our
people."

That paragraph led to one of the most colourful scenes in the
history of Anglo-Irish relations.   Harry Boland and Joe McGrath
brought the letter to Gairloch in the Scottish Highlands, eighty miles
west of Inverness, where Lloyd George was fishing.   On that day,
13th September, the British Prime Minister was in a happy mood.

He had just caught a salmon and was as proud as seven peacocks. When Harry and Joe appeared, he greeted them fondly, and sent for the salmon that they might see it. The personification of good humour, he led the way into the house, telling them of his particular joy to be with Celts, the English were so stodgy. After the emissaries had refused his offer of drinks, he beamed on them and asked had they brought him good news.

They handed him the letter. He opened it, and still smiling, began to read. Then he leapt up, and in the attitude of complete despair, he cried out : " My God, my God." Pacing the floor, he told them that the paragraph would ruin everything. There could be no conference now. There he was, a fellow-Celt, holding back the English Tories from tearing Ireland asunder, and though he was ready to give de Valera everything he wanted, everything, his own independent nation with Gaelic education, anything he asked, de Valera did this to him. Well, it was all over now. To-day he was Prime Minister, Ireland's best friend, to-morrow he would be but a plain country solicitor, without influence ; and while the Birkenheads and Churchills would make Ireland a desert, he could do nothing to stop them. De Valera, by that one paragraph, had stolen all his power away.

The two emissaries watched him fascinated and not a little impressed. In the midst of his lamentations, Lloyd George thought of a way. He would pretend he had never got the letter. They could race back to Inverness, where there was a telephone—he would arrange for a quick service—they would tell de Valera that the paragraph was unacceptable, and the letter could be re-sent to him with that omission and all would be well. Nobody but themselves would know.

When he learned from Harry Boland that the Dáil was to meet next day to hear the letter, his despair returned. He was done ; his career was over. But perhaps if they explained to de Valera, he might be able to stop that, too. Would they discuss among themselves how best it could be done ? At that he left the room, telling them to ring a bell when they were ready. To Harry's gleeful mind, this was high drama indeed, the most wonderful situation he had ever lived through. Ireland was doomed, and these two Commandants of the I.R.A. had only to ring a bell and the Prime Minister of England would come running in to save her ! They talked among themselves and pushed the bell. Lloyd George hurried in, and they told him they would tell de Valera over the 'phone what the Prime Minister had said. The old man was charmed. " We will save the day for Ireland," he said.

In Ireland, the message, coming over a bad line, was understood to mean that the emissaries might be bringing the letter back. To prevent that, Bob Brennan was rushed to the boat, and reached Holy-head in time.   The relief of all was great when it was learned that the letter had been left with Lloyd George.   As the party made its way back to Dublin, a minor comedy was being performed at Gairloch. Through over-efficiency, the Premier's own office had circulated to the members of the Cabinet the letter in its original form.   Lloyd George called it back as unauthorised and waited.

The emissaries reached Dublin, and Bob Brennan, early in the morning, brought Harry Boland to the President.

" Do you know what he said to me——" Harry Boland began getting ready to repeat it all.

De Valera stopped him : " I know.   He told you that he was a Celt, and that he wanted us to have our freedom and Gaelic education too and that he was holding back the Tories who wanted to destroy us.   If he accepted my letter he would be no longer Prime Minister and Ireland's enemies would be in power.   He said all that to me in July."   Harry gazed at him open-mouthed :

" If he did not mean what he said," he mused, remembering the dramatic scene, " he must be the greatest actor born."

" Of course he is," said de Valera.

That day at noon—the hour agreed upon with the British for publishing the letters delivered the day before—the letter of 12th September, with the paragraph undeleted, was read to Dáil Éireann, whose members lustily approved it.

Lloyd George, in anger, summoned a cabinet meeting at Inverness, a rare Constitutional departure which ensured publicity for the crisis, and cancelled the conference.   There were more military consultations.   The British press voiced new threats.   In a pained and irate protest, the Premier telegraphed to de Valera on 15th September :

> " On your part you have not come to meet us by a single step but have merely reiterated in phrases of emphatic challenge the letter and the spirit of your original claims."

It was the British way of saying that the Irish leader had stood fast by independence and by the unity of his country.

CHAPTER 58

CREDENTIALS AND INSTRUCTIONS

LLOYD GEORGE, in cancelling the arrangements for the Conference scheduled for Inverness on 20th September mentioned that he had privately asked that the paragraph be withdrawn which described the status of the Irish delegates as those from a Sovereign State. Now, he declared, he must insist publicly on that withdrawal.

The crisis in the correspondence had been reached. De Valera knew that any doubt as to the standing of the Irish delegation would be mercilessly exploited by the British when, at the Conference itself, the vital question came. He must safeguard that position now. He must make possible the task the Dáil had appointed the plenipotentiaries to do. The British knew the value of what he was achieving, and they fought against him like tigers.

One method was to portray the Irish leader as impossible to deal with ; he was holding up discussions for peace by insisting on formalities, by petty assertions which no reasonable person could accept.

Lloyd George, surrounded by Press lords, not only got the British newspapers to accept this thesis and to feed it to their readers. He got the newsagencies, controlled or influenced in London, to try the same deception on world opinion. In such a situation, it needed special caution on the part of the President to go on striving for a free Conference and yet hold the sympathy of the world. Thus it was that, in every letter in which de Valera refused to give way on the principle of freedom, he also expressed the Irish desire not only for peace, but to discuss with the British the best way of securing it. It was essential to make clear to other nations that Dáil Éireann was a responsible Government, always ready to use peaceful means if its ends could be achieved by these.

That he did succeed in conveying this, the cable sent by the Hierarchy of the United States, on 23rd September, to Cardinal Logue, bore witness. It spoke of their pride to see the Irish leaders " conduct themselves with a statesmanship that has challenged the admiration of the world."

Lloyd George, for all his cleverness, was perplexed by the Irish firmness. He cancelled the Conference, but pleaded illness as the excuse for delaying a fuller reply : " I am for the moment laid up here . . . a few days' delay is inevitable."

On 18th September he announced the final decision of the Cabinet :

> " My colleagues and I cannot meet them (the Irish delegates)
> as the representatives of a sovereign and independent State
> without disloyalty on our part to the Throne and Empire. I
> must therefore repeat that unless the second paragraph in your
> letter of the 12th is withdrawn conference between us is
> impossible."

It had all the appearance of an irrevocable decision, set forth in
unambiguous language. De Valera's reply asked sharply :

> " We request you therefore to state whether your letter . . .
> is intended to be a demand for a surrender on our part or an
> invitation to a Conference free on both sides and without pre-
> judice should agreement not be reached."

If it was a free Conference, concluded de Valera, the Irish delegation
was ready to meet the British representatives at any time.

There was a long and embarrassed pause. Ten days passed without any answer to that last query. Meanwhile, the threats poured
out from all sides. Churchill spoke at Dundee on 24th September :

> " If we were sure that Mr. de Valera's rejections of our offer
> were intended to be absolute and final, our course would be very
> unpleasant, but it would also be very simple. . . . Not peace,
> but certain war—real war, not mere bushranging would follow
> such a course . . . "

The British newspapers cried war as lustily. The *Daily Telegraph*
reminded the Irish Army of its fate :

> " They will be technically rebels and murderers and as such
> they will be dealt with."

British agents in Ireland could report no breaking of the people
under these constant menaces, and on 29th September came the somer-
sault. The President received the last communication from Lloyd
George.

The British Premier now announced that they proposed to cancel
all the letters that had passed ! " They cannot enter a Conference
on the basis of this Correspondence." They would begin all over
again.

> " We therefore send you herewith a fresh invitation to a
> Conference in London on 11th October, where we can meet
> your delegates as spokesmen of the people whom you represent
> with a view to ascertaining how the association of Ireland with

the community of nations known as the British Empire may best be reconciled with Irish national aspirations."

No conditions this time : no demand now for any acceptance of King or Crown or divided Ireland. It was the unconditional Conference de Valera had been insisting on.

But if the British wanted to obliterate the memory of their failure to wring a vital concession from the Irish leader, de Valera reminded them that the assertion of status remained, and that the Irish plenipotentiaries were coming in the name of a nation which had declared its independence. In accepting the new offer, the President summarised it all in one phrase :

> " Our respective positions have been stated and are understood, and we agree that conference, not correspondence, is the most practical and hopeful way to an understanding."

It was then that the bonfires should have been lit throughout Ireland. The first great tussle had been won. But if now was the moment to rejoice, it was also the moment to keep that joy within bounds. It was vital to impress upon the people the difficulty of advancing along the road to which the gate had at last been opened.

On Saturday morning, 8th October, the Irish delegation left for London.

Before they set out, the Cabinet had given them their title and their authority to negotiate. It was embodied in a formal State document, signed by the President, for presentation to the British in emphasis of the capacity in which they came :

> " In virtue of the authority vested in me by Dáil Éireann, I hereby appoint Arthur Griffith, T.D., Minister for Foreign Affairs ; Michael Collins, T.D., Minister for Finance ; Robert Barton, T.D., Minister for Economic Affairs ; Edmund J. Duggan, T.D., and George Gavan Duffy, T.D., as Envoys Plenipotentiary from the elected Government of the Republic of Ireland to negotiate and conclude on behalf of Ireland, with the representatives of His Majesty King George V., a treaty or treaties of settlement, association and accommodation between Ireland and the community of nations known as the British Commonwealth. In witness whereof I hereunder subscribe my name as President,
>
> " Éamon de Valéra."

It had been decided much earlier that the President must stay in Ireland. It was certain that, as the Conference proceeded, superhuman efforts would be made by Britain and the Castle to divide the people at home, to take away their one great protection, unity. That the nation might be rallied and given confidence, the President was to stay with the majority of the Cabinet in Ireland, and the Plenipotentiaries were, in their instructions, ordered to sign nothing which had not been approved at home. The final decision would be left, not to men who were necessarily in temporary isolation in London, but to the President and Cabinet in Dublin. Then in every crisis they had one all-sufficient answer—they were bound to consult Dublin and await the decision. On that basis *Instructions* were prepared and given to each delegate in limitation of his plenipotentiary powers.

They were:

> " 1. The Plenipotentiaries have full powers as defined in their credentials.
>
> 2. It is understood before decisions are finally reached on a main question, that a despatch notifying the intentions to make these decisions will be sent to members of the Cabinet in Dublin and that a reply will be awaited by the Plenipotentiaries before final decision is made.
>
> 3. It is also understood that the complete text of the draft treaty about to be signed will be similarly submitted to Dublin and reply awaited.
>
> 4. In the case of a break, the text of the final proposals from our side will be similarly submitted.
>
> 5. It is understood the Cabinet in Dublin will be kept regularly informed of the progress of negotiations."

All realised as they set out on their task the value of these careful arrangements.

On the day before the two groups of statesmen sat facing one another across the Conference table, the President issued a Proclamation. It reminded the Irish people that this was not a moment for foolish hopes, but for preparation and for prayer.

> " Fellow citizens: The Conference in which the accredited representatives of the nation are about to engage with the representatives of the British Government must profoundly influence, and may determine, the whole course of our country's future. . . . Whatever the differences of the past, it is the interest, as it is the duty, of all Irishmen to stand together for Ireland now."

The Proclamation reminded the nation that what was being sought was not easily to be achieved:

" The only peace that, in the very nature of things, can end this struggle will be a peace consistent with the nation's right and guaranteeing a freedom worthy of the sufferings endured to secure it.   Such a peace will not be easy to obtain.   The claim that conflicts with Ireland's rights has been ruthlessly persisted in through centuries of blood.   It seems unlikely that this claim will be abandoned now.   Peace and that claim are incompatible."

De Valera emphasised that only the strength of the people themselves could make the delegates successful.

" The peace that will end this conflict will be secured, not by the skill or statesmanship of leaders, but by the stern determination of a close-knit nation, steeled to the acceptance of death rather than the abandonment of its rightful liberty."

The Proclamation asked everybody to realise the horrors that even one vital surrender would bring on Ireland :

" Were the prospect of further horrors or further sacrifices to cause her to quail or falter for a moment, all would again be lost. The threats that could force a surrender in one vital particular would be relied on to force surrender in another and another till all was gone.   Of necessity, Ireland must stand where she is, unyielding and fearless on the rock of right, or be outmanœuvred and defeated in detail."

De Valera ended the Proclamation with an appeal that the plenipotentiaries be fully trusted :

" The power against us will use every artifice it knows in the hope of dispiriting, dividing, weakening us. We must all beware.   The unity that is essential will best be maintained by an unwavering faith in those who have been deputed to act in the nation's behalf and a confidence mainfesting itself, as hitherto, in eloquent discipline.   For this I appeal."

The day that this statement appeared, two groups of men met in Downing Street.

CHAPTER 59

TWO GROUPS OF MEN

IF ever opposites had met, it was when the Irish plenipotentiaries sat at the Cabinet table in London on 11th October, 1921.

Facing them were statesmen with long practice in world affairs, men who had played with the destinies of nations. They had ruled over an empire in which more than half the inhabitants were denied freedom. They were mostly men of wealth, to whom the fates had been gentle and generous.

The British were led by one of the most gifted and one of the most dishonest of all the Prime Ministers of England. For twenty years he had been in the limelight, first as the stormy petrel of British politics, now he was as crusted a Tory and as belligerent an Imperialist as any Victorian proconsul. The young Welsh M.P., with the corroding eloquence, who had once hung his head in shame at the burning of Boer farmsteads and the crowding of Afrikanders into the deadly concentration camps, had lived to order the burning of Irish farmsteads and the crowding of great prison camps with the freedom-loving men and women of Ireland. All who had associated with Lloyd George knew his capacity for deception and faithlessness, and when, within a year of this gathering, he fell from power, he was never to see office again. Nobody who had worked with him dared to trust him again.

Beside him sat Churchill. He, like his chief, had changed his politics more than once, and he could argue on any side with brilliant and persuasive oratory. At this period of his life he believed in force as an instrument of policy, and but a few weeks earlier had withstood the idea of negotiation and urged that the Irish be broken by the wholesale seizure and execution of hostages. Birkenhead, who had achieved his office by Carsonite treason, was there, and Austen Chamberlain, more honourable than the others, but with a strong family inheritance of almost irrational anti-Irishism. The British Secretary for War, Sir Laming Worthington-Evans, was a member. He had the distinction of few principles and a gifted tongue. There, too, was Sir Hamar Greenwood, the Chief Secretary, whose very appointment dishonoured the Cabinet who made it, and who in his term of office succeeded in dishonouring all England as well. And last, for legal consultation, was Sir Gordon Hewart, afterwards to become Lord Chief Justice.

It was a formidable team, but there was one characteristic shared by the principals—Lloyd George, Churchill, Birkenhead—which rectified the balance from the Irish point of view. They were opportunists and they were eager for success. If threats of war would win for them, they would use that weapon; if deception would do instead, they would practise it with a carefree and experienced agility. But if the Irish withstood both, their anxiety not to fail would impel them forward to such a point that a real settlement would become possible.

On this side of the table there was a body of men who had been shaped and nurtured by very different forces. They had come to this Conference not from mansions but from prison and from hiding. They had given up the good things of life that they might serve their country's freedom and the liberty of mankind. They were led by Arthur Griffith who all his life had selflessly given his talents to resisting British oppression. He had championed the Boers, the Indians, the Egyptians, whom those now facing him had oppressed. He seemed to have been shaped for exactly this moment. For nearly a generation he had preached to his people never to trust the word of a British statesman for he would serve nothing but Britain's interest and use every deceptive and minatory art in that service. It was Griffith who had predicted that the Irish Parliamentary Party would be deceived and destroyed because they had placed their trust in Asquith and Lloyd George. Nobody seemed more certain of reading through all the pretences, the acting, the false promises which the plenipotentiaries were now to meet than this man who had endured such deprivations for Ireland's sake.

Next to Griffith sat Michael Collins, Minister for Finance, Director of Organisation of the Republican Army, who had so often by acts and by words voiced the determination of this generation of Irishmen to resist to the death every compromise of national independence. As de Valera in the field of national leadership and international relations had become the symbol of the Republic, Collins had assumed, in the people's view, the very personification of the armed defence of that Republic and the sacrifices made to maintain it.

There, too, was Robert Barton, competent, cool-headed, learned, who had just come from eighteen months in the strictest English convict prison where for many weeks he had been in solitary confinement on a diet of bread and water. He, as Minister for Economic Affairs and as a member of the religious minority, knew the importance of both unity and freedom if there were to be a new Ireland. George Gavan Duffy, as son of the Young Ireland leader, brought a great

x

name to that table and, as a lawyer, a fine mind. Éamonn Duggan, a member of the I.R.B. and, like Robert Barton, a Commandant in the I.R.A., was also there as a legal member.

All these men, so different in other ways, had stood shoulder to shoulder through the years of struggle, sharing and suffering for the same objective—an Ireland free from sea to sea without King or Crown or any diminution of national right. To the last dark night they would stand thus, champions of liberty, opposing the greed and the violence of the strong.

The British Premier remained in close contact with the owners of the principal British newspapers during the sitting of the Conference and guided these newspapers in their references to issues discussed, and he used this contact as a weapon against the Irish. Other means of clouding the true situation were used and from one of these came the first crisis of the negotiations.

On the night of 20th October, 1921, the President sent for me, who, in the absence of the Minister in London, had charge of Dáil Publicity. He gave me a telegram to despatch from the Central Telegraph Office and then to issue copies to the Press. That telegram reverberated around the world.

His Holiness Pope Benedict XV had telegraphed to the British king good wishes for the success of the negotiations. Lloyd George drafted the king's reply and inserted into it his claim that the Irish were subjects of the king, and that what was to be settled was not an international dispute between Britain and Ireland, but trouble among the Irish themselves. The British Foreign Office gave the telegrams for world publication on 20th October.

The Pope's message to King George V was :—

> " We rejoice at the resumption of the Anglo-Irish negotiations, and pray to the Lord with all our heart that He may bless them and grant to your majesty the great joy and imperishable glory of bringing to an end the age-long dissension."

To this, Lloyd George, in the king's name, replied :—

> " I have received the message of your Holiness with much pleasure, and with all my heart I join in your prayer that the Conference, now sitting in London, may achieve a permanent settlement of the troubles in Ireland and may initiate a new era of peace and happiness for my people."

The suggestion was the old one which Lloyd George had tried, but failed, to make the basis of the Conference, that the Irish were " my people " and that it was not a War of Independence which the Irish were fighting, but a local quarrel " in Ireland."

That same night I despatched the President's telegram.

HIS HOLINESS BENEDICT XV,

Rome.

"The people of Ireland have read the message sent by your Holiness to the King of Great Britain and appreciate the kindly interest in their welfare and the paternal regard which suggested it. I tender to your Holiness their gratitude. They are confident that the ambiguities in the reply sent in the name of King George will not mislead you, as they may the uninformed, into believing that the troubles are 'in' Ireland or that the people of Ireland owe allegiance to the British King.

"The independence of Ireland has been formally proclaimed by the regularly-elected representatives of the people of Ireland and ratified by subsequent plebiscites.

"The trouble is between Ireland and Britain and its source that the rulers of Britain have sought to impose their will upon Ireland and by brutal force have endeavoured to rob her people of the liberty which is their natural right and their ancient heritage.

"We long to be at peace and in friendship with the people of Britain as with other peoples, but the same constancy through persecution and martyrdom that has proved the reality of our people's attachment to the faith of their fathers proves the reality of their attachment to their national freedom, and no consideration will ever induce them to abandon it.

Éamon de Valéra."

The telegram led to a storm in the British Press unequalled even by what had gone before. As if these newspapers did not know that the telegram from King George was, in fact, from Lloyd George, the highest British journals launched a campaign against de Valera coloured by a fierce personal resentment. The London *Times* described his cable as "an act of impertinence to the Pope," and as being "unmannerly even to the point of churlishness" to the King. Under this lead almost every paper in Britain assailed the Irish leader. It was then, from the London gutter-press, that the charge of "wounded vanity" was first made which later was to be heard so often. De Valera was even accused of wanting to "wreck the peace" to which he had so patiently opened the door.

Only a few of the newspapers of Britain refused to take part in the campaign. To its honour the *Daily Herald* gave the facts as they were :

"Eamon de Valera would have connived at a misrepresentation of the essential facts of the struggle between Great Britain and Ireland if he had not replied to it."

Among the ordinary English people, who accepted without criticism what their newspapers told them, there was much anger and with this as his background, Lloyd George at the reassembly of the Conference demanded that Griffith disown the telegram.

Though the delegation did not then appreciate the necessity for de Valera's reiteration of Ireland's status, Griffith manfully replied (as cited by Frank Pakenham in *Peace by Ordeal*):

> " With regard to President de Valera's message, I must demur to the view that it was defiant and insulting. Mr. de Valera only stated the facts. I should say that the message was called for by the phrase in King George's letter in which he refers to troubles in Ireland. This would be taken to mean a fight between Irishmen. The trouble is not a trouble in Ireland, but is one between Ireland and Great Britain."

The threats of war were resumed in the British papers. Griffith answered these too. The Irish in London met in the Albert Hall to pay honour to the plenipotentiaries. This greatest auditorium in the English capital, holding 8,000 people, was filled to the doors and there was an unforgettable scene when Griffith and his comrades entered.

Griffith spoke a few words, reminding the audience that it was not the place nor the moment when he could speak politically, but what he did say indicated Ireland's willingness to go into the shadows rather than yield her independence :

> " When we gaze at this vast meeting of our exiled fellow-countrymen and fellow-citizens we feel the strength, the solidarity and the unconquerableness of the Irish race. We are wishful to make a peace between our country and this country. We hope it may be so. We cannot say . . . . But while we hope for peace, Irishmen and Irishwomen, you must be equal to either fortune."

As in London Griffith was acknowledging the power through solidarity of the Irish race, so in Dublin was de Valera, where he spoke to the fifth Árd-Fheis of Sinn Féin. The representatives of over 1,300 clubs, young people and old who had survived the raids and the bludgeoning, listened as he warned them that every device known to the leaders of an Empire experienced in keeping peoples subject through division would be employed now to break the Irish people's unity, to turn leader against leader, Church against people, group against group.

He went on to tell the Árd-Fheis that there would never, in any settlement, be allegiance to the English King, for that question was closed for ever. The finality with which he spoke brought the delegates to their feet in a demonstration which disclosed how deeply pledged to independence the rank and file of the movement were. The President's warning was concentrated in the phrase the delegates carried from him to all parts of Ireland : " As sure as the nation is divided, the nation will be tricked." It is a remarkable thing that in a few months, while all the rest was falling to ruin, Sinn Féin as an organisation remained undivided, and held its place as the reflection of the people's will.

CHAPTER 60

A SECRET MEMORANDUM

IT was within a few days of the manufactured crisis over the telegram to the Pope that another kind of tension arose, this time unknown to any but the Cabinet in Dublin and the Irish Delegation at 22 Hans Place, its London headquarters.

The Irish plenipotentiaries did not go to meet the British without constructive proposals for a settlement. That is one of the most interesting facts about that famous Conference.

They carried with them the heads of a Treaty of Association between the Republic and Britain to which the Cabinet had unanimously agreed. It had the approval no less of Cathal Brugha and Austin Stack than of Arthur Griffith and Michael Collins. In return for a recognition by Britain of the full independence of a united Ireland and the withdrawal of all her military and " police " forces, Ireland would enter into an association with her and the other states of the British Commonwealth covering external questions.

War was not one of these. Ireland, like Switzerland, was to be internationally guaranteed a permanent neutrality and would undertake to keep her defences strong enough to resist any attempt by another Power to use Irish territory as the base of an attack on Britain.

On other questions which affected both Ireland and Britain, there would be consultations between all the Governments concerned so that on matters of common interest a common policy might be sought, though each Government would decide its own course freely.

As to the question of the status of the Six Counties, that was set apart as a matter which Ireland must herself decide alone. But it was indicated that if guarantees from the Irish majority failed to allay the fears created among the national minority as to the protection of their civic and religious rights, the Irish Government would discuss with them a measure of local autonomy within a united Ireland.

That was the Irish counter to the British proposals, being the interpretation by the Cabinet of the Republic as to how " the association of Ireland with the community of nations known as the British Empire may best be reconciled with Irish national aspirations," the accepted basis of the Conference.

Griffith wrote almost daily to de Valera as to the progress of the negotiations and one of his letters, that of 24th October, created the impression that the Irish delegates were discussing the question of allegiance. The President wrote strongly :

> " We are all here at one," he said, " that there can be no question of our asking the Irish people to enter into an arrangement which would make them subject to the Crown or demand from them allegiance to the British King. If war is the alternative we can only face it, and I think the sooner the other side is made to recognise that the better."

And in the same letter he made the offer—so much concealed by the propaganda of later days as to be even still little known—to come to London if the delegates thought it imperative that he should be with them to handle the situation. He was loth to go, he told them, reminding them of the general agreement as to the tactical advantage of his remaining in Dublin. But if they thought it necessary, he made it clear that he would come.

The reply of the plenipotentiaries was in part protest and in part explanation. With an asperity not hitherto shown they asked that they be allowed to exercise their negotiating powers free from interference, subject only to the written instructions with which the whole Cabinet had restricted those powers. They explained that if there was to be a treaty of association between a free Ireland and Britain it was natural that the position of the British King in regard to it should arise and be discussed. As to de Valera's joining them, they said if he could come to London privately, without its being known, it would be good that he should be with them, but they were unanimously against his coming publicly. It was a time, of course, when de Valera's going to London, or anywhere else, unnoticed was out of the question as indeed the delegates themselves presumably realised.

De Valera ended the dispute with soft words, telling the delegation that they should regard the memos he sent them as his comment on the events reported to him unless he expressly said otherwise. But he did not modify what he had said about facing war rather than accepting any form of allegiance.

However, in this exchange of letters, the delegates had set the mind of the Cabinet in Dublin greatly at rest. Their acceptance of the limitations put upon their negotiating powers by their instructions was complete. They acknowledged themselves as free to discuss but unable to sign anything or accept other than the policy of External Association unless the Cabinet at home had first approved.

Another development came about this time. As a united team the plenipotentiaries were unable to be either outwitted or overawed.

The British problem was how it might divide them or at least separate them from one another without rousing their suspicions.

It began, I think, through Tom Jones. Lloyd George had brought around him, as secretaries, men in his own likeness and they, particularly Jones, were used to prepare Irish minds for some proposal of Lloyd George's, giving it a meaning far wider than it had so that when it was made officially it would seem to have the advantages Jones had already invested it with. It was he who now carried the suggestion that Lloyd George in his anxiety to be generous to Ireland was having trouble with Worthington-Evans and Hamar Greenwood. It might speed things up if they were edged out. This could only be done if some arrangement like the appointment of sub-committees was come to. He suggested that Griffith and Collins should meet Lloyd George and Chamberlain after the full Conference for short, private discussions.

The delegation discussed the matter and though Barton and Gavan Duffy were opposed to it, and Erskine Childers wholly and strongly against, there seemed no solid grounds on which it could be rejected. Thus began a long series of semi-private meetings in which Griffith and Collins were separated from the body of the delegation and later from one another, and were subjected to the constant attentions of not Lloyd George and Chamberlain only, but of Churchill and Birkenhead also.

I think it is in Churchill's memoirs that the scene is described where in an upper room in Sir Philip Sassoon's house in London, Lloyd George, alone, wrestled with Griffith, while in a lower room Churchill wrestled with Collins.

Frank Pakenham, in *Peace by Ordeal*, referring to the difficulty Lloyd George pretended he was having with Worthington-Evans and Greenwood says :

> " Two other considerations surely weighed more with Lloyd George : the desire to reduce the size of a Conference whose extensiveness had hitherto clogged the functioning of the personal touch ; and the determination to exclude Childers, whom the British credited with fanatical opposition to any Dominion settlement."

Aesop's fable of the lion and the three bulls was being enacted in a new setting.

Griffith and Collins might have been tactically at fault in falling in with the British suggestion for these semi-private talks, but there was no reason then to fear from them what eventually happened. If the British statesmen had really wished for a just settlement with Ireland it ought to have meant progress.

It was the British motive that made the method dangerous and that motive remained, of course, concealed. At private discussions of this kind Lloyd George's gift for deceiving his hearers had its fullest scope. The almost angry sincerity which he was able to assume in making his promises, pledging himself with dramatic emphasis— " my life on the table "—to carry out loyally what he undertook, gave the impression of a man passionately concerned to do the right thing and to be faithful to every comma of his bond.

The two leaders of the Irish Delegation had apparently not realised that the British were still acting as a team and that any concession made in conversation either by Griffith or Collins was carefully noted and efforts made later to expand it. This method in the end secured from Griffith an unwitting consent to a fundamental change in handling the Six County problem. The British stored away the concession to be used against Griffith at the right moment.

The Irish Cabinet had from the beginning agreed that if the Conference should collapse the Irish delegation should see that the break came on Ulster since the sympathy of the world could most easily be won for a nation defending its unity and Britain would not dare to resume war on that issue.

How Britain forestalled such a break is as full of drama and duplicity as anything in the history of that whole period.

How to describe Tom Jones' part in it? Like his chief, Jones was a Welshman. He played the part allotted to him and it was a mean and, indeed, a despicable part. His assignment was to worm his way into the confidence of the Irish delegation, particularly of the Chairman of it, and act as Lloyd George's stalking-horse.

He would drop round to see Griffith at Hans Place and, as in this instance, would represent Lloyd George as the only real friend Ireland had in this difficult situation. Lloyd George, he told Griffith, was determined to secure a united Ireland. The Premier was, however, threatened with a revolt among the Conservatives on the Ulster question. Griffith could assist him without, of course, being bound specifically to anything. If, while Lloyd George was showing up the Orange leaders as the impossibilists they were, Griffith would not " let him down," it would be a great help. Lloyd George, he told Griffith, meant to offer the Six-County Unionists an alternative they could be calculated to reject—either an All-Ireland Parliament or a Boundary Commission severely delimiting the area.

> " This arrangement would give us most of Tyrone and Fermanagh, and part of Armagh, Londonderry, and Down," Griffith reported.

If the Orangemen rejected both, then Lloyd George would resign in protest against Orange obduracy.

This was put forward with the utmost caution, not to startle Griffith into seeing the real purpose of it. It was done entirely by word of mouth, and it depended for its success on Griffith's yearning for national unity. Griffith thought if he could get the British Premier down on the side of an All-Ireland Parliament, the day of Ireland's unity was assured.

Would Griffith agree, Jones asked, that while the Orangemen were being put on the spot he would not disown Lloyd George's proposal?

Griffith, reporting these informal talks to de Valera, said:

"I told him that it was his proposal, not ours. . . . I said we would not do that (repudiate Lloyd George) if he meant that he thought we would come out in public decrying it. It was his own proposal."

De Valera, in reply, sounded a warning about this move:

"The danger now is that we shall be tempted, in order to put them (the Orange leaders) more hopelessly in the wrong, to make further advances on our side. I think as far as the Crown-Empire connection is concerned we should not budge a single inch from the point to which the negotiations have now led us."

That warning was received on 9th November.

Lloyd George, the ground having been prepared for him by Jones, invited Griffith to meet him privately at Sir Philip Sassoon's house in Park Lane, on 12th November. Griffith in that talk fell in with the plan of putting the Ulster leaders in the wrong. If, Lloyd George told him, they refused a Boundary Commission—as he was sure they would—he would dissolve Parliament, carry an election against their intransigeance, and pass an Act establishing an All-Ireland Parliament. To this as a wholly British manœuvre Griffith assented.

The moment Griffith was gone Lloyd George sent for Chamberlain, and he, with Jones, re-stated Griffith's promise in a memorandum far wider than in fact Griffith had agreed to. Next day Jones saw Griffith again and showed him, but did not leave with him, the memorandum. Griffith, believing that all this dealt mainly with Lloyd George's tactics towards the Orangemen acquiesced in what he hurriedly read, without seeing that it could be made to mean that he, Griffith, accepted a Boundary Commission in place of Ireland's unity. Lloyd George put it by, and it was never seen again until it was suddenly produced to the consternation of the Irish delegation on the evening of 5th December.

Griffith was so unconscious of having made any vital concession that while he reported to de Valera an account of these talks, he never mentions this memorandum, nor had he mentioned it to his colleagues on the delegation.

On the last night when Lloyd George stealthily produced it, peeping out of its envelope, and challenged Griffith, the other delegates were mystified.

"What is this letter?" Barton whispered to Collins.

"I don't know the hell what it is," Collins characteristically growled back.

Pakenham wrote of this episode in *Peace by Ordeal*:

> "If there had been no 12th of November, there might have been no Treaty."

Meanwhile, hopes were high in Ireland.

CHAPTER 61

A CABINET MEETING

As the talks were going on in London those at home, filled with a great hope, were planning the Ireland which the people's courage had made possible. All would now be requited : the bereaved ones, the thousands who had lost their bread-winners into the great prison camps, the men in those overcrowded and bitter settlements themselves, the young men and women of the fight who had lived their lives on the lip of the grave, the older men and women who had kept Sinn Féin together through the tyranny—all this sacrifice and daring would bear bounteous fruit.

The world would see in the new free Ireland how lovely was liberty ; it would see earnest workers build up from resources long neglected a nation filling its children with pride, to which freemen in every land would look with admiration and the enslaved with a new, unquenchable hope.

De Valera told of those dreams of ours five years later when once more he had gathered around him the thousands who, like him, had come again from prisons and internment camps to begin the work of liberation anew :

"In 1921," he said, "when the negotiations in London were going on and I believed there might be a successful issue to these negotiations. . . . I set out, naturally, to plan for the future. The most urgent need obviously was to secure immediate employment for the large number of young men who had obeyed the call to remain in the country and had given of their best towards the winning of freedom. There was no lack of useful work to be done. Organisation and capital were all that was required to set it going. The whole question of Transport was awaiting to be tackled comprehensively, and water, rail and roadways to be co-ordinated. . . . The remaking of roads alone would have given immediate employment—and employment distributed throughout the country—to large numbers. Then there was the vast work of Re-afforestation . . . of Reclamation and Drainage and the development of our water and fuel power. Again there were our Fisheries which might be built up to be our second great industry . . . the natural staple industry of our Irish-speaking seaboard. The Housing problem called for a great national scheme, and the solution of it would provide continuous employment for all the workers in the building trades over a period of years, until a decent home was provided for every family in the State and the scandal of the slums removed once for all."

But as these great plans were being laid the immediate present was dark with danger. Britain might resume the war at any moment. Churchill had written somewhere that the British alternatives at that time were " war with the utmost violence or peace with the utmost patience." But there was no patience in the British attitude and we who were in the Volunteers felt that the blow, if it were to fall, would come with the suddenness of lightning. Well, what of it, whatever happened, this thing had to be fought out in this generation. Not all the Volunteers felt that way. Many were sure that Britain would not dare to go to war again : she would bully and threaten, but a stout front would stay her hand. There were many, too, being human, who having tasted again the life of peace and the loving warmth of home, did not wish to go back to the cruel hardships and tension of it all. Yet it is true to say that the majority of the fighting units everywhere did feel that one duty outranged all thought of self and comfort : the defence to the last of the Republic of Ireland.

So all over the nation there were drilling and lectures in tactics and strategy—officers, section-commanders, squad-leaders came for special training, instruction in new arms and in explosives were given to selected groups who went back to pass on the knowledge to their comrades. To heighten the morale of the whole body—for with the Truce came the danger of inaction which had broken so many armies in history—there were reviews and inspections by the President himself and by others of the Army Council.

The preliminaries to negotiations had begun in high summer and had been wisely protracted until the coming again of the long nights, Ireland's greatest ally.

In London once Lloyd George had possessed himself of the memorandum with which he felt he could split the delegation at the critical hour, he began to press for an end to the talks. In the last ten days of November he became more and more urgent. A decision one way or the other must be reached in a matter of days.

How fictitious the sense of urgency he created was disclosed by a task which Lloyd George gave Tom Jones on 22nd November. The Irish had replied to the latest British proposals with Heads of Agreement setting out in detail the scheme of External Association.

Lloyd George called his secretary and sent him on an errand. But he must be cautious. Pakenham tells the story :

> " Lloyd George now imposed on him a delicate mission : to present the Irish delegates with an effective ultimatum, yet to see to it that on no account were negotiations broken off. Jones knew that now, as on so many occasions hereabout, he would receive unstinted censure if he allowed the Irish delegation to pack up and go."

Jones, as if he were acting on his own, rang up Griffith within the hour. He was in a state of simulated consternation. He must see Griffith at once, and was round in fifteen minutes to Hans Place. He told Griffith that Lloyd George was in despair and was thinking of bringing the negotiations to an end there and then. Jones wondered could Griffith help him to ward off that disaster. If the document just handed in were withdrawn or a new one substituted for it ?— Griffith promptly said no. But Jones had succeeded in creating that atmosphere of needful haste under menace which was to bear fruit a little later.

Under methods such as this, Griffith became more and more convinced that there might be war, and as Lloyd George had, as he thought, pledged himself and his colleagues to Irish unity, he thought there should in return be some allegiance by Ireland to the Crown. That was his view when on the morning of 2nd December, 1921, he crossed to Ireland after another semi-private meeting between himself and Collins on the one side and Lloyd George, Chamberlain, Churchill and Birkenhead on the other. The remaining plenipotentiaries followed him that night, bringing with them the latest edition of the British terms.

The vital Cabinet meeting was held in the Mansion House, Dublin on Saturday, 3rd December. It sat all that day until the delegates had just time for departure for London. It is only its main decisions which need interest us now.

The delegation was clearly divided with Griffith and Éamonn Duggan taking one view, Barton, Gavan Duffy and the Delegation secretary, Childers, another. Collins at that time seemed to stand midway between, leaning towards Griffith's view, but not then accepting it. The discussions were grave and long. There was controversy over the British having been permitted to divide the Irish team, but the major part of the day was spent trying to get the British proposals into the mould of external association. It was difficult, for much had been conceded in the semi-private talks, though nobody —so all felt—was yet unalterably bound.

Three of the delegates, the three who had seen most of Lloyd

George, Churchill, Chamberlain and Birkenhead, were convinced the British would make war if Ireland refused allegiance. Barton and Gavan Duffy were sure the British were bluffing. All the time de Valera, presiding at that Cabinet meeting, tried to draw Griffith away from his present attitude and back to Ireland being associated solely in externals. Repeatedly, through the negotiations, he had warned that unless the stand on both unity and independence were firm both would be lost. And, said de Valera, in the latest British proposals, set out now in the form of a Treaty, " you have got neither this nor that."

It seemed for a long time to be a vain effort to re-unite the delegation, and at last Barton proposed that de Valera himself go to London. The President was turning this over in his mind. He had already shown by his letter of 25th October that if the need were vital, he would go. But before he had given any decision the incident occurred which changed the face of everything that day.

Griffith had said that he would not take the responsibility of breaking with the British on the question of the Crown. He wished the Delegation to accept and sign the British proposals with certain amendments. He was ready to break only on the question of partition. The Government, Griffith said, could then reject the Delegation's agreement, but he wished the final decision to rest with the Dáil which " was the body to decide for or against war."

It was here that the whole scene altered. Cathal Brugha, at one of the most tense moments of that tense session, turned to Griffith and said :

" Don't you realise that if you sign this thing you will split Ireland from top to bottom ? "

As the scene was described to me by one of the plenipotentiaries not long afterwards : Griffith was silent, and there was for a moment no sound in the Cabinet room. Then the Chairman of the delegation replied :

" I suppose that is so," Griffith said, speaking slowly, " I tell you what I will do. I will go back to London. I will not sign that document, but I will bring it back and submit it to the Dáil and, if necessary, to the people."

It is not easy to realise now what this undertaking meant at just that moment.

The majority of the delegates believed that if they did not accept allegiance to the Crown, Britain would break off negotiations and wage war. The majority of the Cabinet on the other hand were agreed that there must be no allegiance, that a stand must be made on unity and independence, war or no war, most of them believing that if Ireland stood firm there would in fact be no war.

For Irish leaders to sign proposals containing allegiance to the Crown meant a division in the ranks at this critical hour. When Griffith dropped this proposal and recorded as well his own decision not to sign, there came a relief into the Cabinet room which seemed a reward for that long and anxious effort to come to a united understanding. For now the British could be told that even if some of the delegates favoured their scheme the Cabinet did not, and without anybody being finally committed the Dáil could take the decision, and at that stage there was no doubt what that decision would be.

Griffith's pledge was equivalent to Ireland regaining the initiative and the equivalent, also, of the unity of the people being preserved to see the crisis through.

Pakenham measures thus the undertaking the Chairman of the delegation had given to Cathal Brugha :

> " That," he says, " was quite satisfactory to everybody. There was felt to be no necessity now for ' substituting delegates ' to go over and break off the negotiations. De Valera, in particular, abandoned the idea of going over himself, assured now that nothing would be signed which committed Ireland to allegiance or inclusion in the Empire."

No official record was made of that long day's discussion. Later, it was to have many interpretations, each coloured in an hour of calamity by the emotions of the participants. But there was an official record of decisions. One was that on the refusal of allegiance, Ireland was ready to " face the consequences assuming that England will declare war." Another was :

> " Mr. Griffith to inform Mr. Lloyd George that the document could not be signed, and to state that it was now a matter for the Dáil. (He was to try and see that the break came on Ulster)."

It had been a racking day, but it ended better than it had begun.

CHAPTER 62

" WHERE IS COLLINS ? "

A MYSTERY will always lie behind what occurred in Downing Street on 5th-6th December, 1921.

All the main facts are believed to be known. In that twenty-four hours Ireland suffered one of the greatest calamities in her history. The one thing of all things happened that seemed least likely. It was not later or by something done at some other time that Ireland was doomed to a decade of heartbreaking division in which brother turned on brother and the glory was covered with fratricidal blood: it was at 2.30 a.m. on the morning of Tuesday, 6th December, when with strained faces the Irish delegation, not one, or two, but all five, signed their names to allegiance and the dismemberment of their land.

Watching them at the table were Lloyd George, Churchill, Birkenhead and Chamberlain, the men who had called the Black-and-Tans into being to savage Ireland into submission. There they stood now, triumphant—at last.

How could it possibly have happened, this dire event? Only two days earlier, the Cabinet of the Republic had instructed these plenipotentiaries to get back to solid ground, to stand on an independent Ireland associated with Britain in externals only. That Cabinet had received a pledge from the Chairman of the delegation that he would sign nothing; to the Dáil would be left the free decision. What malevolence achieved so contrary a conclusion?

By the time the delegates got back from Dublin, Lloyd George probably knew the broad outline of what the Cabinet had decided. Cope, the Assistant Under-Secretary at the Castle, had crossed over, though quietly, on the heels of the delegates, and crossed back again after them. A few well-placed questions would have got him the truth and he would have passed it at once to Lloyd George: the Irish were given instructions to stand on External Association and to break on Ulster.

In Hans Place there was confusion on the morning after the return. The delegates remembered different parts of the long day's discussion, and there was conflict as to what was now to be done. Barton, Gavan Duffy and Childers had no doubts. The Cabinet had ordered that the External Relations proposals should be re-submitted.

A new draft was prepared embodying points of detail arising from the Cabinet talks. But when this draft was submitted to Collins and Griffith the intention to present it met with vigorous opposition. It had to be recalled to the two leaders that it was a definite Cabinet instruction that the Irish alternative be put forward again as the limit to which the Irish Government would go.

Griffith asked what was the sense or the use in presenting once more what the British had so often rejected. He did not, apparently, appreciate that these were exactly the tactics being used against himself and to which he was submitting. Lloyd George, Churchill and the rest came back always with their own scheme, rejecting the Irish counter-proposals, insisting on Crown and Empire, Crown and Empire and by that repetition seeking to wear the Irish down.

Something like complete despondency settled on Collins and he and Griffith refused to present again the Irish proposals. It was only when Barton and Gavan Duffy had put on their coats and were setting out alone for Downing Street that Griffith consented to join them. Collins would not come.

Griffith's greatness came out in that hour. Though he had now little belief in what he was doing, he faced up to the British, argued and parried, asserted and interpreted with all his reserves and resources massed.

The astonished British saw him, whom they thought they had won over, renewing the fight on the principles of two months ago. He was offering as the limit to which the Irish would agree, not acceptance of allegiance or empire, not a new form of Dominion status, but Ireland a free nation in association with Britain only from the outside.

Lloyd George and Churchill faced him with: "But haven't we told you——" Griffith brushed that aside, and stressed that it was not any fixed form of settlement they were longing for, but true peace, and there could not be true peace if Ireland's freedom and unity did not survive in the terms. Gavan Duffy and Barton watched the performance with admiration, wishing that more of Griffith's heart was in what his head was directing. Griffith used the moment to try again to get the break on Ulster. If he got it now, the Cabinet instructions would be completely fulfilled.

He did not get it. Gavan Duffy said something about the impossibility of Ireland entering the Empire. Chamberlain, as almost at a pre-arranged signal, jumped up and cried: "That ends it." It did. The other British delegates were on their feet, too. The two sides parted. The break had come. The negotiations were over.

The Irish delegation when they were back in Hans Place thought the main thing was to pack for home. But Lloyd George's mind was on something other than war. He wanted an Irish settlement, and though he and his colleagues were now almost in despair at the toughness of those Irish, he guessed that Griffith was only playing an instructed part. And where on earth was Collins ? If Collins had become so much opposed to the Irish scheme that he would not even come———? With a new light in his eye, Lloyd George decided that he must see Collins, alone, completely alone and at once. He summoned Jones. Jones must somehow, anyhow, bring Collins to him, Collins by himself.

Lloyd George, showman to the last, had fixed Tuesday, 6th December, as the day on which the crisis must come, and it was now late on the evening of 4th December. The British Premier's pretence was that he had promised to inform Craig one way or another—a settlement or a break—by 6th December, and that that promise must be kept. This, as can be seen now and ought to have been seen then, was purely a manufactured crisis date. Lloyd George's dealings with Ireland had long ago shown that when it suited him the keeping of promises had never kept him to a time-table. He just broke the time-table, unless breaking the promise was easier. But his plan now required a zero hour. If he had that, and for weeks he had been building towards it, he could say : " Choose now : in a few hours these terms will be no longer available : the alternative is war." He could, of course, say all this merely by word of mouth. But Lloyd George was an actor : he worked best with the right " props." He arranged a special train, a destroyer with steam up, a messenger panting to be off. Atmosphere was everything.

There was an important preliminary first—Michael Collins. No sooner were Griffith, Barton and Gavan Duffy out of the room than Jones went in search of Collins. He was at Hans Place at 10 p.m. and saw Griffith. He begged the Chief of the Irish delegation to get Collins to see Lloyd George. Collins, as if a breath of the future had blown chillily on him, refused to go. No pressure could shake him. Hardly had dawn come on 5th December than Jones was on to Griffith again. Lloyd George simply must see Collins not later than 9.15 a.m. Ireland's welfare depended on it and Jones of course, was devoted to Ireland's welfare. But still Collins could not be persuaded. Griffith and Jones together laid siege upon him but it was a strong city, and it was not until after the latest hour Lloyd George had fixed that the conquest was made.

At 9.30 Collins went to Downing Street. Lloyd George said nothing truer than that he was pleased to see him. The memo of 12th November was Griffith's doom—that morning meeting with the British Premier was Collins' fate. No one else was present but these two only : the craftiest statesman in Europe and a brave young man, a fine organiser, an able administrator, but—where politics were concerned—guileless and inexperienced.

There is a memorandum of Collins' in witness of what passed between them but it is impossible to get the atmosphere, the actual words and terms of the pledges given. It is certain, however, that in forty minutes Lloyd George had convinced Collins that by accepting the British proposals the territorial unity of Ireland would be restored. The Boundary Commission would liberate Tyrone, Fermanagh, South Down, South Armagh and Derry City; what was left would fall into Ireland's lap through very lack of territory. Let Collins be in no doubt. Lloyd George himself, Birkenhead, Churchill would see that that would happen. Collins left Lloyd George with an unshakable belief that the British themselves had provided the means, and would see them operate, by which the partitioned area would be so reduced in size that it could not continue to exist.

It has nowhere been proved, but it is not inconceivable, that it was Lloyd George who insinuated the stepping-stone idea into Collins's head at that meeting: to yield the Republic only to re-possess it more completely. Not only was Lloyd George the kind of man who would promise Collins to help him to dish Craig, but he was perfectly capable of pointing out to Collins that he could dish the English, too, by accepting the Treaty and then using its clauses to get back the Republic. At any rate, Collins returned to Hans Place a different man. He promised Lloyd George that morning that he would get the Irish delegation to meet him again at 2 o'clock p.m. He now begged his colleagues to come. Great things were going to happen in Downing Street. Barton and Gavan Duffy refused. The British had the day before rejected the only proposal the Cabinet had authorised. If the British had new proposals, let them submit them in writing. The argument went on for hours. In the end, Griffith persuaded Barton to come with himself and Collins by holding out the opportunity this new meeting would give of achieving that break on Ulster that the Cabinet had instructed should be made.

That afternoon saw the last, and the fatal, meeting between some of the Irish delegation and some of the British. For this, despite the issues that were decided at it, was not a full Conference. Had it been, Childers would have been there, and the British did not want Childers at that hour, of all others. The sitting began at 3 o'clock. It halted soon after 8 p.m. It began again at 11.20 p.m. The Treaty was signed at 2.30 a.m. It was eight hours for the British; it was twelve for the Irish, for though the battle was lost at 8 p.m., Gavan Duffy and Barton fought on until, in the end, they, too, were overwhelmed.

Lloyd George's strategy for this, his supreme moment, was simple, and had been long decided. He had detected during the negotiations that Griffith was intensely sensitive about his personal honour, especially in regard to pledges he had made to those with whom he was negotiating. He could be angered or humbled most by being accused of a breach of faith. The memorandum of 12th November, offering a Boundary Commission, instead of insisting on Ireland's unity, had been, as we have seen, accompanied by a promise from Griffith not to let Lloyd George down.

As already shown, that promise, when given, meant merely that while Lloyd George was engaged in his manœuvre to corner Craig, Griffith would not spoil the game by repudiating him publicly. Lloyd George had expanded this into a general pledge to stand by Britain's Ulster policy, and it is doubtful if now, nearly a month later, Griffith remembered the terms of the Memorandum, for he had seen them briefly and but once. He would, however, remember that he had acquiesced.

In the case of Collins, Lloyd George felt he had brought him most of the way by his pledges of that morning's secret meeting. Duggan, the British thought, might follow Griffith and Collins.

Barton and Gavan Duffy were the difficulty, and, with Childers, might yet prove a rallying ground for all. But they might be overcome by a concentration against them, at some stage, of all the British delegates together with the leaders of their own delegation. That was as Lloyd George planned it; to that end the atmosphere of crisis was being created.

Griffith would be broken first; then the others would, it was hoped, be so dismayed and weakened, realising their unity was gone, that they might topple. Whoever refused after that would be told that on him must rest the guilt of the universal outrage and savagery that the instant unleashing of the Terror would mean for the Irish people. It was a dread responsibility to be asked to bear. Lloyd George would see to it, if he could, that it was Irishmen who would work on one another to break down their brothers' resistance to compromise. So the stage was set for the culmination of the effort of a small nation to break free. At 3 p.m. on Monday, 5th December, in the Cabinet Room in Downing Street, London, the actors assembled —for Ireland, Griffith, Collins and Barton; for Britain, Lloyd George, Churchill, Birkenhead and Chamberlain. Seven out of the original seventeen took part in this final act.

CHAPTER 63

THE ULTIMATUM

W HEN the three Irish delegates crossed the threshold of 10 Downing Street that afternoon of 5th December, 1921, can they have foreseen the events of the next twelve hours ?

The answer almost certainly is, " No." Griffith seemed to believe that, with great luck, he might yet get the break on Ulster; or else that the British would concede something more—a share of defence, the right to build up Irish industries by tariffing British imports, a milder oath. Lloyd George had hinted at some such concessions to Collins. When these new points had been added to the British proposals, Griffith would say that he would recommend the agreement to the Dáil, and the two sides would part, not further committed.

Lloyd George, who had other plans, was all the time conscious of the danger to Britain of a break on Ulster. He dare not threaten to make war on the Irish majority for the sake of the Orangemen. He must get the break on something that could be represented to the world as, "Free partnership in the Empire." So, no sooner were the delegates seated at the table than the British Premier opened the Ulster question. He must have that out of the way before he launched his ultimatum.

He recalled the circumstances in which the proposal for a Boundary Commission came into this British draft, reminding Griffith of his agreement. Griffith stood his ground, asking where did Craig stand in all this ? Until Craig replied, nobody knew what the Ulster clauses in the British proposals were really worth.

Lloyd George and Chamberlain brushed the objection aside; it did not matter what Craig said or did; the British would see the Ulster clauses through. Birkenhead chimed in to add that in these Ulster clauses (which all through this discussion were represented as assuring Ireland of unity), he and his colleagues were risking their political reputations. They did that on the undertaking Griffith had given them.

Collins and Barton were mystified by this constant reference to an undertaking, and Collins, in anger, charged the British with trying to manœuvre the Irishmen out of " essential unity," which had been the basis of every Irish concession. He supported Griffith's demand for a reply from Craig. Lloyd George, realising that he had come near the precipice which he must at all costs avoid—a break on Ulster —released his pressure and swung attention to the other parts of the British proposals.

The two sides ranged again over the whole document. There were many minor changes, all in favour of the Irish delegation's point of view. The wording of the Oath was changed, to make it seem outwardly more ambiguous, but concealed in it now was a double pledge of loyalty and fidelity to the Crown. They argued hither and thither over defence. They discussed modification of the trade clauses.

Then the British withdrew to allow both sides to confer privately. The decision come to by the three Irishmen in that interval is revealing. They prepared for three endings to the talks. If the British demanded an immediate acceptance of the proposals, they would break off negotiations; alternatively, they would reject the terms pending a decision from Craig; if they could not apply either of these solutions, they would demand a reference of the points remaining in dispute to the Dominion Premiers. Nobody spoke of signing.

The British, on their part, were almost in despair. Here were the Irish again fighting for a break on Ulster. Lloyd George especially was mortified. He had been sure that he had only to mention that memorandum to Griffith and he would collapse. The one way now, he thought, was to face Griffith with the document itself.

He sent for it. But the document could not be found! The files of the secretariat, their own papers, their offices, their rooms were searched. That precious document of 12th November was gone! Then somebody, probably Tom Jones, remembered the habits of Lloyd George; the memorandum must be in one of his old suits. It was.

Everything was bustle now. While it was being re-typed, Churchill, Birkenhead and Chamberlain returned to the Cabinet room and resumed the negotiations. They were in a generous mood, for the plan now was to yield in detail, and then the moment Griffith again attempted to break on Ulster, to fasten on him as a pledge-breaker. If they got Griffith down, the ultimatum would be issued with the demand that every one of the Irish delegation must either sign now or have war straightway resumed on his people.

Ten minutes after Churchill and the others, Lloyd George came into the room. He had an envelope in his hand, and, watching for his opportunity, he suddenly faced Griffith He asked him if he remembered an undertaking he had given; that it had been put into writing; that Tom Jones had shown it to him, and that he had agreed to it. Griffith, probably not recalling how far he had allowed himself to be tricked in that upper room of Sir Philip Sassoon's house in Park Lane, was clearly embarrassed. He had not told his colleagues of this. Lloyd George told them now, by getting Chamberlain to pass the contents of the document across the table to them. Read in this present setting—so different from that to which the undertaking really applied—it must have stunned Collins and Barton, with its seeming abandonment by Griffith of " essential unity."

This was the moment! Lloyd George capped the dismay on the Irish side by exploiting Griffith's sensitiveness as to honouring his pledges :

" Mr Griffith," he said, shaking the envelope at him, " you undertook that in this matter you would not let us down."

Griffith's reply has been variously reported, but it was complete. Speaking with anger, he said : " I have never let a man down in my whole life and I never will."

Griffith at that moment seemed not only to abandon his attempt to break on Ulster, but his attempt to break at all. Lloyd George could safely use the threat of war now.

The British speedily turned the discussions to other parts of the proposals : the atmosphere of haste was being created. The Irish delegates were reminded of the need for the messenger to be off to Belfast to keep the Premier's promise to Craig. When the discussions had not ended by the time of the departure of the ordinary boat train, a special train was ordered to stand by. The sense of urgency began to fill the room. The British made quick concessions.

They gave in completely on the Irish right to tax British goods, decisions must be come to quickly, quickly : that train could not be kept waiting. No time to haggle over small things. Yes, the Irish could have a share in their own defence ; yes, there could be another modification of the Oath, but hurry, hurry, the time was slipping, the chance was going. The pace was terrific, almost a panic for speed enveloped them all ; that steaming train became an obsession ; that destroyer straining at its anchor at Holyhead.

Into this tumble to get everything fixed suddenly broke the cold voice of the Welshman : the end had come ; the British could concede no more ; the Irish must settle now here in this room, no reference back, there was no time. They were Plenipotentiaries. They had the power ; they must not only settle, but sign ; they must not only sign, but recommend. Or they must quit now, this instant, and on their heels would come such a war as Ireland had never known.

The swiftness of the change of atmosphere ; the solemnity with which the threat was issued made the hour so sinister that the chill of it lived on in Barton's mind, and a fortnight later his speech in the Dáil describing it still rang with the horror of that moment. I was in the Dáil that day when Barton spoke. To me it was the most poignant of all the speeches, though he spoke so quietly, less than six hundred words, to a House in which no man stirred.

"Arthur Griffith sought repeatedly to have the decision between war and peace on the terms of the Treaty referred back to this assembly," Robert Barton told the tense House. "This proposal Mr. Lloyd George directly negatived. He claimed that we were Plenipotentiaries and that we must either accept or reject. Speaking for himself and his colleagues, the English Prime Minister with all the solemnity and the power of conviction that he alone, of all men I met, can impart by word and gesture— the vehicles by which the mind of one man oppresses and impresses the mind of another—declared that the signature and recommendation of every member of our delegation was necessary or war would follow immediately."

Lloyd George gave the delegates an hour to make up their minds. In the sound of the voice that spoke that base threat there merged the tones of many voices which in this same room had menaced Ireland in the past : Pitt and Peel, Forster and Balfour, the other Chamberlain and the other Churchill.

There was a frozen silence after the ultimatum, and then Griffith spoke the fatal words :

"I will give the answer of the Irish delegation at nine to-night. But, Mr. Prime Minister, I personally will sign this agreement and recommend it to my countrymen."

Even Lloyd George was astonished at his victory, and, careful actor though he was, he showed his surprise :

"Do I understand, Mr. Griffith, that though everyone else refused, you will nevertheless agree to sign ? "

Griffith answered :

"Yes, that is so, Mr. Prime Minister."

Since the Rising, Lloyd George had been seeking ways by which Ireland could be robbed of her strength by division. It had been a long journey. With Griffith's words the delegation there before him was finally broken and he had reached his goal.

As the three men, Griffith, Collins and Barton, rode back to Hans Place, Barton was stunned to hear Collins (a deep friendship had existed between them) say that he, too, would sign.

The delegation did not come back to Downing Street at nine, or at ten, or at eleven ; and if they could only have seen into the

Englishmen's hearts they would not have come back at all, For the British did not expect them. Churchill has confessed in his memoirs :

> " No one expected that anyone but Griffith would agree and what validity would his solitary signature possess ? "

Birkenhead records that he was so sure of their not returning that he set about preparing for a blood-and-thunder speech for the morrow. Lloyd George's surprised question to Griffith showed that he, too, thought all but one would refuse.

It was an hour at which destiny called out for a Tone or a Davis or a Parnell to speak for the Irish delegation. If on that December morning the answer had been, "We will not sign," the probability is that there would not have been war, not the slaughter of brother by brother, but a new union of the great brotherhood of freedom and with it the precious things for which all that generation had striven, the liberation and ennobling of the homeland, and, as would then have been certain in the enthusiasm of the time, the saving of the Irish language.

As the British Ministers waited at Downing Street, in the dimming hope that the delegates would ever return, scenes were enacted at Hans Place which can never have left the minds of all who took part in them, of whom three of the six main characters were to die within the year, and five are now dead.

Griffith had yielded beyond recall. Collins, but not in the presence of the British, had announced that he would sign. Éamonn Duggan soon declared that so, too, would he. But Barton and Gavan Duffy, who had agreed to act together, would not give way. For hours the struggle to overcome their wills went on.

Griffith and Collins had become so convinced that war would descend like a lightning stroke on their people that they battled for the conquest of these two minds with all the consuming energy of their personalities. In that heart-rending argument, scenes of outrage and terror were recalled from the years just passed and the defenceless Irish people were pictured as again to be riven by savagery, more terrible now than ever. Barton and Gavan Duffy had been, one in prison and one as diplomat abroad, separated from the more recent horrors now described. They were told that the possibility of the Volunteers being able to meet the kind of war Lloyd George threatened was slender, indeed.

The two stood firm through this tempest. It was urged on them that what the delegates were being asked to do was not final : that the final decision would be left to the Dáil, which would, by their signatures, be given a chance to prepare the national defence before the new blows fell.

Hours passed, and then, in the tension of that room, Éamonn Duggan broke down. Wildly, he spoke of the horrors he had seen when the hangman came to Mountjoy to take out the young Volunteers and slay them as murderers. He recalled the conversations with those about to die. Pakenham records :

> " He poured out an appeal to Barton not to cast away the chance for which these simple martyrs had died, and plunge once more in blood the country they loved so well. Unsophisticated, from the heart, utterly unlike the fierce preceding exhortations, it touched some chord in Barton, not far from breaking himself. The claims of living humanity overcame those of abstract nationhood : he agreed to come round to Downing Street and sign the Treaty."

All through this tragic scene, which lasted nearly three hours, nobody suggested lifting the telephone and talking of their dilemma to the President in Ireland. Had they done so, the whole scene could have been changed in an instant, and the waiting British might not even have got that " solitary signature," of whose validity Churchill was in such deep doubt.

CHAPTER 64

LONDON AND LIMERICK

THE importance of what happened in London on 5th-6th December was not that Griffith or Collins yielded or that Barton and Gavan Duffy were overborne. The tragedy was that on that night was given away that one desire which had filled, not this generation only, but every generation of Irishmen down into the long past. Neither now nor then had the patriots of Ireland asked for Home Rule or Dominion status. They had asked that their nation be independent, that their people, like free peoples everywhere, have the right to rule their land, asking leave of no other Power or Government. They had asked that that free Ireland be the whole island, for all parts of it had suffered the long passion, in equal anguish and with equal hope. Pearse had said it at Rossa's grave—"Ireland unfree shall never be at peace."

In every generation, for hundreds of years, men had laid down their lives for that truth, gladly taking exile or death rather than deny it. In the direst woe, the common people had clung to it with the same silent tenacity as they had clung to their Faith. Many arose to promise them happiness and well-being with less than freedom; these, when the test came, the people rejected, and turned, not to the leaders who had such panoply in their day, but to the lonely bands who struck for independence: not Grattan but Tone; not O'Connell but Davis and Mitchel; not Butt but the Fenians; not Redmond but Pearse.

The leaders of the Irish delegation had lived through the exaltation of the Rising and of the words Pearse had spoken from the steps of the G.P.O.:

> "In every generation the Irish people have asserted their right to national freedom and sovereignty . . . again asserting it in arms in the face of the world, we hereby proclaim the Irish Republic as a Sovereign Independent State. . . ."

In angry love of these all but unknown men, who had paid in the red coin of life for the words Pearse had spoken, the nation swept from office all who would accept less and called into being a National Parliament of the people's elected, who, formally asserting the independence of Ireland, made the great Declaration:

" Now, therefore, we, the elected Representatives of the ancient Irish people in National Parliament assembled, do, in the name of the Irish nation, ratify the establishment of the Irish Republic, and pledge ourselves and our people to make this declaration effective by every means at our command."

Everything in the grim years that followed was grounded on that Declaration : the erection of the functioning Republic, with its President, its Government, its Army, its Courts and its Departments of State. War had been fought in defence of that Republic, life given and taken by the authority of its legitimate Government ; aid was asked from the generous of the world to maintain this Sovereign State, and recognition sought for it from the nations everywhere. The name of Ireland became great to all races because, under savage persecution, she would not abandon her independence. Terence MacSwiney bore his long death agony to make the Republic deathless : Cork City burned through the night to illumine it : Kevin Barry saluted his mother in its name and walked to the scaffold fearlessly.

And now, three Irishmen, near to midnight on 5th December, 1921, came to Downing Street and accepted what all the generations of patriots had rejected. Those three and the two who later signed were all five quadruply bound to the Republic : by oath, by office, by election, by service. Two days before they had been formally instructed by the Cabinet not to yield if there were Allegiance or Partition in the compact. There were both.

Was it something that happened in Ireland in those days that brought all hopes into the dust ? On the contrary, in Ireland there was clarity and strength. One of the Plenipotentiaries, since dead, had a hurried dinner in the Bailey Restaurant with me on that Saturday night, 3rd December, after the Cabinet had taken the formal decision to refuse the proposals. We talked of Griffith's earlier attitude that the Plenipotentiaries could sign and the Cabinet and the Dáil then reject. With an intensity which pierced me, he said : " I promise you on my life that I will never sign a settlement with an Oath of Allegiance in it." As he felt, so did we all. And that feeling was spoken aloud by de Valera in those days of tension.

The President had interrupted a tour of inspection of the Western Divisions of the Army to hasten to Dublin for the Saturday Cabinet. He had said at Galway :

" There are things, no matter what the cost, no matter what the alternative, those who are charged with the direction of affairs in this country can never give up. . . . When we started out on our programme we knew what it meant and we counted the cost. We are not going to quail now even if we are certain that the full price of our freedom has to be paid."

De Valera was speaking then, not only to the men and women in Galway, but also to Lloyd George and Churchill, Birkenhead and Chamberlain. His words made it easier for the Plenipotentiaries to stand their ground.

And now, after that decisive Cabinet meeting, fortified especially by Griffith's pledge to sign nothing, he hastened back to the West that, in continuing his tour, he might rally the national forces at this supreme hour, and thus face Britain with a nation strong behind a re-united Cabinet.

At the Agricultural Show Grounds at Ennis, accompanied by the Minister for Defence, Cathal Brugha, and the Chief of Staff, Richard Mulcahy, he reviewed on Sunday, 4th December, the First Western Division, made up of the 1st and 2nd Galway Brigades and the 3rd, 4th and 5th Clare Brigades. He spoke earnestly to them of discipline, unity and obedience. Their primary duty now was to prepare themselves, each Volunteer individually, for the crisis.

" At any moment," said the President to that great gathering of young men, standing eager-faced in ranks that stretched, this raw December day, over that wide field, " at any moment you may be called upon to do your duty as soldiers of Ireland. These are days of stress, and your answer is to be ready at a moment's notice."

He reminded them that there were fourteen other divisions standing ready for Ireland, and behind them were the people. With discipline and unity they could meet any challenge.

Next day, 5th December, de Valera was in Limerick. There, in a decorated city which had declared the day a public holiday Mrs. Tom Clarke and he were made Freemen. In returning thanks, de Valera spoke gravely. At any hour, the word might come either that the British had yielded or that the Plenipotentiaries were on their way back. He prepared his audience :

" We mean," said de Valera, " to achieve exactly what we set out to achieve and we will not be deflected from it by any threats whatever."

He gave a pledge for the Irish nation :

" There is one thing that the enemy can never hope for and that is success. Never. It may have years of terror, one after the other. It had them before and when it was all over they were as far from achieving their main purpose as they were at the start. . . . This is a separate nation and they will never, not till the end of time, get from this nation allegiance to their rulers."

The demonstration this pledge evoked that day in Limerick was extraordinary even for those tense days. The old city was filled with the echoes of it.

By the time the Press correspondents had wired these words to London, Lloyd George had the three principal delegates in the Cabinet Room preparing his trap for Griffith, his threat for the others. Before they had got back to Hans Place, Griffith had made his personal surrender, his promise to sign even if no one else did.

But if in the three hours of agonised discussion anybody at the Delegation's headquarters said, " But de Valera in Limerick to-day laid it down that we cannot accept any such document," the crisis would have been over. Did they know of de Valera's words, did they remember even those at Galway, or did they think only of how they might avoid war ? Lloyd George had achieved a complete mastery of their minds ; they were as men fixed by the eye of the Basilisk.

Gavan Duffy and Barton at the Cabinet meeting on Saturday (and this was but Monday) had stressed that Lloyd George with his threats was bluffing—that there would be no war if they stood their ground. How right the two men were was to be proved when every-thing was lost.

In Lloyd George's plan to sweep the delegation off its feet by the creation of a sense of urgency, the young man who was to go by special train to Holyhead and by destroyer to Belfast was Mr. Geoffrey Shakespeare, one of the members of the Downing Street secretariat. Thirty years later, that young man, grown old, wrote his memoirs. In his mind for that long spell had remained a question unanswered.

" I have never understood," he wrote in 1949, " why the Irish accepted the ultimatum at its face value. Why did they not call the bluff ? Lloyd George stated over and over again that he had promised to let Sir James Craig know next day (Tuesday, 6th December) one way or the other. Supposing Arthur Griffith had said : ' What is sacrosanct about Tuesday ? We have waited hundreds of years for a settlement. Ask Craig to wait one week. If you feel you must inform him to-morrow, telephone direct to Dublin Castle, or direct to Belfast, and explain the delay. Are you really going to break the Truce and plunge Ireland again into war without giving the Irish Cabinet the chance even of dis-cussing your latest proposals ? ' How could Lloyd George have persisted with the ultimatum if Arthur Griffith had argued like this ? But the Irish delegation did not counter the ultimatum with logic. They bowed to it and signed."

Alas, they had not to wait thirty years to learn that had the Chairman of the Irish delegation faced Lloyd George there and then it is the Welshman who would have yielded. Next day's English papers contained the proof that the well-staged ultimatum was indeed bluff.

Nothing was Lloyd George more conscious of in these negotiations than the power of the Press. He had always recognised it. He had raised to the Peerage every principal newspaper owner in Britain whose support, he thought, such an honour might buy or enmity blunt. He was in close contact with the main London dailies and newsagencies and, either directly or indirectly, he influenced their comment on events at the Conference. That night of 5th December, as we have seen, he did not expect that the Irish delegates would submit. He thought they would never come back to Downing Street at all. Did he suggest to the British newspapers close to him to follow up his threat of war ? He would have if he had meant it, for he knew the political importance to himself of preparing public opinion for such a development.

He did not do so because he knew the British public had been sickened to the soul by the excesses of the Black-and-Tans, and he well understood that the international situation would not permit him to launch a new offensive against the Irish people, whose resistance had won them many friends. So the British Press were guided into urging that there be no war. It was not possible to change the comment after 2.30 a.m., when the Delegates signed, and thus, on the very morning that the news columns carried short reports of an "agreement," the editorial columns and the political correspondence, all written earlier, stand as permanent witness that there would have been no war.

The *Daily Chronicle* was Lloyd George's own paper at this time. On 6th December it published what was its view late the previous evening when it was believed that the Plenipotentiaries were not coming back :

"If the negotiators prove still unable to sign a compact, let them adjourn their negotiation for a fixed period of weeks."

The Lobby Correspondent of the *Daily Express*, believing that all had ended in an Irish refusal to submit, declared :

"Nothing remains but to discuss the terms of an extension of the Truce."

The *Central News*, one of the leading British news agencies, circulated this to the papers of the world :

" The gravity of the situation is manifest. The most earnest efforts will be made, even if the negotiations break down, to maintain the Truce. . . . Negotiations will not be definitely abandoned, but a suspension may occur for a certain number of weeks in the hope of new inspiration and that in the interval both sides will agree to keep the Truce in being."

The *London Times* in an editorial anticipated that by the time the words were in print the end would have come by an Irish insistence on freedom, and said:

" Therefore, even if the Conference were now to end its labours, it should not be permitted to have been in vain. . . . Whatever the difficulties, the Truce should at all honourable costs be kept alive."

All these comments had obviously their origin in one common source. That source was almost certainly Lloyd George himself. He believed his ultimatum would misfire; that the Irish would not yield. He wanted an Irish settlement desperately. The Truce was the way to it. It must be kept in being. If the Chairman of the delegation had made the stand the President and the Cabinet had instructed him to make, peace rather than war would have been the outcome.

CHAPTER 65

A RUMOUR BY THE SHANNON SIDE

THREE of the British signatories (Lloyd George, Churchill and Chamberlain) have described the scene that took place in Downing Street in the early morning of 6th December, 1921.

Each of them is writing under restraint: he must not say too much about the war threat. The Treaty must be represented as a voluntary compact. It was easy for the then junior fry, like Geoffrey Shakespeare, to say thirty years afterwards: " But for the ultimatum we might have had no Treaty." The active participants dare not use so blunt a phrase. The alternative of war, though mentioned, is therefore not given a major part in the story, except by Chamberlain, and he is writing ten years after the event. In Lloyd George's and Churchill's accounts the ultimatum is smothered over. All three stories establish, however, either by admission or by clear implication, that the threat of war was the dominant thing that night. The joyful surprise of the British that the Irish had come back at all is confirmed.

Lloyd George in *Is It Peace?* echoes Churchill in *Aftermath*:

> " He (Griffith)," says Lloyd George, " asked for a few hours to consider, promising a reply by nine o'clock. Nine passed, but the Irish leaders did not return. Ten, eleven, and they were not back. We had doubts as to whether we should see them again."

When they did see them again, the snarers were cautious lest the victims observe the net closely. Churchill records how the British kept the discussions to lesser things for fear that, if the big questions of allegiance or unity were raised again, Collins and Barton might shy off. " Soon," Churchill writes, " we were talking busily about verbal corrections and holding firmly to these lest worse should befall." It was deceit and manœuvring to the end.

Then came the moment for signing. Only seven were present. From the subsequent descriptions, it is evident that none but Griffith signed willingly: Collins was torn with conflicting emotions and Churchill records the agony in his face. Barton signed because Griffith, Collins and Duggan had filled him with their own dread of instant war, and because at this crisis Griffith's promise to Lloyd George had broken the great unity. Duggan signed later in Hans Place; Gavan Duffy had to be waked from his sleep to sign. If even,

358

at this moment of tattered ending, one of the five had, in a blaze of anger, written across the document: "I sign this under duress of war," his name would to-day be spoken of with honour wherever freemen dwell. Robert Barton did almost that during the Treaty debates. But now there was no protest: it was done, as the British have recorded, shamefacedly.

Of Childers, each of the British accounts shows how deeply it was feared that he might communicate his strength to others. Lloyd George records that Childers' early memoranda disclosed a mind the British could not hope to master.

Nobody will ever know fully what passed between Lloyd George and Griffith at those secret meetings in Park Lane and elsewhere. We can, however, justifiably assume that wherever they saw an opportunity for exploiting the inevitable differences that arise among a group of exceptional men the British used their opportunity.

There was a strong difference in personality between Arthur Griffith and Erskine Childers, and at the end this had on Griffith's part become akin to hatred. (Erskine's tribute when Griffith died eight months later shows that he never ceased to venerate what the founder of Sinn Féin had done.) Towards the close of the negotiations Griffith would not even read the memoranda prepared by Childers, who was a wise constitutional lawyer as well as an expert in defence matters. They had to be given to Griffith as if written by Barton! Lloyd George, if we can guess anything of this period of his dark career, used the secret talks to prise open this rift.

Early in the discussions the British had perceived where the strength against them lay. It should have lain in Griffith. Though the British never pretended to have found out that the obstacle was not there, they soon began the work of isolating the three whom they regarded as "difficult": Barton, Gavan Duffy and Childers. These, from the end of October, found themselves cut off from the major discussions. Gavan Duffy was sent to Dublin to protest to the Cabinet at this turn of events. Pakenham records him as having failed completely in his mission. Despite the motive which inspired it, it could hardly at that stage have been a success. The Plenipotentiaries were barely a fortnight gone, and the Cabinet could not have taken away from old colleagues like Griffith and Collins the right to decide the method of negotiation. Nobody dreamt that those Republican Ministers would ever act contrary to the instructions they had received and the purpose which inspired the British in dividing the delegation lay then wholly concealed. And now at the fateful hour Gavan Duffy was not there, Childers was not there; Barton was there, but with a mind very different from that of the two leaders.

The British were determined the Treaty would be signed before the

Irishmen would leave the room. It was 1.30 a.m. when the arguments over this word and that had ended. If this had been truly an instrument of peace, proudly come to by men of good-will, the delegations would have separated and relaxed until the whole intricate document had been retyped. But the British had had one narrow escape in the delegates returning at all : did they part now some of the Irishmen might get in touch with Dublin and all the British hopes collapse. So they held these weary men in the Cabinet room while they rushed the typists in some nearby office. So hastily was the work done that next day several mistakes and omissions were discovered in the text. At 2.30 a.m. the revised copy was brought to the table and the seven in the room put their names to it.

Three of the leaders of the Sinn Féin movement, three of the Ministers of the Government of the Republic, had surrendered the independence of their country. The British thought it was an occasion for a special grace. Chamberlain records it :

"As the Irishmen rose to leave, the British Ministers, under a strong impulse, walked round and for the first time shook hands."

As Chamberlain wrote this ten years later, he seems even then to have no relish in the memory. Though he praises Griffith, it is with the air of one patronising, and he uses the epithet "corner boy" obliquely for some of the others. More terrible were Churchill's words :

"We had become allies and associates in a common cause."

Lloyd George tells how, as the seven signatories walked from the Cabinet room they met the man who had with such care been shut out from this last scene. Lloyd George speaks of him with harshness, as all the British accounts do, but there is, thank God, no patronage. Underlying their abuse of Childers there is respect, as if Lloyd George knew it was not the face of Childers he saw but the face of Ireland ! Here is his picture of the scene as the two delegations issued, in the middle of the night, from that room in 10 Downing Street :

"Outside in the lobby sat a man who had used all the resources of an ingenious and well-trained mind, backed by a tenacious will, to wreck every endeavour to reach agreement—Mr. Erskine Childers, a man whose slight figure, whose kindly, refined and intellectual countenance, whose calm and courteous demeanour offered no clue to the fierce passions which raged inside his breast. At every crucial point in the negotiations he played a sinister part. He was clearly Mr. de Valera's emissary and faithfully did he fulfil the trust reposed in him by that visionary. Every draft that emanated from his pen—and all the first drafts were written by him—challenged every fundamental position to which the British delegates were irrevocably committed. He was one of those men who, by temperament, is incapable of compromise."

Triumphantly, the British passed him on their way to humiliate Ireland as even in her history she had seldom been humbled.

*   *   *   *   *   *

When de Valera set out from Limerick for Dublin on the morning of 6th December, there was a strange rumour running by the Shannon-side. Something had been agreed to in London. When his friends ran to him with the story, his heart swelled with a happiness that rewarded him for these long months of strain when he held with such constancy to the plan that had been decided on and to the belief that if we stood firmly by unity and independence we would win both without further war. Never to yield on essentials, that was part of the plan; but to be ever ready to meet the British on what did not involve either the integrity of Ireland's territory or the acceptance of allegiance, that was part of it, too. As an independent nation, Ireland could have what foreign policy she liked. If a treaty of association of that free Ireland with Britain would make it possible for Lloyd George and the others to recognise the sovereignty of Ireland, then to propose such a treaty were wise.

Lloyd George, de Valera was aware, had rejected external association several times already. But de Valera knew his man and knew the rejection was nothing more than the expression of the Welshman's hope that he could settle for less. If he could not get his " less," he would accept the Irish " more." After Griffith's pledge of 3rd December, de Valera felt certain that the only thing that would now be signed would be an Agreement containing both unity and independence. Anything less would be brought back unsigned. His comment as the rumours persisted was : " I did not think the British would yield so soon." But as he came nearer the capital the rumours grew sinister.

That day in Dublin remains for me and many others a nightmare of memory. I was in the Mansion House in the afternoon when the first definite word came of a surrender. It would be impossible now to give any picture of the depth of the grief that spread through the capital of Ireland as the afternoon wore on into evening, and with it the truth came. Men and women would not believe it, and they crowded with white and often tear-stained faces into the Mansion House looking, vainly looking, for word that it was a lie ; that it had not happened ; that this hateful ghost of history, the spectre of disunity had not risen again on the very eve of Ireland's victory.

They wanted to be reassured that terms had not been accepted that would bring everything to nought, mock us with our dead, humble us with the taunt that Sinn Féin, like the other gang, never meant freedom, that we asked others to die, but we would knuckle under to save ourselves; that the English had only to threaten hard enough and we would all run like hares.

For scoffers had said these things from the beginning, the cynics had decked them with wit and sent them brightly spinning through the drawing-rooms of Dublin. But as sacrifice followed sacrifice, as the nation took its blows and stood its ground, the ranks of the scoffers thinned out. Generously, many of them joined us, saying: " They *do* mean what they say : they *will* give their own lives for it." And now, in shame, we saw their faith broken : the Unionists who had become Republicans, the Presbyterians of the North who had come from their farms in Armagh and Down to vote for Sinn Féin because, at last, men had arisen who would stand unshakably for freedom with justice for all. And now, and now——

That evening, in the Dublin Mansion House, I saw men and women cast themselves down and writhe in woe itself at this surrender. Some came to my door and just looked, and said, " Well ? " and, when I shook my head, they went away. the heart crushed out of them. The daylight died with the procession still coming, questioners who could hardly command their trembling lips to ask.

All that we knew then was that some kind of false peace had been signed—that the British were rejoicing, and the Irish were silent. There was Allegiance in it. Full details came with the evening papers : there was the Oath to the Crown ; there was the permission to the Orangemen to hold what Britain had torn from Ireland. Allegiance and Partition, the two things that these five men had been most pledged to refuse.

Everybody was looking for de Valera. He came at last. Count Plunkett, the Minister for Fine Arts, had organised a commemoration of the sixth centenary of Dante's death, which the whole world was honouring. De Valera was to preside at it.

The Mansion House, where so many brave things had been said for freedom, was crowded. De Valera hurried up the steps, towards the room where, but three days ago, Griffith had restored unity with his dramatic promise to sign nothing. As the President was passing through the door, Stack and Cathal Brugha were waiting for him.

" Is there an Oath of Allegiance in what they signed ? " he asked. " Yes," they answered. " Partition ? " " Yes." He turned from them, . and at that moment Éamonn Duggan, who had crossed by boat, came and proffered him a document. It was 7.15 p.m.

" What is this ? " de Valera asked.

" It is the Agreement," Duggan said.

" What do I want of it now ? " de Valera asked bitterly.

" We have arranged with the British that it be released for publication at 8 p.m." (It had, in fact, already been released.)

" Do you mean that it is to be published whether the President has seen it or not—whether I approve of it or not ? " de Valera asked, his voice deep with the contempt he felt at this sharp practice, this breach of the long comradeship of life and peril.

He turned away and went in to the Round Room to preside at the Dante celebration. He sat there on the platform, immobile, gaunt, his face the colour of death, his eyes looking out on that gathering of learned men and women, unseeingly, unheedingly. He was thinking of the chance that had been lost, of the folly of what had been done, of the weakness that is hidden in every man. He did not scold, he did not storm, he was passing his hands through the vast darkness, seeking a door, a way back to the unity that had been lost, a way out of the disaster that had so suddenly come upon Ireland, a nation divided, riven with the suddenness of a lightning flash into two angry sections, each with arms in its hands. All that night, his world fallen to pieces around him, he tried to grasp the meaning of it all, to plan some escape for the gallant people who had suffered so bravely and who, he knew, would not surrender now.

CHAPTER 66

" THE GHOSTS OF MY SONS "

THE days that followed the signing of the Treaty were days swaying between hope and despair. The President thought he could rally the Cabinet : three Ministers had signed, three were unalterably opposed. He expected that the seventh member, Cosgrave, would stand with Brugha, Stack and himself behind the policy all had so recently pursued. Then with a Cabinet majority he would go to the Dáil and beg of the Deputies to reject this false peace. At Cosgrave's earlier urging he had suppressed his first impulse to dismiss those Ministers who, by abandoning the Republic, had broken with the source of their authority, and by signing had disobeyed their written instructions as Plenipotentiaries and the most recent direction of the Cabinet. The Plenipotentiaries should first be heard in their own defence, Cosgrave said. The President called them home and after a long and stormy discussion Cosgrave went to their side.

I have cause to remember that Cabinet meeting. The President had not yet spoken publicly on the Treaty. Those close to him knew his attitude, but anxious for the unity of the movement and of the Dáil, he did not give voice to his feelings lest harsh words should end the chance of saving all. When the delegation returned, therefore, and the Cabinet assembled, the foreign correspondents, British, American and others, were trying to predict the future. I used to meet them in that oak-panelled room at the Mansion House, which immediately adjoined the Drawing-Room in which the Cabinet now sat, with but a door separating us. Through that door on 8th December, just as the room filled with enquiring journalists, came angry voices. Placing myself close to the door so that the others were as far from it as the small room would allow, I spoke that morning loudly and of everything that came into my head. To every question from the Pressmen I gave a voluble answer. They did not perceive the raised voices, which in my ears were again and again an orchestration to what I was saying, nor did they suspect why I talked so loudly and so much. Their reports to the papers of the world that evening were free of any hint of the reality. As de Valera struggled a few feet from them to draw back a united Cabinet to solid ground, they were as yet unaware of any division.

They knew only when, all efforts having failed, the President in a Proclamation late that night urged discipline in this great crisis :

" You have seen in the public Press the text of the proposed Treaty with Great Britain," he told the people. " The terms of this agreement are in violent conflict with the wishes of the majority of this nation as expressed freely in successive elections during the past three years.

" I feel it my duty to inform you immediately that I cannot recommend the acceptance of this Treaty, either to Dáil Éireann or to the country. In this attitude I am supported by the Ministers for Home Affairs and Defence.

" A Public Session of Dáil Éireann is being summoned for Wednesday next at 11 o'clock a.m. I ask the people to maintain during the interval the same discipline as heretofore. The members of the Cabinet, though divided in opinions, are prepared to carry on the public services as usual.

" The Army as such is, of course, not affected by the political situation and continues under the same orders and control.

" The greatest test of our people has come. Let us face it worthily, without bitterness and, above all, without recriminations. There is a definite constitutional way of resolving our political differences—let us not depart from it, and let the conduct of the Cabinet in this matter be an example to the whole nation."

Free of personal criticism and condemnation, without any note of anger, the statement reflected the President's dominant thought that somehow the nation must be reuninted behind the struggle for Independence, somehow the British must be deprived of their terrible victory.

If the Dáil could consider the Treaty on its merits, if the people were given a fair chance to decide the real issue, then " the definite constitutional way of resolving our political differences " would result, many of us were convinced, in an overwhelming rejection of what had been signed. De Valera was certain—and that view was to be confirmed as soon as the storm of propaganda was over—that the people were faithful to Independence and would endure for its maintenance as much as they had suffered for its establishment. What was most to be feared now was that the issue would be put to them falsely—the Treaty represented as Freedom and Unity for Ireland and the only alternatives to it chaos and bloodshed ; that the appeal would not be to the high things in the nation, but to fear.

Cast down by his failure to hold the Cabinet majority, de Valera sought desperately for a new way out. I remember the day that what seemed a workable plan for re-uniting Parliament and people suggested itself to him. It was on 13th December, 1921, the day before the Dáil was to meet to discuss the Treaty. All of us around him noticed the new energy and as he went by me in the Mansion House that day, hope in the already lined face, I said something of encouragement to him. His response has not left my mind. He put his hand on my shoulder and said : " It is young men like you who make it worth while going on." It was not to me personally that he spoke but to thousands of young men everywhere.

> " The fact cannot be concealed," said the pro-Treaty *Cork Examiner*, " that there is amongst the young men an intensive support for President de Valera and a strong expression of opinion against the acceptance of the Treaty."

The Presidential Office was at that time at 53 Kenilworth Square, whither it had been moved after the raid at Blackrock. There he now placed the plan before the Cabinet colleagues and others who stood with him. Late that night he began to put it into documentary form. Erskine Childers was there up to midnight and early next day as the drafting went on. I remember his astonishment at Kathleen O'Connell's efficiency, that in the midst of chaos—Ministers, T.D.s, callers of all kinds sweeping through these rooms—every draft and revision came up immaculately.

De Valera's plan was essentially a simple one. He would counter Treaty with Treaty. So much had been given away that he could not save everything, but in the redrafted proposals the core of it all— Ireland's independence and unity—would be safeguarded ; there would be no Allegiance ; no Crown ; the Republic would stand.

To make British acceptance of it possible he would retain much of the wording of the Treaty. Then he would present the new draft to the Dáil and ask them to accept it so that simultaneously with the rejection of the Treaty a sound peace set out in full treaty form and already approved by the National Parliament would be offered to Downing Street. If it was done swiftly there was a chance of success. As all can realise now it was the solution the Dáil should have accepted, but then the fear of war, fanned from every side, had become almost a panic as the people saw the leadership divided.

So that it would be discussed freely the President submitted his alternative next day to a Secret Session. He explained it was a " bad best," he had not had time even to complete the draft, there were in it things he would himself change, but what was before them would make the general purport of his plan clear : that the Dáil could reject the London Treaty yet rob Britain of any excuse for war by offering at the same time a settlement which Ireland could accept.

This redrafted Treaty was given the name " Document No. 2"

and for a little while was seriously discussed. Then it was perceived by somebody what an opportunity it provided for propaganda, and the alternative so hopefully drawn up was turned into a deadly weapon, not against the British, but against de Valera and all who still stood for Freedom.

The wording used to equate it with the Treaty so that its acceptance by Britain might be made easier was pointed to as implying that there was no difference between the two Documents, and that de Valera and his colleagues, too, wished to give away the Republic. The fact that there had been time only to revise part of the Treaty, that other Treaty clauses, including those about the Six Counties, were allowed to run on as the changes in the first part would show what changes were necessary in the rest, was proclaimed an acceptance of Partition. After this unpromising discussion de Valera withdrew the rough draft and said he would submit a completed text later, a text over which he would stand personally. He did so on 4th January but that same evening the hostile Press were handed a copy of Document No. 2. It was not the completed Document No. 2 but the provisional, confidential draft submitted three weeks earlier to the Secret Session.

It was shameful but it was effective. The daily Press gave full publicity to this and other deceptions and these remain in many minds to this day. The implication that the whole heroic movement was a sham, a competition between two rival groups as to which would sell out first, perfectly suited those who had failed in their national duty by taking no part in the struggle. Their own lack of patriotism would be minimised if the reputation of all who did take part were soiled. Newspapers which had remained against Sinn Féin for the whole period of the Revolution now passed on this apparent proof of Sinn Féin hypocrisy with relish. " Tweedledum and Tweedledee," the headlines shouted. " Look at the men who say they stand by the Republic."

Faithful Republicans, soon to prove by new and terrible sufferings the reality of their devotion to Independence, knew the profound difference between Document No. 2 and the Treaty but the people left without one Republican daily paper were misled, confused and dismayed. It was all grist to the propaganda mills of Britain. Churchill himself recorded how he felt immediately after the Treaty had split the sturdiest Irish national movement for a century. " It appeared to me," he said gleefully, " as if the tables were turned. Ireland, not Britain, is on her trial before the world." And in that tragic trial to prejudice the verdict, an incomplete, confidential document was made public and deliberately misinterpreted to suggest that nobody had stood for Freedom at all. It was as conscienceless as the trick

Lloyd George had played upon Griffith on 12th November, and it had the same corrupt character.

It was in the Council Chamber of University College, Dublin, that these debates on the Treaty took place. None of those who attended them will forget those crowded, painful days. At the beginning the hall was full of earnestness : everyone understood that a parting of the ways had come and if the dead and the dream were not to be betrayed some bridge must be thrown across the divide. It was the moment for the redraft of the Treaty and de Valera submitted it. Many thought the Dáil might unite behind it and say to Britain : " Come war, come woe, here we stand in defence of the ultimate right." But it was not to be. Fear took hold of the assembly —not an unmanly fear, but, nevertheless, a disastrous one—and to read the debate now is to see Deputy after Deputy in the bleak dread of war supporting the Treaty, even though he gave up the Republic with reluctance. Nobody could speak of the Treaty itself with warmth :

> " None of us want this Treaty," said Richard Mulcahy. " None of us want the Crown. None of us want the representative of the Crown. None of us want our harbours occupied by enemy forces, and none of us want what is said to be Partition ; and we want no arguments against any of these things. But we want an alternative. We want the road open to us to show how we can avoid this Treaty. The only alternative put before us is the alternative put forward by the President, and I want to say that that alternative has not been treated fairly on the side who are for the Treaty."

That was the tone in which those spoke who supported what was done in London, and into their speeches crept more and more a dread echo.

" I support it because the alternative is war."

" If we don't vote for this Treaty the people will be driven to the shambles."

" I am swallowing a bitter pill in having to vote for this Treaty."

" I do not want the Treaty myself : I do not like it : I will vote for it under protest."

" We are going to have a ' March through Georgia,' like Sherman, when he burned every town and village and haggard on his path. You would have thirty-two Shermans marching through Ireland for the difference between this Treaty and Document No. 2."

" Had I believed that this Treaty would leave Ireland a permanently-divided country, I would vote against it."

" I dislike the Treaty as much as any man or woman here, but that is not the point. No man is entitled to sentence the Irish people to death."

" I believe rejection means war."

" I can't take the responsibility for committing the men and women who sent me here to a war of extermination, which I think would result if this Treaty were rejected."

" I think it unwise and unstatesmanlike that England's representatives have thought fit under threat of war to insist on certain clauses of that Treaty."

Each one of those quotations is from a separate speech for the Treaty. As we sat there in the hall, we heard many Deputies plead that the Dáil must abandon Independence to save the people. But for Ireland's honour, be it said, there were other voices. The mother of Pádraic and Willie Pearse spoke with a simple majesty :

" It has been said here on several occasions that Pádraic Pearse would have accepted this Treaty. I deny it. As his mother I deny it and on his account I will not accept it. If I accepted that Treaty I feel in my heart—and I would not say it only I feel it—that the ghosts of my sons would haunt me."

CHAPTER 67

" A VOICE IN RAMA——"

As the discussion of the Treaty continued the scene was marked more by sadness than by the anger which so often glowed on the surface.

The hall itself seemed to take on this air of melancholy. My memory is that it was low-ceilinged and narrow : a place without dignity. The Deputies were crowded at one end and the Press of the world at the other. Somewhere down in the basement there were dining-rooms, and many an evening at the tea adjournment I sat there as these men of national renown were discussing among themselves what was to happen now, and I remember my pride as I was taken for Seán Moylan, then one of the most daring and gallant of our brigade commanders.

In the House itself the division was not yet of Party. A few like Seán Milroy had adopted partisan methods. But so wholly out of place was this tricky play with words that even his supporters seemed to draw away from him. The general body of the Deputies spoke as individuals and the tenor of their speeches was that this was a moment not of victory, but of defeat. Most of those who were for the Treaty named the hour a tragic, a calamitous one.

In later years some of them, many of them, came for a time to boast of the Treaty. That was from the very human desire to put themselves right with the tradition from which they had broken. The burden of what they had done was too heavy for them to bear, so they convinced themselves that this settlement which destroyed the Republic was a wonderful thing. Since then they have succeeded in writing their view as the history of that day, and what is written here comes newly to many.

But in the terrible hours of 1921 they did not pretend. Twenty or thirty deputies referred openly to the chaos into which they had been delivered. They allowed themselves to be comforted with false hopes, that the Treaty would provide the nation with the means of having its own back on England, that what the Treaty lost the Constitution drafted under it would win back again for Ireland.

Well-loved voices warned them that Liberty once abandoned would not easily be regained. Liam Mellows, who within a year was to die for his fidelity to the dream that all had shared, spoke these words :

> " We placed Ireland upon a pedestal for the first time in the history of this country. For the first time we had a Government established by the directly declared will of the people. Ireland was put forth to the world as a headlight, as a beacon beginning to shine for all time to guide all those who were struggling. . . . Here in this country of ours is contained the germ of great and wonderful things for the world. It has fought a fight which will ring down through the ages, and maintained itself well against all the tortures and inflictions that a foreign tyranny knows so well how to impose. It maintained its way up to this stage and now, not through the force of the British Government, not because of the weight of the British armies, but through the guile of the British Government and the gullibility of ours, we are going to throw away the Irish Republic."

Harry Boland's words stay in my mind as, quoting Pearse, he traced the Independence movement, flowing through Irish history like an apostolic succession :—

> " The veterans of Kinsale fought at Benburb, the veterans of Benburb fought with Sarsfield at Limerick, and the veterans of Limerick kept the fires of the nation burning from Limerick to Dungannon ; the veterans of Dungannon of '82 fought in 1798 ; Robert Holmes, the friend of Emmet, was also the friend of Tone ; the man who defended Emmet lived to be a Young Irelander ; three veterans of the Young Ireland Movement then founded Fenianism ; and the veterans of the Fenian Movement stood with the Volunteers of 1916. We picked it up in 1916 and we brought the Irish Republic out of the backwoods, away from the dark rooms of secret societies, and preached the gospel before the Irish people. Many Deputies in this House know that my father himself had to fly from this country because he believed in a Republic. His son was privileged to stand on public platforms to ask the Irish people to subscribe to the Republic— and they did."

He spoke with the old Republican faith in the people :—

> " I, for one, am quite easy in my mind that those who will come after us will deal kindly with the men who vote against the Treaty . . . no demand that you make to the people will be denied. If we are prepared to carry on this fight, the people of Ireland will support us."

I remember de Valera's answer when the *Freeman's Journal* taunted him with not knowing the Irish people :

"I was reared in a labourer's cottage here in Ireland. I have not lived solely among the intellectuals. The first fifteen years of my life that formed my character were lived among the Irish people down in Limerick ; therefore, I know what I am talking about ; and whenever I wished to know what the Irish people wanted, I had only to examine my own heart. . . . I am not a member of the Irish Republican Brotherhood, but I hope when I die I will get a Fenian grave. . . . I stand definitely for the Irish Republic as it was established—as it was proclaimed in 1916—as it was constitutionally established by the Irish nation in 1919, and I stand for that definitely, and I will stand by no policy whatever which is inconsistent with that."

De Valera pleaded with those old comrades of his to take the high road and make a real peace :

"One of my earliest dreams, next to securing Irish Independence, was that there might be a reconciliation between the peoples of these two islands—this (Document No. 2) is a genuine offer of peace, a peace that can be as lasting as human peace can be. We offer them that, and if they turn it down, then . . . we will deny the right, we will oppose the will of the British Parliamentary power to legislate for Ireland ; and we will make use of any and every means to render impotent the power of England to hold Ireland in subjection. . . . If there was not a gun in Ireland, we could carry out that programme. If we were bound hand and foot, we could still, by our voice and our will, stand by that programme."

I can hear again Cathal Brugha on this last day of the Debate foretelling of his own death :

"Here, when we are so strong . . . and England so weak, and with so many enemies as she has now, we are asked to do such a thing as this. Why, if instead of being so strong, our last cartridge had been fired, our last shilling had been spent, and our last man was lying on the ground and his enemies howling around him and their bayonets raised, ready to plunge them into his body, that man should say—true to the traditions handed down—if they said to him ' Now, will you come into our Empire ? ' he should say, and he would say : ' No ! I will not'."

I remember Griffith's final speech and the power of it

"This Treaty gives the Irish people what they have not had for a century; it gives them a foothold in their own country; it gives them solid ground on which to stand; and Ireland has been a quaking bog for three hundred years, where there was no foothold for the Irish people. Well, reject this Treaty; throw Ireland back into what she was before this Treaty. . . . I know where Ireland was twenty or thirty years ago; I know where Ireland was when there was only a few of us up in Dublin trying to keep the national ideal alive . . . a few of us who had faith in our people and faith in our country stood by her—you are going to throw Ireland back to that; to dishearten men who made the fight and to let back into Irish politics the time-servers and men who let Ireland down before and who will, through their weakness if not through their dishonesty, let Ireland down again. You can take this Treaty and make it the basis of an Irish Ireland."

In that speech, with which the great Debate closed, there was an incident which clings to my mind. Griffith had said that those who stood against the Treaty would not dare to say to their constituents what they said to the Dáil. Instantly on his feet was Seán T. O'Kelly: "I would," he said. In a second or two many were up: "So would I," said Erskine Childers. "And I," said Mary MacSwiney, "And I," said Countess Marcievicz.

As the Debate was in progress, a propaganda campaign swept through the nation which for unscrupulousness eclipsed anything of the past. Every newspaper that had access to the people's minds was behind it. The daily papers everywhere, even the Nationalist daily in Belfast, condemned those who stood against the surrender, demanding that they, too, yield.

The British threat of war was taken up, magnified and sent booming through the land. Michael Collins' theme became the burden of a hundred editorials: "By rejecting the Treaty you declare war." War, war, savage war—it was in great capital letters, in headlines, on posters, on the hoardings. Thousands of prisoners were still held by the British, scores of them under sentence of death, and the Dáil was told they must bow to the Treaty or these men would die. Cartoons appeared of broken men in prison, and it was foully said that those who held them there were those who stood against the Treaty. Photographs of children crippled in the fight were headed: "The Treaty—or This."

The people were preached to that it was their moral duty to accept the Treaty, and out of many a Bishop's statement the morning papers made captions:

2A

" No Hope Except In Treaty—Irish Bishops' Advice "

" The Cardinal—Treaty Ireland's Only Hope "

Special meetings of the public bodies were summoned and their declarations for the false peace was used to overawe T.D.s into voting for it. Every propagandist trick was played by illustration, use of type, half-quotation, juxta-position. Those who four years before had shouted that Sinn Féin was Ireland's enemy now shouted the same of de Valera and those who stood beside him. The Nationalist North was told the rest of Ireland wanted the Treaty and they must yield; the rest of Ireland was told the Nationalist North wanted it. De Valera tried to stop the stampede: "a stampede that would expose you to the attacks of the enemy no less than to the pity or contempt of the world whose admiration your heroism has just won," In a Proclamation of 4th January, he appealed to the people:

> " If you give way you are undone—all you have gained will be lost and all the sacrifices you have made will be in vain. . . . It is easy to induce a rout—it is hard to check it once it has begun. . . . Stand fast, fellow-citizens, by what you know to be right. . . . If you quail at the consequences—what will they not ask you to surrender next to ignoble fear?"

But now the enemies of the Republic were in full cry again and they howled him down while their emissaries sped among the people shouting: " War: War: save yourselves: save yourselves."

It was incessant, violent, virulent—and it won. But the day of that bitter victory, heralded by the flaming headlines, the panic-creating posters, was one of the saddest and most moving in the history of Dáil Éireann.

The counting of the votes on that dark night of 7th January, 1922, over thirty years ago, changed the destinies of Ireland and interlaced our individual lives with sorrow and the death of friends. We who had watched that tense Debate from among the Pressmen had tried to predict the outcome of the voting but it was unpredictable. Many Deputies had not spoken at all. Some had spoken for the Treaty but announced that they would abstain. Some spoke against, but ended by saying that they felt compelled by their constituents to vote for. The side a man would take remained in doubt until he had voted. Two or three Deputies who had been against the Treaty when the Dáil adjourned over Christmas came back to tell us with heavy hearts that they would vote for it, so tortured had they become by the fear that had been engendered everywhere. So when the fell hour came and the Clerk stood up to call the roll no man knew for certain what the outcome would be. As it proved, four men changing their minds would have altered the decision. (And within a little time more than four men who voted for the Treaty were back in the ranks of the movement against it.)

The method of voting was that the Deputy's name was called and, standing in his place, he answered in Irish " For " or " Against " to the proposition that the Dáil approve of the Treaty. Now one side, now the other was in the lead ; but, as the waverers came down on the Treaty side, the victory for the Surrender became certain. All eyes were on the leaders as they rose to vote. The reporter of the *Irish Independent* described de Valera's answer:

> " And the voice was that of a man . . . who stands over the coffin of one whom he loved above all else in the world."

And what he loved was the unity of brothers that had brought them all so far and was now dissolving before his eyes.

Every woman who was a member of the Dáil rose in her place and said " No " : the mother of the Pearses, the twice-bereaved Mrs. Tom Clarke, the sister of Terence MacSwiney, the widow of the murdered Mayor O'Callaghan, the dauntless Countess Markievicz, the faithful Dr. Ada English.

Eventually the 121 Teachtaí had voted. The Speaker cleared his throat. There was a piercing stillness in the room. " For approval of the Treaty, 64 ; against, 57." Was there a shout of triumph in the House ? There was complete silence. Nobody moved, nobody cheered, nobody even spoke. Minutes passed.

Then Éamon de Valera rose to his feet. He was very pale. He was heard to say : " The Republic still goes on until the Nation itself has disestablished it." He paused and then continued, speaking with obvious difficulty :

" Before we rise, I should like to say my last word. Up to this we have had the record of four glorious years, years of magnificent discipline in the nation."

He paused again, struggling to master his words : " The world is looking on at us now. . . ."

The voice died away. He stood there looking out over that assembly, white-faced, haggard. The silence was complete as every eye held its gaze upon him. His outstretched hand fell to his side and he collapsed into his seat, and throwing himself forward he buried his face in his arms, and this man, who had never before shown his feelings, sobbed aloud.

> " The strong man who had defied the might of an Empire," said the *Independent* report, " faced its armies, scorned its jailers, had broken down."

And then a remarkable thing happened—and before that year was half gone it took on for me the substance of a dark prophecy. Deputy after Deputy broke down in that strained room, not on one side, but on both, and the passing of the Treaty was accompanied by the sound of brothers' weeping who till now had stood by one another in death's face. The men in that room, nearly all young soldiers, knew the vastness of the tragedy that had overwhelmed them. A British statesman had divided the men of Ireland who had held together so magnificently, had divided them irrevocably, uncontrollably. Those who for four years had fronted every danger, never yielding, never quailing, never parting, were now at one another's throats despite every effort to turn this English victory aside. The passing of the Treaty which saw Irish unity melt away and the nation lie helpless at last before the will of her enemy, was greeted only by tears.

It was the chief protagonist of the Treaty that described the scene. The *Irish Independent* reported :

> " The painful silence was soon broken in every part of the Chamber, and not only women, but stalwart men, sobbed and wept like children."

Then the House rose. The Four Glorious Years were over.

Epilogue

THE SPIRIT LIVES ON

THE story has been told. No similar period in Irish history shone with such idealism and such self-sacrifice. Not for a century had the common people borne trials so great or endured an agony so long drawn out.

They did this without feeling that they were doing anything more than the duty citizens owe to their Motherland. That this heroic drama ended in darkness was not their fault. They would have gone on if the leadership had not been broken. They did, in fact, go on, tens of thousands of them, hundreds of thousands of them, though now neighbour's hand was raised against neighbour, and the Volunteer could no longer be sure that many doors, or even any door, would open to him when death and capture were on his heels.

Most of those who abandoned the fight did so in honest belief that what had been signed was something else. Every hour of the waking day they heard that this was what Pearse had died for, what Terence MacSwiney had fasted unto death for, what Kevin Barry had desired. From Press, from platform, from pulpit the assurance came incessantly. That any at all of the ordinary people should have penetrated this vast misrepresentation would have been strange; that hundreds of thousands did was wonderful.

Despite the deafening chorus " This is Freedom: this is Independence," men and women, boys and girls stood firm everywhere, and when six months later they had to choose between submission or prison, submission or death, they did not falter, thousands everywhere. The list of executions grew to paralysing length, the Volunteers who in the British time had fallen in scores now fell in hundreds; the prison camps were filled to overflowing by ardent men and women who loved Ireland and were faithful to her Freedom. The young men in the field, in the camps, in the jails, the young women, too, were denied the Sacraments, and in many places church doors were locked against the bodies of the dead. Spiritually and physically they were deserted. And yet their faith did not falter, their faith in God or in Ireland.

I was a prisoner in Griffith Barracks in the October of 1922. Under the leadership of Seán Forde all the Republicans imprisoned there fasted for the whole day of the 25th to commemorate the death of Terence MacSwiney. I was in Gormanston internment camp in 1923, and in the hut next to mine were Seán T. O'Kelly, Seán MacEntee, Oscar Traynor. Later that year I was on hunger-strike in Kilmainham Jail. In the cells around me were Tom Derrig, Gerry Boland, Austin Stack. Those who could have been the rulers of Ireland were the prisoners.

Everywhere through these camps and jails were the men who had fought the fight: Ernie O'Malley, Andy McDonnell, Joe MacHenry, Peadar O'Donnell, Mick Smith, George and Jack Plunkett, Stephen O'Mara, David Robinson, Pax Whelan. I could go on with the list for ever. They did not rail at their imprisonment— they watched for the chance to escape, to get back to the fight: they built tunnels, they refused parole, but they did not complain. It was all in the day's work.

I was taken to Mountjoy, and for some act of defiance I was put into the basement. I could see through a broken pane in the little window of that shadowy cell the boots of the other prisoners, exercising in the courtyard above. A pair of boots stopped at my window; a voice said: "Who are you?" I told him. The voice was that of Robert Barton, one of the Plenipotentiaries, now a prisoner, too, for he had rejoined the Republican movement at once. I had met him a year before, on 8th December, 1921.

He asked me then:

"Why weren't we arrested when we came down the gangway from the boat this morning and shot for treason?"

"Who," I asked, after a little while, "would arrest you?"

"The Army, of course," he said.

"What company?" I asked.

"Any company," he said vigorously.

"Chosen by whom?" I asked. "By a Collins officer or a Cathal Brugha officer?"

He looked at me for a long long time: "I see," he said slowly, "the Army is divided, too." And the terrible words formed themselves in both our minds: Civil War.

And here it was.

Some of the noblest Romans of them all soon filled the graves, men we had daily known.

Cathal Brugha was dead. On 5th July, 1922, when the Hammam Hotel, which was the Republican headquarters, was burning and being evacuated, he stayed on. Then, alone, he came fully armed from the building. Silhouetted by the flames and smoke, he stepped into the street, which was swept by machine-gun fire, the favourite Peter the Painter in his hand. Fire from every quarter converged on that lonely figure, standing there in the street, the embodiment of the assailed Republic, a target for all who had deserted it. He fell, as he had foretold in his speech on the Treaty, in fiery protest to the last.

And Harry Boland was dead. Harry, the gay, the gallant, who had striven with such feverishness for peace. He was surprised in a raid at Skerries, and though unarmed, was shot.

On 7th December, 1922, I spoke to Rory O'Connor in Mountjoy Jail over the "telephone" rigged up between the wings. I was in B Wing, he in C. Where the wings came close to the central building, as spokes to the hub of a wheel, there had been fixed a "line" with tough twine and the wooden covers of paste jars for mouth-pieces and ear-phones, the efficient installation of Jack Plunkett and Dick Macaulay.

Then, not to attract attention, one stood in a darkened cell and spoke across the space. That night of 7th December, not gloomily but happily, we spoke, Rory and I, of everything, even some words about the new Ireland that would come out of all this suffering. A few hours later that deep voice was stilled for ever. The I.R.A. outside had shot Seán Hales. Four men, who had been in prison for five months, were taken out and killed in a " reprisal." Among them were two members of the General Headquarters staff who had directed the War of Independence, Rory O'Connor and Liam Mellows. Joe McKelvey, Commandant of the Third Northern Division, who had directed the defence of the Nationalists through the savagery of the Belfast pogroms, was the third ; and the fourth was Commandant Dick Barrett, who, as he sat in his cell waiting for the dawn that was the signal for his execution, wrote to us, his fellow-prisoners, the unforgettable sentence : " Death is terrible only from a distance."

They did not die in anger, or with any sense that Ireland was ungrateful to them, these men. Liam Mellows wrote to his mother :

" The time is short, and much that I would like to say must go unsaid. But you will understand ; in such moments, heart speaks to heart. At 3.30 this morning, we (Dick Barrett, Rory O'Connor, Joe McKelvey and I) were informed that we were to be ' executed as a reprisal.' Welcome be the Will of God, for Ireland is in His keeping, despite foreign monarchs and treaties. Though unworthy of the greatest human honour that can be paid an Irish man or woman, I go to join Tone, Emmet, the Fenians, Tom Clarke, Connolly, Pearse, Kevin Barry, Childers. My last thought will be on God and Ireland and you. . . . Let no thought of revenge or reprisals animate Republicans because of our deaths. We die for the Truth. Vindication will come, the mists will be cleared away, and brothers in blood will, before long, be brothers once more in arms against the oppressors of our country. . . . The path the people of Ireland must tread is straight and true, though narrow. Only by following it can they be men. It is a hard road, but it is the road our Saviour followed—the road of sacrifice. The Republic lives ; our deaths make that a certainty. . . Go to Mrs. Pearse. She will comfort you. . . ."

A few weeks earlier, Erskine Childers had been executed. Before he died, he wrote in a letter to his wife :

" My beloved country, God send you courage, victory and rest, and to all our people harmony and love. . . . It is 6 a.m. You will be pleased to see how imperturbably normal and tranquil I have been this night, and am. It seems perfectly simple and inevitable, like lying down after a long day's work."

No complaint, no personal regret ; why should a man not give his life for freedom and for Ireland ?

But Dick Barrett, Liam Mellows and Erskine Childers had the gift of words. They had been used to command, inured to danger, accustomed to solve national problems. They could well have these high feelings and be able to die without bitterness. What of the rank and file, the young lads, to whom life was just opening ; the boys of the work-bench, the factory, the farmyard ?

Yes, their letters have been preserved, too, and in them is the self-same generous offering of their lives, with no regrets or self-pity. Among the first to be executed was James Fisher, a typical Dublin lad, aged 18. He, taken prisoner some weeks before, was shot on 17th. November. He wrote :

" Dear Mother,

" I am now awaiting the supreme penalty at seven in the morning ; but I am perfectly happy, because I've seen the Priest and I am going to die a good Catholic and a soldier of the Irish Republic. Don't worry or cry for me, but pray for the repose of my soul and my three comrades. . . . To my Mother, whom I dearly love, good-bye, good-bye, good-bye. We will meet again in Heaven, please God, Mother. God strengthen me in the ordeal."

And then in a burst of pride the words :

" I am to die for Ireland."

In Dundalk there were executions on 13th January, 1923. One

of those who was shot was Thomas McKeon. He wrote to his mother :

> " Let there be no weeping for me when I am gone, for it is for Ireland I die. Tell my comrades to pray for me and be true to their faith and to the Republic, and I will pray for you all in Heaven. So now good-night, mother, and good-bye for ever."

In every barrack square, where, as dawn broke, men and boys died, the same ideal sustained them ; the gentle and the simple alike, the learned and the worker, the ideal of Ireland free, of the Irish Republic, which weak men were then saying had never existed. These are not the letters of '98 men or of Emmet's time or of 1916. These are the letters of 1922 and 1923, the same continuity, the same pride in death for Ireland, the same unquestioning service to Independence.

The conflict is written of and spoken of as a Civil War. In the mere physical sense it was that, but more deeply it was simply part of the age-long effort to make Ireland free. It was a continuance, not a new thing. It was 1803 after 1798 in a new form, a much harder form, calling for courage of a special order. Those who would not submit were many—the majority of the General Head-quarters Staff, a majority of the Commandants in the field, the great majority of the Volunteers, and I believe a majority of the people too. For there was never a popular vote on the Treaty. That there was, is one of the fictions that have been accepted as history.

Those who opposed the abandonment of the ideal that had so recently bound all did not seek the war that followed. I have told the story of Document No. 2, that brilliant effort to retrieve a position almost hopelessly lost. That came from the Republican side. In the succeeding months, there were many committees, negotiations, meetings of the leading men of the two wings of the army. When, after the division on the Treaty in the Dail, de Valera, in fulfilment of Parliamentary procedure, resigned the Presidency, Griffith was elected. He pledged himself to fill the same position de Valera had held, and to maintain Republican institutions. It was because of this pledge that Collins, and not he, became Chairman of the Provisional Government set up to implement the Treaty ; and this pledge, too, strengthened the hope that somehow in the end the Republic would survive.

As well as de Valera, Seán T. O'Kelly, Harry Boland, Dan Breen, and many pro-Treaty T.D.'s, too, let not a day pass without seeking to open some road back to unity. There were many failures. Then the Pact of 20th May was accomplished—that great document which

de Valera and Michael Collins signed. Britain had been pressing
for an election on the Treaty. Many saw that as the final calamity.
It would drive the division into the very hearts of the people. By a
miracle, de Valera had held Sinn Féin together through the vast
divide. The special Sinn Féin Árd-Fheis of 22nd February, held to
consider the Treaty, had adjourned for three months, during which it
was agreed that no elections would be held, and then only when the
Constitution, to be drafted under the Treaty, was in the people's
hands, that they might see if the promises were kept to regain in the
Constitution what had been lost in the Treaty.

Now, the adjourned Árd-Fheis was about to meet, and the national
pressure for peace became intense. The Pact met the situation
triumphantly. The election, so the Pact decreed, would not be
fought on the Treaty, but on the protection of the nation from civil
war. To effect that, the pro-Treaty and anti-Treaty sections of Sinn
Féin would unite and go forward together, not as opposing candidates, but as members of the one Panel, each supporting the other.
When the elections were over, a National Coalition Government
would be set up, in which the relative strengths of the two groups
would be reflected by five Ministers from the majority and four
from the minority, with the Minister for Defence chosen by the
Army and the President chosen by the Dáil. Thus, the war of
brothers, whose imminence had darkened the whole sky, would be
averted. Seán T. O'Kelly and Dick Mulcahy were foremost among
those who got the Pact accepted by every group, and when Griffith
proposed it in Dáil Éireann, and de Valera seconded, it was unanimously made the law governing the elections. " The definite
constitutional way of resolving our political differences " had been
found.

Thus, when the adjourned Árd-Fheis met on 22nd May, it was
to herald the Pact with joy. Collins at that Árd-Fheis told the British
who had viewed the Pact with the deepest anger, that if need be he
would stand by the Pact against the Treaty. It was a wonderful
hour for Ireland, and that Árd-Fheis received Collins' speech with a
rapture inexpressible.

Then the British machinations began again. Griffith and Collins
were summoned to London. The British found Griffith pliant;
Collins defiant. Collins soon returned to Ireland, and the British
threatened they would resume military hostilities. The evacuation
of the Twenty-Six Counties was suspended.

Collins left no doubt where his sympathies lay. Back in Ireland,
he spoke and worked for the Pact. The British summoned him to
London again when, on 6th June, they saw the Constitution drafted

by the Committee of which he had been chairman. He refused to go, and on 9th June addressed a Pact meeting at the Dublin Mansion House over which de Valera presided. It was clear that he was happy to be back among the old comrades. The summonses to London became more insistent. The British tore up the Constitution —they insisted on one with Oath and King and Privy Council. They demanded of Collins that he come. Four days before polling day he went. He saw Churchill on 13th June. On 14th June he returned to Ireland—and he repudiated the Pact that he had signed, and advised the people to ignore it.

The elections were held, and it was not until the actual morning of the polling that the now-riven Constitution was published. The people overwhelmingly approved the Pact. Of a House of 124 members, 94 were elected from the Sinn Féin Panel, and 17 Labour T.D.'s, who supported the re-union of pro-Treaty and anti-Treaty forces, were returned. Because, as had been anticipated, a majority of the 94 were pro-Treaty, Britain claimed that the elections had ratified the Treaty, and demanded that its terms be implemented straightway. De Valera and his colleagues waited to see if any call would come to form the National Coalition decreed by Dáil Éireann. But the call they heard were British guns bombarding the Republican headquarters in the Four Courts. Republicans everywhere sprang to arms to defend the institution which Pearse had founded and for which countless lives had been given.

And so the old struggle began again. The veterans of the War of Independence had withstood the British, but the British, and their old comrades, they were unable to withstand. After incomparable bravery, they were beaten.

But their faith never died ; all things they suffered, but not despair, and so in those great prison camps, in those frozen jails, in the overcrowded and fetid cells, while the world outside shouted " murderers," " gunmen," " bank robbers," " thugs," they planned again to win for their people that Freedom which they had thought had been purchased at a great price. I remember how into the internment camp where I was in 1923 there was smuggled one day a thin sheet of paper with a message written in a familiar hand. It suggested that the prisoners from each county should come together and prepare to re-establish Sinn Féin in their areas as soon as they got out. The writing was that of Éamon de Valéra. The rebuilding had begun.

It was terrible, but it was beautiful, this fidelity of those weary men and women to their nation ; the determination of so many of that great generation never to lose hope, but to go on and on until Ireland was free.

No word that has been written here has been set down to recall the bitterness of those days or that any should taste again the hot anger of that time. It is recorded so that the present generation, and those who come after them, will always remember how nobly Ireland was served during the FOUR GLORIOUS YEARS—and after.

THE END

INDEX